Foundation Macromedia Flash MX 2004

Kristian Besley and Sham Bhangal

friendsof

DESIGNER TO DESIGNER™

an Apress· company

Foundation Macromedia Flash MX 2004

Distributed to the book trade in the United States by Springer-Verlag New York, Inc., 233 Spring Street, 6th Floor, New York, NY 10013 and outside the United States by Springer-Verlag GmbH & Co. KG, Tiergartenstr. 17, 69112 Heidelberg, Germany.

In the United States: phone 1-800-SPRINGER, email orders@springer-ny.com, or visit http://www.springer-ny.com.
Outside the United States: fax +49 6221 345229, email orders@springer.de, or visit http://www.springer.de.

For information on translations, please contact Apress directly at 2560 Ninth Street, Suite 219, Berkeley, CA 94710.
Phone 510-549-5930, fax 510-549-5939, email info@apress.com, or visit http://www.apress.com.

The source code for this book is freely available to readers at http://www.friendsofed.com in the Downloads section.

Credits

Technical Editors:
Andy Corsham, Marlene Spector

Editorial Board:
Steve Anglin, Dan Appleman, Ewan Buckingham,
Gary Cornell, Tony Davis, Jason Gilmore,
Jonathan Hassell, Chris Mills,
Dominic Shakeshaft, Jim Sumser

Assistant Publisher:
Grace Wong

Project Manager:
Kylie Johnston

Copy Editor:
Nancy Depper

Production Manager:
Kari Brooks

Production Editor:
Kelly Winquist

Proofreader:
Lori Bring

Compositor:
Molly Sharp, ContentWorks

Indexer:
Michael Brinkman

Artist:
Christine Calderwood, Kinetic Publishing Services, LLC

Cover Designer:
Kurt Krames

Manufacturing Manager:
Tom Debolski

CONTENTS

Chapter 5: Working with Color and Images **117**

Chapter 6: Motion Tweening **157**

Chapter 14: Publishing 349

Chapter 15: Intermediate ActionScript Part 1 369

Chapter 16: Intermediate ActionScript Part 2 403

MACROMEDIA FLASH MX 2004 AND THIS BOOK: THE TRUTH

This book aims to give you a solid foundation in the most essential skills you need to use Macromedia Flash MX 2004—both the Standard and Professional versions. By the end of the book, you'll understand how the components of a Flash movie fit together, you'll have used all of the key tools, and you'll have integrated all your learning in a series of detailed creative exercises. Our mission is to launch you into orbit around planet Flash, equipped with all the tools and knowledge you need to make a safe landing.

Flash is one of the hottest content-creation technologies on the Web. From its origins as an animation package, Flash has grown stronger and planted deep roots. It is already used to create all kinds of content, such as website front-ends, interactive games, animated cartoons, movie trailers, and PDA interfaces. Perhaps its most significant role, however, is in creating *interfaces* for all these different areas. Its ability to present a clean, friendly, and functional front-end to the user is coupled with its power behind the scenes. Designers love Flash for its speed, quality, ease of use, and clearly structured functionality, and at the same time, both programmers and designers can use its ActionScript programming language to produce phenomenal results. Whatever kind of interface you want to build, Flash has the answer. If you've never used Flash before, you're in for a real treat.

As the Internet has changed, Flash has moved with it, evolving into a two tier system. The timeline-based animation is still there, but this is underpinned by a stronger emphasis on functionality that enables you to create the large, code-heavy sites required for today's e-commerce front ends and other intelligent user interfaces. This second tier doesn't consist only of ActionScript but also includes a new *authoring environment for programmers*, as provided by the Professional version. Don't worry of you are not a heavy-duty programmer though, you can still build Flash sites using the new, code-free *behaviors* with which you drag and drop elements to build interfaces without getting bogged down in code.

This book will take you step by step through every aspect of designing your own Flash interface, building your knowledge and skills with each chapter. We'll also look at the pitfalls and practicalities that every web designer faces, teach you how to make your designs web friendly, and ensure that you know how to get your hard work up on the net. But before we dive into these complex issues, let's make sure you know the basics of how Flash works, and why it's such a capable authoring tool.

Flash—the big picture

When you create a Flash movie for the Web, you're pulling together images, sound, video, text, and animation, and bundling them in a file that gets posted up on a website.

The Flash software you install on your computer is the authoring environment in which you create your masterpiece. The work in progress is stored in a file with the extension .fla. Once you're happy with your movie and you want to publish it to the Internet, Flash will convert the FLA file into a playable file with the extension .swf—pronounced *"swiff"* in the Flash community. The SWF file is then embedded in an HTML file on the server that hosts your site:

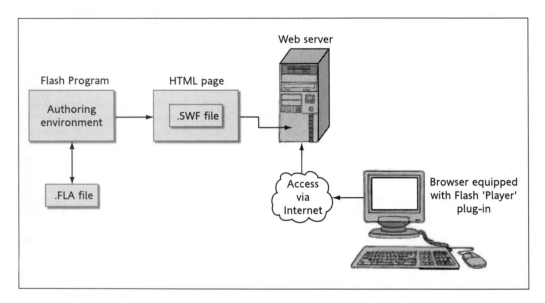

When a user visits your site, the SWF file is downloaded into their browser and your movie is played back. All the viewer needs is the Flash player installed on his or her machine. This player is a reasonably compact download, and the vast majority of the world's browsers are equipped to play back Flash content.

One of the reasons that Flash is such a popular tool is that it uses **vector graphics** technology. There are two main graphic standards on the Internet: **raster** (bitmaps) and **vector**. The majority of static images that you see on the Web are raster images, composed of files in formats such as BMP, GIF, and JPG. Raster images do a good job, but a big raster image usually requires a large file size, and a large file size means a long download time. And on the Web, download time is *everything*. Internet users are picky—if a site's packed with raster images and is taking too long to load, they'll just skip it and go somewhere else. This is where vectors come in. They're small, fast, and funky.

> *Vector images describe the image in terms of coordinates and mathematical transformations. That sounds complicated, but it's really as simple as saying, "put a dot here, put a dot there, and draw a line between them." This compares with the raster technique of describing the color and position of every single pixel in the image.*

Vector graphic files are much more compact and efficient compared to rasters, and Flash is the main tool for delivering vector graphics and vector-based animations on the Web. The files that Flash creates are therefore comparatively small, which is one of the reasons for Flash's success.

A well-constructed Flash file will also **stream** onto the user's computer. That means it will load the first part of the animation and start playing it back while the rest of the animation loads in the background. Streaming a file correctly is an important technique for a Flash designer because it means that a visitor is presented with something visual and enticing almost immediately—removing the danger that he or she will get bored and go elsewhere instead of wait for the site to download.

Another disadvantage of raster images is that they're *display dependent*, meaning that if you create them to look just right on one particular display, the image could come out significantly altered if someone uses a different display resolution to view it. In addition, if you *zoom in* on a raster image, the pixels just get bigger and bigger until you end up with a screen full of squares of color that are completely unrecognizable as the source image. Vector images though, can work independently of the display because the line will always be the same relative length and clarity no matter what resolution you use to view it. Also, no matter how far you zoom into a vector, the image will still stay crisp and at full resolution.

Why would you ever want to use a raster? Raster formats are good for images with thousands of different colors. Can you imagine trying to describe a photograph in terms of vectors? It would be horribly complicated, and have a far bigger file size than the raster equivalent. Luckily, Flash has the best of both worlds: the vast majority of its drawings and animations are vector-based, but when you need the extra richness that you can only get with a raster, Flash will allow you to import a bitmap and use it in conjunction with the dominant vectors.

What's significant about Flash MX 2004?

If you've used a previous version of Flash, the first thing you'll notice when you open the program is that the basic interface has changed slightly. Macromedia implemented a more standard interface that is common through the Studio range. Each file you are working on is represented at the top by a tab, allowing you to move quickly between your separate works in progress. There are also new panels. The most important one for the beginner being the Help panel, which has the helpful ability of knowing when there are updated help files available and downloading them for you at the click of a button.

One of the most significant new enhancements for designers is the way Flash now handles bitmaps, sound, and video files. These three kinds of files have a number of things in common—they make your site look and sound better, and they can take ages to load. You can now use ActionScript to dynamically load video, MP3, and JPG files directly into the Flash player, meaning that you can incorporate rich media content into your website and still keep the user's download time to a minimum as the large video and sound files are not included in the final SWF.

Flash now also supports subsets of HTML and CSS (cascading style sheets), two of the big technologies of traditional web design, as well as better support for small font sizes. These go together to give you *much* finer control of how your text and graphics will look in the browser.

Flash MX 2004 has also built upon the core scripting capability that came of age with Flash 5—a hugely powerful but easy to use programming language called **ActionScript**. Flash ActionScript is a deep and professional tool that allows you to add mind-blowing effects to your sites but keep that minimal file size. You can use ActionScript to program flexibility and complexity into your Flash websites and pass information backward and forward between the movie and the web server with greater ease. In Flash MX 2004, Flash ActionScript has moved on to version 2.0, which represents a major upgrade to previous versions. Although many beginner books gloss over these changes, this book shows you the fundamentals of class-based programming in ActionScript 2.0.

This may sound quite complicated for the novice user, but there's no reason to be intimidated by it. Although you're taking your first tentative Flash steps, by the end of this book you'll have used ActionScript to produce an interactive website with content that's rich and dynamic. Although ActionScript is far too big a topic for us to cover definitively in a book of this size and scope, you'll learn the essentials of using ActionScript in four dedicated chapters that allow you to expand your knowledge as you explore Flash further. As ever, we're aiming to give you an accessible, secure foundation.

Our aims and philosophy in this book

As its title suggests, the aim of this book is to give you a solid, extensible foundation in Flash design, implementation, and programming. We believe that Flash is too complex a tool to cover definitively from scratch in 1000 pages, let alone 500. We want to provide a rock-steady foundation: an in-depth treatment of the core aspects of using Flash MX rather than an overview of each and every feature.

We believe in creating a reliable foundation so you can understand Flash more fully and absorb and internalize the material we cover. We're not going to list every menu option and cover every single ActionScript command in immense detail. We're going to concentrate on the core of learning Flash successfully, taking you from a zero knowledge of Flash to being able to put up a website you can be proud of.

Everyone knows that the best way to learn is to play and practice. It's no good if someone just *tells* you what to do—to master Flash, you have to *use* it. This book follows that philosophy by providing examples and tutorials in every chapter, and on every topic we cover. It's another well-known fact that although small examples are fun and can help you learn, it's difficult to apply those examples in the real world when you've finished the book. So, at the end of most chapters, you'll be able to apply the things you've just learned to the **case study project**. Each case study is an opportunity for you to put the information you learn in each chapter into building a complete and fully functional website that you can use as your online portfolio:

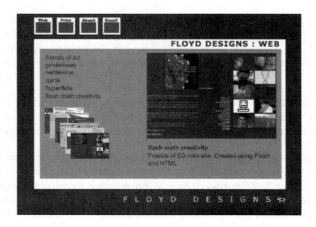

The website you'll create will have a full navigation menu and animated content, and it will dynamically load in images and text files using ActionScript. As it's created, this real world example will reinforce the core skills you learn in this book.

We believe that by learning the Flash skills you need in context, you'll build the knowledge and mental adaptability to fit your expanding knowledge and specialization into a structured and reliable framework.

How to use this book

To use this book, all you'll need is a copy of Macromedia Flash MX 2004 and a computer to run it on. If you want to publish your Flash movies onto the Internet, you'll also need a connection and some web space to publish them to. Your Internet Service Provider (ISP) will be able to sort this out for you if you have any problems.

The case study you'll create contains an animated introduction, interactive buttons, examples of dynamic masking using ActionScript, and it will be fully optimized for publishing to the Web. It's modular nature means that you can easily go back and find the specific functionality that you're looking for and modify it or replace it with something completely different. If, for example, you want to use the buttons in a different website or reuse any of the animated effects, you can easily flip to the relevant chapter for a recap on how to do it, and then just pull the desired part out of the one movie and incorporate it in the other.

You don't have to download anything to use this book, but we've supplied support files containing the sounds and images that we've used to allow you to recreate the worked examples exactly as they are in the book. The case study files, and all support material, can be found in the **Downloads** section of our website at **www.friendsofed.com**. We'll point you at the relevant files in the chapters as necessary.

The case study project files are there so you can pick up the project at any stage in the book and work through it, or you can use them as backups if you've lost your files and don't want to have to re-create them all again. You may just want to check that your results are the same as ours. The files are arranged so that you have a pre-prepared project as the starting point for any chapter. For example, if you want to start from Chapter 5, you'd go into the appropriate folder and use the `for chapter5.fla` file, which contains all the work done on the case study from the beginning through to Chapter 4. Likewise, if you've just finished the Chapter 5 case study and want to check it against ours to make sure it looked right, you would use the `for chapter6.fla`.

We also have some optional sound and video files that can be downloaded if you want to try your hand at the compression material we cover in Chapter 11. These (uncompressed) sound and video files are quite large, though, and could take a long time to download on some connections.

Support: friends of ED designer forums

If you have any questions about the book or about friends of ED, check out our website http://www.friendsofed.com. There are a range of contact e-mail addresses there, or you can just use feedback@friendsofed.com.

There are also a host of other features up on the site: interviews with renowned designers, samples from our other books, and a message board at www.friendsofed.com/forums where you can post your own questions, discussions, and answers, or you can just look at what other designers are talking about. So, if you have any comments or problems, write us—it's what we're here for and we'd love to hear from you.

Layout conventions used in this book

We've tried to keep this book as clear and easy to follow as possible, so we've only used a few layout styles:

- When you first come across an important word it will be in **bold** type, then in normal type thereafter.
- We'll use a different font to emphasize code and `file names`. We'll also use this font when we want you to `type some text`.
- Menu commands are written in the form Menu ➤ Sub-menu ➤ Sub-menu.
- When there's some information we think is really important, we'll highlight it like this:

> *This is very important stuff—don't skip it!*

- Worked exercises are laid out like this:

1. Open Flash.

2. Start a new movie file, and save it as `TestMovie.fla`.

3. Etc....

PCs and Macs

To keep the book as easy to read as possible, we've used PC commands as a default so that every time you come across a command you don't have to read something long-winded like, "right-click (on the PC) or *CTRL*+click (on the Mac)."

We've written instructions for both formats only when there is a difference between the standard Mac substitute command and the actual command required.

When we tell you to click something, we mean *left*-click on the PC or simply *click* on the Mac. The common substitute commands are:

PC	Mac
Right-click	*CTRL*+click
CTRL+click	Apple+click
CTRL+*Z* (to undo)	Apple+*Z*
CTRL+*ENTER*	Apple+*ENTER*

The images of the Flash interface are shown using either Windows Classic or Windows XP Silver operating system. Windows Classic is a common Windows interface for most non-XP machines. Windows XP Silver is not the XP default, but it has the advantage of being the most color-neutral operating system interface so it will not detract from your Flash designs. To change your Windows operating system appearance: Right-click anywhere on the desktop, select Properties, and click the Appearance Tab. The following images show Windows XP set up for Classic and XP Silver via this tab:

Flash MX 2004 and Flash MX Professional 2004

Although there are two versions of Flash, most of the stuff we talk about in this book are common to both. When we say Flash or Flash MX 2004, you can assume we mean both versions, unless we mention Flash MX Professional 2004.

Let's get to work.

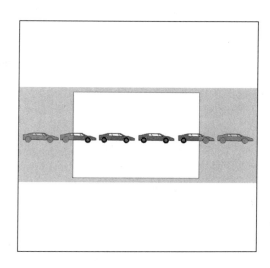

Chapter 1

FLASH MOVIE ESSENTIALS

What we'll cover in this chapter:

- The Flash **stage**: exploring the area where you create your movies in Flash.
- The **Properties panel**: finding and using tool and object properties guaranteed to make authoring in Flash easier.
- The **Document Properties panel**: manipulating the size of the stage and changing your movie's overall background.
- The **timeline**: controlling the playback of your movies.
- **Frames**: creating and arranging the content of your movie.
- **Animation**: making content move.
- **Layers**: adding depth to your movie keeping track of complex content.
- **Scenes**: creating separate scenes that contain distinct chunks of your movie.

Macromedia Flash is the gateway to state of the art web content. Flash is the standard file format for delivering interactive, visually rich content and animation on the Web. (This is the SWF file format we talked about in the Introduction.) It's also the authoring environment that lets you create and publish the SWF files.

In this chapter, we're going to introduce you to the authoring environment—the Flash MX 2004 interface—and take you through the essentials of creating visual content in Flash and making it move. In doing this, we'll start building a picture of the main components of a Flash movie and see how they fit together.

Taking time to understand the core elements at the heart of a Flash movie will pay off later—after you have a firm grasp of the foundations, you'll be able to build on them.

So let's begin by looking at the first thing that almost everybody wants to do when they open their copy of Flash—create a movie and make interesting things happen on the screen.

The authoring environment

If you don't already have Flash up and running, start it now.

When you first open Flash, you see an array of screen elements: icons, menus, toolbars, panels, and status bars:

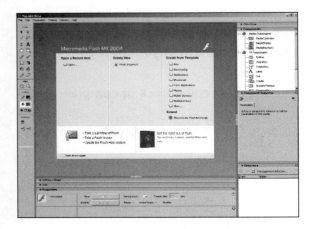

If you've already explored Flash a little, your screen setup might look a little different from the previous screenshot. For the purposes of this book, it's best to reset to the default setup. Don't worry too much about this for now; we'll show you how to do that in a moment.

This is the feature-rich authoring environment (Flash's studio, workshop, and test track combined) that lets you create your Flash movies and export them so they can be published on the Web and accessed by the adoring multitude.

If you've never used a Macromedia product before, you might be intimidated by the unfamiliar interface the first time you open Flash—don't be. Before long, you'll be navigating the interface with ease. And there's an added bonus to learning the Flash interface: Macromedia uses a common interface across their software, so once you're familiar with Flash, you'll have no trouble finding your way around other Macromedia Studio MX 2004 Suite programs such as Fireworks or Dreamweaver.

There's a tremendous amount of detail and power tucked away in the Flash interface, and at first it can seem a little daunting if you're new to the software. To avoid a sense of clutter, and in order to "turn down the volume" a little, let's clear some of the elements out of the way. Then you can concentrate on the bare essentials. (Don't worry, you won't be missing a thing—we'll explain all the core features during the course of this book.)

Configuring the authoring environment

1. Select Create New ➤ Flash Document from the central window or File menu ➤ New ➤ Flash Document (see figure on the next page):

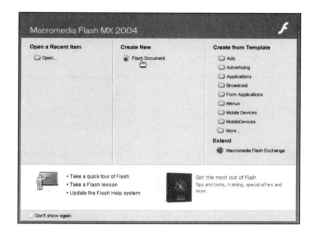

number of things. You can use the panels and menu options to alter their characteristics and the way they behave. All the panels are dockable; you can drag them around the screen and dock them to the other panels.

Draggable Handle

Panels can also be separated from their peers and go it alone. A lone panel has a slightly different appearance than one docked with other panels because single panels have an extra bar added at the top:

> Flash MX Professional 2004 users will see a number of available document types in the center column of the startup screen. Most of these document types are beyond the scope of this book. For all the exercises throughout the book, select the Flash Document type.

2. If you used Flash before picking up this book, reset the default setup by selecting Window ➤ Panel Sets ➤ Default Layout.

3. Minimize all the palettes—called **panels**—on the right side of the screen. You can do this by clicking the black text at the top of each panel until all the panels are stacked up.

Floating panels are used to help you modify and manipulate the content of your Flash movie after you've created that content. This content can be graphic images, pieces of animation, text, and any

> For the benefits of clarity in screenshots throughout the book, you will often see our panels going it alone. This enables us to clearly focus on that single panel.

Now let's customize the authoring environment. If you decide at a later stage that Macromedia's preset Flash panel layouts (Window ➤ Panel Sets) aren't particularly to your liking, you have the option of saving your own customized layout (Window ➤ Save Panel Layout).

Each element you create in your movie (such as pictures and text) is treated as a discrete object: each element has its own attributes, such as color, transparency, and size, and you can use the panels to change these attributes. Additionally, changing panel settings can alter the way an object behaves. You'll look at all of these attributes as you progress through the book. At the moment though, you don't have any content to work with, so let's move the panels out of the way.

5

4. **Windows users**: click the arrow button on the side of the panel to minimize it:

You can also click the arrow belonging to the panels on the bottom of the screen to hide the Properties, Help, and Actions panels. This hides the panels from view and provides you with a great deal more screen space to play with.

To redisplay the panels, click either of the arrow buttons. Although we've put them out of the way for now, we'll come back to them later.

Mac users: You can close panels by clicking the close button in the top left of each panel.

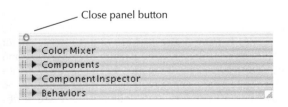

Close panel button

After you've hidden the Properties panel and right-hand panels, maximize the main window.

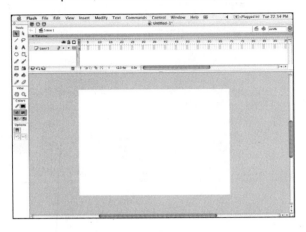

On both platforms, you can close individual panels by right-clicking (CTRL-clicking on Mac) the title bar and clicking Close Panel, *or choosing the* Close Panel *option from the drop-down menu when the panel is maximized.*

Alternatively, selecting Window ➤ Hide Panels *or pressing F4 will also close all panels onscreen (including the Tools panel).*

Next, you want to make sure that you can see all of the area where you're going to create the visual content in your Flash movie.

5. Click the Magnification drop-down list box near the top right of the screen above the timeline.

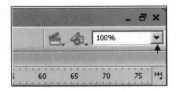

6. Click the Show Frame option:

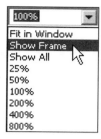

Notice that the white area in the center of the screen is now visible in its entirety:

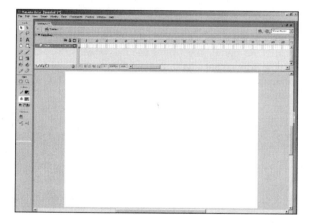

This white area is called the **stage**, and it's where all the action in your movie takes place. The gray area around the stage is called the **work area**. Let's talk a little about these different areas.

The stage

The **stage** can be likened to what a movie director can see in the viewfinder of a camera. What the director sees in the viewfinder is what will appear onscreen when the audience views the finished product. In the motion picture world, the action takes place on the film set (the stage), while actors are waiting off stage, ready to make their entrance.

At various times in the movie, different people and objects will be visible on the stage, and consequently, "in the shot." The stage in Flash works on the same

principle: at any given point in your Flash movie, the things that are on the stage are what the viewer will see when the movie is rendered in their browser. Keep in mind that the movie set can be much larger than the camera's field of view, and the camera can move around and seek out previously hidden corners.

If you want the end user to see something in the Flash movie that plays in their browser, that something has to be visible on the stage area when you create the movie. This also means that movie content can move onto the stage from the "wings." For example, an animated actor could enter stage left, walk across the stage, and exit stage right. In the Flash authoring environment, any visual element that moves beyond the boundaries of the stage winds up in the **work area**.

The work area

The work area surrounds the stage. You can place content in the work area, but only content that actually appears on (or moves across) the stage will show up in the finished movie. When you're designing your movie, you need to think about whether the visual elements it contains will spring into existence directly on the stage, or whether they're going to wait in the wings and then move onto the stage at some point.

Another example of this would be a car that starts its journey in the work area to the left of the stage, moves across the stage (and into the viewer's sight), and then accelerates off into the work area on the right:

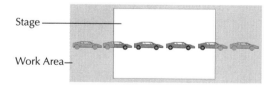

While the content is on the stage, the viewer sees it in the browser. When it's "in the wings", it's invisible to the viewer.

So far you've used the Magnification box to change your view of the stage **in the authoring environment**. Any changes you make by zooming in and out and making the stage look bigger or smaller in the authoring environment will **not** be applied to the finished movie seen by the end user. These magnification changes are just to help you see things more clearly when you're creating and modifying your movie.

To alter the size and proportions of your finished movie when it's displayed in the user's browser, you need to change the **properties** of the stage itself. Flash MX has a resource that enables you to do that easily. It's called the **Properties panel** and we'll take a quick look at that now.

The Properties panel

The Properties panel makes working in Flash a whole lot easier. With the Properties panel, you can easily manipulate all your movie's contents from one place. We'll be using it frequently throughout this book and it will come to be your best friend when creating movies in Flash.

By default, the Properties panel is positioned at the bottom-center of the screen (you might recall minimizing it when you hid all the panels). If you've followed our lead and hidden it, you can retrieve it by pressing the arrow button at the bottom center of the screen.

If you don't already have it open, you can access it with the Window ➤ Properties menu option.

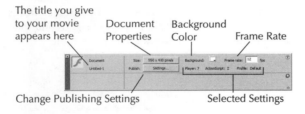

The title you give to your movie appears here · Document Properties · Background Color · Frame Rate

Change Publishing Settings · Selected Settings

You don't have any content on your stage yet, so this is how the Properties panel appears.

The Properties panel is split into two parts: the upper and lower sections. You'll see in the next chapter that when using an item from the Tools panel, the upper section has properties related specifically to that tool, whereas the lower section is related to an item you have selected in your work area. The lower section can be opened and closed using the arrow in the bottom-right corner.

Let's move on to see how you can use the Properties panel even though you have no content on your stage yet.

The size of the stage

When you're planning your Flash movie, you should consider how much browser space you want the finished movie to take up. You'll need to decide what size you want the movie's window to be, based on factors such as the kind of content you're displaying, what else will appear alongside the movie in the host page, and so on. When you've made that decision, you can alter the size of the stage to match your plan.

You can view the stage's current dimensions and global characteristics by clicking the **Size** button in the Properties panel. This opens the **Document Properties** dialog box, where you make global changes to the **properties** (or *characteristics*) that affect the whole movie.

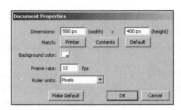

> *You can also display the* Document Properties *dialog box clicking the* Modify ➤ Document *menu option or by right-clicking the stage and selecting* Document Properties...*from the context-sensitive menu.*

You can see that the default dimensions of the stage are 550 pixels wide by 400 pixels high. When you change the dimensions of your stage, Flash will always measure them from the top-left corner. For example, if you change the width of your movie to 750 pixels and the height to 600 pixels, Flash will simply add 50 pixels to the right side of the stage and 50 pixels to the bottom:

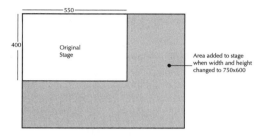

If your brain doesn't translate pixel-speak easily, you can always change the units of measurement that Flash uses throughout the entire movie by picking a different measurement option from the Ruler Units drop-down box:

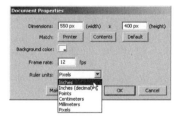

Whichever option you choose will be applied throughout the movie until you choose a different option.

When you set the Dimensions of the stage in this dialog box, you are directly affecting the size of the window that your Flash movie will be displayed in on the user's browser. It's good practice to think about this before you start creating your visual content on the stage. You can always change the size of the stage as and when you like, but the more planning you do, the smoother your movie creation process is likely to be!

Note that the Match: Printer and Match: Contents options will automatically change the size of the stage if you select them: Match: Printer will set the stage size

to reflect the default paper size for your default printer, and Match: Contents will change the stage so that it is large enough to contain all the content elements that you've created (even those that spill over into the work area outside the stage).

As you can see, there are a number of other global properties that you can change for the whole movie. We'll cover all the important properties as they come up during the course of building the example movies in this book. At this stage, let's just observe that the Frame Rate property influences the playback speed and smoothness of your movie. The default frame rate is 12 fps (**frames per second**), which will be fine for most of the movies you'll produce.

The next movie property we want to concentrate on is the Background Color option. You use this option to set the background color your movie has when it's rendered in the user's browser.

The movie's background color

Again, the background color is something you should probably think about when you're *planning* your movie. The questions you might ask yourself include: What size will the display window be in the browser? Will the movie take up the whole display in the browser? Do I need to stick to a color scheme that matches the site in which my Flash movie will appear?

You can change the background color simply by clicking the Background Color box in the Properties panel and selecting a color.

The background color can't change **throughout the entire movie**. You can't change the color in different parts of the movie.

Another thing you need to think about in this context is the background color of the web page in which your movie will appear. If your finished movie is embedded in an HTML page, the choice you make for the background color of the movie is important. By default, Flash will take the background movie color you specify and use it as the background color of the HTML page in which your movie appears.

> There are a number of options you can use when you're exporting your finished movie for publishing on the Web. We'll talk about the built-in publishing features of Flash in more depth later in this book.

For now, let's start a little movie project that you'll be working on over the next couple of chapters. This will be a simple movie that will get you started practicing your Flash skills—and it'll also give you the chance to start expressing your creativity in the Flash authoring environment.

Creating the movie background

The test movie is set at night. The cicadas are doing their thing, there's a cool breeze, the moon is up, and there's the faint aroma of fresh mushrooms rising from a garden mushroom patch. You're going to start creating that scene in Flash.

The background for your little movie scenario is going to be the night sky, so you need to choose a suitable background color to reflect that.

1. If you don't already have it open, display the Properties panel (Window ➤ Properties or press CTRL+F3). Because mushrooms only grow at night, select a deep midnight blue from the **Color** box in the Properties panel (revealed by clicking the Background down arrow):

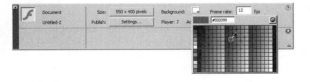

2. Clicking your color will adjust the color of the stage accordingly. You'll notice that when you move the cursor over each color, its identity is displayed with a pound sign (#) followed by a **hexadecimal** value (made up of numbers and letters). These hexadecimal (hex) values are the same ones that people use when writing HTML web pages, and each combination of numbers and letters represent a unique, universally recognized color. This makes it very easy for you to match your background and host web page colors.

Global movie settings

The values you set for this particular movie in the Properties panel are saved automatically. If you want these settings to be applied to **all** of your Flash movies, go to the Document Properties box (Modify ➤ Document or press CTRL+J) and click the Make Default button:

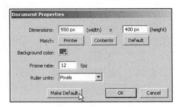

Flash assumes that you want to use these settings whenever you create a new movie. You can change these default settings as and when you need to.

Having set the global properties for your movie, the next step is to create some content. You're going to do that by walking through a basic creation/modification/animation scenario in the context of your nighttime movie. This will familiarize you with some essential techniques and give you the chance to stretch those creative muscles.

While introducing you to the creation/modification/animation process, we need to cover two absolutely critical features of the Flash authoring environment: the **timeline** and **frames**.

The timeline

The **timeline** is one of the most important parts of the Flash interface, and one of the most important things to understand as you learn Flash.

When a web surfer visits your site and your movie starts to play, Flash "interrogates" the timeline encoded in the SWF file and "reads off" what should be displayed in the user's browser. The relationship between your movie's content and the timeline is absolutely vital in coordinating the end effect that the viewer sees.

You've already seen that the Flash stage has height and width. The Flash movie also has another critical dimension—**time**. Although Flash movies can have a high degree of user interaction and change the way they run based on choices that the user makes, the essential experience of seeing a Flash movie is that it **starts** when you open a web page or click a link, and it **finishes** when the movie has run right through or when you exit the web page where the Flash movie is stored.

What the user sees in their browser between the start and end points of the movie is determined by the **content** that you create in your movie and by how you use the timeline to **organize** that content. The length of your movie's timeline will control how long the movie runs and how content changes in the movie over time. As the movie's author, you control all this by using the Flash timeline in conjunction with the content you create.

To help you visualize this, picture a simple movie scenario: imagine a time-lapse nature movie that shows a mushroom growing in slow motion. At the **start** of the movie, you'd have the tiny head of a mushroom poking up from the soil, and at the **end** of the movie, you'd see a full-grown mushroom, standing tall above the grass:

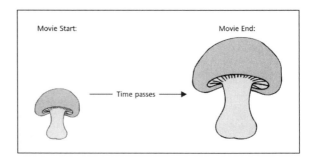

Clearly, your movie won't consist of just those two images, and your movie won't just jump from tiny stalk to full grown instantaneously. In between the two points, time passes, and your mushroom moves through the intermediate stages of growth until it attains its full-grown state. In between the start and end-points of the time-lapse movie will be a whole series of images that represent the mushroom at the different stages of its development:

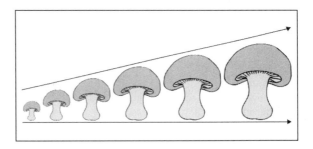

In the real world, mushrooms have a natural growth rate, which is determined by mushroom DNA or by divine guidance (depending on who you ask). In a Flash movie, you have to *imitate* the effect of time passing—and that's where the timeline comes in. To create the effect of time passing, you need a start point, an end point, and some space in between that represents the passage of time. The timeline lets you do this and gives you complete control over the length of your movie, the speed that it plays at, and what you see on the screen at each point in time. How? By using **frames**.

Frames

Let's take a look at the timeline in the Flash authoring environment. If your timeline is closed, open it with the Window ➤ Timeline menu option. After it's open, you'll see this:

Now concentrate on the left part of the timeline:

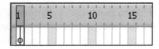

You can see that the top part of the timeline (the solid gray part) is divided up into numbered segments, and there are corresponding divisions in the lower part, consisting of groups of four white rectangles separated by single gray rectangles.

Each of these little boxes on the lower part represents a **frame**, and the numbers on the top part give you a frame number reference: frame 1 on the left, through to frame 45 (and beyond) on the right. Your movie can be 1 frame long, or it can be thousands of frames long. The length of your movie is determined by the highest numbered frame that has content.

The red rectangle with the line coming out of it on the timeline is called the **playhead**.

The playhead

The playhead indicates where you currently are in your movie. You can click the playhead and drag it back and forth along the timeline, and the stage will change to show the contents in the selected frame. At the moment, of course, you don't have any images or objects on the stage, but as you start to add content you'll see how you can spool through your movie using the playhead.

The playhead lets you anticipate what will be seen when the movie plays back in the browser. When you position the playhead over a frame, you see what will be displayed on the screen at that point during playback.

Your movie begins in frame 1. By default, when it loads into the user's browser, your movie will start at frame 1 and play through the rest of the frames in sequence until the end point. Each successive frame on the timeline represents a moment in time, a moment that will be played back when your movie runs.

At the moment, all the frames in the timeline shown here are empty—that's because you haven't created any content yet. If you were to play your nighttime movie now (by pressing *F12*), you'd see just a block of color displayed in the browser window. This is Flash displaying the background color of the movie that you set using the Properties panel. To make your movie more interesting, you have to add content at various points along the timeline that can play back in the browser. This is where frames come in.

By placing content in frames at different points along the timeline, you imitate the passing of time, make animations, and generally make things happen in your movie. Just like that time-lapsed mushroom movie mentioned earlier, you can create start and end points and show all the intermediate stages in between. When the movie plays, Flash looks at each frame on the timeline and renders what it finds there in the user's browser. To achieve the effect of content appearing and disappearing, animating and morphing, Flash provides different types of frames.

To see the nature and effects of the different types of frames that Flash provides, you first have to get some content onto the stage. So without further ado, it's time to start drawing.

Making mushrooms

First let's create a mushroom that will live out its life under the midnight sky that you created as your background.

1. Select View ➤ Snapping ➤ Snap to Objects menu option.

Windows users can also toggle Snap to Objects using the Magnet button in the Main toolbar at the top of the screen. This toolbar is not visible by default, but you can display it by selecting the Window ➤ Toolbars ➤ Main menu option.

Turning on Snap to Objects invokes Flash's ability to help you make your drawings more precise. This feature automatically snaps the drawing cursor to certain points as Flash anticipates what you're trying to do. For example, when you activate Snap to Objects and draw with the Oval tool, Flash jumps to a perfect circle when you get close to it, but with Snap to Objects off, it will let you draw the oval to whatever dimensions you want. Whether you use Snap to Objects or not is entirely dependent on personal preference and what you're trying to achieve. If you're drawing perfect circles, it makes sense to leave it on, but for most freehand drawings it is easier to leave it off. Experiment and see what works best for you in different circumstances.

Next, you need to select the drawing tool that you'll use to draw your mushroom. All the drawing tools are accessed in the Flash **Tools panel**. We'll detail more aspects of the Tools panel and its contents in the next chapter, but you'll start using some of its features as you work through this example.

2. The Tools panel is located (by default) on the left side of the authoring environment. If you hold the mouse pointer over any of the tool buttons in the Tools Panel, a **tool tip** will pop up with a description of what that the button does:

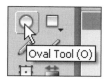

The letter in brackets next to the tool's name is the shortcut key for that tool. In this case, pressing *O* will select the Oval tool. Each of the tools will be

covered in the next chapter, but you'll dip into them now as you set about creating some content.

3. Click the Oval tool.

   Now you need to select a color for the outline of the shape you're going to draw.

4. If you're not already displaying it, bring up your Properties panel by pressing *CTRL+F3*. You'll notice that some of the aspects have changed from those previously seen in the Properties panel. The Properties panel now reflects that you selected the Oval tool:

   Stroke Color   Fill Color

   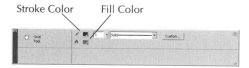

   From here, you can pick a color for the outline (**Stroke color**) of the object you're drawing. Similarly, the **Fill color** box allows you to select the color you want to use to fill the area **inside** the outline. By default, many of the objects you draw using tools from the Tools panel have an outline and a filled interior. You can control and modify these outlines and fills to a very fine degree, as you'll see as you progress through this book.

5. Set the stroke color to a dark brown.

6. Click the **Fill color** box and set the fill color to a lighter, mushroom-like brown.

7. Now for the actual drawing. At the bottom of the stage, about half way across, click and drag with the Oval tool to make a small stalk for your mushroom:

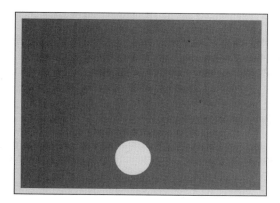

8. Using the same click and drag action, draw a flatter, larger oval just above the stalk. Make sure that there's a gap—a small one—between the two ovals:

This larger oval will be the cap of your baby mushroom.

9. If you look at the timeline now, you'll notice that the first frame has changed:

If you look closely at the lower part, you'll see that this frame is now shaded a darker gray, and that it contains a little black circle. Why is that?

In a new movie, Flash assumes that you want the action to start in frame 1. When you started drawing on the stage, Flash assumed that the oval was the first piece of content you were creating for this movie, so it put the drawing in frame 1.

Flash created the starting point for your movie based on the drawing you made. This is the first fixed point in time for your movie—the first image in a sequence of images that you want to display changing over time. If you like, consider this the first snapshot in a sequence that you want to show to the user.

Flash uses a particular type of frame to store fixed points in time that hold visual (or other) content: this type of frame is called a **keyframe**.

Keyframes

A keyframe indicates that something important happens at the point in the timeline where the keyframe is located. For example, it indicates a point where you displayed some content, made something disappear, or

made a transition from one piece of content to another. Keyframes are markers in time, indicating start and end points for different pieces of action.

Essentially, a keyframe alerts Flash about a point where something significant is placed. Your Flash movies will consist of a series of keyframes spaced out along the timeline, with each keyframe flagging the start and end points of distinct pieces of content that are to be displayed in the user's browser.

Think back to the time-lapsed nature movie that we discussed earlier. Remember how we said that the start and end points of that movie would be the baby mushroom and the full-grown mushroom?

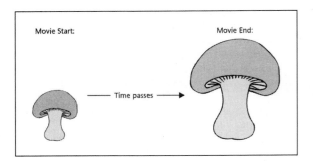

In Flash, those start and end points are defined by **keyframes**. You need a keyframe in frame 1, which contains the baby mushroom image, and a keyframe in a later frame (say frame 15), which will contain the image of the fully developed mushroom:

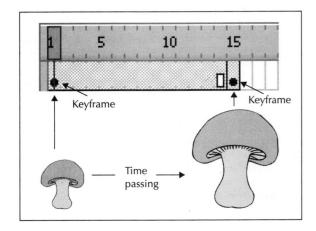

These two keyframes will tell Flash that you have images of your mushroom in two different states: "starting to grow," and "finished growing." After you have those two keyframes in place, you can get Flash to help you create and animate the intermediate growth states for the mushroom that should exist between the start and end images. We'll be looking at how to do that in more detail very shortly. For the moment, remember this:

> *If something significant changes onscreen in your movie, there'll probably be a keyframe involved. Keyframes are the key to making things happen.*

Much more on frames in a moment. First, a bit of housekeeping.

Saving your movie

It's good practice to save your work often—just in case your dog eats it or the computer crashes and burns. The way to save your embryonic Flash movie is the same way you save files in most other programs.

1. Click File ➤ Save in the main menu.

   You'll be prompted with a dialog box asking where you want to save the movie, and what name you would like to give it.

2. Choose (or create) a suitably named folder to save your work in, type Mushroom in the File name box, and click Save:

Flash automatically saves the movie as an FLA file, which is the extension used for Flash authoring files.

> *Remember that there's a distinction between the file that you work on in the authoring environment (the FLA file) and the file that's loaded and played when a surfer visits your site (the SWF file). As an author, you create and modify your content inside the FLA; the SWF is created when you publish your movie. The publishing process takes all the drawings and other content that you created in your FLA file and compresses and encodes them into the SWF format. The SWF file is much smaller and more compact than its parent FLA file, and is thus much quicker and efficient to download for the end user.*

Now that you have your example movie safely saved, you can continue your exploration of frames.

You've already drawn a couple of ovals in frame 1: these represent your baby mushroom—the starting point for your movie. If you were to play the movie now, you'd see a static image of your baby mushroom in the browser. (You can do this by pressing *F12*. This will open your default browser and render your movie. You'll need to close the browser or click back into your Flash window after you've finished viewing your masterpiece.)

The reason you see this static image is that you have created only a single frame with any content in it—the movie has nowhere to go except this single keyframe. When Flash plays back the movie and looks at the timeline, it finds only this single keyframe. Flash's default publishing settings tell it to **loop the playback** of your movie, so what you're seeing in the browser is the same single frame, being shown over and over again as Flash repeatedly loops through the timeline. Flash will continue to do this until you close the browser or move onto another web page.

Next, you're going to see how to add an **end** point for your "mushroom growth" movie, and how to create the sequence of images that imitate the passage of time and show the mushroom growing. This means you'll have a proper movie to play rather than a single-frame loop.

Animation

You've already seen that keyframes mark the beginning and end points of pieces of action in your movie. In this sense, Flash can be compared to traditional animated cartoons. In traditional 'toons, the animator plans out the action sequence that she wants to create—for example, a car driving from one side of the screen to the other. She creates the background for the action—maybe a desert setting with some distant mountains—and this background typically remains static.

Next, the animator creates her start and end images of the car, that is, the car on the left of the screen, and the car on the right of the screen. Clearly, she'd also need to have a series of intermediate images that show the car in progress across the desert. Each image would be drawn onto a separate sheet of transparent acetate. The plan would be to use a movie camera to photograph the start, intermediate, and end images against the static background to create a number of different frames of film. Running the frames in sequence would show the car in motion against the static background.

This is a time-consuming business, and cartoon production companies wouldn't want to make their star animators slave over frame after frame of minutely changing action. The solution is to get the lead animators to create the key images—start and end points and important transitional images—and then use specialized "in-betweeners" to draw the images that come in between the keyframes that the expert animator created. These in-between frames are critical to ensuring that the cartoon action was smooth and convincing.

In Flash, you do things similarly. You can create keyframes that define significant stages in the action that you want to show, and then get Flash to generate the in-between frames that link the keyframes together. This saves us a lot of time and effort in creating the transitional frames, and is an important factor in making Flash the successful animation package that it has become. (Note that you *can* mimic the traditional animation method in Flash if you want, by hand-drawing each frame individually. This can be a powerful way to express yourself and create great

animation, but it's too big a subject to tackle. Maybe in another book....)

> *Throughout the book you'll hear us refer to animation in Flash as* **tweening**. *As you might have guessed, this is short for "in-betweening," or the process of creating the transitional frames that go in-between the keyframes.*

Let's get back to your mushroom movie. Currently, you have that single starting keyframe containing the baby mushroom. Next, you want to create a keyframe that holds the fully grown version, and then get Flash to create all the in-between frames that show the mushroom growing over time. Let's work through that in an exercise now.

Working with frames

As we've said already, a keyframe marks a significant change in your movie. In order to create the image showing your mushroom when it's fully grown, you need to add a keyframe to the timeline. This will tell Flash that you have some important new content that it needs to be aware of.

To insert a new keyframe into the timeline, you simply click the timeline at the position where you want to add your keyframe. After you've selected the frame position, you can choose the Insert ➤ Keyframe menu option, or use the keyboard shortcut *F6*, and a new keyframe will appear.

You might wonder how far along the timeline you should put your second keyframe. The answer to this depends on how long you want your piece of action to last. The thing to remember here is the **frame rate** setting that you saw in the Properties panel—12 frames per second by default. This frame rate setting means that **for every 12 frames your movie takes up on the timeline, there will be one second of action when the movie plays back**. The math is fairly simple: estimate how long you want the action to last in seconds, and multiply the number of seconds by the frame rate. You can always change the position of the keyframes later on if you need to tweak the timing of different pieces of action.

Let's make that mushroom grow.

1. Click frame 14—parallel to the first keyframe—of your mushroom movie and press *F6* to insert a keyframe.

   You'll see immediately that the timeline has changed:

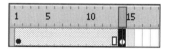

Frame 14 now has a black circle in it and a black border (note that the circle is white and the frame black in the image above because the frame is selected), and all the frames between frames 1 and 14 have turned gray. Additionally, there's a small white rectangle in frame 13, and the playhead has jumped to frame 14. Let's take a look at what this all means:

- The black border around frame 14 indicates that it is a keyframe. You're going to use this keyframe to hold some content that's different from the frames that precede it.

- The white rectangle in frame 13 tells us that it is the last frame before a new keyframe, and that all the frames to the left of this rectangle contain the same content as the **previous** keyframe—in this case, frame 1. The frames are grayed to show you that they contain the same content as frame 1. Every frame in the black-bordered box running from frame 1 through frame 13 contains the same image of the baby mushroom you created in frame 1.

- The black circle in the keyframe at frame 14 indicates that this frame contains some content. But how come? You didn't add any content to this frame yet, did we? What's happened is that Flash has carried over the content from the

previous keyframe (frame 1). This is the default behavior when you add a new keyframe. This feature can be very useful, as you'll see in a moment.

There's one other thing to note here: when you move the playhead backward and forward through your movie, the current frame number is indicated in the area just underneath the timeline:

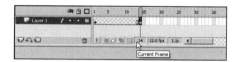

So far then, you've got an opening keyframe (frame 1), followed by some intermediate frames (frames 2–13), and a new keyframe (frame 14) that will soon contain the image of your fully grown mushroom.

All the frames from 2 to 13 now "belong" to the keyframe in frame 1 and reflect what is in it. If you changed the image in frame 1, the "slave" frames (2–13) would change to reflect the new picture. Frame 14 would remain as it is, however, because you told Flash that you want this frame to be self-contained so that it can contain new content.

2. Double-click anywhere on the timeline between the two keyframes. You'll see that frames 1 through 13 turn black:

This shows you that these frames all hold the same content—they're all dependent on the content in the keyframe at frame 1. You can't alter the content in frames 2 through 13 by editing them directly—you can change their contents *indirectly* by amending what's in frame 1. You can directly edit only content that's in a keyframe.

3. Deselect the black-highlighted frames by clicking away from them. Next, click anywhere between the

keyframes. This time, only the frame you clicked is selected:

4. Use the Insert ➤ Timeline ➤ Frame menu option or press the *F5* key twice to insert two new frames into the timeline at the position where you just clicked. This will add two frames to the timeline, and these new frames will inherit the contents from the preceding keyframe (frame 1).

Using the playhead to move through your movie, you can see that it is now 16 frames long, and each of the frames contains the same picture of a mushroom. We promise that your mushroom will grow soon, but first there are a few more tricks we can show you with frames.

5. Click between the keyframes again to select a single frame.

This time, rather than inserting slave frames, you're going to insert a **blank keyframe**. A blank keyframe is just what its name suggests—a keyframe that has no content in it. It is, however, independent of the content of the keyframe that precedes it.

6. Use the Insert ➤ Timeline ➤ Blank Keyframe menu option or press the *F7* key to convert one of the normal frames in your timeline into a blank keyframe:

A blank keyframe is represented in a similar way as a keyframe except that it shows an unfilled circle in the timeline. This is because it doesn't yet have any content. The remaining white frames are all dependent on the blank keyframe you just inserted.

7. If you now scroll through your movie using the playhead, you'll see that all the dependent frames after the blank keyframe are also blank, reflecting the fact that the keyframe before them is empty. Blank keyframes are useful for stopping animations or dividing different pieces of content that exist on the same layer. (Stay tuned, there's more on layers later.)

You'll also see that the keyframe at frame 16 still has the baby mushroom image in it. That's because it inherited the content of frame 1 when you created it. However, there is no link between the inherited image and the current (possibly amended) content of frame 1—frame 16's keyframe is completely independent.

8. You don't want half of the frames in your movie to be blank, so somehow you'll have to get rid of that blank keyframe and its dependent frames. There are two ways to do this: you can either delete the blank keyframe or convert it into a normal frame. Let's do the latter—the advantage of this is that the movie's length remains the same.

9. Click the blank keyframe and use the Modify ➤ Timeline ➤ Clear Keyframe menu option or press *SHIFT*+*F6*. The white frames become shaded again, and if you run the movie through now, you'll see that they've all been refilled with your baby mushroom picture.

You now have 16 frames in your movie, all filled with exactly the same mushroom image. You want the movie to last for 15 frames because it's a nice round number, so you'll have to remove one of those frames now.

10. Click to select a single frame anywhere between the two keyframes and use the Edit ➤ Timeline ➤ Remove Frames menu option or press *SHIFT*+*F5* to delete the highlighted frame. You should now be left with two keyframes on your timeline (in frames 1 and 15) and a set of identical normal frames between the keyframes that contain the same image of your mushroom you created in frame 1.

The normal frames that separate the keyframes may appear to be plain and boring at the moment, but don't dismiss them: they're the Flash equivalent of pawns on a chessboard or foot soldiers in an army—not as glamorous as the other elements, but just as important.

In Flash, there are three methods for adding, converting, and deleting frames, each with its own advantages and disadvantages. The first and most formal method is to use the Timeline section of the Edit, Insert, and Modify menus. These menus contain all the manipulation actions associated with frames.

The second and probably most commonly used method is the keyboard shortcuts that mimic the menu options. The major problem with this is that you have to learn them first, although this is something that most people pick up quite quickly.

The third method is to right-click the relevant frame in the timeline to highlight it, and then to select the appropriate command from the context-sensitive menu that appears. Throughout the tutorial sections in this book, we'll use a mixture of these methods. There is no single best method—whichever one you find easiest is the one you should use.

As promised, let's make your mushroom live and…well, breathe.

Making the mushroom grow

Frame 15 is going to be the final frame of your movie, which means that you need to populate it with the content that represents the final growth stage of your mushroom. Let's add the fully grown mushroom image to the keyframe in frame 15.

1. Click frame 15 in the timeline. Notice that when you click the frame the whole mushroom (the two ovals you drew earlier) is already selected. Remember, these ovals were inherited from the keyframe in frame 1, so they are identical in shape and position to the mushroom in frame 1. This in turn means that you don't have to worry about positioning the image of the mushroom in frame 15—it's in exactly the same place as it in frame 1. This will make your animation easier to create.

A related and very useful feature in Flash is the ability to copy (or cut) and paste content into exactly the same location on the stage. This is particularly useful when you want to paste images or other components into other keyframes or other layers and still have them occupy the same coordinates on the stage as the original image. To achieve this, copy (or cut) the original component, and then use the Edit ➤ Paste in Place *menu option. This way you are sure to place your object exactly where you want it. We guarantee that you'll find this feature immensely useful in your Flash career.*

2. Click the Selection tool in the top left corner of the Tools Panel and then click the background of the stage to deselect the mushroom.

3. Double-click the middle of the cap of your mushroom. This will select both the stroke and the fill. If you had only clicked once in the middle of the cap, you would have selected only the fill.

4. Click the mushroom cap and drag it up to where you want the cap of your full-grown mushroom to be. (Alternatively, holding *SHIFT* and using the arrow keys makes your selection move in units of 10 pixels):

If you hold down the SHIFT key while you drag, Flash will help you drag the mushroom cap upward in a straight line (provided that you've turned on the Snap to Objects option).

5. Double-click the stalk (the lower oval) to select it, and then press *BACKSPACE*. This will delete the baby version of the stalk from frame 15 (although the old, smaller stalk is still intact in frames 1 through 14).

Your next task is to create the fully grown version of the mushroom stalk.

6. Click the Oval tool in the Tools panel again, and draw a long thin oval from the bottom of the cap of your mushroom down to the bottom of the stage, again ensuring that there's a small gap left between the edges of the two ovals. This is your adult mushroom stalk:

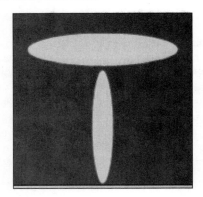

If you need to move your new stalk after you've drawn it, select the Selection tool, double-click the stalk, and drag it to the desired position. If things go wrong, you can always use the undo option by selecting Edit ➤ Undo from the menu bar, or pressing CTRL+Z.

7. Press the *ENTER* key to preview your movie. Hmm...not *particularly* convincing, is it? You're

getting the same picture for 14 frames, and then a sudden jump to a fully grown fungus. What you really want is a smooth transition from baby mushroom to big mushroom, and Flash can do that for you. You're about to see how Flash can perform as an underpaid, unappreciated "in-betweener."

8. Double-click between the two keyframes on the timeline to select the first keyframe and all the normal frames that depend on it:

What you're going to do now is change the behavior of these frames. You're going to tell Flash that you want to create an animation that smoothly transforms the small mushroom in frame 1 into the fully grown version that you just created in frame 15. Your ability to do this is entirely dependent on the existence of your two keyframes. The keyframes define the two different states of the mushroom, and you're asking Flash to create all the in-between frames that will represent the growth of the mushroom. Let's do that.

9. If you don't have your Properties panel open, open it with the Window ➤ Properties menu option. Then click the frames. The Properties panel will now change to reflect your choice:

Now you're going to use the Properties panel to give these frames a label and create your growth animation.

10. Click inside the far left box (under the word Frame) in the Properties panel and give your frames a Name label that identifies them—we've called ours Mushroom Growth. This attaches the label to frame 1. Now if you look at your frames, you can see a little red flag to draw your attention to the label:

Using labels makes it easier to identify specific bits of action inside a large and complex movie. If you keep objects on separate layers and name those layers, you should not need to use large number of labels. They will come in useful later on when we start to deal with actions, but this will be discussed in greater detail when we come to it.

11. Click the drop-down menu next to Tween, and select Shape.

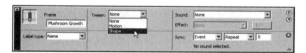

This will automatically create a **shape tween**: Flash will understand that you want the stalk in frame 1 to morph into the stalk in frame 15, and that you want the cap in frame 1 to morph into the cap in frame 15, and it will automatically generate the in-between images in frames 2 through 14 that will produce this effect.

12. Click the playhead and notice that the tweened frames on the timeline have now been colored green by Flash, indicating a shape tween. There is also an arrow pointing from Frame 1 to Frame 15 that indicates the length of the tween.

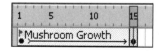

(For clarity, we've removed the label from subsequent screenshots.)

13. Slowly drag the playhead back to Frame 1, noticing that Flash has automatically filled in all the animation frames between 1 and 15. Press *ENTER* to preview the movie, and the mushroom will steadily grow to its full-size.

14. Save your happy-grow-lucky mushroom.

We've spent some time looking at frames in Flash, and started to see how they can help you achieve the effects that you're after in your movies. What we'll do next is introduce you to another vital element of Flash authoring files—**layers**.

Layers

Whereas the timeline and its frames help you organize and manipulate content over time, layers help you add depth to the movie and allow you to separate out pieces of content and action that would otherwise get tangled up. If you had to place your entire movie content on a single layer, it would be horrendously difficult to achieve anything complicated. By separating the action onto different layers, you can create much more convincing and complex movies, and make full use of the flexibility and power that Flash's timeline gives you. Multiple layers mean that your movies can have a host of different elements on the stage, all acting completely independently of each other.

A traditional animator would have a different set of sheets of acetate for each part of her cartoon. For example, the background forest would be on one set of sheets, Red Riding Hood would be happily skipping on another set, and the Big Bad Wolf would be stalking her from yet another set. By keeping the parts separate, the animator has much greater control over the individual aspects of their cartoon. If something needed to be altered, the animator could change just one set—say, adding an evil twinkle to the Wolf's eye—without having to redraw the forest or Miss Riding-Hood as well. Another benefit of having separate animations on different sets of acetate is that the sets can be reused later in the cartoon, or indeed in a completely different cartoon, so while Jack and Jill are running up the hill in cartoon two, cartoon one's Little Red Riding-Hood can be happily skipping along below them without having to be redrawn. The content on the different layers is independent and portable.

In Flash, layers are shown to the left of the timeline. Each new Flash movie comes with a single layer by default:

Insert Layer Folder
Insert Layer Button
Delete Layer

This layer—Layer 1—is the default layer you've been working with in your mushroom movie so far.

In Flash, layers are the equivalent of those separate sheets of acetate containing different visual components. Layers make movies easier to alter, and allow for much greater richness of content. Let's take a look at what layers allow you to do in your sample movie.

Working with layers

It's good practice to keep each element of your movie on a separate layer for ease of editing and for neatness. Let's see how this works in this exercise.

1. The **active layer** in Flash is the highlighted layer with the pencil icon next to its name. This pencil icon indicates that this layer is currently selected.

2. Click the Insert Layer button. Flash will create a new layer above Layer 1 and call it Layer 2.

3. Notice that Flash has automatically made Layer 2 15 frames long to match the length of Layer 1. If you look at any of these frames though, they will still all be empty:

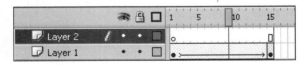

Flash always calls a new layer **Layer** *n* where *n* is sequential from the last layer you created. This means that even if you subsequently delete a layer,

Flash will still increment the next layer's number as if the deleted layer still exists. For example, if you delete Layer 2 and then add another layer, the new layer would be called Layer 3 even though there is no longer a Layer 2. Luckily, the good people at Macromedia understand just how confused you are at the moment, so instead of trying to work out which layer is which, they've given you the ability to uniquely name each layer, which means that you can forget about the whole numbers shebang and work with meaningful, descriptive layer names instead. Giving names to your movie's layers is another good habit to get into, and it will save you a lot of heartache.

4. Double-click the name Layer 1 in the timeline. When you double-click it, it will become editable, allowing you to change the name of the layer:

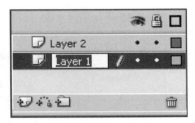

5. Type mushroom and press *ENTER*.

6. You want Layer 2 to contain a picture of the moon in front of your night-sky background, so double-click where it says Layer 2, type moon and press *ENTER*. You now have your two layers meaningfully named and you can instantly infer what's on each of them.

7. Click the Oval tool. Your moon will be a full one, so you'll use this tool to create the celestial body.

8. Click the Black and White button under the two color boxes at the bottom of the Tools panel:

   This button resets the colors to a black stroke with a white fill, Flash's defaults.

9. Still on the moon layer, use the playhead to go to the final frame of the movie, and then draw a circle (remember, you can hold down the *SHIFT* key to help you draw a perfect circle) over the top of the right side of your fully grown mushroom cap:

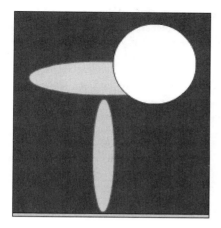

If you look at the timeline, you'll notice that Flash has automatically created a keyframe at frame 1 of the moon layer, and that it has also populated all the frames on this layer with the image of the moon. This is a handy effect, because you want the moon to be visible in the sky throughout your movie. If you'd wanted the moon to appear in the movie from frame 15 onward (but not before), you'd have needed to create a keyframe at frame 15 in the **moon** layer.

10. Press *ENTER* to play your movie. Flash has zipped through the timeline and displayed the content of both layers for you.

But something looks slightly wrong, doesn't it? The mushroom seems to be further away than the moon, and bigger, too. If you're going to get the perspective right, you'll need to put the moon *behind* the mushroom. You need to get the layers' stacking order right.

The higher up a layer appears in the layer list on the left of the timeline, the closer the contents of that layer appear to you on the screen. To get your mushroom in front of the moon, you just have to move its layer above the moon's layer in the layer list. Let's do that now.

11. Click the name of the mushroom layer in the layer list and drag it above the moon layer. You'll see a shaded bar appear while you're dragging the layer:

This indicates where the layer will go when you release the mouse.

12. Now when you play your movie, the mushroom will rise in front of the moon. Perspective has been returned, and the tale of the very big mushroom and the very small moon has been consigned once more to legend.

Deleting a layer is as easy as adding a layer—it only takes the click of a button. To delete a layer, click the layer to highlight it, and then click the **Delete Layer** button, which is indicated by the trash can icon underneath the layer listing. You should note that Flash won't let you delete **all** the layers in a movie; there must always be at least one layer. If you're trying to delete everything from a movie and start again, it's easier to close the current movie and start a new one.

> *As you've seen, layers are a useful way to manage and control your content. Flash has the added ability of using layer folders to bundle together similar layers for further ease—more on these in Chapter 4.*

Layer modes

Layer modes define how you view and use specific layers in the authoring environment. There are three layer modes in Flash and, by default, they're all turned off. You control the three modes by clicking the icons in the columns after the layer name. The status of the modes for a particular layer is indicated by the two dots and the square next to that layer's name:

Show/Hide All Layers — Lock/Unlock All Layers — Show All Layers as Outlines

The first column controls showing and hiding a layer, the second controls locking and unlocking a layer, and the third column is used for viewing the contents of that layer as outlines. Let's take a look at how these different modes interact in the authoring environment, and see what benefits they offer.

Working with layer modes

With all three of the layer mode selector icons in the off position, the authoring environment will behave exactly as it has done so far. If you were to draw a circle with the Oval tool right now, it would appear as normal on the currently selected (active) layer. Let's see what happens when you start switching the layer modes on.

1. In the mushroom layer, click the dot underneath the picture of the eye.

   Three things happen:

   ■ Because you hid the layer, its contents disappear from the stage in the authoring environment

   ■ A red cross replaces the dot in the eye column, reminding you that this layer is currently hidden

   ■ The pencil icon gets a red line struck through it, indicating that the contents of the hidden layer cannot be edited. If you try to draw on the stage now, you'll find that the cursor has changed to a pencil with a warning circle next to it:

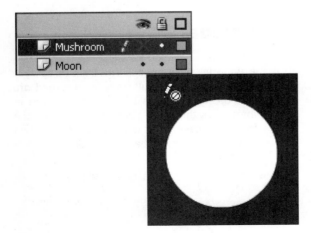

The warning circle tells you that the currently selected tool can't be used at the moment. The logic here is that if you *were* able to draw on the hidden layer, you'd be able to unwittingly draw all over the content that you've created so carefully already. Flash is protecting you from yourself.

If you were to click the stage with the Oval tool, you'd get an error prompt:

Hiding layers is very helpful when you need to concentrate on content on a particular layer and you don't want the contents of other layers to obstruct your view. For example, in the final frame of your mushroom movie, the mushroom covers part of the moon. If you wanted to draw a face on your moon, it would be hard to see what you were doing because the mushroom would be in the way. By hiding the mushroom layer, you can see the whole of the moon, select the moon layer, and draw to your heart's content. You could then click the cross in the eye column and the mushroom layer would be visible again.

2. Click the cross in the eye column to return everything to normal. Then click the dot in the lock column. A small padlock replaces the dot, and the pencil again has a line through it. This time though, although the layer is locked and you can't draw or select objects on it, the mushroom is visible.

   Locking layers allows you to work with objects above or below them without accidentally selecting anything in the locked layers. This is useful when you're drawing or modifying on one layer and you want to see the contents of the other layers to keep things in context. Locking the surrounding layers means you can draw and edit confidently, secure in the knowledge that you won't mess anything up on the other layers.

   The final mode allows you to display all objects on a layer as **outlines only**, rather than as filled shapes.

3. Unlock the mushroom layer by clicking the small padlock across from the layer name. Click the colored box to the right—the mushroom is reduced

to just an outline. The outline takes its color from the color of the box that you just clicked. Each layer will have its own dedicated outline color (automatically allocated by Flash), so you can easily make out which objects belong to which layer.

4. Click the outline button on the moon layer and (on your monitor, at least!) you'll see that the moon's outline is a different color than the mushroom's.

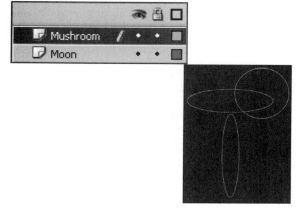

Outline mode is useful for helping you get a grip on exactly what's in your movie across all layers. Things start to get complicated when you have lots of different things on lots of layers and you can't quite see what is going on. Outline mode lets you step back from the jumble and get a clear view. Outline mode is also helpful for previewing your movie because it's easier for Flash to render outlines than filled shapes, meaning that the movie preview displays quicker.

You can easily change the layer mode for **all** the layers by using the icons at the top of each of the columns. To turn outline mode **off** for both of your movie's layers, just click the black box next to the eye and the lock: This will instantly return your mushroom and moon to their full-color glory.

If you're working with a lot of layers and want to lock every layer except the layer you're currently working on, it is easiest to click the **Lock/Unlock All Layers** button to lock every layer, and then click the small padlock on the layer that you want to use to unlock that layer. The same principle applies to the show/hide feature invoked via the eye icon.

Using layer folders (see Chapter 4), it is possible to lock or hide the content of a folder with one click. Locking or hiding the folder layer also affects all the content within the layer in the same way. This makes it easy to show/hide or lock/unlock similarly grouped elements while editing other content on the stage.

Layer modes affect only how you see the layers as you are constructing them. They have no effect on the final movie that you create, so layers that are hidden in the authoring environment will be visible in the final movie. Similarly, layers that are in outline mode will be seen in full color when they're rendered in the browser.

Now let's move on to the last Flash concept that we want to introduce into this chapter—**scenes**.

Scenes

Scenes are used to organize your movie into sections that you can view as independent pieces of the whole movie. The ability to have a multi-scene movie allows you to break up your content into logical chunks and helps you organize things efficiently.

Flash movies can be large or small, simple or complex. Small, simple movies can usually be contained in a single scene with no problem, but when you're creating a large movie with many components, or one that has long animations or multiple navigation elements, multiple scenes can be the way to go.

You can think of scenes as an extension of your timeline; they give you the facility to break up the action and continue from one scene to another. The benefit to you as an author is that your authoring files are more manageable. The benefit to the user can be a more navigable movie. Many developers simply use separate scenes for their preloader (an element of a Flash movie that downloads movie components in advance of their being used), the introduction, and the main movie.

Some developers also use separate scenes in the same way that traditional designers use HTML pages on their sites—one scene is equivalent to one HTML page. This can be a useful model when you're designing a whole site in Flash—you can create a front page for your site and then jump to different scenes (pages) depending on which buttons the user presses.

Each new Flash movie starts out with one default scene, named **Scene 1**. You can tell what scene you are currently in by looking at the scene name directly above your layers:

You can view, add, or delete scenes as you like by using the Scene panel (Window ➤ Design Panels ➤ Scene or *SHIFT+F2*).

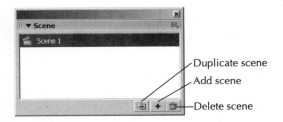

Here, you can use the buttons to manipulate scenes, and you can drag scenes to change the order of playback. You can also double-click any scene in the Scene panel and give it a meaningful name. Once again, this is useful for bringing clarity to your movie authoring files.

By default, Flash always plays the scenes in the sequence in which the scenes are listed in the Scene panel, so make sure you keep the right scenes in the right order. However, you can also use Flash ActionScript to jump from scene to scene and play them in different sequences.

Another way to switch between scenes in the authoring environment is to click the Scene button directly above the frames on the right, and click the scene you want to edit in the drop-down list:

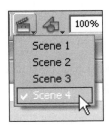

There's yet another way of navigating between your movie's scenes in the authoring environment: the **Movie Explorer**.

The Movie Explorer

The Movie Explorer gives you the ability to browse your way through your whole movie at different levels of detail. You can open the Movie Explorer by choosing the Window ➤ Other Panels ➤ Movie Explorer menu option or by pressing *ALT+F3*.

The Movie Explorer window looks something like this:

As you can see from this view from your mushroom movie, the Movie Explorer reveals the contents of your movie in depth, in terms of its component scenes, layers, and keyframes (provided that you've chosen the relevant options from the Show buttons along the top). You can click any node in this displayed hierarchy and view that point in the movie. This is a powerful way of helping you navigate through your movies—especially as your movies grow in size and scope. You'll be seeing more of the Movie Explorer as you progress through the book.

For now, though, let's recap what you've seen before you move on to the next chapter.

Summary

In this chapter, we've introduced you to the Flash authoring environment and demonstrated some of the essential elements of Flash movie creation.

You saw that:

- You create movie content on the **stage**, which has a surrounding **work area**.
- You can use the Properties panel to change the global characteristics of your movie, such as size and background color.
- You add content to the stage, and it is displayed in the viewer's browser when the movie plays back.
- Your movie is a series of points in time. These are played back in sequence as the playhead moves along the timeline.

- You use keyframes to hold new or changed content, and to indicate to Flash that something significant is happening. Keyframes are separated by normal frames that influence how long the action between keyframes lasts.
- You can create Layers to add depth and manageability to your movies.
- You can use Scenes to separate your movies into distinct chunks.
- You can use the Movie Explorer to navigate through your entire movie and browse through its content.

In the next chapter, we're going to look in more depth at the built-in Flash tools that let you create movie content. As you've already seen, these tools are found in the Flash **Tools panel**.

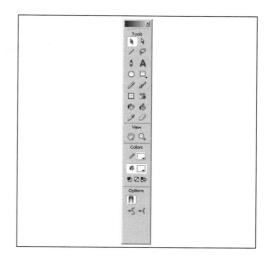

Chapter 2

THE FLASH TOOLS PANEL

What we'll cover in this chapter:

■ The Flash **Tools panel:** where you find Flash's integral drawing and manipulation tools, and what they're capable of

■ How to use these tools to create and amend movie content: images and text

■ Precision drawing and fine-tuning with Bezier curves

In the previous chapter, you looked at the key structures contained in every Flash movie—the stage, the timeline, keyframes, frames and layers. In this chapter, you're going to start exploring Flash's built-in facilities for creating and manipulating movie content.

To do this, you'll examine each of Flash's drawing and editing tools in context by creating a Flash illustration. These tools are the integral means that Flash gives you for drawing pictures, creating text, and manipulating these and other visual elements on the stage.

All these built-in content creation tools are accessed via the Flash **Tools panel**.

The Tools panel

The Tools panel is where you'll find all Flash's drawing and editing tools. Using these tools in conjunction with Flash's Properties panel and other panels, you'll have at your disposal everything you need to design and manipulate the visual components and building blocks of your movie.

By default, the Tools panel is situated on the left side of the screen when you open Flash for the first time, but you can move it around or hide it, just like any other window. The Tools panel itself is subdivided into four sections—Tools, View, Colors, and Options:

- The **Tools** section is where all the basic design and manipulation options are found. These tools can be used to draw pictures, create text elements, select objects, and move them around the stage—amongst other things.

- The **View** section contains tools for two main functions: zooming in and out on the stage, and changing the stage's position on the screen. These changes of view and position apply only to the screen display in the authoring environment where you're creating the movie—any changes you make to the view here don't have any effect on the

way the finished movie itself is rendered in the user's browser. You might, for example, want to shift the stage around onscreen so that you can see other screen elements—such as open panels—more clearly.

- The **Colors** section is used to control the color of the stroke (line) or fill of an object. For instance, if you want to have a blue circle with a black outline, you choose those options in the Colors section. The top tool in the Colors section determines the stroke color, and the tool below it (the one with the paint bucket icon) controls the object's fill color. Reading from left to right, the three remaining tools in the Colors section are responsible for setting the stroke and fill colors to black and white; switching off the stroke or fill (depending on which of them is selected); and swapping back and forth between black stroke/white fill and white stroke/black fill. You can also assign your own colors to stroke and fill—more on that later.

- The **Options** section is where you can change some of the properties of the selected tool. For example, you can change the size and shape of the Brush tool to make different kinds of brush marks. Note that not every tool in the Tools panel has options that modify their characteristics, so don't worry if this section appears blank for some tools.

> *The position and featured icons in the toolbar can be customized using* Edit ➤ Customize Tools Panel *on the PC and* Flash MX 2004 ➤ Customize Tools Panel *on the Mac.*

If you're working in Windows, you'll see that the modifiers in the Options section of the Selection tool are duplicated in the main toolbar at the top of the screen:

These options become visible on the main toolbar after you've selected an object on the screen using the

Selection tool. You'll look at how to use these modifiers as you progress through the book.

> Remember that you'll need to have the main toolbar activated—otherwise, you won't see these options. To activate the main toolbar, choose the Window ➤ Toolbars ➤ Main *menu option*.

Later in this chapter, you'll flex your muscles with the tools to create a vector drawing of a boat. By the end of this chapter, you'll have a working knowledge of all the basic tools and have a sense of how to apply them to achieve the results you want.

Let's start with the Selection tool, which is used for manipulating visual elements of the movie.

The Selection tool

The Selection tool is perhaps the most important tool in Flash, and probably the one that you'll use most often when creating and amending visual content on the stage. Here's what the Selection tool looks like in the Tools panel:

Essentially, the Selection tool is used to select objects on the stage for editing, and to move and place those selected objects just where you want them. The Selection tool has a few little quirks that are important to understand. Let's take a look at them now.

Using the Selection tool

First let's examine the basics of using the Selection tool. To do this, you'll need something drawn on your stage.

1. Open a new movie, and click the Oval tool in the Tools panel.

2. Select a black stroke and a fill color of your choice from the Properties panel. To choose a color for strokes and fills, simply click the relevant color selector box to bring up the color palette and make your choice:

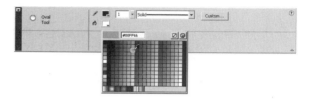

3. Click the stage and hold down the mouse button, dragging the mouse so that you draw a nice big circle on the stage. (Remember that holding down the *SHIFT* key while you drag will result in a perfect circle.):

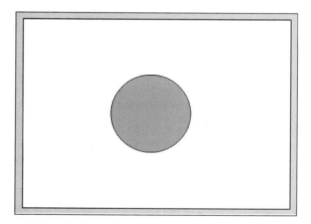

4. Select the Selection tool by clicking its icon in the Tools panel:

When you select the Selection tool, its three associated modifiers appear in the **Options** section of the Tools panel:

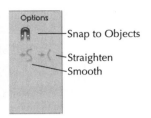

These modifiers can be applied to the objects that you select with the Selection tool—you'll see how to use each of these later.

5. Point to the center of the big circle you've drawn:

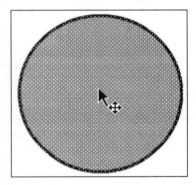

Note that when you move the Selection tool over the center of the circle, a cross with arrows on each of its arms appears next to the mouse pointer. This indicates that you're hovering over an object that can be selected and moved simply by pressing and dragging.

6. Click the colored part of the circle (it'll be highlighted as soon as you click it) and drag it off to the side. Then release the mouse button:

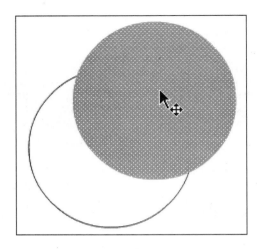

This action separated the fill part of the shape from its enclosing line (stroke)—the circle has become two separate objects.

Note that by default, the enclosed shapes you draw using the tools in the Tools panel consist of an outline and a fill. You can choose to have no outline or no fill by selecting the Stroke Color or Fill Color box in the Properties panel and then clicking the No Color selector.

7. Select the Oval tool from the Tools panel and click the Fill Color box. Above the palette of colors is a white box containing a red diagonal line. This is the No Color selector:

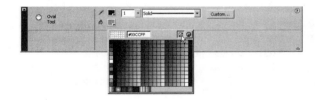

Selecting it will put a red slash through the Fill Color box in the Properties panel, indicating that the color for that drawing element (stroke or fill) is switched off:

It's easy to accidentally separate the stroke and fill elements of a shape when using the Selection tool as a selection device, and this points out the need to take care when selecting objects. Furthermore, if you now click away from the highlighted disk of color, then click it and drag it again.

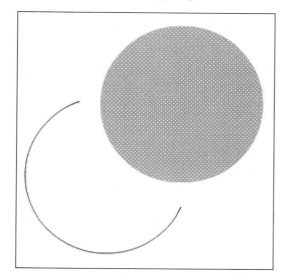

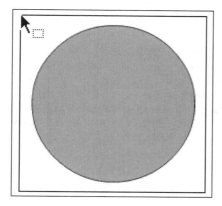

You can see that it's taken a bite out of the original stroke that used to surround the circle. Dang.

What's the solution to this? You can always undo the change you just made using *CTRL+Z*, and then try again. A less haphazard way to avoid separating an object into its component pieces is to make sure that you select both the colored fill and the surrounding stroke before moving the object. The way to achieve this is to double-click the object you want to move—this will select its stroke and its fill. By double-clicking a shape like this, you ensure that you can drag it around as a single entity.

Another solution is to **group** the components together so they are treated as a single shape. To do this, you can choose one of two methods: you can double-click your shape with the Selection tool (thus selecting both the fill and the stroke) and choose the Modify ➤ Group menu option or the *CTRL+G* keyboard shortcut; or you can select the Selection tool and use it to draw a rectangle around the shapes that you want to group together:

Again, this will select both the stroke and the fill, and you can use the same Modify ➤ Group option to group them together.

Whichever method you use, the result will be the same: your objects will be grouped together—in this case, the circle's surrounding stroke and color fill.

Grouped objects, when selected, will be highlighted by a colored line that indicates that they are a group. (The color of this line is determined by the global **Highlight Color** setting that you choose via the **General** tab of the Flash MX 2004 Preferences (Edit ➤ Preferences on Windows and Flash MX 2004 ➤ Preferences on the Mac).

To separate grouped items back into their component parts, select the group, and then choose the Modify ➤ Ungroup menu option.

There's another common mishap that can befall you when you're using the Selection tool to select and move objects. Take a look at this:

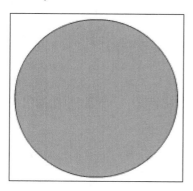

Yes, it's that familiar circle, drawn once again using the Oval tool—this time with a green fill (honest) and a black stroke.

Now, let's suppose you want to use the Selection tool to select the circle so you can move it. I remember that you need to select both the fill and the stroke, so you decide to use the Selection tool to draw a selection box. You click and drag the mouse to draw the box...

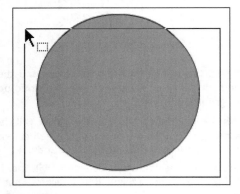

...but, sadly, it's easy to misjudge the starting position for the drag, and you can accidentally missed the top of the circle. If you decide to persevere, at the end of the drag, when you release the mouse button and click the center of the circle and try to drag it away to the right...

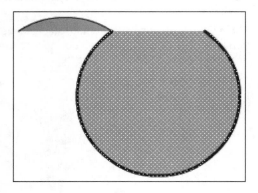

Hmm...not *quite* right. Flash thinks that you want to *carve up* you circle rather than move it as a single entity. Again, this problem can be avoided by grouping the stroke and fill segments. Take care—those selection boxes can be sharp!

You've looked at the selection and moving of objects, both here and in the last chapter when you constructed your first mushroom-oriented Flash movie. The Selection tool has one other important use, though—it can help you change the shape of objects by dragging their outlines. Let's take a look at this functionality next.

Extending your mushroom's cap

Let's modify the mushroom-based movie that you started working on in the previous chapter.

1. Open `mushroom.fla` from the end of the last chapter.

2. Click your keyframe in frame 15 of the mushroom layer.

3. Choose the Selection tool from the Tools panel.

4. Click the stage, away from the drawn shapes, to ensure that you've got nothing selected.

5. Position the point of the arrow on the edge of the mushroom cap—that is, touching the line around the filled shape:

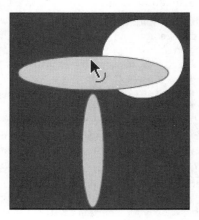

You'll notice that when the arrow point touches the line, the mouse pointer changes to an arrow with a curved line underneath it:

This change of mouse pointer indicates that you are now in a position to click and drag a point on a line, thus changing the shape of that line. A mouse pointer with a right angle underneath the pointer, like this...

...means that you are in a position where you can drag a *corner*.

6. Click the line and drag it upward to create a domed, more natural-looking cap for your mushroom. Notice that when you release the mouse button, the fill expands to flood the modified shape with color:

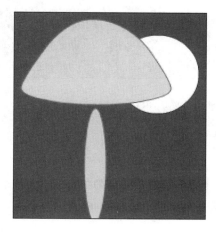

The little bit of genetic modification is complete.

7. Play the movie. You'll see that Flash has automatically modified all the frames between the keyframes so that the animation shows the smooth growth of your newly amended mushroom cap. Flash is great at making life easy for you in this respect. If you change the start or end points of your animation—the keyframes—Flash will recalculate all the in-between images without even asking you.

Next, let's take a look at a tool that lets you see objects in fine detail—the Zoom tool.

The Zoom tool

Here's the Zoom tool in the Tools panel, along with its related modifiers in the Options section:

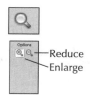

The Zoom tool is very easy to use: clicking the screen with the Enlarge option selected will zoom in on the screen, and clicking with the Reduce option selected will zoom out. Simple.

After you've selected your zoom in or out mode, you can temporarily switch from one state to the other by holding down the *ALT* key in Windows or the *OPTION* key on the Mac. When you click the screen with this key pressed, the zoom will operate in the opposite direction from what's selected in the Options section. This saves you from having to keep changing the mode in the Options box whenever you want to zoom in and out.

With the Zoom tool selected, you can also drag a box around an area, and Flash will enlarge that area to fill the screen.

A feature related to the Zoom tool is the **Pixel Zoom.** When you zoom in beyond 400%, a pixel grid appears that allows you to draw shapes and objects more precisely. For this feature to work, you need to select the View ➤ Snapping ➤ Snap to Pixels menu option. You can see the pixel grid here when you zoom in to 1600% at the bottom of your mushroom movie:

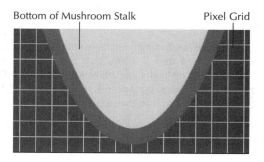

Bottom of Mushroom Stalk   Pixel Grid

1. Still in your `mushroom.fla` file, hide the mushroom layer by clicking the dot in the eye column next to its name:

2. Use the Zoom tool to enlarge the moon until it fills the screen. Look at the edge of the moon and notice that the quality of the image doesn't degrade as you zoom in, however much you increase the magnification. This is one of the wonders of working with vector graphics—you never lose any detail.

   Also, note that any changes in magnification you make inside of the FLA file don't affect the finished movie. The zoom features are just there to help you when you're creating your movie.

The next tool you're going to look at is also a relatively simple one—the Hand tool.

The Hand tool

The Hand tool is used for moving around the segment of the stage that's displayed on your screen. It's most useful when you're zoomed in and not able to see the entire movie all at once. Remember that any changes in view you make in the authoring environment will not have any effect on the display of your finished movie.

Using the Hand tool, move the stage around in the window, making sure that you finish up with the moon in the middle again. You can achieve the same effect using the scroll bars below and to the right of the stage, but the Hand tool feels somehow more controlled and intuitive.

The tools in context

In this section, you're going to utilize Flash's drawing and modification tools to create a picturesque scene. The actual scene is a colorful fishing boat out on the ocean. The beauty of this exercise is that it familiarizes you with all the tools in the Tools panel, and what's more, it doesn't require you to be Van Gogh.

Ahoy matey...

You'll start by creating the boat's hull by using the Rectangle tool. Before you begin, close the `mushroom.fla` file because you no longer need it.

The Rectangle tool

The Rectangle tool, as the name suggests, is used for drawing squares and rectangles.

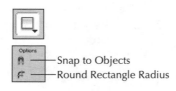

To draw a rectangle, select the Rectangle tool and simply click and drag a shape to the required size. Similarly, pressing the *SHIFT* key while drawing will snap the rectangle to a perfect square.

As you can see in the screenshot, the Rectangle tool has a couple of modifiers in the Options section of the Tools panel. The second modifier, the grandly named **Round Rectangle Radius**, controls the extent to which the corners of the rectangle you're drawing are rounded.

Let's put the rectangle tool to use by creating the hull of your boat.

Making your boat

You're going to make the skeleton of your boat with three rectangles.

1. Open a blank Flash document. Open the Document properties window and change the background color to a light blue (#66CCFF).

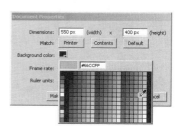

2. Rename the existing layer boat.

3. Click the Rectangle tool, and select a red fill and no stroke outline color.

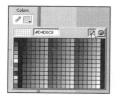

4. Draw a large red rectangle for the hull of the boat.

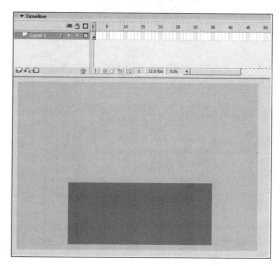

Next, you'll draw the boat's control room on the same layer. (Well, boats *do* have GPS these days.) Because you're going to draw this on the same layer, you need to switch on the Snap to Objects feature for the Rectangle tool. This will enable you to draw the control room without overlapping the hull.

5. With the Rectangle tool still selected, click the magnet icon in the tool's list of Options. This switches on Snap to Objects.

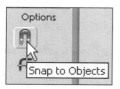

6. Draw a green (#33CC66) rectangle with no stroke outline color above the hull, stretching the square until the mouse pointer snaps to the top of the

hull. The snapping here makes the possibility of overlapping smaller because the mouse pointer is attracted to—and sticks to—the existing line.

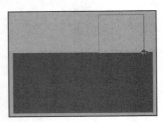

After you are done, draw a smaller rectangle in a dark green so that your boat looks something like this:

At the moment your boat is a little blocky and Lego-tastic, but you'll enhance it a little using other tools later. For now, that's all you require of the Rectangle tool. The next thing to add to the boat is the porthole for the cap'n to watch the storms 'a coming. You'll do this with the Oval tool.

The Oval tool

You've already used the Oval tool a couple of times:

The Oval tool allows you to draw oval shapes naturally, and circles when holding the *SHIFT* key. Let's use it to add a porthole.

Making a porthole with the Oval tool

1. Create a new layer above the boat layer, and name it porthole.

2. Use the Zoom tool to zoom in to the control room. This will allow a little more precision when drawing the porthole.

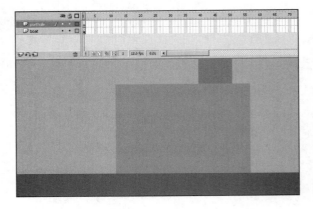

Let's start by creating the shiny porthole frame.

Select the Oval tool, click the fill color selector in the Tools panel, and choose the leftmost gradient fill.

We'll cover gradients and colors in detail in chapter 5.

3. Select a gray stroke color.

4. Place your mouse pointer directly in the center of the control room and click and drag to start drawing an oval.

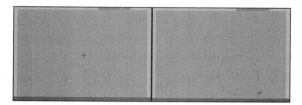

You'll notice that the oval tool draws shapes from the top corner down. This isn't much good if you want your porthole centered, but luckily there is a way to get the Oval tool to work in your favor: by using the mouse pointer as the center of the circle.

5. While drawing the oval, hold down the *Alt* key. The oval will now be drawn using the initial clicked point as its center.

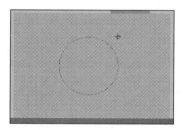

Remember to hold down the *Shift* key for a perfect circle.

6. When you are happy with your circle, release the mouse button.

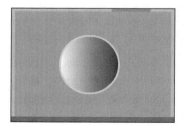

Now you need to draw another oval for the window.

7. With the oval tool still selected, select a light blue color fill and keep the same gray stroke color.

8. This time, click the center of the window frame, and hold down *Alt* and *Shift* while you draw your window.

You now have a porthole, and the boat's captain can look out for any giant calamari on the horizon.

Before you look at the next tool, let's add some sunshine.

9. On a new layer called sun, draw a circle in the top left corner, give it a yellow fill and no stroke.

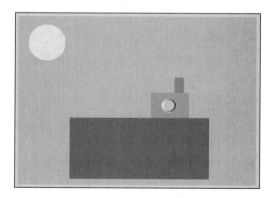

That's it for the Oval tool for now. Let's move on to the next tool.

The Line tool

The Line tool is used for drawing lines; it really is as easy as it sounds. Here's the Line tool icon in the Tools panel:

To use the Line tool, select it, click (and hold) the starting point of your line, and then drag the mouse and release at the end point. To help you work with the Line tool more effectively though, the Properties panel will let you closely control the characteristics of the line that you draw. Let's look at that in a short exercise.

Making a flagpole with the Line tool

1. Make sure that the Properties panel is open (open it with Window ➤ Properties).

2. Choose the Line tool from the Tools panel. The Properties panel is updated to show the current properties for the Line tool, showing line color, height (size), and style, as well as a button that allows you to further customize your line:

Stroke Color   Custom Button
Stroke Height   Stroke Style

These modifiers also work in conjunction with the other drawing tools; this means that you can alter the characteristics of the outlines of your ovals and rectangles after you've drawn them.

Next, you're going to use the Line tool to draw a flagpole for the boat.

3. Click the Stroke Color box to bring up the Properties panel's standard color palette, and select a dark woody brown for the flag post.

4. Click the down pointing arrow to the right of the **Stroke Height** box:

5. A slider pops up that you use to control the height of your line. (You can also type a precise height into the box if you prefer—the maximum size is **10**.)

6. Set the stroke thickness to 8 by moving the slider up.

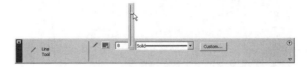

7. To fix your size choice, release the mouse button.

8. To preview the line, click the Custom button. In the Stroke Style window that appears, a simple preview is displayed on the left:

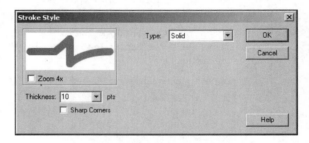

Don't worry about the rest of this window for now; you'll take another look at it shortly.

9. In the Line tool's options, click the View ➤ Snap to Objects option (indicated by the magnet icon).

10. This feature ensures that when your line gets close to a vertical or horizontal orientation, the line will automatically snap to a perfectly straight position. As you draw your line, you'll see a small circle at the end of the line, and when the line snaps into place, this circle grows bolder to signal to you that you've reached the desired angle. When you're in Snap to Objects mode, you can also hold down the *SHIFT* key while you're dragging; this will snap your line in increments of 45 degree angles.

11. Insert a new layer called flag pole. Make sure this layer is below the boat layer.

12. Draw a flag pole at the front of the boat by clicking and dragging a line. Make the pole a little taller than the funnel. When you are happy with its

length, snap the line to vertical, and release the mouse button to fix the line.

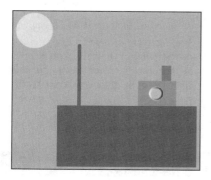

Now you have a pole, it needs a flag.

13. On the same layer, draw a green triangle an inch or two away from the pole using the Line tool with a thickness of 1. You'll fill in the rest of it later:

Even though the Line tool in Flash is not rubber-banded—that is, it does not continue the next line from where you drew the last one—because you have the Snap to Objects option selected, Flash will automatically snap to any previously drawn line making continuous drawing easy.

14. After you have a triangle, use the Selection tool to move it to the flag pole so that they are touching.

When you're done, save the movie as boat.fla.

Earlier on, you got a quick look at the **Custom Stroke Style** window when you used it to preview the height and color of your line. Let's take a closer look at it now.

Creating custom stroke styles

If you don't want all your lines to be perfectly straight, you can create a **custom stroke style**. Flash allows you to easily change contents of the stage—including more

than just changing the color and size of your stroke. Let's see how it works in practice:

1. Open a new, blank document.

2. Draw a simple line of any color with the maximum stroke thickness (10) using the Line tool.

3. Choose the Selection tool and click the line. When the line is selected, the Properties panel changes to show the properties of the stroke.

4. Click the Custom button in the Properties panel. A new window opens with some stroke options visible:

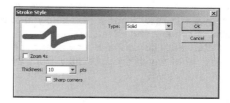

The preview on the left shows possible variations of the line—from a perfectly straight to a variety of curves and edges. This will show you how your line will look in almost any situation.

You're going to make the line look rickety and old from many years of wear by creating a customized stroke style that is textured and rough.

5. Click the Type drop-down menu and select Ragged. When you do this, a number of other drop-down menus appear that you can use to further customize the line. The preview pane displays these options as you select them:

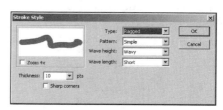

6. We won't go through all the menu options here, but there are a variety of options for each **Type** style. Have some fun and experiment with the other options later on.

Let's change the line a little so you get a ragged effect.

7. Select Solid from the Pattern drop-down menu, Very Wavy from the Wave Height drop-down menu, and Short from Wave Length. The line in the preview pane of the Stroke Style window will look like this:

8. Click OK and take a look at your line on the stage. It looks like a twisted branch right now.

Even though we haven't covered them all here, some of the Custom options will give you some pretty wacky results, and others help you to quickly achieve some useful effects, such as the creation of a dotted line. Flash also has a number of preset line styles, all of which are accessible from the Stroke Style drop-down.

That's all for the Line tool. Let's make some more modifications to your scene, this time using the Paint Bucket tool.

The Paint Bucket tool

The Paint Bucket, commonly known as the Fill tool, is used for filling in empty shapes or changing the fill color of existing shapes.

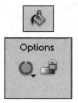

We'll talk about these modifiers later in the book when you come to use them "in anger." For the moment, let's stick with the core functionality of the Paint Bucket tool.

The Paint Bucket tool is used in conjunction with the Properties panel's color palette. You select the Paint Bucket tool, and pick a color from the color palette, and then click the area that you want to fill with that color.

Let's do that now in the context of your boat.

Filling the flag with color

1. Select a bright green color from the color palette—you're going to fill your flag.

2. Click the Paint Bucket tool, and then click the flag triangle to fill it instantly with the color you selected.

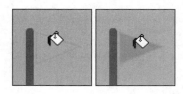

Every mouse pointer has a point, called a **hotspot**, that tells the computer *exactly* where you're clicking the screen. The hotspot for the Paint Bucket tool is the end of the paint spilling out of the can.

hotspot—

You've quickly made your flag—not bad for a minute's work!

Later in the book we'll take a closer look at the Fill Transform tool, which is closely related to the Paint Bucket tool. For now though, we're going to move on and look at the Ink Bottle tool.

The Ink Bottle tool

The Ink Bottle tool works hand in hand with the Paint Bucket tool. Where the Paint Bucket tool changes *fills*, the Ink Bottle does the same for *lines* and *strokes*.

In addition, if a fill does not have a stroke outline, the Ink Bottle tool can be used to give it one. This is where the Ink Bottle tool comes in handy.

The hotspot for the Ink Bottle is at the tip of the spilled ink. Let's use it to give your sun a glowing orange outline.

Adding a stroke to a fill

1. Select the Ink Bottle tool and ensure that the Properties panel is open (Window ➤ Properties).

2. In the Properties panel, select an orange stroke color.

3. Change the Stroke height to 2.

   The reason you make these selections is to specify the stroke color and thickness that will outline the sun.

   Now, let's apply it.

4. With the Ink Bottle tool still selected, click the sun. The orange stroke has now been applied to the yellow fill.

Having seen a couple of ways of applying changes to different objects on your stage, let's now look at how you can copy characteristics from one object to another. The tool you use to do this is the Dropper tool.

The Dropper tool

This tool is used to copy the colors and styles of fills (or lines) from objects that you've already created. When you use the Dropper to copy an object's attributes, Flash automatically switches to the tool you use to apply these attributes to another object. That is, if you copy a *fill* style, Flash will switch to the Paint Bucket tool, and if you copy a *line/stroke* style, Flash will switch to the Ink Bottle tool.

The Dropper tool can also be used to copy bitmaps and gradients, and we'll cover that in more detail later.

Let's now apply the Dropper tool to your example movie.

Copying colors from lines and fills

Bad memory? Can't remember what color you used for the sun or its stroke outline? Use the Dropper tool to retrieve the colors.

1. Click the Dropper tool and move it over the sun's fill. Notice that a little picture of a paintbrush appears next to the mouse pointer: This indicates that if you were to click that spot, you copy a fill style. When the mouse pointer is held over the sun's stroke rather than a fill, a little pencil icon is shown:

2. Click the sun's fill. The Dropper switches to the Paint Bucket tool. Notice that the fill color in the Tools panel has changed to the color you just selected.

This selected color—inherited by the Tools panel—can be used by any of the other tools.

Let's hoist the flag!

The PolyStar tool

The PolyStar tool is new to the Flash MX 2004 toolset. Its curious name is a fusion of the shapes that it creates: polygons and stars. In essence, the PolyStar tool is two tools, but because each one is a little obscure, Macromedia bundled them together.

If you are having trouble finding the PolyStar tool it is because it's hidden under the Rectangle tool. To select it, click and hold the Rectangle tool icon until the menu appears and select it.

If you intend to use the PolyStar tool regularly and find its hiding place unintuitive, you can move it to its own place by customizing the Toolbar (Edit ➤ Customize Toolbars on Windows and Flash MX 2004 ➤ Customize Toolbars on the Mac).

The PolyStar tool works in a very similar way to the other shape tools. To draw a shape, just click and drag until you are satisfied with the result, and then release the mouse button.

The only major difference with the PolyStar tool is the option to set the number of sides on the star and polygon shapes. Let's see how this works.

Adding a star to the flag using the PolyStar tool

In this exercise, you're going to add a star to your flag. It might not be as cool as skull and crossbones, but this is a friendly vessel.

1. Insert a new layer above the flag pole layer called flag star.

2. Using the Zoom tool, draw a box around the flag to zoom in to that specific area.

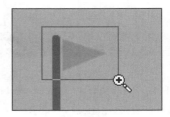

This will make your flag decorating a little easier.

3. Select the PolyStar tool and select a red outline and an orange fill.

4. In the Properties panel, click Options.

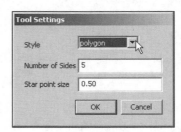

This displays the settings for the PolyStar tool. This is where you can create a star or a polygon using the drop-down menu. These settings also allow you to customize the number of sides on your shape and the star point size (or thickness). The default star point size is 0.5:

Star Point Size   0.1   0.5   1

5. Select Star from the drop-down menu and leave the other options as they are. Click OK to close the dialog box.

6. Select a solid line style from the Properties panel and draw a star on the flag.

7. Use the Zoom tool to zoom out and view your handiwork. When you are happy with your star, we'll proceed on to something completely different...

The Pencil tool

The Pencil tool is used to draw freeform lines.

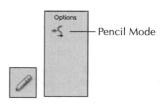
Pencil Mode

You use the Properties panel to set the Pencil tool's characteristics, such as stroke height, style, and color. The Pencil tool also has one modifier in the Options section of the Tools panel—the Pencil Mode modifier. This modifier is an important one—it controls how the line behaves when you draw by clicking and dragging with the mouse.

Clicking this modifier reveals that there are three Pencil modes to choose from:

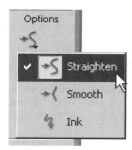

Let's see how these work in a short exercise.

Using the Pencil tool

Here you're going to see how Flash's pencil tool works.

1. Save your boat movie and create a new movie by choosing the File ➤ New menu option or by pressing CTRL+N. This will open a fresh, blank white movie in Flash.

> When working with more than one Flash file, Windows users will notice that a tab at the top of the Flash interface represents each Flash document. This is a very nice interface enhancement and speeds up any Flash work dramatically.

> Mac users will have to get used to living without tabs and must work with multiple windows. This might explain your boat's sudden disappearance. If you're unsure where your boat movie has gone— don't fear! The boat Flash movie is still there, it is just hidden behind your new document window. To switch to it, look at the very bottom of the Window menu for the appropriate document—you will see a list of currently open files—and select it.

2. Using the Pencil tool, draw a series of similar lines with the different Pencil modes and notice the results.

- **Straighten mode** will flatten some of the curves in your line. This tool will also automatically complete simple shapes that you draw. For example, if you draw a rough circle with Straighten mode on, Flash will snap it to a perfect circle:

- **Smooth mode** will refine the curves in your hand-drawn shapes, **rounding** out kinks and generally softening awkward shapes. It's a good mode to use if your freehand drawing is a little shaky.

- **Ink mode** is the basic Pencil mode. If you want to draw something on the screen and have it appear onscreen *exactly* the way that you drew it, **this** is the mode to use. In this mode, you'll notice that Flash does seem to smooth the lines a little bit—this is just a result of the process of converting the line from the bitmap line that Flash uses while you're drawing to the vector version that Flash will store and render.

3. Close the movie that you've been using to experiment with the Pencil modes: don't save it (unless you really did like it), and your original boat movie will be displayed again.

Now we'll take a look at the Pencil tool's larger sibling, the Brush tool.

The Brush tool

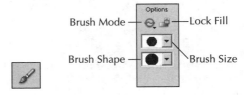

The Brush tool is very similar to the Pencil tool, but instead of drawing lines, you're painting fills. Every time you use the Brush tool on your movie, you're simply painting a fill with no enclosing border line.

The Brush tool has four options:

- The **Brush Mode** option controls the way that your brush strokes are painted. This option has five modifiers:

  - **Paint Normal** paints over anything else that's on the screen (provided it's on the same layer as the one you're drawing on, of course).

  - **Paint Fills** paints fills and leaves lines in place and visible through the fill that you just painted.

  - **Paint Behind** paints only on blank areas of the current layer—any objects on that layer will not be painted over.

  - **Paint Selection** paints only on areas of the screen that have been highlighted with the Selection tool.

  - **Paint Inside** paints only inside the lines. This is the tool you needed when you had those coloring books as a kid. When you start painting, Flash will ignore any marks you paint when your brush crosses a line:

- The **Brush Size** option changes the width and spread of the brush strokes.

- The **Brush Shape** button opens a menu containing a selection of shapes to paint with—round, flat, and so on.

- The **Lock Fill** button works in the same way the Lock Fill button for the Paint Bucket tool does, and its use will be covered in a later section.

Drawing with the Brush tool

Here you're going to add some waves to your scene; you're setting sail at last.

1. Select the Brush tool and pick a dark blue fill color from the Properties panel. Remember that the Brush tool draws fills—not strokes.

2. Choose the middle brush size from the Tools panel options, and ensure that the Brush Mode is set to Paint Normal.

3. In the Properties panel, set the Brush smoothing option to 100.

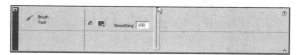

This determines the amount that drawings with the brush are smoothed and sharpened. This is very much like the pencil smooth mode. If this setting is low, the result will be rough edges. A setting too high however, will remove the curves from your drawings:

4. Create a new layer, name it waves, and place it above all the other layers.

5. Use the Brush tool to draw two lines of waves across the body of the boat. Make sure your waves run off the stage on either side.

Don't worry about drawing off the edge of the stage—remember that viewers only see the contents of the stage.

6. Draw a line either side of the waves connecting them to make a closed shape.

The reason you are doing this is so that you can fill the gap in between the waves with a lighter blue. Let's do that now.

7. Select the Paint Bucket tool and choose a mid-blue fill color (#0099FF).

8. Click the space in between the waves to fill the area.

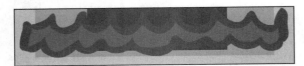

Now you need to create a space for filling below the bottom wave because at the moment you can't fill the space at the bottom of the screen. You can do this by creating a closed shape around the wave.

9. Select the Brush tool and choose the wave color.

10. Draw a line off the bottom of the stage parallel to the waves.

11. Connect the new line to the side of the waves above it. This creates another closed space, ready to fill with the Fill tool.

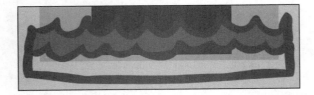

12. Use the Fill tool to fill in the space with the same fill color as before (#0099FF).

You've almost completed your waves. Almost? Well, they look a little dull, don't they? Before you move on to the next tool, let's give the waves a little detail—some white foam.

13. With the Brush tool still selected, choose a white fill color.

14. Select a smaller Brush size from the Tools panel options.

15. Draw some highlights on the left side of each wave. This will give the illusion of the sun and sky reflecting on the sea.

That's about it for your waves. Simple and fast! Now then, having seen how to paint, let's see how to erase any mistakes you might have made.

The Eraser tool

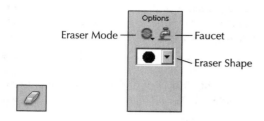

The Eraser tool is similar to the Brush tool—it just erases rather than paints. It has three modifiers:

- The **Eraser Mode** button has five modifiers. These are the same as those for the Brush Mode button on the Brush tool, and they behave in the same way.

- The **Eraser Shape** button lets you change the shape of the eraser's "footprint."

- The **Faucet** button changes the Eraser tool so that it will erase an entire fill or line at once. In this mode, you just touch the Eraser tool hotspot to the target line or fill, and the whole thing is erased.

Next, let's take a look at the Text tool.

The Text tool

The Text tool is used in conjunction with the Properties panel. Together, they allow text entry and editing in your Flash movie. In Flash, text fields can also be used as hyperlinks—more on this later.

For now though it's time to name the boat.

First, you'll define how your text should look.

1. Create a new layer above boat and name it text:

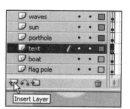

2. Click the Text tool in the Tools panel. This will open the Text tool properties in the Properties panel. Make sure that the drop-down menu on the far left is set to Static Text.

The options displayed are similar to those in a word processing program, and many of them will probably be familiar to you. For now, let's concentrate on the top section of the Properties panel—if the lower section is visible, close it using the arrow at the bottom right of the Properties panel. The options in the top section are:

Text Type—The type of text box you are creating (more about this later).

Font—The font you want to use. Note that Flash previews the fonts when you open the font list:

Font Size Position—This is where you can choose to display the font as subscript or superscript.

Auto Kern—Kerning is the gap between pairs of characters. Most fonts will have built-in kerning so that the gaps between certain characters will be different sizes. For example, the gap between an **A** and a **D** will be larger than that between an **A** and a **V**. The default is to use the font's built-in kerning, and in most cases you will want to leave this on.

Alias Text—This determines whether the text is anti-aliased (smoothed out) or not. If this is switched on, text will be aliased (unsmoothed) and will appear pixellated.

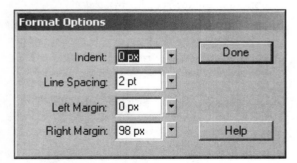

Rotation—The amount of rotation applied to your text.

Format—This provides increased control over the format of individual lines of text. This includes the amount of the indent, line spacing, left margin, and the right margin of each line. Individual lines of text are given their own settings here:

![Format Options dialog box: Indent: 0 px, Line Spacing: 2 pt, Left Margin: 0 px, Right Margin: 98 px, with Done and Help buttons.]

The **Bold** and **Italic** modifiers will make the text either bold or italic, and the **Color** button will open the standard Flash color palette so that you can choose the text color.

Note that in Flash, there is no text modifier that will underline text. If you want to have underlined text in Flash, you will have to manually draw a line underneath it.

3. Select the Text tool and click near the stern of the boat.

A small text box appears with a blinking cursor at the text insertion point. Don't worry if your insertion point is not in exactly the right place—you'll be able to position the text precisely later.

4. In the Properties panel, choose a font that you like the look of (we used Arial Black), and choose a font size that will fit nicely. Notice that as you move the Font Size slider up and down, the text box on your stage is automatically resized. This guide will help you to choose how large a text size you should select to fit on your boat.

5. Set the color of your font to white.

6. Type some text into your text box. Feel free to call your boat what you like! We called ours The StarFlower.

7. Click the Selection tool.

The white box around the text disappears and is replaced with a thin, colored highlight (this is the color that you have set as your default Highlight Color on the General tab of the Edit ➤ Preferences menu). You can now pick up this text with the Selection tool's mouse pointer and move it around until you are happy with its position:

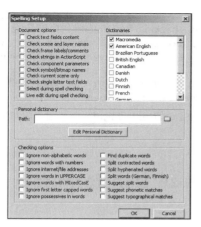

To go back and edit the text again, click the text with the Text tool.

Save the boat movie before you move on.

Checking spelling

Users of Flash MX 2004 rejoice—Flash now has a spell checker! Well, it took long enough, but there is finally a way to proofread text within Flash. This will make proofreading projects easier, because you won't have to rely on your eagle eye and a hefty dictionary.

Let's see how it works.

1. Open a new Flash document.
2. Use the Text tool to type the following text (or something equally crass!):

> My spellin is pretty awful

Before you can ask Flash to correct your spelling, you have to set a few options.

3. Select Text ➤ Spelling Setup and you'll see a great number of options and a selection of dictionary languages:

Many of the options available here will be extremely useful throughout your Flash career, but only a couple of them are of interest right now. The first of them is at the top of the list.

4. Check the Check text fields content option from the list. This option specifies that Flash should examine all the text fields in your movie.

5. Check Suggest phonetic matches from the bottom right of the window. This will allow Flash to suggest any corrections where relevant. Click OK to close the window and confirm these options.

6. Select Text ➤ Check Spelling to run the spell checker. Flash's spell checker will run through all the text fields and check for any errors.

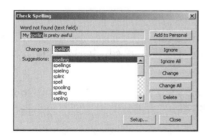

It's no surprise then that Flash has found an error (or two). From here on, the procedure will most likely seem familiar to you from all the other applications with spell checking functionality. The most important thing you did here was to switch the spell checker on and notify Flash that you want it to do some work.

7. When you are done correcting your spelling, save it and close the Flash movie.

Next up is an extremely useful tool, the Free Transform tool.

The Free Transform tool

The Free Transform tool is used to manipulate different properties of your content. It can be used to resize, rotate, and perform some pretty impressive tasks on elements on your stage.

Clicking this option reveals four different options in the Tools panel:

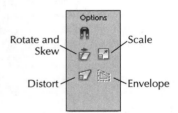

Rotate and Skew—this limits the function of the Free Transform tool exclusively to rotating and skewing objects.

Scale—this allows the Free Transform tool to scale your objects.

Distort—this allows scaling from each point giving maximum flexibility, and as the name suggests, distortion.

Envelope—this uses Bezier curves (more on these later) to manipulate simple shapes. Like the Distort option, this cannot be used on grouped objects.

By default, none of the options are selected and the tool allows you to rotate, scale, and skew. Let's give it a try.

Using the Free Transform tool

In this exercise, you're going to modify a simple square using the Free Transform tool.

1. Open a new Flash movie.

2. Select the Rectangle tool. (If you just worked through the previous exercise, its icon will be hidden beneath the PolyStar tool.) Draw a square with a red fill and a black stroke. Give it a stroke height of 5. If you still have rounded corners set from earlier and want a straighter rectangle, click the Round Rectangle Radius button in the Options section of the Tools panel. This brings up the Rectangle Settings window. To draw a rectangle with no rounded corners, enter 0 in the Corner Radius box.

3. Double-click the square to select its fill and stroke, and select the Free Transform tool in the Tools panel:

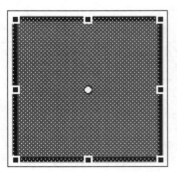

4. A number of anchor points will appear around the shape. These points can be moved to manipulate the scale of the shape in different directions. Let's make your square a rectangle.

5. Place your mouse pointer over the top-center point. When you do this, the mouse pointer changes to a double-ended arrow, indicating that you can resize your selection.

6. While the mouse pointer is a double-ended arrow, click and drag upward. You'll notice that Flash shows you a ghostly outline preview of your target shape. This affects none of the other sides; only the side you are dragging will change.

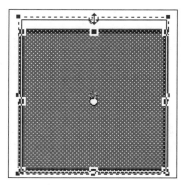

When you release the mouse, the shape is updated and you now have a rectangle. You resized the square in one direction only—if you had chosen any of the corner anchor points, the square would be resized in both height and width. Let's give that a try.

7. Move your mouse pointer over the top-right corner anchor point. Your mouse pointer changes into a four-headed arrow. Click and drag to manipulate the shape in both width and height.

If you look at the square on the stage, you'll probably notice that it isn't centered. You can center it by putting your mouse pointer over the square so that it turns into the familiar arrow with which you can drag the shape:

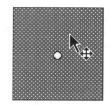

One of the other default actions of the Free Transform tool is rotation. Let's experiment a little with it.

8. It would help if your square had an identifier for your rotations. Choose the Text tool with a yellow text fill color and place a large N at the top-center—you'll use this as your north indicator:

At this point you'll need to **group** your objects so that they act as a unit—otherwise your north will remain north while your square goes south.

9. Click the Selection tool and select all the objects on the stage by drawing a box around them. Choose the Modify ➤ Group menu option or press CTRL+G to bundle them together as one unit. Now that your objects are grouped, you can manipulate them all at once.

10. Select the grouped objects with the Selection tool and then click the Free Transform tool. The familiar anchor points should appear, so place your mouse pointer just outside any of the corner points and notice that it's been replaced with a circular mouse pointer:

11. Click and drag right to rotate the square 90 degrees. Again, if you hold down the *SHIFT* key Flash gives you a helping hand and snaps in increments of 45 degrees:

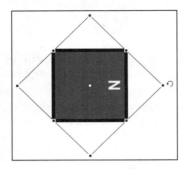

An extra feature of the Free Transform tool is the ability to adjust the center pivot of your rotation. When the square is selected, you will see a small white circle in the center—that's the pivot for the rotation. You can move that white circle anywhere you like and the shape will still rotate around it—even if the pivot is off the stage.

Let's take a look at the final basic function of the Free Transform tool—the **skew**.

12. Make sure the group is selected and place the mouse pointer over the perimeter of the square between any of the anchor points.

You'll notice that the mouse pointer turns into a peculiar shape that on closer inspection is two arrows pointing in different directions:

13. Click and drag to see the skew in action:

Let's now take a look at the **Distort** modifier option. This can only be applied to simple elements and not grouped objects.

14. Return your skewed square back to its original square shape by pressing *CTRL+Z*. Select the square using the Selection tool. To ungroup the object so that you can use the Distort option, choose the Modify ➤ Ungroup menu option.

15. Select the square again, click the Free Transform tool and then select the Distort modifier from the Options section at the bottom of the Tools panel:

16. When your square is selected, you'll see those familiar anchor points again. Placing the mouse pointer over the anchor points will change the mouse pointer to a small white chevron. Select the top-left corner anchor point and drag it toward the center of the square:

The shape reflects the new location of the anchor point.

To conclude your look at the Free Transform tool, you'll now quickly use the Envelope modifier option. Like the Distort option, this cannot be used on grouped objects.

17. Return your shape to its original square by pressing *CTRL+Z* to undo the distortion.

18. Select the square, and with the Free Transform tool selected in the Tools panel, click the Envelope modifier option:

You'll notice that when you select the square with the Envelope modifier option, there are many more anchor points around the perimeter of the shape.

19. Drag as many anchor points as you like in whatever directions you want.

Some experimentation with the last two options of the Free Transform tool will enable you to create some wild, as well as some subtle shapes.

20. Close the current Flash document without saving changes.

What's next? The mighty Pen tool, that's what!

The Pen tool

The principles embodied in the Pen tool are an example of how high science and math can have unforeseen spin-offs. The space race gave you microprocessors and non-stick pans, but a lesser known spin-off comes from the automobile industry of the 1970s. Designers had just started using CAD/CAM packages to design cars, but there was a problem—the computers couldn't draw squiggly lines. They could do straight lines and simple curves, but they couldn't come up with a way to draw squiggles. Squiggly lines are difficult because the equations that define them—unlike those for straight lines or regular curves—are extremely complex.

Bezier curves

The solution to this problem was a special kind of curve called a **Bezier**, named after a mathematician by the name of Pierre Bezier. Monsieur Bezier's curve is used in all sorts of computer applications today, from designing curved cars to displaying postscript fonts.

The difference between a Bezier and a normal curve is that a normal curve is made up of points. A Bezier curve, on the other hand, is made up of points that include two additional pieces of data that we will call *direction* and *speed*.

Bezier curves are drawn using the Pen tool—let's see how the Pen tool works in practice.

Working with Bezier curves

1. Open a fresh Flash movie to experiment with.

2. Select the Pen tool, and make sure you have the fill color and line color selected. The mouse pointer changes into a pen nib with a little cross next to it:

3. Drag in the general direction you want the curve to go:

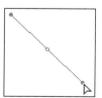

A line starts to appear as you drag. This line consists of three points—one at the center and one on each end—so there's a kind of bow tie look to the line. The center point of the line is where your finished curve will start.

4. Don't let the bow tie get too big; once you're happy with it, release the mouse button. You've now created the starting point of the curve.

5. Position the mouse pointer at another point on the screen where you want your curve to pass through. In the same way you did before, drag out another bow tie, keeping the mouse button pressed as you position the bow tie:

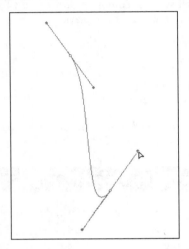

Notice that as you drag the second bow tie around, the curve between the two center points of the bow ties changes in real time. The way it changes is pretty difficult to explain, but once you have seen it, it somehow looks totally natural. The direction of the bow tie defines what *direction* the curve goes in, and the *length* of the bow tie affects its curvature.

A good way to think of it is that the bow ties represent the position (via the center point of the bow tie) and the speed (via the length of the bow tie) of a car trying to move in a straight line between the two points. As it gets faster (bow ties get bigger) the car travels in a curved path. Some of you may recognize the bow tie as the car's *velocity vector*,

but the rest of us will be having fun making the squiggle dance to care too much about the math. In fact, practicing drawing the curves using the bow ties is the best way to get the feel of what's happening.

6. Keep adding bow ties to form a roughly puddle-shaped squiggle as shown here:

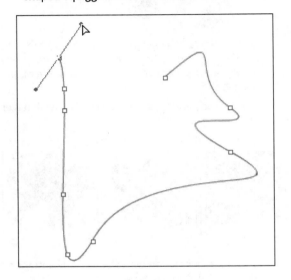

As you put the pen near the original starting point of the first bow tie (or near *any* point on a line that would make a closed area), the Pen tool changes to show an **O** where it was previously an **X**:

This is Flash's way of saying that the next point you add will create a closed shape. This sounds a little complicated, but try it. As with most everything associated with Beziers, it's easier to do than it is to explain!

Sometimes when you're constructing shapes with the Pen tool, you don't want a shape composed completely of curves, but rather a mixture of curves and sharp corners. If you want to create a corner rather than another curve, you simply click the stage with the Pen tool rather than clicking and dragging. This will give you a mix of curves and straight lines:

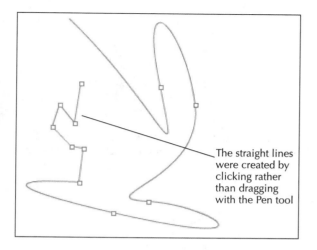

The straight lines were created by clicking rather than dragging with the Pen tool

Close the movie without saving it.

Now that you've had a little experience with the Pen tool, let's enhance your scene.

Making smoke with the Pen tool

Even though the Pen tool has some really beneficial uses for illustrations and high graphics work, we're just going to create a few clouds of smoke with it.

1. Return to your boat movie and create a new layer called smoke.

2. Select the Pen tool, and choose a white fill and stroke.

3. Use the Zoom tool to zoom in and use the Pen tool to create a sequence of simple curves on the stage—remember to click and drag to shape a curve, and release when you are happy with it.

4. When you have a few decent curves, close the shape by clicking the starting point. (The mouse pointer will change to show a 0 when your mouse pointer is over the start point.) When you do this, the shape will be closed and filled. Now you have some smoke emanating from the boat's smokestack.

5. Draw smoke clouds up to the top of the screen.

6. Save your movie.

If any of your clouds are less than perfect, you can edit them with the Subselect tool.

The Subselect tool

This tool is certainly worth getting to know. It allows you to select and alter specific points on a curve, which means you can control how you modify the curves that you created.

When you choose the Subselect tool from the Tools panel and click a Bezier stroke, a skeleton-like structure appears inside your shape. This shows you the

57

start and end points of the curves, and the shape of the curves that underlie the displayed drawing:

> You might have to zoom right in to see this clearly—it's easier to see this if you have a big fat line like the one in this graphic.

And there's more: if you click one of the little nodes on the skeleton, the Bezier bow ties will appear, allowing you to modify the curves with precision and confidence.

There's another application of the Subselect tool that's extremely useful: you can use it to modify shapes that weren't drawn with the Pen tool.

In the boat movie, choose the Subselect tool, and then click any of the smoke clouds.

The same skeleton and node structure appears. Click a node, and those familiar bow ties spring into view again:

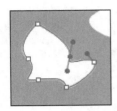

This reveals that all the shapes you've drawn using Flash's drawing tools are composed of Beziers that you can modify. By dragging the bow ties, you can rework shapes:

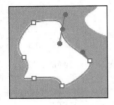

This tool is very useful for reforming shapes.

Shaping the boat using the Subselect tool

Until now, your boat has been a square mass. It would never carve through the water! It's time to shape the hull.

1. Hide the waves layer from view so you can work with the boat a little more easily.

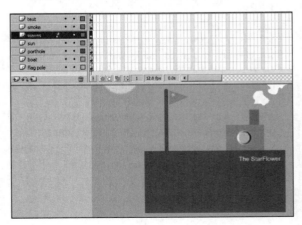

2. Select the Subselect tool and click a corner of the hull. The four corner points of the boat appear.

3. Click and drag the bottom left point to create a slight angle. Then release the mouse button to apply it.

Repeat the same process for the bottom right point. The boat scene is now finished!

From here you can use the tools to add more detail or alter what is already in the scene.

Beziers and animation

One thing about Bezier curves that doesn't become apparent until you play around with them is that they're not just a fancy drawing tool: they can be used to simulate real world movements much better than standard curves. For example, imagine a tennis ball hitting a net. When the ball makes contact with the net, the ball's weight and momentum will drag the net with it, changing the net's shape. If you draw your net with Beziers, the fine control you have with the bow ties lets you regulate a significant parameter—the *tension* of the net:

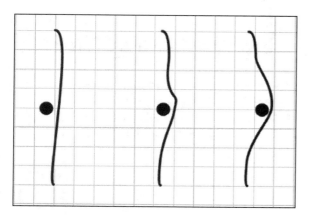

As you'll learn in detail later in this book, these images could be animated with a *shape tween*. The Bezier curve bow ties can be used to set the tension of the net, and therefore show its acceleration. Acceleration is a fundamental attribute of good animation because it's the direct result of forces acting on the shape—which is what animation should try and express. With Beziers you can animate the effects of these forces more easily.

The use of Beziers used for *animation* rather than just for shape creation opens up a whole new facet to expressive animation. If you stop thinking "tennis net" and start thinking "eyebrows and mouths" for example, you can begin to see how these curves could help you animate a face as its expression changes.

In this chapter we've taken a long look at some of the more important aspects of Flash's integral tools. We haven't covered every single option, but you'll see more as you progress through this book.

Case study

In this exercise, you're going to set up the layout and begin to create the basic interface for your portfolio website. You'll be using this portfolio website throughout the book to implement the things we discuss in each chapter, and this will help you see the Flash components you're learning about in context.

Creating background and base elements

Let's start by creating the background for your movie. First, you'll set up your movie's global properties.

1. Open a new Flash document. Open the Document Properties dialog box using Modify ➤ Document and change the dimensions of the movie's stage to 500 (width) x 400 (height) pixels.

2. Select a dark blue color (#003366) for the movie background color and click OK.

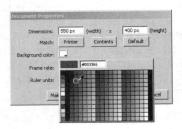

3. Change the name of the movie's default single layer to white rectangle.

4. Before you proceed, save your movie with a suitable name.

5. Use the Rectangle tool to draw a large white rectangle with a white fill and stroke color roughly in the center of the stage—don't be too fussy about its location because you'll correctly center it later.

6. Open the Properties panel (Window ➤ Properties) and select the white rectangle. The Properties panel displays the rectangle's width and height, shown as W and H respectively. Typing in these text fields will allow you to change the size of the rectangle:

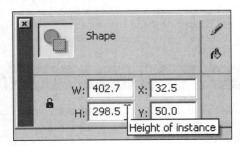

7. Click the W text field (representing Width), type 485 and press by ENTER. Change the value in the H text field (height) to 300, and press ENTER again. The rectangle changes to the size you specified:

Specifying a particular size will allow you to work with the same settings we are using, and make the case study creation easier throughout the book.

This will act as your main viewing area—or page:

8. Create a new layer called colored rectangles and select the Rectangle tool.

9. Select no stroke color and a fill color of #66CC00. To select this color, click the color selector in the Properties panel, click the text field at the top, and type 66CC00.

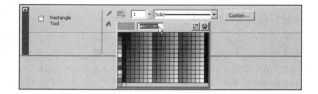

10. Draw a single tall rectangle and change the size of the shape to a width of 113 and a height of 258 using the Properties panel:

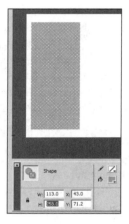

11. With the rectangle still selected, copy and paste it three times. When you do this, make sure to move each rectangle into its own space, so it doesn't overlap another rectangle. Use the Selection tool to position them roughly in their own space within the white rectangle.

Don't worry too much about their precise alignment for the moment—you'll place them correctly later.

12. Select each of the rectangles individually and change the fill colors to #99FF00, #FF9933, and #00CC66.

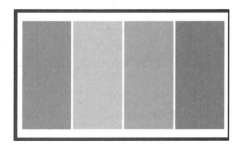

These four rectangles will expand to show your four pages.

13. Insert a new layer called logo + text.

14. With the Text tool, add your name or company name below the white rectangle. Set the font to Verdana, its size to 14, and its color to white. Change the Character Spacing of the text to 14 and position the text roughly at the bottom right edge:

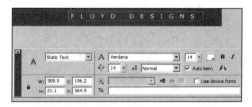

15. Zoom in and draw a symbol or icon for your company alongside the text with the Pencil tool. We've drawn a dog.

Here's how it looks in context:

16. Create a new layer called buttons. Not surprisingly, this will house all your buttons.

17. On the new layer, use the Rectangle tool to draw a small square with a white stroke and fill in the top left corner.

18. Select the square and resize it to a width and height of 34 pixels using the Properties panel. This will form the basis of your button.

19. To finish the button, draw a smaller red rectangle—30 pixels wide by 22 pixels high—away from the white square.

20. Drag a copy of this rectangle into the white square. Leave a bit of white space above it, where you'll put the text later:

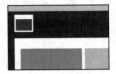

In the next chapter, this shape will be converted into a navigational button.

That's all for the case study in this chapter. This might seem simple so far, but as you work through the case study exercises at the end of each chapter you'll see the concepts and content build bit by bit. This is the way any Flash movie is built: first you have an idea, then you create the building blocks that you need for your movie, and then you splice them all together.

Summary

In this chapter, you worked through some of the main features of the Tools panel and used different tools to add and amend movie content. You'll continue to do this throughout the book.

You saw that:

- Drawn shapes in Flash consist of **strokes** and **fills** that can be moved and modified separately.

- Flash's drawing tools have modifiers that control how drawn elements look and behave.

- You can use tools (such as the **Ink Bottle** and Paint Bucket) with their modifiers to change the attributes (color, height, etc.) of strokes and fills.

- You can use the **Properties panel** to change the characteristics of drawn objects.

- You can create **text fields** and customize them using the Properties panel.

- The Pen tool allows you to draw precise and amendable **Bezier curves.**

- You can select and alter the curves and lines that make up any drawn shape in Flash with the Subselect tool.

Now that you've seen how to create simple shapes and text in Flash, let's look at how you can convert them into components that you can reuse. These reusable content components are the subject of the next chapter—**Symbols**.

Chapter 3

FLASH SYMBOLS AND LIBRARIES

What we'll cover in this chapter:

- **Symbols**—what they are, why they're useful, how to create them, and how to store and reuse movie content elements in the **Library**.
  - **Graphic symbols** contain simple moving content and are the cornerstone of cartoon animation in Flash.
  - **Button symbols** are the easiest method to achieving interactivity.
  - **Movie Clip symbols** are independent, self-contained movie components that free you from the linear tyranny of your movie's main timeline. They can contain as much interactivity as buttons and are the most powerful of Flash's symbols.

In Macromedia Flash, a **symbol** is a particular kind of movie content component—a piece of self-contained content that you can save and reuse time and time again. Symbols add life and richness to your movies by allowing you to break free of a rigid static timeline. Now that you know how to get around the stage and main timeline and you have a working knowledge of the Tools panel, you can begin to really make Flash come to life. **Symbols are a vital part of making great Flash movies.**

Typically, you create symbols when you know that you're going to have particular elements that you'll use repeatedly in a movie or in a number of movies, or when you want to encapsulate a little piece of action or animation and use it independently of what's going on in the rest of the movie—and you can *share* the saved symbols from one movie with your other movies, too.

Using stored symbols rather than uniquely created content for every element in your movie has at least three advantages: first, symbols allow you to create far more interesting, flexible, and extensible movies; second, they give you the benefits of mass production and reusable components; and third, they help you keep your movie file size small and the end user happy and attentive to your site.

In this chapter, you'll learn about the three types of symbol that Flash employs, and create and use an example of each. We will also cover the more complicated aspects of critical symbols in more detail later in the book. Here, we'll give you a solid grounding in the basics of symbols that will stand you in good stead.

Symbol essentials

A **symbol** at its most basic level is a thing in Flash that you can use time and time again. That thing could be a simple picture, an interactive button, or even an entire mini-movie that runs within your main movie. You can convert your existing movie content into symbols, or you can create symbols from scratch. Either way, you save the completed symbol so that you can use it again later:

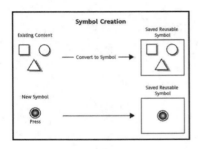

Every time you create a new symbol in Flash, it's added to a **Library** that's attached to your FLA authoring file. The Library is where all the reusable symbols are stored for the movie that you're working on:

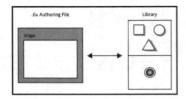

To use one of the saved symbols in your movie, open the Library, select the symbol that you want to add, and drag it onto your stage. The original symbol remains in the Library, however, Flash creates a copy of the stored symbol and renders it on the stage for you. The stored symbol kept in the Library is like a template that Flash uses to create a brand new copy of the saved symbol. When you create a new, individual copy of a stored symbol on your stage, it's known as an **instance** of that stored symbol.

Each new instance is a unique object—an exact copy of the stored symbol that the instance is based on. There's also a default link between the symbol and its instances. If you amend the underlying symbol, the amendments ripple through to the instances too. However, you can change the properties (tint, size, and so on) of individual instances without affecting the original symbol.

One way of picturing the relationship between the stored symbol and the copy (or copies) of it that you create on the stage is to think about that familiar kitchen tool—the cookie cutter. A cookie cutter is designed to turn out multiple copies of cookies that are the same size and shape. The cookie cutter is a template for mass production of identical objects:

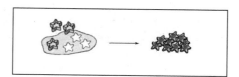

You apply the cookie cutter to the cookie dough and produce identical cookies every time. In Flash, the stored symbol is the cookie cutter, and the instance copied onto the stage is the identical individual cookie derived from the cookie cutter. With cookies, you can add toppings to specific cookies, and in Flash you can change the characteristics of individual instances via the Properties panel.

One of the nice things about creating instances of symbols is that you can customize each instance on the stage individually. For example, suppose you need a series of buttons in your movie that the user clicks to navigate through your website. Rather than create the same button 15 times, you can just create one button symbol in your Library, and then customize each instance of the button on your main movie stage.

Let's start creating some symbols and see how to implement them in practice.

Symbol types

When you create symbols in Flash, you have three basic types to choose from:

- Graphic symbols
- Button symbols
- Movie Clip symbols

Each type of symbol has different capabilities and levels of complexity, and the type of symbol you decide to create will be based on your judgment of what you want that symbol to do—how you want it to **behave**. For example, if you just want to reuse a static graphic that's essentially inanimate, the graphic symbol is the best fit. For a symbol that has some animation and

maybe some sound, you'd choose to create a movie clip symbol. Each of the different symbol types has its own range of possible behaviors—from the simple graphic symbol to the potentially very complex movie clip symbol.

All three types of symbol are created by one of two methods: you can convert an existing drawing or other object (such as a text field) into a symbol, or you can create a new symbol from scratch. You'll use both these methods to construct symbols in the following examples.

Let's begin with the simplest kind of symbol—the graphic symbol.

Graphic symbols

Although graphic symbols are not as feature-rich as button or movie clip symbols, they're no less important. They are used for static images throughout your movie so if you know that you are going to use an object over and over again and you don't need it to be interactive or animated, a graphic symbol is your best bet.

Let's create a simple graphic symbol now.

Creating a graphic symbol

Here, you're going to create a new symbol.

1. Open Flash and create a new blank movie by clicking the File ➤ New menu option.

2. Select the Text tool from the Tools panel, ensure that you have Static Text selected in the left-hand side of the Properties panel, and click the stage. In the text field that appears, type the words Graphic Symbol. Click the Selection tool so that you can select the text you've just placed on the stage, and then choose the Modify ➤ Convert to Symbol menu option. The Convert to Symbol dialog box appears:

This is where you choose the **type** of symbol that you want to create. Notice that Flash labels the categories of symbols using the term Behavior because each type of symbol has its own repertoire of behaviors.

3. If it's not selected already, change the behavior of the symbol to a graphic by clicking the bottom radio button next to the word Graphic.

4. Change the name by deleting Symbol 1 in the Name field and typing Graphic Symbol.

5. Also in this dialog box, you'll see the Registration matrix—a grid composed of nine small squares, one of them black. You can click any of the squares to define the point that Flash will consider the center of your symbol. If it's not already selected, click the center square because you want the **registration point** to be in the very center of your symbol. Finally, click OK.

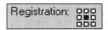

Your text field now has a registration point—a small cross—in the center:

Graphic⊕Symbol

So far you've created a new graphic symbol, assigned it a registration point, and given it a symbol name. This is the name that the symbol will be stored under in the Library.

6. Double-click the Graphic Symbol text field. When you do this, Flash opens a separate editing window. You're no longer looking at the main stage—instead, you're in the Edit Symbols window for your graphic symbol. Flash indicates this to you by highlighting the name of your symbol above the timeline, next to the name of your movie's default first scene:

The blue arrow on the left is Flash's equivalent of the ubiquitous Back button; it gives you a shortcut to move back a level from wherever you are. In your current scene, the Back button will take you back to the main timeline in Scene 1.

This symbol was created by converting content using the Modify ➤ Convert to Symbol menu option. However, you can also create a symbol from scratch by choosing the Insert ➤ New Symbol menu option.

When you create a symbol from scratch using Insert ➤ New Symbol, rather than converting existing content, Flash automatically starts Edit Symbols mode. The contents of a symbol created in this way are not modified on the main stage—you can only alter the symbol's content in Edit Symbols mode.

You'll see that in Edit Symbols mode, the timeline and layer list are displayed. This is very important: it shows you that **each symbol has its own internal layers and timeline**. If you add extra layers while inside Edit Symbols mode, this would affect only that one symbol, not the entire movie.

It can sometimes be a bit confusing to see whether you are in Edit Symbols mode or normal editing mode. The only way to really be sure is by checking above your timeline to see if the symbol name appears there. If it does, you're definitely in Edit Symbols mode, and if it doesn't, you're not. Additionally, creating symbols from scratch in Edit Symbols mode prevents you from seeing the rest of your movie. You are more likely to achieve the continuity you want by designing your symbol on the main stage and converting it after you're happy that it fits with the rest of your movie.

7. Click the Back button or the Scene 1 button to return to the main timeline. (These are to the left of your graphic symbol name, just above the main timeline.)

You're now back in normal edit mode, and you're looking at the stage and the main timeline.

8. Select the text field with the Selection tool and delete it. Your symbol disappears—to see it again you must open the **Library**. Flash automatically created a place to store your new symbol in the Library that's associated with this authoring file.

9. Open the Library by using the Window ➤ Library menu option, and take a look at the window that pops up:

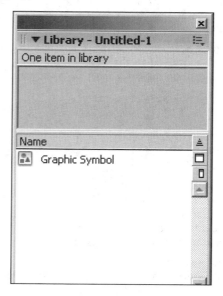

10. The entry for your new graphic symbol is in the white box in the lower half. The small icon with the circle, square, and triangle on it next to the name is the identifying tag for a graphic symbol.

11. Double-click the icon next to your new symbol's name in the Library window. This will redisplay Edit Symbols mode, where you can work on the content of your symbol.

12. Back in Edit Symbols mode (you'll see a blank screen containing your Graphic Symbol with the

registration point in the center), select the Text tool from the Tools panel.

13. Using the text properties in the Properties panel, change the symbol's font's color. Then click the blue Back arrow or the Scene 1 button to return to the timeline and normal editing mode.

Although there's no text anywhere on the stage because you deleted it earlier, if you look in the Library and click your Graphic Symbol, you'll see the changes you made to your symbol in the Preview pane of the Library. To put the symbol back on the stage, you can simply click and drag it out to the main stage.

The Library works like a mini file browser. You can use it to find and use symbols, create new symbols, or delete symbols you no longer need.

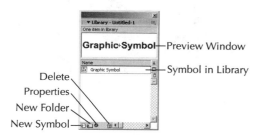

An alternative way to convert an object to a symbol is to use the Library as a shortcut, and drag an object into it from the stage. Let's give this a try.

14. On the main timeline, use the Rectangle tool to draw a square anywhere on the stage.

15. Using the Selection tool, double-click the square to select its fill and stroke.

16. Drag the square to the lower part of the Library. A small rectangle (or a plus sign, depending on your system) appears at the bottom of your cursor, suggesting that you want to add something to the Library:

When you release the mouse button to confirm, a familiar dialog box appears:

Yes—it's the Convert to Symbol dialog box again.

17. Name your symbol Square Symbol, click the center-left square of the Registration matrix, and give the symbol a Graphic behavior.

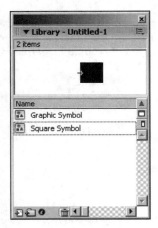

Notice that your new symbol has been added to the Library, and that you can see a preview of the symbol in the Preview pane. The preview also shows the square to the right of the registration point.

Dragging an object into the Library to convert it into a symbol is another one of Flash's shortcuts. There is no standard way to create a symbol—just use the way that suits your way of working. The useful thing about this particular approach is that you can choose where in the Library you want to put the new symbol by dropping it into a specific folder. You'll look at how to create folders in the Library in a moment.

Before you move on to the next part of this chapter, let's take a quick look at manually adjusting the registration point of a symbol.

18. Double-click your new Square Symbol in the Library so that Flash displays Edit Symbols mode.

19. Choose the Window ➤ Design Panels ➤ Info menu option to bring up the **Info panel**:

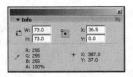

The X and Y boxes on the right are the coordinates that determine the position of the registration point.

20. Enter a value of 14 in the Y box and press *ENTER*. You'll notice that the registration point is now closer to the top-left corner of the square:

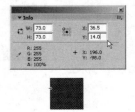

The Info panel provides you with greater flexibility when positioning your registration point.

You might be wondering why you have these various options for positioning the registration point of your symbols. Well, if you wanted to make a loading progress bar, you would set the registration point to the center left point, and if you were animating a flower growing from the ground, you would set the registration point to the bottom center of the flower symbol.

Registration points other than the center point are more commonly used (but they are not exclusive to) ActionScript scenarios such as building a preloader bar. You'll see how it can have a beneficial effect when animating content a little later in the book.

Let's now go back to the Library window and see what else you can do with it.

Working with the Library

The **New Folder** button allows you to create folders in your Library as a means of organizing your symbols.

1. In the Library window, click the **New Folder** button (second from the left at the bottom of the window). A new folder appears in your Library with its name highlighted:

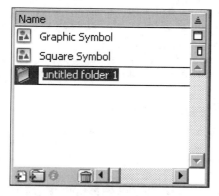

2. Type Circle Folder as new folder's name and press *ENTER*. Flash automatically sorts the contents of the Library into alphabetical order, so your new folder will jump above the Graphic Symbol.

3. Click your Graphic Symbol in the Library and drag it onto the Circle Folder icon. As you'd expect from a file browser program, the Graphic Symbol is now located inside the new folder:

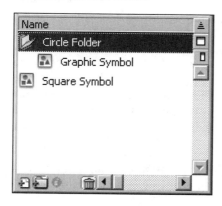

You can tell it's inside the folder by the level of indentation.

4. Double-click the Circle Folder icon to close the folder and hide your symbol. Double-click it again to reopen it. Double-clicking the name of the folder now will allow you to rename it—if you do this by mistake, just press *ENTER* to leave it as it is.

5. With the folder open, click the Graphic Symbol to highlight it and then click the Properties button in the Library:

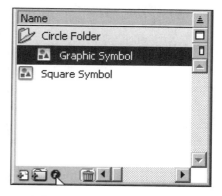

This will open the Symbol Properties dialog box, from which you can rename your symbol or change its behavior—that is, its *type*:

6. Click Cancel to close the dialog box without making any changes.

7. Click the Square Symbol to select it. Next, click the Delete button (the trash can icon) in the Library. You'll be prompted with a dialog box asking whether you really want to delete the Square Symbol:

Flash always gives you this prompt, just as a fail safe. If you happen to delete items by mistake, you can Undo the action. By default, Flash removes all instances of the deleted symbol from the stage.

8. Click Yes to get rid of the Square Symbol.

9. Select the Graphic Symbol and drag it out of the folder so that the Graphic Symbol icon is at the same level of indentation as the Circle Folder icon, then delete the folder:

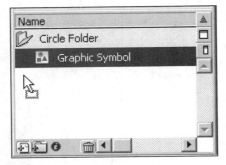

You'll now be back where you started with just the single original Graphic Symbol in the Library. Let's put an **instance** of this symbol on your stage.

10. Click the blue arrow to go back to the main stage.

11. To get an instance of your symbol onto the stage, drag the name of your symbol out of the Library and release it on the stage. Don't worry about placing it too precisely—you can always move the symbol around again later.

You now have a single instance of your symbol on the stage.

12. To illustrate how easy it is to reuse symbols, drag another couple of instances of the Graphic Symbol and put them anywhere you like on the stage:

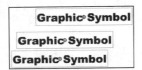

That's a lot easier than making each component separately every time, isn't it? Notice that you've selected all three instances on the stage, and that each one displays a little cross, indicating that they're symbols.

Perhaps the best thing of all here is that even though you now have three images on the stage, they still only take up the space of one picture in the final SWF file. This is because the instances of the symbol on the stage are really just coordinates that tell Flash where to put a copy of the content of the master symbol stored in the Library.

Now you have your instances of the symbol on the stage. What if you decide that you want to change the symbol in the Library that they're based on?

Modifying symbols

When you change the symbol defined and stored in your Library, all the instances of that symbol on your stage will change as well.

Modifying a symbol in the Library

1. Select the Graphic Symbol in the Library, and then double-click its picture in the Preview pane. This will open Edit Symbols mode.

2. Select the symbol on the (Edit Symbols) stage and then select the Text tool from the Tools panel. In the Properties panel, choose a text color that's obviously different from the original color.

3. Click the Scene 1 tab below the timeline to return to the main stage. Here you'll notice that all the instances of your graphic symbol have changed to the same color as the master in the Library.

This is clearly a very powerful feature that makes it easy to redesign and amend significant parts of your movie without having to edit each and every symbol throughout the movie. You can just change the symbol in the Library that the individual instances are based on.

Let's now experiment with the second, slightly more complex type of symbol—the **button symbol**.

Button symbols

Buttons are essential features of any interactive website, and they're the key to any good menu or site navigation interface. Why? Because you're used to clicking buttons and having them do things for you—it's almost an unconscious action. Using buttons is such an obvious thing that you're often unaware you're doing it when you're interacting with a website or software application. However, if you ever go to a site whose navigation architecture doesn't provide you with buttons, you'll quickly become aware just how vital they are.

It's amazingly easy to create buttons in Flash and include them in your movies, and they're one of the components that take Flash from being a great animation package to being a web application development tool. Flash buttons are important because they take you into the world of true interactivity where your site visitor can control their experience. Whether it's jumping from movie to movie or kicking off a series of complex actions, buttons can be the way in. In Flash, button symbols embody the behaviors that open up the interactive world.

To get you started, you'll build a simple button and go through a button's basic features and capabilities. Later in the book, you'll see more extremely interesting and important things with buttons.

Creating a button symbol

Let's create that button symbol. First, you need a shape to convert to a symbol.

1. In the movie where you created your graphic symbol, select the Oval Tool and draw a circle with a stroke and fill of your choice. (Delete the instances of Graphic Symbol from your main stage to give you a clean space to work in.) To adjust the properties of the circle, select it with the Selection tool and go to the Properties panel. You'll see the circle's dimensions in the W and H boxes in the bottom half of the Properties panel. If you can't see the bottom half of the Properties panel, click the arrow on its bottom-right edge to extend it:

We've made our circle 120 pixels across to create a big hefty button.

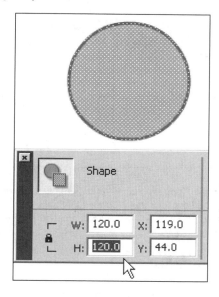

2. Select the circle and change it into a symbol, either by using the Modify ➤ Convert to Symbol menu option or by pressing the *F8* shortcut.

3. In the Convert to Symbol dialog box, choose the Button behavior type. Name your button Button Symbol, give it a central registration point, and press OK:

You should notice three things: your circle on the stage now has a bounding box around it, indicating that it's now a symbol; the new symbol appears in your Library; and if you bring up the Properties panel, the symbol's name is displayed next to a pointing finger over a rectangle icon—this is the icon for a button symbol:

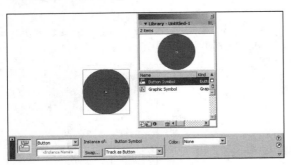

4. Double-click the instance of your Button Symbol on the stage to open Edit Symbols mode again.

> *Editing a symbol by double-clicking its instance on the stage sends Flash into Edit in Place mode. This mode is particularly useful for changing a symbol when you need to view it in relation to other symbols on the stage.*

5. You may have noticed that your timeline has changed:

Whenever you create or edit a button symbol you will see this *button-specific* style of timeline. This timeline is only visible in Edit Symbols mode, and every button symbol has this same kind of special internal timeline. This timeline controls how the button will behave when you interact with it.

> *A button symbol's internal timeline is nested inside the symbol. When Flash comes across an instance (copy) of the symbol on the stage, it is aware of the button's timeline, but the button only does anything when the user interacts with it.*

Every button timeline has only four frames, each of which controls a different aspect of the button's behavior. The names above the four frames—**Up**, **Over**, **Down**, and **Hit**—refer to the four possible conditions that a button can be in. These conditions are called **button states**.

Button states

The states of a button are defined in the four frames of the button's timeline. Each frame describes what the button will look like and what it will do when the button is in that state.

This is what each state means:

- **Up**—This is how the button looks in its static state when it is in the movie interface waiting for a user to interact with it.

- **Over**—This is what the button will look like when the user runs their mouse over it.

- **Down**—This is what the button will look like when the user clicks it.

- **Hit**—This is a special state that you can't see in your finished movie. The *hit* state is the part of the button that is clickable. Think of it as a target for the mouse—hitting this target will make the button work. Make sure that whatever part of the button you want people to be able to click is defined in the Hit state. It doesn't have to be pretty, but it's important to clearly define the Hit state.

Let's see how these states work by defining them for your circular button symbol.

Making your button work

At the moment, your button is just a single-state, lifeless circle that might as well be a static graphic symbol. What your button needs is that extra something that makes a button a button—interactivity. You define this interactivity in the four frames of the button's timeline.

Notice that only one of the frames on the button's timeline is actually a **keyframe**—the first frame, which represents the button's Up state—the other three frames are currently blank:

This is because Flash assumed that you wanted to display the circle you'd drawn when the button is in its Up state. You can edit this keyframe and change the image that's displayed if you want to.

To create the other three states for the button, you first need to convert the three blank frames in the timeline into keyframes. Remember, a keyframe is what defines a significant change to a piece of Flash content. By defining these keyframes and their content, you're telling Flash how you want your button to behave.

1. Click each of the three blank frames individually in the button timeline and press *F6* to insert a keyframe. You now have a full timeline:

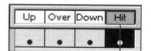

2. Click the Over state in the timeline. Your button will automatically be selected.

3. Select a color from the Properties panel that's different to the original button symbol color. The color of your button automatically changes to reflect your new choice.

4. Select the Down state keyframe in the timeline and change it to another color in the same way. Leave the Hit state as it is for now.

5. Test your movie by using the Control ➤ Test Movie menu option, or by pressing *CTRL+ENTER*. This opens a new window showing what your finished movie will look like when it's rendered in the web browser.

6. Move your mouse over the button and it changes color. This color is the color you defined for the Over state.

7. Click the button. While you hold the mouse button down, the button displays the color defined in the Down state keyframe.

8. You just created your first button and taken your first steps towards interactivity. It was pretty easy, wasn't it? But remember, what you're learning here about button states is the basic foundation on which you can build an infinitely complex universe of interactivity.

9. Close the Test Movie window to display Edit in Place mode.

At the moment, you haven't defined a Hit state for your button: Flash is currently using the image from the preceding keyframe to define the Hit state. Let's be more explicit.

10. Click the Hit state keyframe on the timeline and use the Rectangle tool to draw a big rectangle (any color you like) around your button:

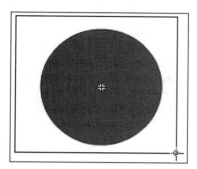

11. Open the Test Movie window again.

This time, even though everything looks the same, when you run the mouse over your button you'll see it change color before you get to the actual button itself:

This is because you defined the Hit state (invisible to the user) as a larger area than the (visible) button. You may be wondering why you would ever want to do this—normally you wouldn't, but there is one case where this technique is incredibly useful: when you want to use text as a button.

Making buttons from text

1. Click the Scene 1 tab below the timeline to get back to the main stage.

2. Using the Text tool, find a clear part of your stage and type Hello in any font and color.

3. Click the Selection tool, select your text, and then convert it to a button symbol (*F8*), naming it Hello. As normal, give it a central registration point.

4. Insert a keyframe (*F6*) into each of the button states as you did before, and test your movie.

This time when you move your mouse over the text, it seems to flicker on and off. This is because the Hit state of the button is defined, by default, as the actual text itself—the gaps between the letters and the holes in the letters don't respond to the mouse. If all text buttons were like this, nobody would be able to use them. This is where the Hit state comes in handy.

Go back to Edit Symbols mode and click the Hit state keyframe. Using the Rectangle tool, drag a rectangle (make sure it has a fill) that just covers all your text:

Don't worry about not being able to see your text in the authoring environment. As you saw before, the Hit state image is invisible in the movie.

5. Test your movie again. As your mouse moves over the text it stays highlighted because there is now an (invisible) border around the text, which means that the whole of the text is now defined as the Hit area.

6. Close the Test Movie window, and then click the Scene 1 tab to return to the main stage.

There's an easy way to see, and edit, all the symbols in your movie. There are two buttons below the timeline on the right:

Edit Scene 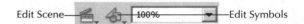 Edit Symbols

If you click the Edit Symbols button, a drop-down menu will appear with a list of all the symbols available to you in your movie's Library:

When you click one of the named symbols, editing mode for that symbol opens. Try it with your three symbols and see. You can go back to the main stage by either clicking the Scene 1 tab as you've done before, or by clicking the Edit Scene button and then selecting Scene 1 from the menu that pops up.

If you look at the Properties panel when you're in Edit Symbols mode, you'll see on the right that there are options to add sound and script to your creations. You'll look at this later in the book. Next though, let's take a look at the third type of symbol in Flash—the **movie clip symbol**. You'll use movie clips more and more as you progress through the book.

Movie clip symbols

The **movie clip symbol** is the third and final member of the Flash symbols set. Movie clip symbols—usually referred to as **movie clips**—are vitally important components in Flash movies. The simplest explanation of movie clips is that they are a movie within a movie. You can use them to create entirely self-contained pieces of action that you want to run independently of the rest of the things on the main timeline. Movie clips can have multiple layers just like the main timeline, and they can contain many graphic, animation, and sound components. An example of a typical movie clip would be a clip that encapsulated a logo with some background music. You can have the music playing and the logo fading in and out repeatedly throughout your whole main movie while other action changes around it.

> *Like the button symbol, a movie clip symbol has its own internal timeline. However, a movie clip's timeline is not limited to the four standard frames. As you progress through this book, you'll find that movie clips are flexible and multi-talented members of the Flash team.*

Movie clips can be very complicated, containing all manner of actions and animations. In this section we'll just introduce the basics of what movie clips are and how to use them.

Creating a movie clip symbol

1. You need an uncluttered stage, so close the current Flash document and create a new one.

2. On the main stage, use the Rectangle tool and draw a square—any color you like. Select the square and convert it to a symbol. Make sure the symbol's behavior is set to Movie Clip and its registration point is at the center. Name the new symbol Square Clip:

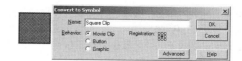

3. Double-click the square with the Selection tool to open Edit Symbols mode.

   Notice the timeline inside your new movie clip. This timeline works like the one above the stage in the main movie. The difference is that your movie clip symbol's timeline applies only to what happens inside the symbol itself. Any action and animation you create using this timeline will be encapsulated inside this movie clip. Anything you can do in your main movie, you can do inside a movie clip. That means you can create completely self-contained units of movie content that you can add to your main movie by dragging the movie clip symbol onto the main stage.

   Let's make a quick shape tween as an example.

4. Still inside your new movie clip, click frame 20 and press *F6* to insert a keyframe.

5. Click outside the square in frame 20 to deselect it, and use the Selection tool to pull out the sides and make an irregular shape:

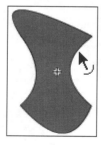

   Now that you've got two keyframes with distinct content in them, let's animate the shape tween.

6. Click frame 1 and go to the Properties panel. Select Shape from the Tween drop-down menu to create a shape tween between the two keyframes (just as you did with your mushroom movie in Chapter 1).

7. Click the Scene icon above the timeline to get back to the main stage.

8. Open your Library if it's not already displayed. It contains your Square Clip:

The blue sunburst next to the symbol's name is the icon that identifies movie clip symbols.

9. Click the icon for the Square Clip.

There are two controls in the top right of the Preview pane:

10. These two VCR-type controls are used to preview your movie clip inside the Library window. (These controls are also available when you select a button symbol in the Library.) If you click the play button, your movie clip will play in the Preview pane. You can use the stop control to halt playback.

11. Drag a couple of copies of your Square Clip from the Library onto the stage.

12. Press *ENTER* to preview your movie—nothing happens. This is because movie clips are not rendered in preview mode.

If you want to see your movie clips play, you have to use the Control ➤ Test Movie (*CTRL+ENTER*) menu option. Alternatively, you can publish your movie by pressing *F12*. If you do this you'll see your animations. Movie clips can do much more than this, but you'll have to wait until the later chapters before you can find out just how powerful they really are.

13. Save your movie as `movieclip.fla`.

14. Close the `movieclip.fla` movie.

It's probably worth mentioning here that graphic symbols have similar functionality to movie clips. The main difference is that movie clips can be scripted, whereas graphic symbols cannot. The file sizes of graphic symbols are slightly smaller than those of movie clips, so if you want just a symbol with a simple tween, it's probably worth using a graphic symbol.

Movie clips and the main timeline

When you drag an instance of a movie clip symbol onto your stage, you bring with it all the action you've added to the movie clip's timeline. When Flash finds the instance of the symbol in a keyframe on the main timeline, it digs down into the symbol and plays the content that it finds encapsulated in the symbol's internal timeline. Simultaneously, Flash continues along the main movie's timeline, rendering any content that it finds there. In this context, you can think of movie clips as separate loops that start and then run their course while the main movie's playhead continues along the main timeline. Your movie clip is still integrated with the main movie, though—it shares the host movie's frame rate and background color, for example.

Another way of thinking about movie clips is that they're the "children" of the main movie. The main "parent" timeline plays in sequence, and when it comes across a movie clip symbol in a keyframe, it spawns a movie clip. After Flash has 'given life' to the movie clip, that movie clip has an independent life of its own while the main timeline continues separately.

Imagine a movie where you create a static background layer (a gradient) that lasts for fifty frames:

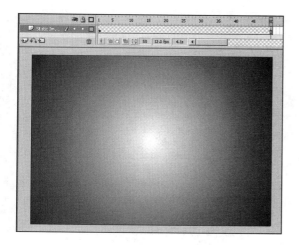

When you test your movie, you see the static image displayed for fifty frames, and then the movie loops and starts again. Now suppose that you create a keyframe at frame 10 and drag a morphing square movie clip from your Library into it. Next, you could add a morphing circle movie clip in a new keyframe at frame 25:

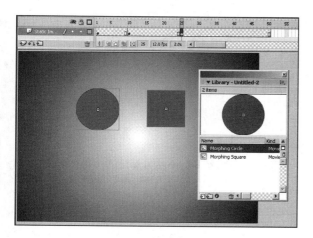

When you test your movie, you'd find that the static background will appear for a few frames, and when the playhead hits the keyframe at frame 10, the morphing square movie clip is triggered. The main movie playhead will continue along the main timeline until it

encounters the morphing circle at frame 25, at which point it will start that movie clip before continuing to display the static background until frame 50—the end of the movie. It's very important to remember that launching these movie clips doesn't pause or stop the playback of the main timeline—all three playback elements (the main timeline, plus the two internal movie clip timelines) play simultaneously:

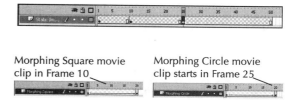

Morphing Square movie clip in Frame 10

Morphing Circle movie clip starts in Frame 25

A movie clip has a mind of its own; that is, its behavior is embedded in its internal timeline. However, the parent timeline can have the authority to tell the child movie clip what to do. It can use ActionScript commands to tell the movie clip to stop, start, change position and so on. You'll see this in practice after you've learned some ActionScript.

So far, you've dealt exclusively with symbols in the Library that are attached to the specific movie that you've been working on. But you can also reuse symbols from other movies' Libraries.

Sharing symbols

An extremely useful feature in Flash is the ability to import symbols from other movies libraries. This is particularly useful for projects in which you might be working on a number of Flash movies at the same time and want to share the symbols from one movie to the next. You might also consider creating a library that stores commonly used symbols for a number of Flash movies.

One other benefit of sharing symbols is that you can also share fonts. If you are working on a Flash presentation with someone who has fonts that you don't have, you can share your partner's font symbols.

Let's see how symbols are shared.

Using symbols from other movies

1. Select File ➤ Close All to close all the other Flash documents that are currently open. When you are prompted to save the various documents, save whichever ones you want.

   Closing all the other documents will help you focus a little more in this section.

2. Create a new Flash document from the startup screen's Create New ➤ Flash Document option, or the File ➤ New menu option followed by Flash Document.

3. Open the new movie's Library window. As you might expect, it's currently an Empty library:

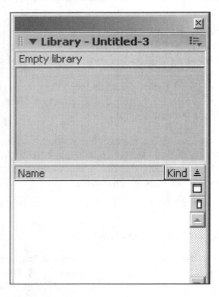

4. Go to the File menu and choose the Import ➤ Open External Library option.

5. In the resulting dialog box, navigate to the folder where you stored your movieclip.fla file and select it:

6. Click the **Open** button, and then take another look at your Library window:

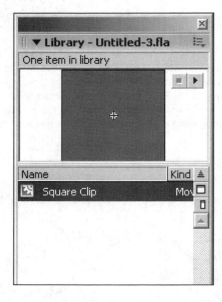

You now have the symbol from the first movie you made available to use in your new movie. This means that you can build up a collection of common symbols and share them between different movies—another labor-saving device from Flash! Flash also includes a feature you can use to share Libraries across networks and even over the Web, but this is a little beyond the scope of this book.

Sharing fonts over Flash movies

Font symbols allow users to share fonts through different Flash files. They are very useful when working with other people who might have a different set of fonts. Let's see how to share and retrieve fonts.

1. Open a new Flash document.

2. Open the Library (Window ➤ Library) and select New Font from the Library options drop-down menu.

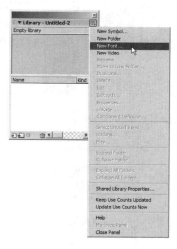

3. In the dialog box that appears, enter Midnight Train in the Name field, and select Georgia from the Font drop-down:

4. Save the movie as font_share.fla and close it.

5. Open a new Flash document (yes, another!) and select File ➤ Import ➤ Open External Library.

6. Select the Font_Share.fla file. After you confirm this, the Library of the Font_Share file will open.

7. Drag the Midnight Train font symbol onto the stage. The font dubbed Midnight Train will now be available on the Font drop-down menu suffixed with an asterisk.

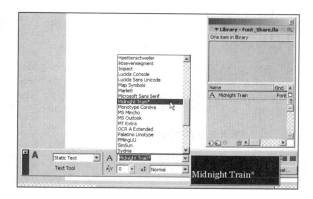

It can now be used just like any other font.

8. After you are done with this file, close it.

There are lots of pre-made buttons and other symbols already stored in Flash. You can access them via the Window ➤ Other Panels ➤ Common Libraries menu option. Open some examples and check out their construction in Edit Symbols mode.

Finally in this chapter, let's work on your case study project and implement some of the things we've just discussed.

Case Study

Creating symbols

1. Open the case study movie you worked on at the end of the previous chapter.

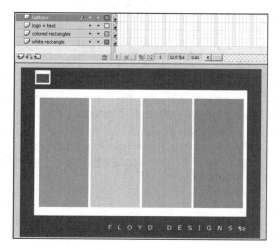

At this point you should have your interface objects sitting on their separate layers. You need to convert some of your objects into symbols.

2. Select the shape in the top-left corner and select Modify ➤ Convert to Symbol. In the dialog box that appears, name it generic button, and give it a center registration point and a button behavior.

3. Double-click the button on the stage to edit it. This will allow you to edit the symbol within the context of the rest of the document.

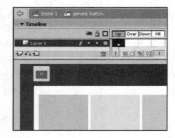

You might notice that the other elements of the stage are washed out; this is to help you to concentrate on your active symbol alone. This mode of editing symbols is called **Edit in Place**.

4. Select the Over state and insert a keyframe (Insert ➤ Timeline ➤ Keyframe or *F6*).

5. On the Over state, use the Paint Bucket tool to change the red square to green.

6. Still in the Over state, use the Line tool to draw a white line from the bottom of the shape up to the large white rectangle. Use the Properties panel to set a stroke thickness of 3.

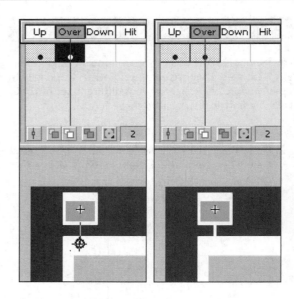

7. Return to the main stage and drag three copies of the generic button symbol onto the stage. Place these next to the first button.

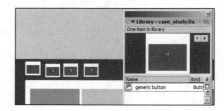

Test the movie using Control ➤ Test Movie. Hover the mouse pointer over the buttons to see the red change to green and the added white line.

8. Select the name/company text and your representative icon using the Selection tool and convert them to a single graphic symbol called logo.

> *Remember: to select more than one symbol or item, hold down the SHIFT key when making subsequent selections.*

9. Save your Flash document and close it.

Summary

In this chapter, you took a preliminary look at the nature, creation, and storage of symbols in Flash.

You saw that:

- **Symbols** are self-contained pieces of movie content that you can create once and then use many times in your movies.
- When you create a copy of a symbol on the stage, it's called an **instance**.
- Symbols are stored in a **Library**, and you can organize the Library and use it to share symbols between different movies.

- Symbols have their own **internal timeline**, which allows them to work independently from the main movie's timeline:
    - **Graphic symbols** are typically used for still graphics.
    - **Button symbols** have a standard four-frame internal timeline. This timeline includes the different button **states**.
    - **Movie clip symbols** are the multi-talented superstars of the symbols world. Their internal timelines are infinitely customizable. You can embed the same kind of multi-layered graphics and sound content in movie clip symbols that you can on the movie's main timeline. It's also possible to have graphic and button symbols as well as other movie clips within a movie clip symbol.

You'll see much more of symbols and their use later in this book. In the next chapter, you're going to examine the features that Flash gives you to help manage and arrange multiple pieces of content on the stage.

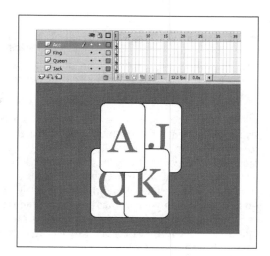

Chapter 4

MANAGING CONTENT

What we'll cover in this chapter:

- Assembling and placing content precisely on the (three-dimensional) Flash stage
- **Grouping objects** for consistency and convenience
- Using **grids, rulers, guides** and **alignment tools** to place objects exactly where you want them
- **Transforming objects** with control and confidence
- **Stacking** multiple objects inside a layer
- Splitting content with **Distribute to Layers**
- Managing layers with **folders**
- Tracking your actions with the **History panel**

In this chapter, you'll examine the tools and facilities that Macromedia Flash gives you for aligning and arranging objects on the stage. In doing so, you'll be working on the stage in **three dimensions**: width, height, and depth.

When you create movies that have only a couple of visual components, arrangement and alignment is not so much of an issue, but if you build larger-scale movies or if you want to make your movies look more elegant, you need to ensure that the components in your movie are effectively and harmoniously set up. Additionally, when your movies are growing in size and complexity, you need ways of grouping content elements together so that they are easier to maintain and amend. Flash provides you with plenty of tools in these respects, and getting a handle on these tools will save you a lot of pain and frustration.

Let's begin by seeing how Flash can ease the burden of moving things around and editing them while maintaining proportions and relative positions.

Grouped objects

You've already seen that grouping objects can help prevent you from cutting objects in half or picking up just the fill. Here, you'll look more closely at grouping objects and the benefits that it brings. You can think of grouping as an easy way to organize and manipulate multiple objects.

Grouping multiple objects

1. Open a new Flash document using File ➤ New and selecting Flash Document.
2. Using the Rectangle tool, draw a square shape anywhere on your stage. Then draw a smaller circle on a nearby part of the stage with the Oval tool.

3. Use the Selection tool to drag a box around both objects to select them, and then group them using the Modify ➤ Group menu option (or *CTRL+G*). Now when you move one of the objects, the other will move with it, staying in exactly the same position relative to the other object:

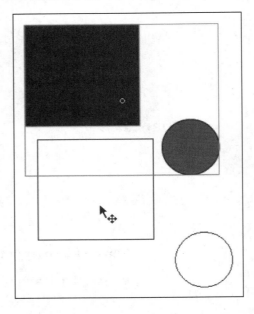

This is clearly a useful feature when you're dealing with large numbers of objects and you don't want to move them around individually by hand, and it'll help you maintain the design and look of your movie when you're amending it.

You can group lines, fills, buttons, graphics, movie clips, and text—pretty much anything you can put on the movie stage. A sure way to tell whether an object is part of a group is that a thin colored highlighting line appears around the outer edges of grouped objects. You can change your default highlight color using Edit ➤ Preferences menu option (Flash MX 2004 ➤ Preferences on the Mac) and amending the Highlight Color option on the General tab:

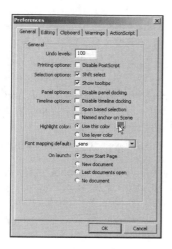

It's also extremely easy to ungroup objects in Flash:

4. Click your grouped shapes with the Selection tool to select them and use the Modify ➤ Ungroup menu option. They will be returned to two distinct objects with their own separate lines and fills.

5. Use the Line tool to draw a triangle on your stage, and fill it with color.

6. Drag a box around all three of your objects with the Selection tool and group them all together.

It would be a laborious process if every time you wanted to edit a specific line or fill within a group, you had to ungroup it, edit it, and then group it again. Flash gets around this by having an **Edit Group** mode. This mode is used to add, subtract, or change elements in groups.

Editing a group of objects

1. To enter Edit Group mode, simply double-click your group or select the group on the stage, and use the Edit ➤ Edit Selected menu option.

2. When you're in Edit Group mode, notice that something has changed below your timeline. In the same place where the symbol name is displayed in Edit Symbols mode, it now says Group with an icon next to it similar to that of a graphic symbol:

This is Flash's visual cue to let you know that you're currently editing a group of objects. Another visual cue is that when you're in Edit Group mode, as with Edit in Place when editing symbols, all the objects on the stage apart from the group you're editing will be dimmed and inaccessible.

3. In Edit Group mode, change the shape of your triangle using the Selection tool and move it to somewhere else on the stage:

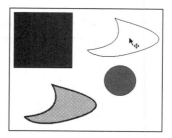

4. Return to the main stage by using the same method as you would from Edit Symbols mode—by clicking the Scene 1 button or the Back button to the left of the Scene icon.

Back on the main stage, everything is still grouped together and moves as one object, but your triangle shape is now happily sitting in its new position in the group.

5. Save your file as group.fla and then close it. You'll use it later in this chapter.

There's no limit to the number of groups you can have in Flash. In fact, you can have symbols within groups, groups within groups, and even groups within symbols within groups—the possibilities are endless.

Symbols within symbols

Nested symbols are easily manageable from within the Flash interface.

87

A hierarchy of nested symbols

1. Open a new Flash document with File ➤ New. Select the Line tool and set the stroke width to 4 in the Properties panel. Draw a rough sketch of the body of a car on the stage.

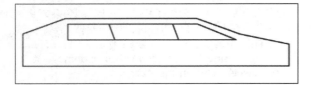

2. Fill the body of your car using the Paint Bucket tool, selecting your favorite color from the Color palette in the Properties panel.

3. Draw a box around the car with the Selection tool and select Modify ➤ Convert to Symbol, or press F8, to make the car graphic a symbol. Name the new symbol car, select Movie Clip as its behavior, and give it a central registration point:

4. Double-click the car symbol in the Library to enter Edit Symbol mode.

   When you look at your beautiful automobile, you might notice something key missing from it, something vital to making that baby move.

   Your car has no wheels! Time to put it right.

5. Rename the current existing layer car and lock it to prevent any changes. This will keep your car getting scratched while you do other things to it:

6. Create a new layer by clicking the Insert Layer button:

   Double-click the new layer name and rename it wheels, because that's what your car needs more than a flame paint job right now.

7. On the wheels layer, use the Circle tool to draw a circle near the rear of the car—holding down the SHIFT key to keep it in proportion. When you are happy with your circle, select it and make it into a symbol with Modify ➤ Convert to Symbol menu option.

8. Make it a graphic symbol with the name static wheel and a central registration point:

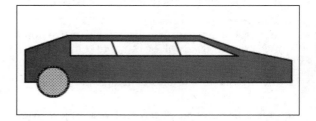

   At this point, your car is a little more able, but is more suited to being towed to an auto shop than speeding down the highway. Let's give this baby a much-needed helping hand.

9. Go to your Library (if it's not open, open it using Window ➤ Library) and drag an instance of the static wheel symbol onto the stage. Use the Selection tool to select the new wheel and position it at the front of the car, finally making it stable:

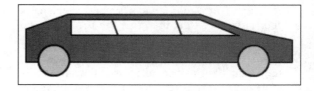

   Now, if you were to animate your wheels, you'd have no idea if they were rotating or not. Let's give them something to show a little rotation.

10. Double-click either of the wheels to edit the static wheel symbol:

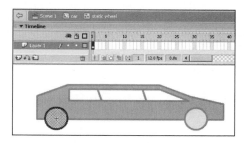

Remember, when you double-click any symbol within another symbol, you are taken to the **edit symbols mode**—inside the previous symbol. You can tell you've gone one level deeper by looking at the icons above the timeline:

To return to the previous symbol, click the symbol name to the left of the one you are currently in, or use the Back button. This can be a bit confusing at times, but as long as you keep an eye on the icons below the timeline, you should be able to work out where you are. If in doubt, return to the main stage and work your way through your nested symbols to reach the one you wanted.

11. In the static wheel edit mode, create a new layer and select it so you can work on it. Use the Line tool to draw a black horizontal line across the center of the wheel:

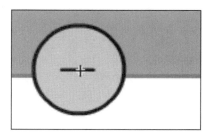

This line will be used to show the wheels of the car in motion. The next bit may seem a little tricky at first, but will be explained fully in a later chapter—so bear with it.

12. Click the Back button to return to the car editing mode:

13. Select the rear wheel and use the Modify ➤ Convert to Symbol menu option. Name it animated wheel, with movie clip behavior and a central registration point.

This will place your original static wheel, which is already a graphic symbol, within the timeline of a movie clip called "animated wheel." You've nested the static wheel graphic symbol within the animated wheel movie clip symbol. Within this movie clip you'll animate the wheel a little.

14. Double-click the animated wheel on the stage to edit it. The bar above the timeline will look like this:

Finally—let's animate your wheel.

15. Click frame 20 of the timeline and press *F6* to insert a keyframe.

This time you'll use motion tweening to make the wheel rotate a little—there'll be more on motion tweening in Chapter 6.

16. Click frame 1 and make sure that the Properties panel is visible (use the Window ➤ Properties menu option if it is hidden). In the Properties panel, select Motion from the Tween drop-down menu:

The frames in the timeline should have turned a blue color and there should be an arrow from frame 1 to 20:

17. In the Properties panel again, select CW from the Rotate drop-down menu. (If you can't see the Rotate drop-down menu, click the white triangle in the bottom-right corner of the Properties panel.)

18. In the box to the right of the Rotate drop-down menu, type 3:

This will set the wheel to rotate 3 times in a clockwise direction over the designated 20 frames. Remember, we'll explain motion tweens in detail a little later in the book.

19. Test the movie with the Control ➤ Test Movie menu option.

If all went well, the left wheel should be turning—the car is almost moving! To make the other wheel move, you need to replace the static wheel graphic symbol with the animated wheel movie clip.

20. Click the Back button to enter the car movie clip's editing mode.

21. Click the front wheel and delete it with the Backspace key. Then drag a copy of animated wheel from the Library and place it on the stage at the front of the car.

If you now test the movie with Control ➤ Test Movie, you'll see that both wheels are turning in the same direction, at the same speed. Your car is driving on a treadmill and is going nowhere fast.

22. Save the movie as car.fla and close it for now. You'll give your car traveling independence in Chapter 6.

Now that you know how to create and manage groups and symbols, how can you get them lined up neatly and evenly on the stage? You could always do it by eye of course, but Flash gives you a couple of quicker and more precise methods. You'll start with something you might have come across already, **Snap Align**.

Snap Align

One of the great new additions to Flash MX 2004 is the Snap Align option. Snap Align works by snapping objects to the edges of other objects.

When snap align is switched on (View ➤ Snapping ➤ Snap Align) and one object is being moved in the vicinity of another, Flash will snap the moved object to the edges of the static shape and will indicate this with a dotted line. One particular use of this is the ability to ensure that objects do not overlap on the stage. A quick example will help show how this works in practice.

In the following screenshot, we dragged a rectangle just above a square. When it is near enough to the square, a dotted line appears, and snaps the rectangle to the square's top edge.

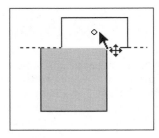

A little more to the left, and the Snap Align kicks in again, showing a dotted line for the left edge of the square.

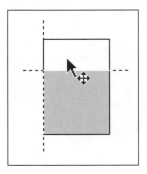

So far so good. The next screenshot does the same thing, but uses the opposite edges of the rectangle.

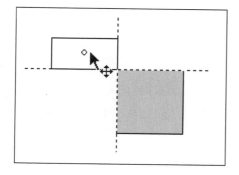

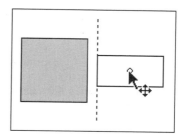

Snap to Align also works in a few other ways.

It snaps objects at a distance from other shapes:

Where more than one shape is involved, the snap align will check all the available edges for a match:

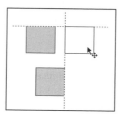

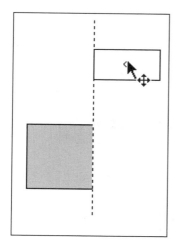

Creating an emerald using Snap Align

Let's use Snap Align to make an emerald shape from a number of small shapes.

1. Open a new Flash document.

2. Draw a square with the Rectangle tool and give it a black stroke and any fill color. We used red.

3. Select the square using the Selection tool and create four copies of the square using Edit ➤ Copy followed by Edit ➤ Paste In Center. Alternatively, you can use Edit ➤ Duplicate (*CTRL-D*). Each time you make a new copy, make sure you move it away from the any of the other squares, otherwise they'll be fused together.

It snaps other (non-rectangle) shapes:

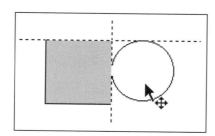

Snaps objects parallel to other objects (at a 10 pixel offset):

After you've done this, all squares should be spaced apart on the stage:

4. Select one of the squares using the Selection tool and drag it to roughly the center of the stage. This will be your center square.

5. Click and drag on one of the other squares and position it above the center square until both the vertical and horizontal Snap Align lines appear.

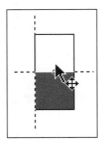

6. Position the other three squares at the other three sides of the center square. Make sure each time that the both vertical and horizontal Snap Align lines appear. The last maneuver should look like this:

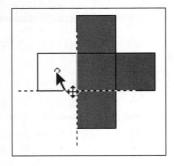

Now you have a cross shape, all you need to add are 45 degree angled corners. To do this, you need to create a triangle for copying and rotating to angle off each corner. And to make that triangle, you need to work with a square!

7. Use the Selection tool to double-click and select an existing square and its fill.

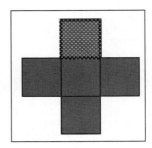

8. Select Edit ➤ Duplicate or *CTRL+D* to copy the square.

9. Position the new square away from the others so that it can be modified separately.

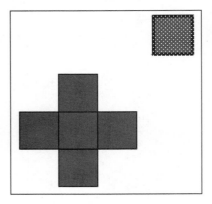

10. Choose the Subselection tool.

11. Click the new square once to reveal the vector points.

12. Click the top-right vector point. After you select it, the vector point will appear solid—as in this screenshot:

13. Press *DELETE* or *BACKSPACE* to remove the point. Et voila, a perfect right-angle triangle!

14. Double-click with the Selection tool to select the triangle and it's fill. Then copy and paste (or duplicate) the triangle three times, taking care to drag each new copy away from the others.

15. Drag one of the triangles to the top-right corner of the cross. As before, make sure that both vertical and horizontal snap align lines appear.

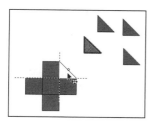

The remaining three triangles must be rotated or flipped to fit the remaining corner plots.

16. Select a triangle and choose Modify ➤ Transform ➤ Rotate 90° CW. Alternatively, type 90° into the Rotate text field of the Transform panel (Window ➤ Design Panels ➤ Transform):

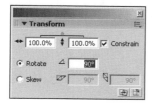

17. Select the next triangle, and choose Modify ➤ Transform ➤ Rotate 90° CCW, or type -90° (minus 90) into the Rotate text field in the Transform panel.

18. Select the last triangle, and choose Modify ➤ Transform ➤ Flip Horizontal followed by Modify ➤ Transform ➤ Flip Vertical.

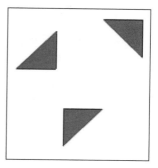

19. Drag the modified triangles into their respective slots, remembering to use the snap align option to correctly position them.

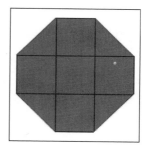

To improve on that dull, flat look, you need to add a little depth. You'll do this using a gradient.

20. Select all the shapes by drawing a box around them with the Selection tool.

21. Click the fill color selector in the Properties panel and select the green gradient along the bottom.

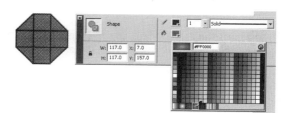

After your eyes have adjusted to it, you have an enchanting emerald.

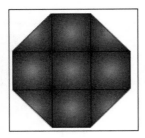

22. Close and save this Flash document as `emerald.fla`. You'll improve it in a later chapter.

As you can see in this exercise, the Snap Align option is extremely useful for placing objects in line with each other using their edges.

Now that you've seen how to align objects and shapes relative to each other, let's learn how to work with Flash's **grids** and **rulers** for finer placement from the start.

The grid

By default, the grid in Flash gives you a background of fine-lined squares that you can use to guide the placement and alignment of objects.

Using the grid

1. Open the `group.fla` file you were working on earlier.

2. Switch off the Snap Align option with View ➤ Snapping ➤ Snap Align. This will make it easier to work with the grid.

3. To access the grid in Flash, use the View ➤ Grid ➤ Show Grid menu option. The stage now has a series of grid lines across it:

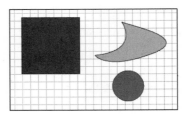

4. Turn on Flash's grid snapping feature by clicking View ➤ Snapping ➤ Snap to Grid.

5. Select your square, making sure you select both the fill and the stroke. Carefully click the center of your square and drag it around—it will snap to a grid line when it gets near one:

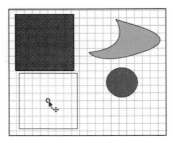

If you miss the middle of the square when you click and drag, the square won't snap to the grid. It can be deceptively difficult to find the middle of an object; the only solution is to try and try again. When you click the center of an object and drag it, a small black ring appears next to the cursor. This is called the **snapping ring**. When you drag an object close to a grid line, the ring will jump to the grid line and become larger and darker:

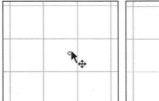

The snapping ring snaps to any gridline, but is easiest to snap to the grid at an intersection—where vertical and horizontal grid lines meet.

Experiment with moving your square around the stage with snapping turned on and off, and see the different effects. Also try zooming in and moving the object again. Notice that it gets easier to position things precisely the more zoomed in you are. The trade off for this is that you won't be able to see your whole image. The best solution is to experiment until you find a happy medium—this will, of course, be different for each movie you work on.

When you're aligning your shapes, you won't always want to do so by dragging the shape at the center. Flash caters to this by allowing you to drag the shapes by their corners as well. When you drag shapes by the corners, a similar snapping ring appears:

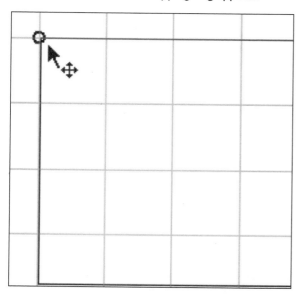

These are the default behaviors of the grid. Flash also gives you the ability to customize the grid and its settings to suit your every need.

Changing the grid settings

1. Open the Grid dialog box by using the View ➤ Grid ➤ Edit Grid menu option:

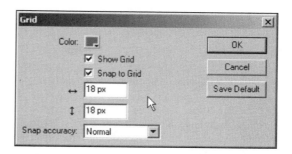

From here, you can change the spacing and the color of your grid lines.

It can be useful to change the grid color if the current grid lines are merging into the color of your movie background, or if you just prefer another color aesthetically. The units of measurement will be the same movie-wide values that you set in the Properties panel and Document Properties dialog box.

The Snap accuracy option allows you to alter how close the snapping ring has to be to something before it will snap to it. So, if you find those lines are just too sticky, you can set it to Must be close. On the other hand, if you want to be seriously snap happy (sorry) you can set it to Always Snap and never get left with those middle-of-nowhere-blues again. Again, you can experiment with these settings at different levels of zoom.

The option to Save Default is the same as Make Default in the Document Properties box—using this will apply these values to all the Flash movies you create.

2. When you're finished, close the dialog box by clicking OK. To turn off the grid, go to the View ➤ Grid ➤ Show Grid menu option again—there'll be a

check mark next to the Show Grid option, indicating that it is currently turned on:

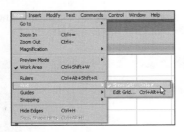

3. Click the Show Grid option and the check mark will disappear along with the grid lines. Try moving your square around. Even though the grid is no longer visible, your square will still snap to it if the Snap to Grid option is on. To stop this, you have to go into the View ➤ Snapping menu again and click the Snap to Grid option.

As you might expect, the grid is not shown in your final movie. If you want to see a grid effect in your finished movie, you have to draw one yourself. This is easily accomplished by drawing over the grid in the authoring environment on the back layer using the Line tool with snapping turned on for precision.

Flash has yet more ways of making drawing and alignment easier. Among these are **rulers** and **guides**.

Rulers and guides

Guides are an extremely useful feature of Flash, and when used in conjunction with Flash's rulers, they give you a powerful, customizable, and easy-to-use set of alignment tools. Let's see them in action.

Using rulers and guides

1. Use the View ➤ Rulers menu option to display Flash's rulers. As soon as you do this, a pair of vertically and horizontally-oriented rulers appear around the stage:

Zero point
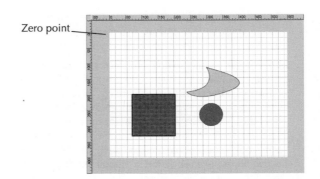

These rulers are marked out in the units currently defined in the Document Properties dialog box. The **zero point** for your rulers (where everything is measured from) is always at the top left-hand corner of your stage.

2. Using the Hand tool, move the stage around and notice how the zero point moves with it.

Rulers are not just handy for alignment—they're also useful for seeing how big your object is and how all the changes you're making are affecting it.

3. Grab your square with the Selection tool and move it around the stage, keeping an eye on your rulers as you do so. Two black lines on each ruler shift position as your shape moves. These lines indicate the dimensions and position of your shape on the stage:

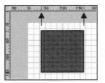

These lines mark the shape at its widest point, so if you have a big irregular shape, Flash will put an invisible bounding box around it at its edges and use them for reference:

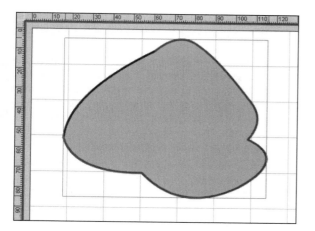

Another feature of rulers that you might have seen before is that you can use them to line up your **guides**. Guides are reference lines that help you with shape alignment. The great thing about guides is that—unlike grids and rulers, which are in a fixed position—you can put guides wherever you like, and add as many as you like. This means that no matter where an object is or what shape it is, you can always use a guide to help you line it up precisely with another shape.

4. Click anywhere on the ruler at the top of the stage and, still holding the mouse button, drag a horizontal guide down onto the stage:

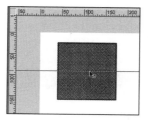

(We've turned off our grid so that you can see the guides more clearly.)

5. Release the mouse button anywhere on the stage to fix the guide at that point. The color of the guide defaults to a rather lurid green, but it can be altered via the View ➤ Guides ➤ Edit Guides

menu option. To get a vertical guide, drag a line from the left-hand ruler in the same way:

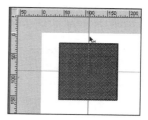

A guide's position is never set in stone. Whenever you move your mouse over a guide, the cursor will change:

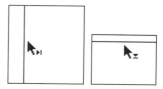

When the cursor looks like this, you can pick up your guide and move it elsewhere; you can even drag it right off the stage to get rid of it altogether.

6. Click your horizontal guide to pick it up, then drag it to the bottom of your square and release it to anchor it there:

Just as you can snap shapes to the grid, you can snap objects to guides.

7. Make sure that this snapping functionality is active by going to the View ➤ Snapping menu and ensuring that the Snap to Guides option is turned on.

8. Click the center of your circle and drag it to the guide line until it snaps to it. Your circle will now be perfectly lined up with the bottom of your square:

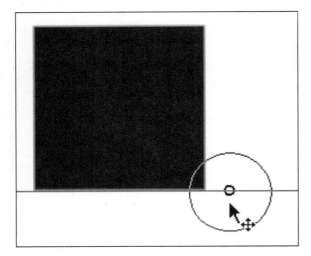

One more circle and you've got a wagon!

To get rid of your guideline, drag it all the way back onto the top ruler and release it. Dropping it anywhere on the ruler will do.

If you have a number of guides on the stage and you want to get rid of them all at once, you can use the Clear All button from the View ➤ Guides ➤ Edit Guides menu option. Using this option allows you to undo their removal by clicking the Cancel button.

Those of you who trust yourself enough can use the View ➤ Guides ➤ Clear Guides menu option. This option is final—so beware!

The Lock Guides option in the Edit Guides dialog will fix all current guides in place, meaning that you will not be able to move them after dropping them in place. This is useful when you're working with a lot of guides for precise placement purposes, and you don't want to pick them up by accident when you're moving other objects around. This may seem a little awkward at first, but with more practice you'll find these guides to be very useful in arranging your work on the stage.

As your movies become more complex, multi-layered, and sophisticated, you'll find guides increasingly useful, particularly because they are visible through all the layers of a movie. But as with a lot of things, Flash offers more than one way to align objects.

Alignment

In Flash, the **Align** panel acts as a hub for a number of alignment features.

The Align panel

With the Align panel, you can fine tune the position of multiple objects on the stage by aligning them, spacing them evenly, and even sizing them to ensure they all have exactly the same dimensions.

You access these features via the Window ➤ Design Panels ➤ Align menu option, or (in Windows), by clicking the Align button on the main toolbar:

This opens the Align panel:

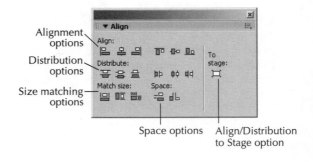

In this panel, you can see all the different alignment options. The seventeen options that take up the bulk of the panel work, by default, on the objects that you have selected on the stage, aligning them *in relation to each other*. If you turn the **To Stage** modifier on and then use the alignment buttons, the selected objects will be aligned *relative to the stage*:

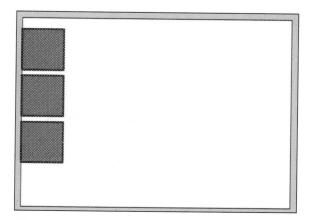

The key to using each of the options is to look at the thin black line on each button and its position relative to the objects shown on the button. This line dictates how the objects will be aligned. For example, look at the first group of alignnment buttons at the top left of the panel:

In the first button, the black line is to the left of the objects, which means that the objects will all be aligned along their left edges. The next button aligns your objects by their centers, and the third button will align them along their right edges.

As you'd expect, if you hold the cursor over any of the buttons, a tool tip will help you check out the basic function of the button:

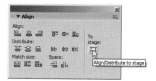

The best way to learn to use the Align panel is with practice and application. Next you'll look at examples of the buttons in each of the categories.

Aligning objects

Let's start by aligning objects in relation to each other with the basic alignment buttons. Make sure the To Stage modifier is turned off.

The Align options consist of two sets of three buttons: one set for aligning horizontally, the other for vertical alignment:

1. In a new Flash document, draw three new objects: a square, a circle, and a triangle. Make the objects different sizes, similar to the ones shown here:

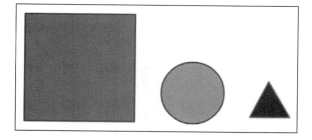

2. Select the line and fill of the square and group them. Repeat this step for the circle and the triangle so that you now have three separately grouped objects. (This will make them easier to move around and manipulate.)

When aligning objects, Flash puts a box around the object or group, marking its boundaries, and then uses this to align by. You see this highlighted box for a grouped object or symbol when you select it. Flash uses the center of this highlighting box as the center of the object or group. This can be a bit confusing at first because we humans tend to credit two-dimensional objects with real-world characteristics—we give them weight and volume, for example. In contrast, your cold-hearted computer sees these objects as just a collection of pixels on the screen.

99

For example, the center of this (grouped) shape is marked by a cross, which is probably not where you expect it to be.

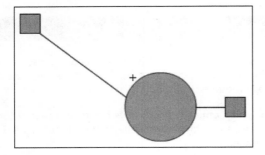

To show why Flash put the center-point there, look at the same object with the bounding box around it:

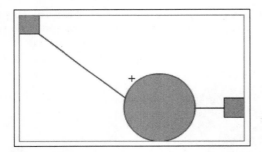

You can clearly see now that the cross is in the center of the box, which Flash treats as the center of the whole object.

3. Arrange all three of your grouped objects on the stage on a rough, unevenly spaced diagonal:

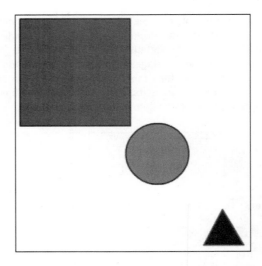

4. Group all your objects together by dragging a box around them with the Selection tool (or press CTRL+A).

5. Click the Align left edge button (the one at the top left of the Align panel) and your objects immediately reposition themselves by aligning with the left edge of the left-most object—in this case, the square:

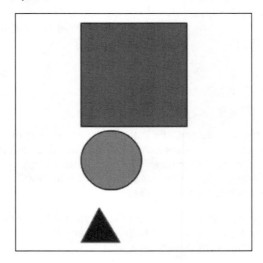

If you had selected the Align right edge button they would have lined up along the right edge of the triangle.

The Distribute options ensure that there's an equal distance between the respective edges of the objects.

6. For example, with all three of your objects still selected, click the Distribute left edge button. Your objects rearrange themselves like so:

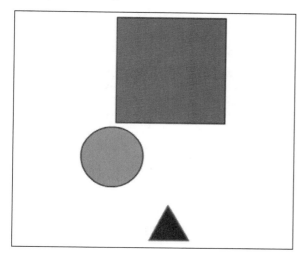

7. To clearly see the effect that this has, turn on the rulers and then drag guides out to each of the left edges of the objects:

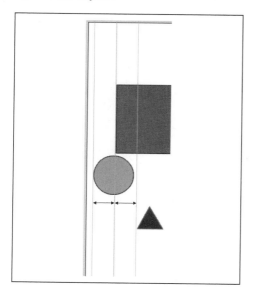

Now you can clearly see that Flash spaced the objects with equal distances between each of their left edges.

8. Remove your guides either by dragging them individually off the stage, or by choosing the View ➤ Guides ➤ Clear Guides menu option.

9. Turn your attention back to the Align panel and click the Match width button (bottom-left in the Align panel). Your circle and triangle suddenly grow in size:

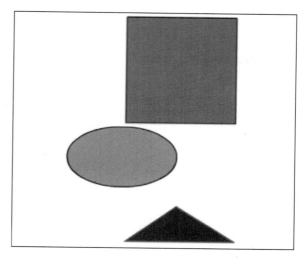

The Match Size option works by making all your selected objects the size of the largest one in the selection. So by clicking the Match Width button, you made all your objects the same width as your square. To ensure all objects on your stage are exactly the same dimensions, click the Match width and height button, and in the blink of an eye Flash will do the job for you. An example of when this comes in very handy is when you're drawing buttons and you want each button a different shape, but the same size in relation to the others.

The two Space options at the bottom-right of the Align panel will ensure that the gaps between the objects are the same size. This means, for example, that you can precisely arrange a set of buttons so that they look just right. Compare the

101

left hand set of buttons with the evenly spaced selection on the right:

Although the differences in spacing are subtle, an accumulation of unevenly spaced objects in your movies can quickly make things look rough and sketchy.

10. Back in your movie, click the Space evenly vertically button. This is another option when using guides can help to clarify exactly what Flash has done:

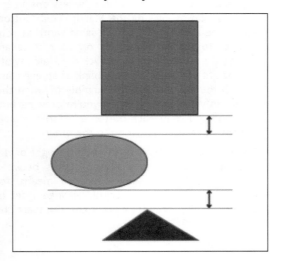

You can clearly see that the space between each of the objects is now the same size.

The final option remaining on the Align panel is the To Stage button on the right side:

This is a global switch that will affect all the other options on the Align panel. As you have already seen, so far Flash aligned all the object to one object, for example, the largest object for matching size, the left-most object for aligning to the left, and so on. When To Stage is turned on, Flash uses the stage to align the objects to instead, so aligning to the left will align the objects to the left of the stage, and matching size will match the objects to the full size of the stage. You could use this latter option to size an imported graphic image to match the dimensions of the stage—for example, if you wanted to use the image as a background layer.

11. Clear all your guides away, and then click the To Stage button to highlight it.

12. With all your shapes still selected, click the Match width button. All your objects are resized horizontally to mirror the width of the stage:

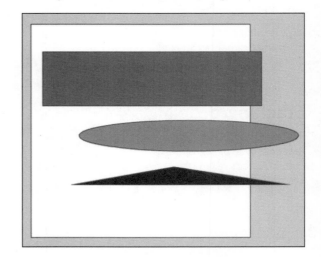

13. You can see that they are all exactly the same width as the stage by clicking the Align horizontal center button. This will align your 3 shapes perfectly to the horizontal center of the stage:

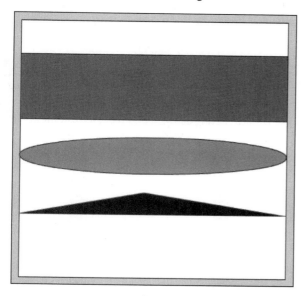

As you've seen in this series of examples, the alignment buttons can drastically affect the way that your objects appear on the stage. You can also see how much easier it can be to use these tools to do the job rather than attempting to align and match everything by eye.

Now let's take a look at how to control objects in Flash in another dimension through depth arrangement and layers.

Stacking order

In Chapter 1 you learned about **layers** and how they function in a background/foreground relationship. In that chapter's example, when your mushroom was growing behind the moon, you simply pulled the moon

layer underneath the mushroom layer and presto, the mushroom grew in correct perspective. There's a similar effect within individual layers, too: Flash's default behavior is to give objects that are on the same layer a front to back order—this is called the **stacking order**.

Only symbols or grouped objects can be stacked in Flash. All other objects—such as hand-drawn shapes—will fall to the lowest possible level of the layer. You can see this effect when you hand-draw two or more shapes on the stage. If, for example, you draw a rectangle and a circle on the stage they'll both occupy the same plane:

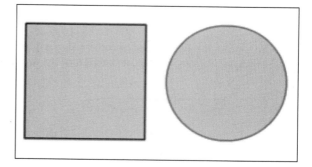

If you drag the circle onto the rectangle and then click away somewhere on the stage, Flash assumes that you want to merge these shapes on this plane:

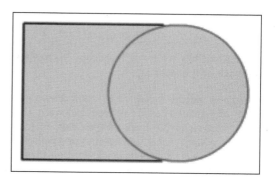

The overlapping areas of these shapes share the same piece of stage real estate. If you click the arc of the circle inside the shape...

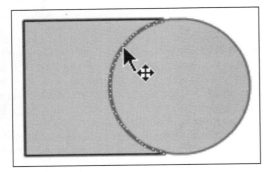

...and delete it; the two shapes become a single, fused entity, with all the lines and fills at the back of the layer:

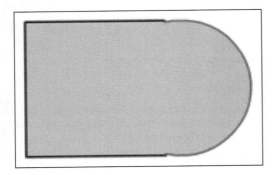

Drawn shapes merge together because their component lines and fills are trying to occupy the same space at the back of the layer.

However, unlike the behavior of hand-drawn objects, symbols and groups can be moved backward and forward in relation to the back of the layer. To facilitate this, Flash assigns each new group or symbol that's added to a particular layer a stack position that determines how far up from the back it sits. Flash assigns these positions based on the order in which the symbols or groups are added to the stage. This means that every time you create a new symbol or group, it's placed in front of the ones that were already there.

Let's look at this principle in action.

Shuffling a deck of cards

1. Start a new Flash document, and set the movie background color to a warm, casino-style green.

2. Double-click the Rectangle tool and set the Corner Radius modifier to 15. You want to create round-edged rectangles that'll represent playing cards.

3. In the Properties panel, set the stroke width to 2, the stroke color to black, and the fill color to white.

4. Draw a playing card-shaped rectangle on the stage:

5. Select the whole shape (fill and stroke) and convert it into a graphic symbol with a central registration point. Name the symbol Card Base:

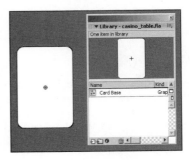

You now have a blank card symbol that you can use for all the cards that you'll show on the stage.

Now you'll create four cards on the stage—the Jack, Queen, King, and Ace. Each card will use the same Card Base symbol as its background but have a different letter on top of that background to indicate its seniority—J, Q, K, or A. You can easily do this by adding separate text boxes on top of each instance of the card base symbol.

6. Select the Text tool and choose an appropriate font and color from the Properties panel.

7. Click the middle of your card—this will help you judge what size the font should be:

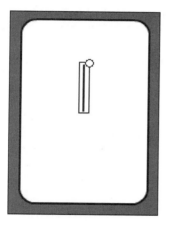

Make sure you don't go into Edit Symbols mode on the **Card Base** instance. All you want to do is create a text box that'll float above the symbol instance.

8. In the Properties panel, use the font size slider to set the font size to something that will look good on your card:

9. Type a capital J for Jack and use the Align panel to center your text in the card:

The simplest way to achieve this centering is by selecting the symbol instance and the text box by dragging a box round them with the Selection tool, and then clicking both the Align vertical center and Align horizontal center buttons on the Align panel.

10. Make sure you have both the card and the text selected and convert them into a symbol using *F8*. Give it the name Jack, a graphic symbol behavior, and a center registration point. Your card and its unique text identifier are now tied together in one symbol.

11. Use the same process to drag three more instances of the Card Base symbol onto your stage. Add the letters Q, K, and A to these three cards, **in that order**. Align the text over each card and then convert all the cards into appropriately named graphic symbols as you did with the Jack card.

When you've finished, you should have four cards on your stage that look like this:

12. Drag each of your cards to the left so they overlap each other:

Notice that the Jack, which you created first, is at the bottom of the stack, and the Ace, which you created last, is at the top. The Queen and King are in the correct sequence, too, so the stacking order is currently J, Q, K, A. Flash has faithfully created a stacking order for the cards based on the sequence that you created them in.

You can change the stacking order of these cards by using the options available through the Modify ➤ Arrange menu option:

Bring to Front	Ctrl+Shift+Up
Bring Forward	Ctrl+Up
Send Backward	Ctrl+Down
Send to Back	Ctrl+Shift+Down
Lock	Ctrl+Alt+L
Unlock All	Ctrl+Alt+Shift+L

13. Click your King card to select it, and use the Bring to Front option from the Modify ➤ Arrange menu. Your King will now jump to the top of the stack, so that the stacking order (from back to front) is changed to J, Q, A, K:

14. Click the Jack and use the Modify ➤ Arrange ➤ Bring Forward menu option.

   The Bring Forward option pulls the selected object up one level in the stacking order, so the Jack will immediately be brought forward one space, and jump in front of the Queen.

15. To test the Jack's position in relation to the other cards, pick it up and drag it between the King and the Queen:

You can see that the jack is in front of the Queen.

16. Drag the Jack between the King and the Ace:

You'll notice it is behind both of them. As expected, from bottom to top, the order is now Q, J, A, K.

17. Click the Ace and use the Modify ➤ Arrange ➤ Send Backward menu option. The Ace is moved backwards one level, jumping behind the Jack:

18. Drag the Ace up next to the Jack, between the Queen and the King.

   The Ace will now be in front of the Queen but behind the King:

The order is now Q, A, J, K.

19. Click the King and use the Modify ➤ Arrange ➤ Send to Back menu option. This will send the King all the way to the bottom of the stack:

The final order is K, Q, A, J.

20. Save the file as `cards.fla` and leave it open.

This exercise illustrates that you can manipulate the stacking order of symbols or groups to a very fine degree, which can be of real help when you're putting together complicated objects and pieces of content.

There will be times when you're building something on your stage and you'll find that one component disappears behind another one. If you have a grasp of stacking order, you'll understand why it disappeared and how to get it back.

However, there is another way to make the card shuffling a little easier.

Distribute to layers

For those of you who found arranging the royal part of the deck a little too much like hard work, there is Flash's **Distribute to Layers** option. Distribute to Layers is incredibly useful for putting order in chaotic situations.

Distribute to Layers takes all the selected objects—symbols, grouped objects, or primitives (simple graphics drawn on your stage that have not been converted to a symbol or grouped with other graphics)—and calculates associations between them before creating and placing them on as many different layers as required.

Distribute to Layers works differently for selected objects:

■ If the selected items are symbols, grouped objects, or text boxes, each individual element is placed on its own individual layer.

■ If the selected items are primitives, Flash will try to make associations at the geographic location of items. If two or more primitives are within touching vicinity, they will be treated as one object and placed together on the same layer.

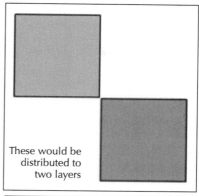

These would be distributed to two layers

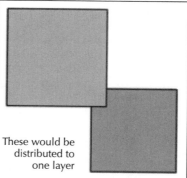

These would be distributed to one layer

The rule is: if the items are touching, they are hitched forever!

■ If the selected items are symbols, the layers they are distributed to are given the symbols' names. This makes Distribute to Layers very useful for cleaning up that Flash mess you've made.

Let's give it a try with your deck of cards.

Distributing your deck of cards to layers

1. Open up your `cards.fla` File (if necessary).

2. Select all the cards with the Selection tool and choose the Modify ➤ Timeline ➤ Distribute to Layers menu option.

   Each card is placed on its own layer, and each layer the same name as the symbol, which resides on that layer. There is also an extra layer that has no content; it's just a blank keyframe. This is the layer that all your symbols were taken from. Let's remove this superfluous layer before proceeding.

3. Select the blank layer in the timeline. Click the Delete Layer icon—the trash can—below the timeline.

   The unused layer is deleted, leaving you with just your card layers.

The order of your cards in the last exercise was K, Q, A, J. It's easy to change their order by dragging and moving the layers up and down in the timeline. Let's put them in their correct order with the Ace at the top where it belongs:

4. Click the Ace layer and drag it to the top of the layer list (above the King layer). This leaves the Ace as the top card—just where it wants to be.

   Your cards are now in the correct order—A, K, Q, J:

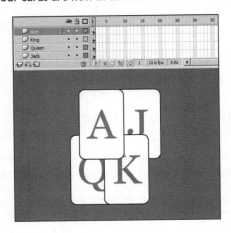

5. Save the movie as `cards2.fla` and leave it open.

Now that you've seen how Flash can save you a few headaches by organizing your content for you, let's see how it can ease the pain a little more by using **layer folders**.

Layer folders

As you've seen, layers are an excellent way of controlling your content. Flash has a way to organize your content even more efficiently—you can now use **layer folders** to bundle together similar layers. A layer folder works just like any folder on your hard drive; it enables you to maintain some kind of control over the chaos of your files.

Let's create a layer folder to place the King and Queen together in their honeymoon suite—away from the prying eyes of the Jack and the Ace—while maintaining the physical depths of all the cards.

1. Select the King layer and click the Insert Layer Folder button:

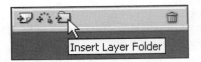

   Flash creates the layer folder above the King layer and names it Folder. Flash automatically suffixes each layer folder name with an incrementing digit as each folder is added. The next new layer folder you create will be named Folder 2. It is worth noting that Flash suffixes layers in the same way.

2. Double-click the layer folder name in the timeline, type in Honeymoon Suite, and press ENTER.

   So far, you have a new layer folder with no content in it. You can tell this because the arrow to the left of the layer folder icon is pointing down, meaning that it's open.

You can toggle the folder open and closed by clicking the arrow.

Let's give your royal couple some peace and put the King and Queen layers in the Honeymoon Suite folder.

3. Make sure the Honeymoon Suite folder is open and click the King layer. Then hold down the *SHIFT* key while selecting the Queen layer. Both layers should now be selected.

To select layers that are not sequential, hold down the CTRL key (COMMAND key on the Mac), and click the non-sequential layers.

4. Drag the layers up to the Honeymoon Suite folder. As you do this, a shaded gray bar appears with a small notch on it. Make sure this notch is indented—the folder icon is also highlighted—and release the mouse button:

If you placed the **King** and **Queen** layers in the **Honeymoon Suite** folder correctly, your list of layers will look like this:

The King and Queen layers are indented and are in the Honeymoon Suite layer. To further prove that they are in the folder, click the arrow to the left to close the folder—now they have some peace and quiet!

With the two layers inside the folder, any actions performed on the folder will also apply to its contents. This applies to locking/unlocking, showing/hiding, moving, or deleting the folder.

Flash gives you three ways of operating in the third (depth) dimension: **layers**, the **stacking order** within layers, and **layer folders**. With experience, you'll develop your own strategies for combining these options, but one rule of thumb is that if you're going to have lots of separate overlapping objects, it's usually best to have them on different layers and keep these controlled in layer folders. The stacking order is particularly useful when you're constructing individual objects and groups that'll always be kept together and that you want to assign to a layer using the Distribute to Layers command.

Believe it or not, it's time to introduce a fourth dimension. Here's a history lesson.

History panel

The History panel records all user actions in Flash. At its most basic level the History panel is a glorified undo list, storing and listing every action—whether it is drawing with the Pencil tool, making a selection with the Selection tool, or changing a primitive into a symbol. Using the History panel is beneficial because it provides you with better control over elements within the Flash environment. If you make an error while creating content, the History panel allows you to quickly backtrack through the actions and revert to a point before the mistake.

The History panel also has some advanced features, which we'll cover in Chapter 9.

The History panel is accessible by choosing the Window ➤ Other Panels ➤ History menu option or Ctrl-F10. When it's open, it looks like this:

If you've been working in a Flash document for any length of time, chances are your panel is a little fuller than this one. By default, Flash stores 100 actions, but this can be reduced or increased in Flash Preferences under the Edit ➤ Preferences ➤ Undo levels option. Undo levels tend to take a lot of system memory, so we wouldn't recommend this figure being much higher.

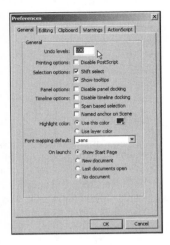

One of the important functions of the History panel is its ability to step back through your actions so you can review them. This is useful in the event you need to undo a significant amount of actions and your fingers become sore from holding down the *Ctrl/Cmd+Z* keys! With the History panel, you can quickly review any actions you've taken. Let's see how it works at in a short exercise.

Using the History panel

1. Open a new Flash document.

2. Open the History panel (if it isn't already open) with Window ➤ Other Panels ➤ History.

3. Select the Text tool and type Flash 4 on the stage.

4. In a new text field below the first one, type Flash MX.

5. Type Flash MX 2004 in a third text field below the previous two. This should leave you with three text fields and three versions of Flash:

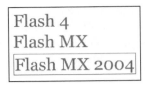

6. Look at the contents of the History panel.

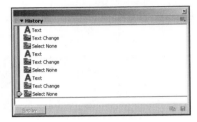

It's not telling you much is it? It shows you that you did something with three text fields, but doesn't really tell you what. Lucky for you, Macromedia included an option to show you specifics. Let's switch it on.

7. Click the History panel menu—located at the top-right of the panel—and select View ➤ Arguments in Panel.

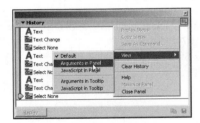

Now the History panel is a little more user-friendly and shows you detail like the position and size of the text boxes, as well as the actual text that you entered (shown as Text Change):

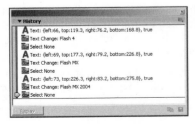

8. Now that you can see some detail, you can see how the History panel really works. Drag the gray arrow on the left up four notches slowly and watch the text on the stage disappear as you do it.

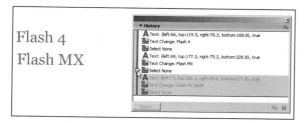

As you move the arrow up, Flash runs backward through the chronological order of actions or events and gives you a snapshot of the stage before the subsequent—now grayed—actions were taken. In the screenshot just shown, the arrow is positioned just before the third text field is added, so Flash shows you only the first two text fields.

9. Drag the arrow back down to the bottom, and the text field reappears. In essence, what you've just done is a number of undos and some redos, the equivalent of six key presses in all. The History panel makes the task significantly easier.

We have to let you in on a little secret we've been keeping from you. The chronological order of Flash releases is incorrect because there was a Flash 5 after Flash 4 but before Flash MX. Obviously, there are a number of ways to rectify this, but you're going to do it using the History panel.

10. Drag the arrow indicator in the panel up to the third action or until only the Flash 4 text is visible.

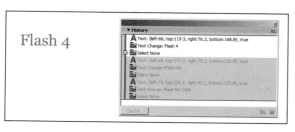

11. Select the Text tool and type Flash 5 below the Flash 4 text. If you look at the History panel now you'll see that something very strange has happened—history has been changed!

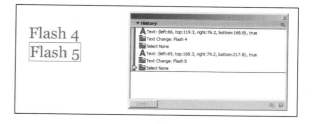

The History panel in Flash works in the same way as time travel: when history is changed, it has a drastic effect. If the Terminator could have removed John Connor in the past, there would be no resistance to the evil machines in the future.

By going back through the History actions and adding new text, everything that originally followed is removed. A word of note—after you've done this, there is no way of retrieving any of the lost steps or their content. At this point, not even the Undo command can help you.

This means that you have to add the remaining releases of Flash again.

12. Use the text tool to add two new text fields containing Flash MX and Flash MX 2004.

13. Select Clear History from the History panel options.

This, unsurprisingly, removes all the actions from the History panel and leaves you with no history and nothing to undo. Drastic? Yes, but Flash requires a confirmation before it completes the deletion:

The History panel is a welcome addition to Flash because of the time saved by using it. To get the most out of it, we recommend that you use it as we have configured it because this allows you have an overview of your actions without having to laboriously examine every step.

Even though we've only scratched the surface of the History panel here, in **Chapter 9** you'll see how it can be used to help automate content creation and modification, making repetitive tasks a cinch for all users. For now though, let's return to your case study.

Case study

You now begin to organize your content into a more manageable form, based on what you've learned so far in this chapter.

In its current condition, none of the case study elements are neatly arranged or lined up. Let's tidy them up, starting with the big white rectangle.

1. Open the case study movie.

2. Open the Align panel with Window ➤ Design Panels ➤ Align and switch on the To Stage modifier:

3. Select the white rectangle with the Selection tool and click the **Align horizontal center** and **Align vertical center** buttons in the Align panel. You're doing this so you place the white rectangle in the dead center of the stage.

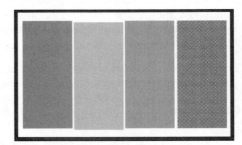

The white rectangle is now centered. Now on to the colored rectangles.

4. Position the two outer rectangles roughly near the edges of the white rectangle:

5. Select all the colored squares and click the **Align vertical center** button in the Align panel. This will position them all at the same vertical position, as well as vertically center them in relation to the stage.

6. With the rectangles still selected, unselect the **To Stage** modifier in the Align panel, and click the **Space evenly horizontally** button.

This will even out the space in-between the rectangles. Your rectangles are now in line with each other.

7. Copy the rectangles using Edit ➤ Copy and insert a new layer above the colored rectangles one and call it content. Lock the colored rectangles layer because you won't need to edit it again.

8. Select the content layer and choose Edit ➤ Paste in Place or press SHIFT + CTRL + V.

9. Select the newly pasted rectangles and choose Modify ➤ Convert to Symbol or press F8. Give the new symbol the name Content, select a Movie Clip behavior and ensure that it has a central registration point:

The reason you have two copies of the rectangles will become apparent in a later chapter. Before you move on to the buttons, let's finish the white rectangle.

10. Use the Selection tool to select the white rectangle and its stroke, and choose Modify ➤ Convert to Symbol or press F8. Make it a graphic symbol with a central registration point and name it white rectangle.

Aligning the buttons and logo

11. Use the Selection tool to move the buttons out of the way, off stage and to the right. This will make it easier to position them with the Snap Align feature:

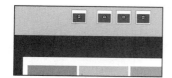

12. Make sure that Snap Align and Snap to Objects are selected on the View ➤ Snapping menu. These will allow your buttons to snap to the edges of the white rectangle.

13. Select the left button and drag it down to the top corner of the white rectangle. Drag it until two

Snap Align lines appear, one along the left edge and one underneath the button.

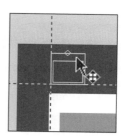

You will notice that there is a gap between the button and the white rectangle. This is because Flash will snap align objects to a 10 pixels away from objects as well as in direct vicinity to them.

14. After you have both Snap Align lines visible, release the button.

15. Drag the next button down and position it to the right of the first button. After you have the two Snap Align lines, release the button.

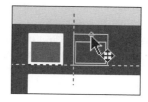

As you might have guessed, you've positioned this button at a 10 pixels offset from the last one.

16. Repeat this process for the last two buttons. When you're done, the buttons should be positioned in excellent regimented fashion.

17. Select the logo and text on their layer and drag it slightly away from its original position.

18. Drag it back to its original position at the bottom right of the white rectangle. As with the buttons, after you have two Snap Align lines, release the button:

Now that your current assets are all neat and tidy, it's time to add some more.

Adding text to the buttons

19. Select the buttons layer and add a new layer called buttons text. This will position the buttons text layer above the previously selected one.

20. Select the Text tool, and click the buttons text layer. Set the font and so on as seen here:

21. Use the Text tool to type the words Web, Print, About and Email anywhere on the stage. They will be repositioned in a moment.

22. Select the Web text field and drag it to the top of the left button. Because Snap to Objects is selected, the text field will snap to the center top of the button.

23. Repeat the same action for each of the text fields, so that the buttons read Web, Print, About and Email from left to right.

24. Select all the text fields and use the down arrow key to move the fields down pixel by pixel. Four little jogs should be about enough.

When the Selection tool is selected, pressing the arrow keys shifts selected objects 1 pixel in any given direction. To move objects larger distances, hold down the SHIFT key to move in 5 pixel increments.

Managing your layers

The last thing to do in this chapter is to organize your layers into layer folders. You'll do this logically by asset type.

25. Select the buttons text layer and insert a layer folder. Give this layer folder named button assets.

26. Drag the buttons text and buttons layers into the button assets folder, ensuring that you keep the buttons text layer at the top:

27. Create a new layer folder called background assets, and drag the layers logo + text, colored rectangles and white rectangle into it. Remember to hold down the CTRL key to make multiple non-sequential selections.

28. Place the background assets folder at the bottom of the layer stack. Your layers now look like this:

Not only is this nice and tidy, but it will also make future modifications, by you or other flashers, a whole lot easier.

29. Save and close your case study file.

Summary

In this chapter, we've introduced you to the integral Flash facilities that help you arrange, align, and nest objects. These features are intimately linked with the ability to arrange content in space on the Flash stage in the three dimensions of width, height, and depth.

You saw that:

- **You can group objects** together to maintain their relative proportions and still have access to them for editing.

- **You can nest groups within groups** and **symbols within groups** and so on, giving you the ability to create hierarchies of precisely arranged, related, objects.

- You can use Flash's **grids**, **rulers**, and **guides** to draw with a steady hand and sure eye.

- You can precisely place and transform objects by using Flash's **Align** panel and the **Transform** menu/panel.

- You can manipulate symbols and grouped objects, which have an implicit **stacking order**.

- You can better manage and arrange your content as well as nest your layers by using **Layer folders**.

You were also introduced to the all-seeing **History panel**, which:

- Stores a set number of user actions within the Flash authoring environment.

- Allows you to easily review your previous actions and change one or more if necessary.

In the next chapter, you're going to drill down inside of some objects and see how to use color to enrich content and effects.

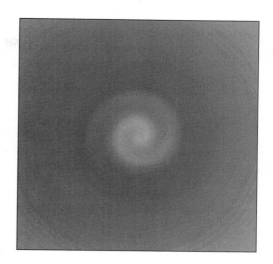

Chapter 5

WORKING WITH COLOR AND IMAGES

What we'll cover in this chapter:

- How Flash **renders color**
- How to create and save custom colors
- How **gradients** work, and how to use them effectively as **fills** on drawn objects
- How to **manipulate** object fills
- How to import and **use bitmaps** and other file formats

In this chapter, you'll see how Macromedia Flash MX 2004 allows you to customize the objects you create by fine-tuning their colors and fill styles. You'll see how Flash handles color, and how you can ensure that the color features are optimized. Additionally, you'll take a quick look at how to import bitmaps and manipulate them in Flash. This is a long chapter with a lot of examples, but stick with it. By the end, you'll handle the color features with confidence and understanding.

Colors, fills, and gradients are the extra paprika on the already tongue-tingling dish that is Flash. If you've used any of the many graphics programs that are available today, you'll be instantly at home with Flash's color-creation methods. If, on the other hand, you're new to the world of swatches and radial gradients, don't worry. By the end of this chapter you'll be whistling *R-G-B, as easy as 1-2-3* while using the Alpha slider to open new windows into your movies.

It's never going to be entirely satisfactory to discuss colors in a book printed in black and white, but with a little bit of imagination and by working through the exercises with Flash open in front of you, you'll get through without any problems.

Let's begin by talking about computerized color in general terms.

Color primer

Color on a computer monitor, like on a TV, is rendered using a mixture of three discrete components of colored **light**:—red, green, and blue—hence **RGB**. When you're working with paint on a white canvas, you know that you need to add colored paint to make the picture. And you've probably also discovered that if you add red, blue, and green paint together in the right quantities and mix them up, you end up with a murky black.

When you're dealing with colored light rather than colored paint, however, the opposite is true. With light, if there's no color present, everything is black, and if you add all the colors together at the right strength, you get white light:

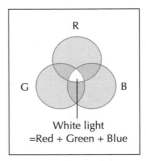

The three color elements can be combined in an infinite variety of mixtures and strengths: blue light on its own will give you a blue screen, but if you add a little green to that blue, you'll see the color change.

Each unique color that a computer monitor displays is composed of different proportions of red, green, and blue. These unique colors can be described numerically by values that specify the amount of R, G, and B that you want to display. These values determine the color on the screen. On a computer, these numbers are expressed in base 16, otherwise known as **hexadecimal** or **hex** for short.

In base 10, which you use every day for counting, your numbers fall into familiar columns: one column is the number of single units (1s), the next column is the number of tens of units, the next column is the number of hundreds of units, and so on:

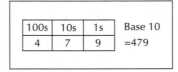

In hex, a different model applies. The right column still expresses the number of 1s, but the next colmn expresses the number of *16*s there are in the number:

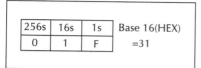

256s	16s	1s	Base 16(HEX)
0	1	F	=31

Because the second column from the right starts at 16, the units in the columns go up to 15 but they are still expressed as a single digit. This is achieved by using letters rather than numbers. In the 1s column, you count from **0** to **9** just like in normal base 10, but the numbers from **10** through **15** are expressed with the letters **A** through **F**. So **A** in hex is equal to **10**, **B** is **11**, continuing all the way up to **F**, which is **15**. After that, the 1s column goes back to 0, and the 16s column increments to 1. Thus, the figure 10 in hex means "1 in the 16s column and zero in the 1s column."

Back to your colors. Each unique color is the result of combining the three base colors, and each unique color has a six-digit identifier. In this six-digit number, there are two digits for each of the base colors. The first two digits describe the amount of red present, the next two describe the green, and the last two describe the blue. This means that black—the absence of any color of light—is expressed as 000000. That's 00 (hex) of red, 00 of green, and 00 of blue:

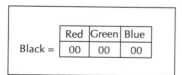

	Red	Green	Blue
Black =	00	00	00

The opposite of this is white, which is a mix of all the colors at full strength, so pure white in hex is FFFFFF.

The largest number that can be expressed in two digits in hex is **FF**, which means (15 x 16) + (15 x 1), making a total of 255. So a color whose number was **FF0000** would be 255 parts of red, zero parts of green, and zero parts of blue—which means that only red would be displayed on the screen. Play around with the hex values of each base color component in a six-digit identifier to create different colors. The different combinations possible with this hex numbering system give you access to a range of over 16 million colors. Enough, I'm sure you'll agree, for most people to find one that they like—even if you can't find a shirt that matches it.

Right now, you're probably thinking, "This chapter is supposed to be about color, but all I've had so far is a math lesson!" Hopefully though, this brief explanation will help you to understand how Flash sees color, and from there, how you can best get the effect you want.

Let's take this knowledge and see how it's implemented in Flash. A good place to start is with custom colors. That's where you create your own mixtures of the base colors that you can use and save.

Custom colors

Bored with seeing the same colors everywhere you look? Want to make your whites whiter than white? Then you need…the **Color Mixer** panel:

This is where you can get Flash MX 2004 to mix exactly the color you're looking for. The Color Mixer panel is partnered with the **Color Swatches** panel, which is used for choosing default palette or custom-made colors:

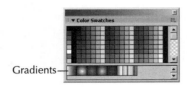

Gradients

On the Color Mixer panel, you can enter the precise RGB values that you want your strokes and fills to have, and then apply these colors to the objects in your movies. The Color Swatches panel shows you all the colors you have available. (A *swatch* is the name given to a single color, and a group of swatches together is called a *palette*.)

The colors shown in the top part of the Color Swatches panel make up the 216 **web-safe colors**, and this is the default palette used by Flash. These web-safe colors are guaranteed to work on any computer using any browser running anywhere in the world, so if you always want your work to render perfectly on any old or superseded browser exactly as you designed it, these are the colors to use.

If you're not sure about using a particular custom color you've created, the best thing to do is to test your movies and web pages in as many different browsers as you think is necessary. Ultimately, there's a trade-off between how certain you want to be that your page looks tip-top *everywhere* and the time and effort it takes to test everything. For most people, testing their movies and sites on up-to-date versions of Internet Explorer and Netscape (or Mozilla) is the norm.

Here's an exercise to take you through the process of creating your own custom colors.

Creating custom colors with the Color Mixer panel

1. Open the Color Mixer panel and the Color Swatches panel from the Design Panels section of the Window menu.

In the Color Mixer Panel, you'll see the familiar Stroke and Fill Color boxes in the same layout as you find in the Property inspector and Tools panel:

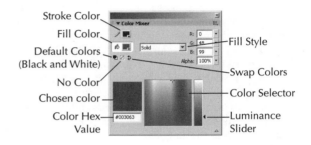

Stroke Color
Fill Color
Default Colors (Black and White)
No Color
Chosen color
Color Hex Value
Fill Style
Swap Colors
Color Selector
Luminance Slider

On the right side, there are four input boxes: three where you can change the RGB value combinations for the current color (using a value of 1–255 for each base color), and one where you can set the **Alpha** value. *Alpha* is essentially another word for **transparency**: 100 percent Alpha is solid opaque color, 0 percent is fully transparent, and anything between will give an intermediate degree of transparency. Alpha is commonly used to make objects fade in and out of movies and to create windows in objects so that you can see through them. How to use alpha in your movies will be more fully explored in the next chapter, when you look at animation in more detail.

The final tools on the Color Mixer panel are the **Color Selector** and **Luminance Slider** bars at the bottom. The Color Selector is a quick, visual way to choose a color. Click anywhere on the bar, and that color will automatically be selected. The Luminance Slider bar lets you fine-tune that selection. Drag the arrow up and down until you get the shade that you want.

2. Click the square next to the bucket icon in the Fill Color selection box. The current color palette appears:

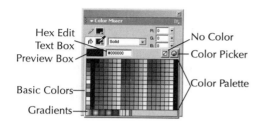

Hex Edit
Text Box
Preview Box
No Color
Color Picker
Basic Colors
Color Palette
Gradients

On the top row of the color selection box (above all the available colors, and to the right of the preview box showing the currently selected color) there's a box showing the hex value of that color:

It can be extremely useful to know the hex value. With that information, you can match the color of your Flash movie to that of the host web page and vice-versa because web page colors are also defined in hex.

3. Click the Color Picker button—it's at the top right of the color palette and has a rainbow-hued circle on it. The **Color** dialog box opens so you can create a custom color:

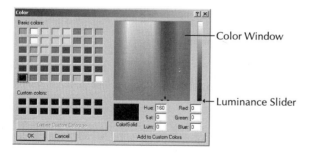

Color Window
Luminance Slider

This is where all your alchemical color mixing takes place. On the left side of the dialog box is a set of basic, solid colors that you can use as starting points. Your attention though, is no doubt already drawn to that lush, color-drenched pane on the right, which looks like a piece of blotting paper used to mop up a rainbow. This pane contains all the colors that you can use in your movies.

The Mac's color picker, shown in the following graphic, is very different from the PC version, but it works almost exactly the same way.

In the **Color Wheel** mode, a color picker takes the place of the color-drenched pane in the Windows dialog box. If you want to adjust the RGB values of your color, simply click the **Color Sliders** icon from the options at the top and select **RGB Sliders** from the drop-down menu.

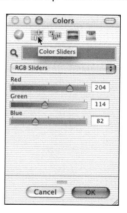

121

The color picking options available to the Mac user are more sophisticated than those on the PC, and they are beyond the scope of this chapter. What the Mac doesn't have, however, is the ability to create multiple custom colors in one visit to the picker—you'll have to mix your new colors one at a time.

4. Click the color pane and drag the mouse pointer around. Everything seems to change at once; the colors in the luminance slider shift like a tie-dyed chameleon and the RGB values rush frantically to keep up with your mouse pointer.

5. Release your mouse button and let the chameleon take a rest.

It's time to explain some more about those numbers. To the left of the RGB values are three boxes indicating the **Hue**, **Saturation**, and **Luminance** (HSL) of the current color:

These three terms are another way to describe color. The *hue* is the actual color, and it's a relative of the RGB settings but with a smaller range.

6. If you drag your mouse pointer carefully in a horizontal line across the color window, only the hue setting changes.

7. If you move the mouse vertically up and down the window, only the saturation setting changes.

> *On the Mac, hue is determined by the angle you select on the color wheel, whereas saturation changes as you move nearer or farther away from the hub of the wheel. If you move your mouse pointer along the radius of the color wheel toward the center, the saturation will decrease from 100% at the rim to 0% at the hub, but the hue setting will stay the same.*

The saturation determines the *amount* of the color. Imagine you've got a bucket of white paint, and you've chosen the pigment (hue) you're going to add to the paint. The amount of saturation is determined by how much you put in—if you put a little in, you'll have a very pale color. If you put all of it in, you'll have a very deep rich color even though you're still using the same pigment.

The final value is the luminance (sometimes called brightness—hence HSB and often called lightness on the Mac). This is the amount of light in the color. So far, you've chosen your original pigment (hue), and you've mixed it into your white base to get the depth of color (saturation). Now you paint it onto a big sheet of glass. You place a light behind the glass—this light determines the *luminance*. If you use a small, dim light, the color will be a dark, gloomy shade, but if you position a huge arc light behind the glass, the color will become so painfully bright that there will be only a negligible difference between it and white. The luminance value is controlled with the slider bar on the right side of the Color dialog box:

It's worth mentioning that in Flash you can use the HSB color model as your default color value display instead of RGB. If you go to the Color Mixer panel and click the white icon on the right side of its title bar, a menu appears giving you the option to switch to HSB. For this chapter, stick with RGB.

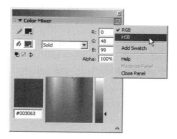

8. Choose a color from the vast spectrum available in the Color pane.

9. Look in the color preview box to ensure that you have the color you want. You may think this is obvious, but it's very easy to choose a color from the color pane and leave the luminance set to 0, which will make everything come out black!

10. Click the Add to Custom Colors button at the bottom of the dialog box:

11. On the Mac, after you chose the color you want in the selected color box, click OK to return to the Color Mixer.

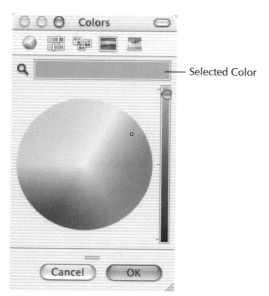

Selected Color

Mac users can go on to the next section—the next load of stuff is for PC users only.

Your color now appears as a swatch in one of the Custom colors boxes on the far left. These boxes serve as a temporary storage area for your swatches. Next time you want to use your swatch, you can come back to this dialog box and it'll be there waiting for you.

> *Beware though, the next time you open the Color dialog box. If you select a color from the spectrum and add it to your custom colors, Flash will automatically overwrite the color in the top left of your Custom color boxes:*

By default, Flash will always save your color into this first box, even if it's currently filled with another color. The only way to specify which box your new color goes into is to click the specific custom color box you want to use, select your color from the spectrum, and then add the color to the box.

12. Click OK to close the Color dialog box.

Notice that your custom color is currently selected in the Fill Color box of the Color Mixer panel. If you were now to use the Oval tool to draw a circle, it would be filled with your beautiful custom color. (Go on; try it…you know you want to…)

> *It's important to remember one thing when creating custom colors: Flash does not automatically save them permanently for you. If you close Flash and reopen it again, all your carefully constructed colors will be gone from the Custom color boxes.*

So the question arises—just how the heck do you make your custom colors *persist*?

Persistent custom colors

Saving custom colors in Flash is, unfortunately, quite a long-winded process. After you've created your color and defined it as a swatch in a Custom color box, you must then add it to the main color palette, and finally save this as a color set. Let's see exactly how.

Saving custom colors permanently

1. Make sure the Color Mixer panel is open. Also make sure that the swatch you want to add is displayed as the currently selected fill or stroke color. This means you need to ensure your chosen Custom color box is selected when you close the Color dialog box after choosing your color from the spectrum.

2. Click the menu in the top right of the Color Mixer panel, and have another look at the resulting drop-down menu:

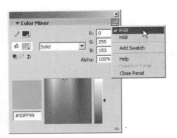

As you already know, the menu contains two options for displaying color values—RGB and HSB, and an option for adding a swatch to a palette.

3. Click the Add Swatch option.

When you open up your color palette on the Color Mixer panel or in the Tools panel, you'll see your new swatch in a fresh row at the bottom of the palette:

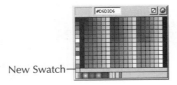

New Swatch

You can now easily select your new color from this palette.

After you've added all your new swatches to the bottom of the palette, you still need to save it so it'll be available to you in the future.

4. In the Color Swatches panel, click the small icon in the top-right corner to access the drop-down menu options:

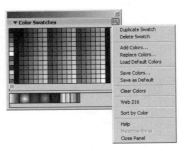

This menu contains all the commands for dealing with swatches and palettes. For the moment, let's just focus on a couple of these options: Save Colors and Add Colors.

5. Click the Save Colors option, which will open up the **Export Color Swatch** dialog box. This dialog box will allow you to save your current colors in a permanent file—a **color set**—that Flash can access in the future:

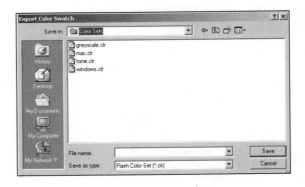

Flash's default location for these files is in the **Color Sets** folder, deep within your user settings folder. The *exact* location of this folder on your machine is typically C:/Documents and Settings/ <Username>/Local Settings/Application Data/ Macromedia/Flash MX 2004/en/Configuration/

Color Sets on a PC, and in your <Hard Drive>/ Users/<Username>/Library/Application Support/ Macromedia/Flash MX 2004/Configuration/Color Sets folder on a Mac.

6. Navigate to the location where you'd like to keep your swatches, give your color set a name, and then click Save. Your swatches are now saved in a Flash color set (CLR) file.

The files that are already in this folder are the ready-made palettes that come with Flash, each one designed to cater to a specific set of requirements. Note that Flash's default behavior is to open the standard color set whenever it restarts. If you want to access your custom color set again, open the drop-down menu from the Color Swatches panel and click the Add Colors button. This will open the **Import Color Swatch** dialog box, where you can select the specific color set you want to use to enrich your palette. Then you can use the slider button on the right edge of the Color Swatches panel to scroll through the newly available colors:

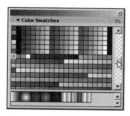

There are many ways of creating and describing color, and a detailed analysis of them is beyond the scope of this book. If you're interested in learning more, there are plenty of resources just waiting to be discovered, ranging from the Internet to your local library. The best thing you can do is experiment and see how the different values affect the final color. It's up to you to decide which method you prefer, but remember that your color will be rendered in Flash and on the web as an **RGB** value.

Your next step is to look at color and **gradients**.

Gradient color

Custom colors is great, but no matter how much work you put in picking and choosing your color values, you still end up with a single flat color. This is where **gradients** come in. Gradients are distinct color features you can apply to your objects' fills.

A gradient consists of a smooth change from one color to another. In Flash, gradients can be simple and pure, with a starting color and an end color, or they can be more complex, with up to eight different colors. In complex gradients, intermediate colors create distinct "steps" in the gradient, giving the effect of a richer and more complicated spectrum:

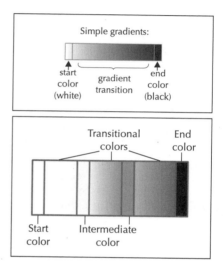

These different types of gradients allow for some pretty spectacular effects, especially when you tween transitions from gradient to gradient. For now though, you'll start with the basics.

This next screenshot shows a simple gradient, which runs from white to black:

This is an example of a **linear gradient**, so named because the gradient runs in a straight line from the first color (white, on the left) to the second color (black, on the right). With linear gradients, you define the start and end colors (and any intermediate ones, if you want a more complex effect), and Flash works out the intermediate colors between them. Flash has a number of predefined linear gradients in its palette, but you can also mix your own, as you'll see shortly.

The other type of gradient is a **radial gradient**:

Radial gradients have their starting color at the center and their ending color at the outside. The gradient radiates out from the center to the edge. Flash has some standard radial gradients but once again, you have infinite customization options at your fingertips.

The choice of which gradient to use for a given task is entirely up to your personal taste. There's no right or wrong gradient type; just use the one you think looks the best for what you're trying to do.

Gradients are really just smooth transitions of color between two (or more) distinct colors. If you've ever tried to create a gradient on paper with colored pencils or paint, you'll know how difficult it can be to get the effect right. Thankfully, Flash gives you a little studio and palette where you can create, preview, and amend gradients to your heart's content.

Making the Gradient

To work with gradients, you need to use the Color Mixer panel.

Creating and modifying gradients

1. If the Color Mixer panel isn't open, open it from the Window ➤ Design Panels menu. You probably already noticed the boxes at the bottom of the Color Swatches panel that don't look like the other solid colors:

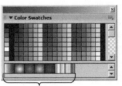

Gradients

These are Flash's predefined gradients. There are five basic (two-color) gradients and two more complicated ones.

2. Open the Color Swatches panel to open the palette. From there, click the black and white linear gradient at the bottom on the left.

Notice that as you select the gradient, the Color Mixer panel automatically changes to reflect this choice:

You've chosen the gradient style that you want to use—a simple, linear, black and white one. You can now either use this as the fill on a new or existing object or you can customize it as you're going to do here.

Let's ensure that you don't overwrite the default linear gradient.

3. Select Add Swatch from the Color Mixer panel's drop-down menu. This will add a new gradient at the right end of the list:

New Gradient

You now have your very own gradient to tinker with.

4. Click the new gradient's box at the bottom of the Color Swatches panel to ensure that this is the one you're working on. The currently selected gradient box will have a white outline around it:

Because you selected a linear gradient, you can see the gradient controls in the Color Mixer panel.

Fill Style

Gradient Range

Gradient Preview

The most important of these is the long bar across the middle. The bar has a white paint bucket hanging from the left side and a black paint bucket

hanging from the right. This bar shows the **range** of your gradient—that is, its start and end points.

5. Click the white paint bucket and drag it to the middle of the bar:

The gradient in the preview window on the bottom left will now be half bleached-out with only a smudge of black creeping in on the right side:

Your selections tell Flash to start the gradient at the white paint bucket and use the black paint bucket as the end point. Notice also that the gradient box in the Color Swatches panel has also changed to reflect your alteration.

6. Click the black paint bucket and drag it all the way to the left side where the white paint bucket used to be:

Your gradient is reversed: it now consists of a small black stripe on the left with a large white mass to its right.

Now you can start adding to the basic gradient and make it a little more interesting. To do this, you have to add some intermediate color stages to the range bar.

7. Place your mouse pointer below the gradient range bar, just to the right of your current white paint bucket. When a plus sign appears next to your mouse pointer indicating that you will add to the current selection, click to place another paint bucket:

Because you clicked underneath a white part of the gradient, the new paint bucket will inherit that color. If you'd clicked in a black area, you'd have got a black paint bucket.

8. Click the same way under the gray gradient between the black and the white buckets:

Again, your new paint bucket will be filled with the same gray as the color immediately above it in the gradient range bar. Notice that the currently selected paint bucket has a black pointer at the top and that the body of each paint bucket indicates what color that bucket represents. Furthermore, the color box to the right of the gradient bar shows you what color is in the current paint bucket.

You can now change the color content of your paint buckets and customize the gradient further.

9. Click the color box above the gradient range bar in the Color Mixer panel to open up the color palette.

10. From here pick a color—say, a pure blue. As soon as you click the color, the current paint bucket will be filled with that color and the gradient bar will change to reflect its new Technicolor glory.

Warning: When you're mixing a gradient, it's tempting to use the Color Swatches panel to pick the color. Don't do it. If you do, Flash will think you want to use a solid color instead of a gradient and it'll take you out of the gradient selection in the Color Mixer. If you do this by mistake, just click the Fill Style *drop-down box and reselect the gradient type you you're editing. Your gradient colors should still be there, exactly as you left them.*

11. Click the paint bucket on the far right and, using the color box at the top right again, change its color to red.

12. Your gradient should now flow from black on the left to blue, with a very thin white bar in the middle that rapidly fades into red on the right:

Now that you've created your gradient, how do you use it? Easy. It's now your selected fill for any objects you draw, and if you click the Paint Bucket tool you can use it to fill existing objects.

13. Draw a square with the Rectangle Tool, and you should see something much like this, but in glowing color:

Radial gradients are created the same way.

14. Go back to the Color Mixer panel and select Radial from the Fill style drop-down menu:

Note that Flash retained the colors you defined on the gradient range bar, but now they're mapped to a radial gradient with what was the left color (black) in the center of the gradient and the right color (red) on the outside.

15. Draw another square next to the first one:

From this, you can clearly see the relationship between linear and radial gradients. They're both based on a spread of colors you define on the range bar, and the way this range is displayed depends on the left-to-right sequence of those colors. You can alter the way the gradients appear by shifting the relative positions of the paint buckets on the range bar.

16. To save your gradient permanently, use the same technique you used in the previous exercise. Open the menu by clicking the top-right icon on the Color Mixer panel, add the new swatch, and save (or overwrite) your customized color set using the menu option from the Color Swatches panel. **Make sure you don't overwrite any of Flash's default color sets.**

17. If your gradients get messed up (as sometimes happens while you're experimenting), you can always revert to your saved color set (using the Add Color option from the Color Swatches panel menu), or reload Flash's default colors:

Now that you have an initial understanding of gradients, let's have a look at how they can be used to create light effects in your movies.

Using light and shade with gradients

By combining simple gradients with drawn shapes, it's easy to create convincing light effects that simulate shadow, shade, and light sources. In reality of course, you won't build true 3D light-sourced objects (you need other packages to create those), but you *can* fabricate an adequate enough illusion to fool the eye. These effects can add real interest and depth to your movies.

Let's explore this by constructing a shaded sphere.

Using gradients to create a shaded sphere

1. Open a new Flash document.
2. Select the Oval tool, and then select the green radial gradient from the bottom of the Color Swatches panel:

Green Radial Gradient

Because you want the sphere to look like a realistic three-dimensional object, you need to remove the stroke line from around the edge.

3. Click the Stroke button in the Tools panel, and then click the No Color button, either at the top of the palette or in the Tools panel:

Now you're ready to draw your circle.

4. Use the Oval tool with the *SHIFT* key held down to keep it perfectly symmetrical. You should now have a black sphere with a green center:

To bring the sphere to life you need to adjust the position of the green center light on your sphere.

5. Reposition the center of the fill—the point from which the gradient radiates—using your Paint Bucket tool. Imagine that the tip of the bucket is your light source, and click the top left side of your circle to re-adjust this source. You'll end up with a sphere like this:

And that's it, your very own 3D sphere just waiting to be moved around on the stage and morphed into something else. With this basic technique, it's easy to make more complicated shapes with multiple gradients. Maybe a festive egg...

...or a metal cube made from two skewed rectangles:

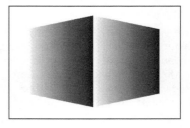

This method can also be used to improve your emerald.fla from the last chapter. Removing the strokes also improves the 3D effect.

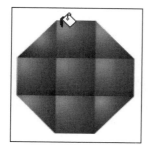

Just in case you aren't sure of the improvement, here's a good old before and after.

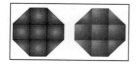

You've seen how to make a basic shape look three-dimensional with a standard gradient. Flash also has features that let you finesse the gradient effects you apply to your objects.

Applying gradients to objects and modifying them

It's all well and good being able to make a perfect linear gradient for your shape, but what if your shape itself isn't perfectly linear? For example, a linear gradient looks fine on a square, but on a skewed parallelogram, the standard gradient doesn't really enhance the impression of a real object with the light falling on it:

Luckily, Flash provides ways of changing your gradient to suit your shape.

The simplest and least painstaking way of applying the gradient in a non-standard way is achieved with the Paint Bucket tool.

If you draw a filled rectangle on the stage after selecting a linear gradient for the fill, you get a dandy-looking gradient:

The only problem is that all your rectangles drawn with the basic gradient as a fill will look the same. However, you can change this. If you select the Paint Bucket tool with the standard linear gradient as the fill, and then drag the mouse pointer to apply the fill to the shape, you can simulate light coming from a different direction:

The angle of your drag will make the gradient flow from a different starting point. This method is one of trial and error—experiment and see the effects you can get with different types of gradient.

You won't be surprised that Flash also has more precise methods of manipulating gradients with the **Fill Transform** tool from the Tools panel:

This tool is your key to modifying gradients professionally. In the next exercise, you'll find out how to fit a gradient to a skewed parallelogram and see the methods you can use to alter gradients in a controlled manner after they're on the stage.

Scaling and rotating linear gradients

First, create your parallelogram.

1. Use the Rectangle tool to draw a square with a black border and no fill. Skew your square using the Free Transform tool from the Tools panel:

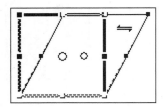

2. Fill the shape with a linear gradient. We've used a custom gradient consisting of two black paint buckets at each end of the gradient range bar, and a white one in the middle:

The effect you're trying to achieve with this shape is to make it look like a length of metal pipe. Right now, it looks more like a sheet of metal than a tube. Let's see if you can model it better.

3. Select the Fill Transform tool from the Tools panel.

Your mouse pointer changes to an arrow with a gradient-filled rectangle next to it. This indicates that you're in **Transform Fill** mode:

4. Click the gradient that's filling your skewed shape and two blue lines appear around your shape. A circle appears in the center, and a square and a circle appear on the right side:

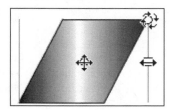

These are the handles used to move and transform your gradient; you can think of them as the **Scale** and **Rotate** commands rolled into one. When you position your mouse pointer over the Center point, your mouse pointer changes to a four-headed arrow. Your pointer becomes a two-headed arrow when positioned over the Resize handle, and it becomes curved arrows around a circle when positioned over the Rotate handle:

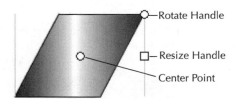

Each of these handles controls a different aspect of the gradient that's filling the parallelogram.

5. Click the Center point and drag it to the left side. When you release the mouse button, the gradient is centered around the new point. Notice also that the lines at either side of your shape have moved as well. These bounding lines act as a quick guide to the position, size, and angle of your gradient:

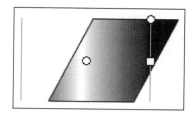

6. Drag the Rotate handle down until the gradient is on a similar slant to the sides of your skewed square:

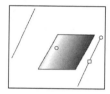

7. The gradient looks a little too big now, and to your eye it seems to be bleaching the shape a bit. You can get around this by squeezing the gradient to fit into the shape better.

8. Click the Resize handle and move it in until you achieve your desired effect—a strip of metal pipe in low light:

And there you have it, a gradient that you've fit perfectly into your skewed parallelogram.

From here, the sky is the limit and it's surely only a matter of time before you start building all manner of objects, such as a metallic ice-cream cone, or maybe a cone of metallic fries:

Radial gradients are also amenable to your creative sleight of hand.

Modifying a radial gradient

When dealing with a radial gradient, you have four parameters to transform the fill rather than the linear gradient's three. The majority of them are the same, but their implementation can appear very different on a radial gradient.

1. Open a new Flash document and draw a circle with any fill color and no stroke.

2. Select the first radial gradient in the list and fill the circle in the top corner using the Paint Bucket tool.

3. Duplicate the circle (Edit ➤ Duplicate) and move the copy away from the original.

4. Select the copy and use the **Transform** panel (Window ➤ Design Panels ➤ Transform) to change its size to 70% of the original. Before typing 70% into either of the top two text fields, make sure that the Constrain option is selected. This will force the transformation to stick to its true circle ratio and prevent distortion:

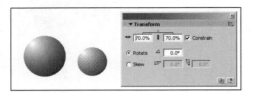

5. Select the Fill Transform tool and click the copy of the (now smaller) circle:

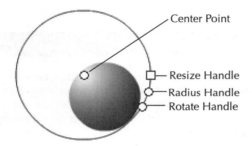

Center Point

Resize Handle
Radius Handle
Rotate Handle

The circle around the radial gradient is the equivalent of the two bounding lines that were on either side of the linear gradient. This marks the shape and the limits of your gradient.

6. Click the Center point and drag it around to experiment. You will notice that the epicenter of the gradient shifts according to the location of this point. (Note that the epicenter was previously located in the top left because of the fill orientation on the original circle.)

7. Drag the center point to the bottom-right corner. So far you have two spheres that aren't talking to each other:

8. Use the Arrow tool to select both circles (or use *Ctrl+A* to select all—assuming you have nothing else on the stage).

9. Open the Align panel (Window ➤ Design Panels ➤ Align).

10. Make sure the To Stage modifier is switched off, and then center the circles over each other—with the smaller one on top—using the Align panel:

Can you guess what it is yet? Yes…it's a 3D button. Let's add a little highlighting to the top left of the inner circle.

11. Add a new layer called highlight and draw a very small oval shape on it. This oval will suggest the highlighting.

12. Rotate the oval to negative 50 degrees using either the Free Transform tool or the Transform panel.

13. Make sure that Snap Align is switched on for the next step (View ➤ Snapping ➤ Snap Align).

14. Drag the oval to the top left of the inner circle and position it when two Snap Align lines appear. Then release the mouse button.

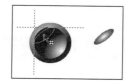

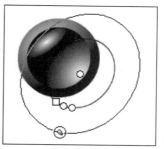

The way the snapping occurs depends on how you've got your snapping preferences set. You can play around with these via the View ➤ Snapping ➤ Edit Snap Align menu option.

At this point you should have a neat roller ball style button with depth created by using gradients. If you are happy with this, save the movie before you proceed.

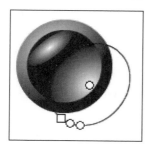

Before you move on to the next section, let's experiment with the remaining radial gradient modifiers.

15. With the Fill Transform tool selected, click the inner circle. The modifier points appear.

16. Click the Resize handle (the circle next to the square) and drag it around.

The size of the gradient is increased or decreased uniformly. After you release the mouse button, the new gradient size will be rendered:

Now it's time for the Rotate handle. Let's illustrate this with a different object.

17. On a new layer, draw a square with no outline and choose a radial gradient fill. Create it away from the button—hide those other layers, if you like.

18. Select the Fill Transform tool and click the fill. Use the Rotate handle to rotate the fill to your hearts content. But nothing is happening!

Yes, that's right, nothing is changing because you're rotating a circle, and as you know, no matter how much you spin a circle, it always remains the same. The secret is to change the shape of your gradient first, so it's no longer a perfect circle.

19. Click the Resize handle and drag it in toward the center of the shape:

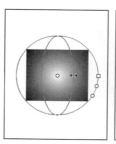

135

Your gradient is now elliptical.

20. Use the Rotate handle to turn the gradient 45 degrees to the right.

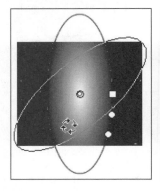

That's better! And better still, that's all for Fill Transform modifiers.

All in all, you've now used all the gradient tools except one. So far you've only been able to give gradients to individual shapes and then modify those, but imagine what you could do if you could apply your gradient evenly to a number of objects spread out over the entire stage? That's just what the **Lock Fill** option lets you do.

Locking fills

By locking the fill, you can make a gradient span across multiple shapes. That is, you can get the effect of a series of cutout shapes that reveal a common underlying background, almost as if you were opening up little windows to reveal a big picture behind them:

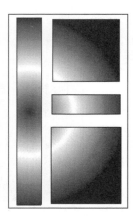

Here's how to use the **Lock Fill** feature.

Locking a fill

1. Select a gradient from the Color Swatches panel. We used the black and white linear gradient for clarity, but feel free to experiment with something a little more adventurous.

2. Use the Rectangle tool from the Tools panel to draw a long, thin rectangle across the stage from left to right:

3. Change the Rectangle tool's fill to No Color and draw six small squares underneath your original rectangle:

4. Select the Dropper tool, and then click your big gradient-filled rectangle. This tells Flash to use this particular gradient (and its orientation on the page) as a fill for other objects.

Flash automatically changes the mouse pointer to a paint bucket with a small padlock next to it, the sign for—you guessed it—a locked fill:

5. Click each of the squares to fill them with the gradient:

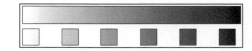

See how the gradient stretches across the six squares as though they were a continuation of the fill in the big rectangle? Flash is intelligent enough to work out the continuation of the gradient beyond the original shape and map it onto the new shapes. This can be a very powerful way to achieve symmetry across your gradients.

To unlock these fills, with the Paint Bucket tool selected, click the Lock Fill icon in the Options area of the Tools panel:

After the lock is unselected, the fill is unlocked and you can color your squares with any fill you like.

We've spent all our time so far talking about ways to draw images directly in Flash, but it's also possible to create images in external programs and import them into Flash.

Bitmaps

Working with vectors is all well and good, but it has some significant limitations from a creative point of view. Don't get us wrong, we think vectors are great, but they aren't going to be much help if you want to make a website for a photographer or someone who needs to show photographic images.

Well, despair not because Flash has a number of import solutions, from bitmap to vector file formats. An especially welcome addition in Flash MX 2004 is the ability to import the ubiquitous PDF file format. In this section, you'll look at the different import options at your disposal with your copy of Flash, and what you can do with the files you've imported when they are on your stage.

As a stand-alone application, Flash MX 2004 can import many major image types, including:

- Adobe Illustrator
- FreeHand
- GIF
- JPEG
- PNG
- PDF
- EPS

If you have QuickTime 4 or later installed (download it for free from www.apple.com/quicktime), you can also import the following formats:

- Photoshop
- PICT
- TIFF

Let's start with probably the most common image type, the *bitmap*.

Using bitmap images in Flash

A **bitmap** image (otherwise known as a **raster** image) is a generic name for an image that's defined by thousands of individual *pixels*. Typical bitmap formats include JPGs, BMPs, GIFs, and TIFs. The difference between the formats is the particular way each one stores the image data. Bitmaps are generally used for complicated images like photographs or paintings in which every single pixel can make a difference in the finished picture. The problem with bitmaps is that the image file has to describe each and every pixel that the image is composed of, which often results in a large file, in turn meaning long download times. (Some "lossy" bitmap formats such as JPG can compress images by describing blocks of similar color rather than every pixel, but does so at the expense of picture quality.)

A **vector** file, on the other hand, describes an image in terms of mathematical expressions—such as the start and end points of a line. This allows vector files to compress a lot of graphical information into a small space. Mathematical line description is great for simple shapes, but it's more difficult to try to describe the Mona Lisa in terms of vectors.

The first thing to remember when you're considering using bitmaps in Flash is that Flash was not designed as a bitmap program. To get the best performance in your movies, it's always preferable to create everything inside Flash using the drawing tools provided or to use vector graphics imported from other software applications. Flash can optimize a vector graphics file to ensure it is the smallest (and therefore the quickest) download possible. Although it's possible to create a flipbook-style movie by using a sequence of imported bitmaps, this will create such a huge file and take so long to download that most people will have moved on to the next site before the first couple of frames of your movie have loaded.

There'll be times when you've got a nice logo that you created in a paint program and you're tempted to just pull it into Flash and animate it. Although you can do this, in the long run you're better off doing it from scratch in Flash. It may not look exactly the same, but the benefits of smaller size and higher speed will probably outweigh the small graphical differences. The first rule of thumb when using bitmaps is to think carefully about the trade-off between file size and the benefit that the bitmaps will bring to your movie.

A couple more rules of thumb. Use bitmaps when:

- You need photos or lifelike images.
- You need screenshots.
- You need pictures of drawings or artwork.

For anything else, draw it inside Flash or another vector program.

> *Warning: Don't forget that the web-safe color rule that applies to the colors you use in Flash also applies to the colors of any images that you import into Flash. If you want your image to be guaranteed to display correctly on all computers, you should use the 216-color palette throughout all the stages of your movie's creation. This means that when you find an image to import, its best to change its colors in a graphic editing program first to make sure it appears as you want it to, and then bring the image into Flash.*

You've considered all the warnings, you've tried your best to draw your picture in Flash, but you've come to the decision that you're just going to have to import a bitmap image into Flash. So how do you do it?

Working with bitmaps

1. Open a new Flash document, and click the File ➤ Import ➤ Import to Stage menu option to open the Import dialog box.

2. Navigate to a **BMP**, **JPG**, **PNG**, or **GIF** file image on your computer (or you can download the example we've used here from this book's download section on our website):

3. Open the file.

4. Your file is imported into Flash and placed both on the stage as an object and in the Library:

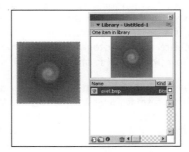

> *Warning: Flash uses the original image stored in the Library as a reference point, so deleting it can cause problems with your Flash movie. Even if you break the image apart and convert it to a graphic symbol, it will still be inexorably linked to the original bitmap.*

After you've imported the image into Flash, there are a couple of methods you can use to modify it.

5. Right-click (or *CTRL*-click a Mac) the bitmap symbol in the bottom pane of the Library. This will open a context-sensitive menu with a list of commands that can affect your image:

You are mainly concerned with the Edit with commands. The first of these (Edit with Fireworks in this example) opens the default image-editing program that your computer has associated with that file type. The second Edit with command opens a dialog box from which you can choose a program to edit your image. Both of these commands open the bitmap within the selected editing program. When you've finished editing the bitmap, save it and close the program to return to Flash, and you'll find that the image in the Library will have been updated to reflect any changes you've made.

The second method of altering bitmaps is to modify them within Flash itself. At the moment, the bitmap on the stage is an instance of the symbol in your Library.

6. Double-click the instance on the stage. You might expect Edit Bitmaps mode to open, but instead, nothing happens.

To alter a bitmap inside Flash, you first have to **break it apart**.

7. Click the Modify ➤ Break Apart menu option.

8. Your bitmap image is now a shape with no outline, and it is filled with the image from the Library. This

shape can be modified as any other shape can be in Flash: you can draw on it, cut bits out of it, and scale or rotate it.

9. Click the Lasso tool. It has three options at the bottom of the Tools panel:

— Lasso Tool

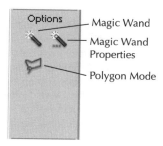

The two important options in the bitmap-editing context are the **Magic Wand** and the **Magic Wand Properties**. The **Magic Wand** is used to select a specific color in the image. For example, if you have a picture of a sky with clouds and you want to select the sky but not the clouds, you'd use the Magic Wand Tool. With this tool, you can select the blue areas and ignore the gray and white clouds.

10. Select the Magic Wand option. If you've downloaded the swirl.bmp from our website, click the top-left corner of your image. (If you're working with one of your own images, click an area comprised of mostly one color.) A small section of the image is selected:

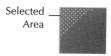
Selected Area

This is because Flash has selected only the sections of the image whose pixels are a very close color match to the original pixel you clicked.

11. Click the Magic Wand Properties option, and a dialog box appears:

From here, you can alter the settings for the Magic Wand Tool.

The **Threshold** box defines the amount of deviance from the clicked-on color allowed when Flash determines the matching pixels to include in its selection. Imagine a bitmap image of a cloudy sky. If your sky ranged from a deep blue to lighter gray-blue, using just the Magic Wand with its default settings would select only a small piece of the sky. A setting of **10** will allow Flash to select the 10 nearest shades of blue to the one you clicked as well. If you put a larger number into this box, Flash would select a greater portion of the sky.

12. Type 20 into the Threshold box and click OK.

13. Click off the stage to deselect the corner of the image, and click again with the Magic Wand in the same place on the image as last time:

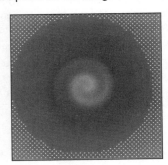

Now you can see that Flash selected a much greater part of the image. If you were to increase the Threshold number again, Flash would select an even bigger portion.

The other option in the Magic Wand Settings dialog is Smoothing. This controls the amount Flash will smooth the boundaries of the selection:

The Pixels setting means Flash will not smooth the boundaries at all; only a very tight range of color will be selected. The other granularity options range all the way up to Smooth, which does as its name suggests—smoothes out the differences between bordering colors.

If you're trying to select a very specific area of color, you should set this to Pixels with a low Threshold (1-2). If you're trying to select a large area with variable color, set Smoothing to Smooth and choose a high Threshold figure.

You've already played with solid and gradient fills in objects; you can also fill objects using **bitmap** images. Using bitmaps to fill shapes in your movie can give some very interesting results. You should always bear in mind that wherever bitmaps are involved, though, a larger file size is sure to follow.

Using bitmaps as fills

1. Working with the same imported bitmap image as before, use the Arrow tool to change the sides of the shape and increase its size:

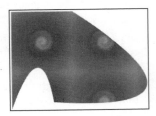

Your image is tiled in the background of the altered shape. Whenever you draw a shape bigger than the bitmap image, Flash tiles the bitmap to fill the shape's outline.

2. Click your shape with the Dropper tool. In the fill color in the Tools panel or Property inspector, a small copy of your image appears inside the box, which means that the current fill color is your bitmap image!

3. To better demonstrate the selected bitmap fill, draw a simple rectangle on the stage next to the original shape:

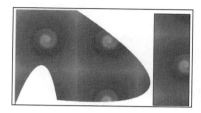

The new shape is also filled with the bitmap, continuing the tiling that appeared when you stretched your original shape. This is because the bitmap image is a locked fill on the stage.

Another useful way to manipulate bitmaps in Flash is to use the **Trace Bitmap** command.

Tracing bitmaps

Tracing a bitmap converts it from a bitmap image into a series of vectors. Although this sounds like a good thing because it gives your bitmap detail with vector scalability, the results can sometimes be problematic. You should experiment with this feature and judge its usefulness for yourself. Let's walk through an example of bitmap tracing.

Tracing bitmaps

1. Delete the contents of your stage, and then drag another two instances of your bitmap image from the Library and onto the clear stage.

2. Select the first bitmap instance and click the Modify ➤ Bitmap ➤ Trace Bitmap command. You'll see this dialog box:

The settings are as follows:

- **Color Threshold**—This works on the same principle as the Threshold setting in the Magic Wand Properties box. A higher number in this field means more colors are considered a match, so your final (traced) image will break down into fewer vector shapes.

- **Minimum Area**—This defines the minimum size (in pixels) that an area can be. The more detailed you want your final image to be, the smaller you should make this number. Keep in mind that more shapes entails a bigger file size.

- **Curve Fit**—This is similar to Smoothing in the Magic Wand Properties box. Setting this to Pixels ensures that the resulting traced curves will stay faithful to the original bitmap, whereas setting it to Very Smooth will rounds out the curves in its selection. The smoother a line is, the fewer vectors Flash will need to define it, which will keep the file size smaller.

- **Corner Threshold**—This performs the same task as Curve Fit, but this setting specifies how far a line can bend before Flash breaks it into two lines with an angular corner. The fewer corners in the image, the smaller the file size.

3. Leave the defaults shown in the screenshot, and click OK. Flash converts the first bitmap instance into a group of vectors using the default settings. The result looks like this:

141

You can see that this isn't particularly faithful to the original bitmap. Let's try and trace an image that's a little closer to the original.

4. Click your second bitmap instance, and open the Trace Bitmap dialog box (Modify ➤ Bitmap ➤ Trace Bitmap) again.

5. This time, set the values to 10, 2, Pixels, and Many Corners respectively, and click OK:

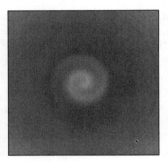

We think you'll agree that this looks virtually identical to the original bitmap. Unfortunately, the price you pay for this accuracy is an enormous file. You'll see just how big this file is when you **optimize** it in the next exercise.

Optimizing bitmaps

Optimizing bitmaps minimizes the number of corners in an image and smoothes out the lines to give a smaller but less precise picture. You can optimize any shape that you've drawn, but the feature is particularly useful when dealing with traced bitmaps.

Optimizing the traced bitmap

1. Select your first bitmap image instance with the Arrow tool and use the Modify ➤ Shape ➤ Optimize menu option to open the Optimize Curves dialog box:

2. Change the settings to those in the screenshot by dragging the Smoothing bar all the way to the right and checking the Use multiple passes box. This ensures that Flash will optimize the curves as much as possible and create the smallest file it can.

3. Click OK:

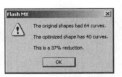

A report window appears, showing the number of curves Flash was able to optimize.

If you look at your image on the stage now, you'll see that it is a lot spikier than it was before because Flash converted all the pixilated smoothness into vector precision. By keeping the Smoothing slider at a lower setting, you kept the image more faithful to the original, but at the expense of optimization.

4. Do the same thing with your second (more accurately traced) image, using the same settings as before:

Clearly, tracing bitmaps accurately can leave you with a huge number of curves, which all add up in the final file size. Although the first image had only 64 curves, the second had 5839 before optimization and 1531 curves after. The final image though, is not too shabby a reproduction of the original, and at a considerably smaller size:

The original bitmap image is on the left, the highly optimized vector image is in the middle, and the accurately traced and optimized vector image is on the right. Again, you're on the horns of that old size vs. quality dilemma—and only you can make the ultimate decision about whether those extra kilobytes are worth it.

> *The Trace Bitmap tool will not always give the best results, and it can leave you with very large files. It is sometimes more useful to import the bitmap onto one layer, lock it, physically trace it using the Pencil tool on another layer, and then delete the original when you're finished.*

You'll now focus on another type of bitmap image— the **GIF** file—and see how Flash treats these when it imports them.

GIF files

The **GIF** (Graphic Interchange Format) file is one of the most commonly used image types on the Internet. What makes GIFs so special is that not only can they be compressed to produce relatively small images, but they can also include animations and single color transparency. When you import a GIF into Flash, you can retain these attributes.

Let's see how, starting with transparency.

Understanding Transparent GIFs

GIF transparency is not as powerful as Flash's Alpha setting. With Alpha, you can have a range of partial transparencies from completely opaque to totally transparent, whereas with a GIF, the transparency can only be on or off. However, reusing transparent GIFs in Flash can still be a useful feature to exploit.

Using transparent GIFs

1. Open a new Flash document.
2. In the File ➤ Import menu, navigate your way to any transparent GIF on your computer or use the downloadable `transparent.GIF` file from this book's support area on our website. You should have a red square on your screen with a hole in the middle:

The hole in the middle is the transparent area of the **GIF**.

3. Draw a line across the image using the Paintbrush tool. The line passes behind the image, but it is visible through the hole:

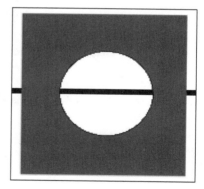

Move the GIF around on the stage. Wherever you put it, you should still be able to see the line through the hole.

Remember that there's not actually a gap in the image such as you'd get if you drew a vector rectangle with Flash's Rectangle tool and then used the Oval tool to cut a vector circle out of the middle. The hole in the GIF is more akin to a window—it's still a solid image, but it's completely transparent.

> *Flash also supports transparent PNG files. PNGs are often useful because the PNG-24 format—a considerably better image quality than that of the GIF format—also retains transparency. We'll cover PNG import later in this chapter.*

4. To test this, click the part of the line that you can see through the window. If there were a gap there, you'd expect to be able to select the line, but instead, you selected the entire GIF image.

Next you'll look at animated GIFs.

Understanding Animated GIFs

An animated **GIF** is a collection of static images that play one after the other at a specified speed. You can import these into Flash and incorporate them into the main timeline or into a movie clip's timeline.

Using animated GIFs

1. Start a new Flash document, and use the File ➤ Import command to locate an animated GIF and bring it into Flash. Again, we provided a file on the website for you called `animated.gif`.

2. When you bring an animated GIF into Flash, you'll notice that your timeline changes:

Flash creates a new keyframe for each frame in your animated GIF, and the number of normal frames between each keyframe depends on the delay specified in the GIF. For example, your original GIF has six frames and a delay of half a second between each frame. This gives you a total running time of three seconds (6 x 1/2 = 3).

In Flash, each keyframe is followed by five keyframe-dependent frames, so each of the GIF frames is displayed for six Flash frames. The movie plays at the default 12 frames per second, so each set of six frames will take half a second to display.

3. Each keyframe reproduces a GIF frame as a bitmap within that frame. Open your Library:

There are six bitmap images, one for each frame of the GIF. The first one is named after the file name of the GIF, and the five subsequent images are named Bitmap followed by a number. If you're going to use animated GIFs in Flash, it is helpful for your reference to create a folder in your Library for the GIFs and store all its frames in that folder.

> *You can create a similar effect by importing a sequence of images into Flash. If you have a number of images named* `slide1.gif`, `slide2.gif`, `slide3.gif`, *and so on in the same directory and you import the first one, Flash will prompt you to import the rest as a sequence of images.*

> *If you click Yes, Flash imports your sequence of images as keyframes, one after another in a straight line.*

JPG files

The **JPG** image format is best suited for photographic images. If you have a photo from a digital camera that you want to bring into Flash, it is probably already in JPG format.

JPGs are imported in the same way as GIF images, but they need to be optimized a little differently. JPG images can greatly inflate the file sizes of your Flash movies if you aren't careful.

Let's bring a JPG into Flash and see how to deal with it.

Importing and optimizing a JPG in Flash

1. Open a new Flash document and choose the File ➤ Import ➤ Import to Stage menu option.

2. Locate a JPG on your hard drive, or use the down-loadable `spiky.jpg` from our website. Click Open to import it.

3. After the JPG image is placed on your stage and in your Library, test the movie with Control ➤ Test Movie.

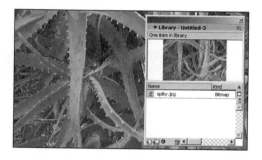

The image looks pretty good, but your Flash movie has a large file size. Flash has compressed the image a little…but not nearly enough.

Let's take a look at the compression settings.

4. Select the File ➤ Publish Settings menu and then click the Flash tab:

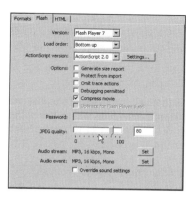

This tab contains the JPEG Quality slider bar. This sets the default compression for JPG images in your Flash movie, usually set to 80. Rather than change this setting and affect any future imported images, override the default document setting and edit the quality of your JPG through the Library.

5. Double-click the image name in the Library to display its properties:

Notice the preview of your image in the top-left corner.

The Allow Smoothing option gives Flash control over whether the compression is smoothed out. Sometimes JPG compression can leave harsh edges or blocky sections. Smoothing eliminates this but increases your image size a little. In most cases, it is better to leave this on, but it's always worth checking your image with and without it to see how much of a difference it makes.

The Compression setting allows you to choose the type of compression applied to the image. There are two options—Photo (JPEG) and Lossless (PNG/GIF). Luckily, Flash shows the most appropriate format (in parentheses, after the file type).

Let's take a look at the last setting and try to shave some kilobytes off your image.

6. Uncheck the Use imported JPEG data box. This will enable the Quality box, which has a default compression quality setting in it. Type 10 into this box and click the Test button:

If you look closely at the image in the preview window, you'll see that it looks pretty granular. Place your mouse pointer over the preview window and when it turns into a hand, drag to see other parts of the image.

The JPEG quality information, directly below the Quality field, shows the amount of compression applied, the size of the original image, the compressed image size, and the size of the compressed image as a percentage of the original.

Although the figures look healthy, the image certainly doesn't.

7. Type 30 into the Quality field and click **Test** again.

The image looks a lot better this time, and the file size is still pretty low. To be sure of the final quality of any image, it is always a good idea to test your movie with Control ➤ Test Movie and assess each image individually. There is no right and wrong when it comes to JPG compression. The choices you make will depend a lot on the JPG image itself, the context in which you are using it, and the file size restrictions for the whole Flash movie.

For example, if you are creating a portfolio website for the aforementioned photographer, you would want to retain as much image quality as possible—a lot of compression just wouldn't show the images as the photographer intended.

If you import a bitmap image in another format into Flash, say a TIFF or PICT, you can still apply JPG compression to it by opening the image's properties from the Library. JPG compression is not only limited to imported JPGs.

You'll now look at importing files from other Macromedia products and get a glimpse of the extended integration between them.

Fireworks files

One of the great things about Flash is its integration with other Macromedia Studio MX 2004 suite products like Fireworks and FreeHand. (We'll cover FreeHand in a moment.) You can import images created in Fireworks and maintain the vector elements from their original form.

The Fireworks native format, PNG, is extremely useful because of its transparency and quality of image, which is far superior to the GIF format. As an added bonus over GIFs, PNG files also support multiple varied degrees of transparency or opacity.

This screenshot displays a single Fireworks PNG file (spiky.png) with opacities ranging from 20 to 100 percent:

Importing Fireworks files is a very simple process. On the File ➤ Import ➤ Import to Stage (or Import to Library) menu, select PNG file. You'll then be prompted with a dialog box:

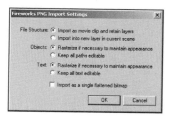

When importing your file, it's wise to retain the original Fireworks file in the best possible format to allow further manipulation in Flash. Here's a run-down of the options available to you:

- **File Structure**—Select Import as movie clip and retain layers so Flash will place all the Fireworks content in one movie clip and retain the original layer format. Flash creates a new folder in the Library called **Fireworks Objects** and places a generically titled movie clip in it. Flash will place all Fireworks imports within this folder.

- **Objects**—Select Rasterize if necessary to maintain appearance when you want to keep the import true to the original file. Select Keep all paths editable to keep all objects editable within Flash.

- **Text**—Select the Rasterize option wherever possible. Use the Keep all text editable option in situations where your text is rasterized in Flash and you want to keep it as a vector object.

If the objects and text options don't give you a satisfactory result the first time around, try using the other option. Sometimes a little trial and error is required.

Enough about bitmaps already! Now let's look at some of the vector import options available in Flash MX 2004.

Importing vector images into Flash

Vectors are beneficial for many different reasons—from providing infinite scalability to helping you maintain the all-important small file sizes. Remember, the smaller the file size of a website, the more visitors will stick around to appreciate it.

You don't have to create all your vector illustrations in Flash; you can import vector graphics as well. You can import virtually every significant vector format into Flash, from Adobe Illustrator native files to Windows

metafiles. In Flash MX 2004, you can also import PDF files, which are comprised mainly of vector text and bitmap images.

In this section, you'll look at a few of the vector import options. You'll start with Macromedia's illustration heavyweight, FreeHand.

Importing FreeHand files into Flash

FreeHand is a vector illustration application that was initially used for print, but it has quickly become the tool of choice for any serious Flash vector or web work. Simply put, FreeHand's illustration tools are far more powerful than those in Flash. Many Flash creations start as a FreeHand page and are imported into Flash later for animating or incorporating into a website.

Importing FreeHand files into Flash is easy. Use File ➤ Import ➤ Import to Stage (or Import to Library) and select FreeHand from the Files of type drop-down menu. After you've selected a file, the following dialog box appears:

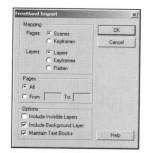

As you can see, you have more options when importing FreeHand files than you did with Fireworks files. Due to its print-industry origins, FreeHand organizes documents into multiple pages. These pages can be imported into Flash as separate scenes with one page in each scene, or it can import them into their own individual keyframes.

You can also tell Flash how you want the layers of FreeHand to be imported. If you want to keep everything exactly as you had it in FreeHand, just keep the Layers radio button checked. Alternatively, you can make Flash flatten out the FreeHand file, but none of your text or artwork will be editable, just like with Fireworks.

In the FreeHand Import dialog box, you can specify which pages of the FreeHand file you want to import. You also have a few extra options to import layers that were hidden in FreeHand, as well as your background layer. You can also make sure that any text is imported as text, and is therefore still editable.

We recommend that you keep the default settings here as well because that will ensure that all your artwork is editable after it's imported (unless it wasn't vector artwork to begin with).

Importing PDF documents into Flash

PDF documents are the cornerstone of the print industry and have fast become the de facto standard for eBooks and sharable documents. The beauty of PDFs is their cross-platform compatibility, small file sizes, and excellent quality text. PDFs truly maintain the fonts and layout from the machine that produced them.

PDFs are comprised of a combination of vectors and bitmaps. Generally, all PDF text is vector-based, whereas images are a combination of vectors and bitmaps. The use of vector text is especially notable because this allows the text to be editable after it's imported into Flash.

Let's see how to import a PDF.

Importing a PDF

You're going to use a tiny PDF portion of Chapter 2 of this book to import into Flash. The file, chapter2.PDF is available for download in the Chapter 5 files on our website, but you can use any PDF for this exercise. One with two or more pages and bitmaps is preferable.

1. Open a new Flash document.

2. Select File ➤ Import ➤ Import to Stage and locate the chapter2.pdf file, or any PDF on your system. The following dialog box appears:

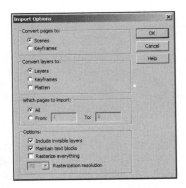

As with the previous import dialog boxes, this is a series of import options. Like FreeHand, PDF files contain a number of pages. The first option, Convert pages to, specifies how pages should be presented. Even though this defaults to Scenes, in most cases, we recommend using the Keyframes setting.

The Convert layers to and Which pages to import options are fairly rudimentary; the default settings are adequate for most situations. The set of Options at the bottom of the dialog box are a little more significant. The first, Include invisible layers, tells Flash to import any visible and hidden layers, and in most cases this is preferable.

The Maintain text blocks option specifies whether the imported text will be editable. You will usually keep the default selection because it allows you to edit the text and text fields. The last option, Rasterize everything, is a no-no! If this is switched on, all the PDF pages will be imported as bitmap images, which not only increases your file size, but also prevents you from editing the content. The one reason for using this option will become apparent in a moment.

3. Set the options as seen here and click OK to import.

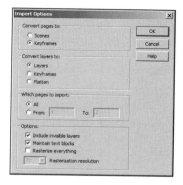

4. After a little processing, you are likely to get the following error message:

This is Flash warning you that some of the fonts in the PDF file are not on your system. Don't panic; this is quite common.

There are two options. The one you choose depends on how close you want the text to be to the original. The easiest option is Use default, which will render the text in one of Flash's default fonts—serif, sans serif, or typewriter (more on these later in the chapter). If you select this, Flash determines the best font from the three for each typeface in the document. Even though this might sound lazy, remember that you can always edit the text fields later and apply fonts at that stage.

The second option is Choose Substitute, which allows you to choose a replacement font for the PDF document:

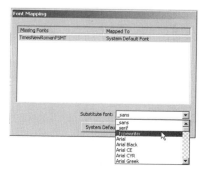

In this particular case, the missing font is a Times New Roman family font, which can easily be replaced with a font from the same family. Job done! In scenarios where you have 10 or so missing fonts, you might not be so keen to replace them all, so go with the Use default option. Guess which option you'll use here?

5. In the Missing Fonts dialog box, select Use default.

After a little while, the content will be on the stage, the timeline will have a number of keyframes, and the Library will contain the bitmaps and other content from the PDF:

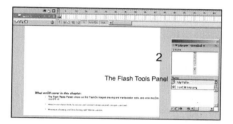

If you are wondering why your content is running into the work area, it is simply because the PDF document was physically bigger than the stage. In most cases, it is usually a good idea to increase the stage size before importing the document.

6. Click the header text field that reads The Flash Tools Panel and open the Property inspector. As you can see, the text here is fully modifiable. Neat!

7. Click the second keyframe in the timeline and click the image of the Tools panel:

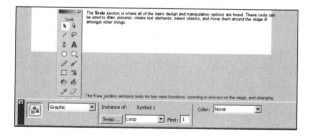

As with the text, this image can be transformed, moved, and modified in any way. Flash has even made it into a symbol for you!

149

You're not going to do any more work on this document because you should now be aware of the possibilities of importing PDF documents. The result of the exercise is available as the file `pdf_import.fla` from the code download for this book.

Macintosh users will especially benefit from the PDF import in Flash MX 2004 because of the excellent built-in support for PDFs in Mac OS X.

You can use the built-in Save as PDF option from the Print dialog box, which allows you to create PDFs from any application, as well as the PDF screen-grab (COMMAND-SHIFT-3 or COMMAND-SHIFT-4). Any of these Mac-created PDF files can then be imported into Flash.

Now, it's time for more vectors.

Vector clip art

Clip art has a wonderful history in print art, presentations, and web pages, so it should come as no surprise that it can be used in Flash as well. The greatest thing about clip art is that, unlike bitmaps, most of it is already in vector format and it can be easily imported and used in Flash.

The easiest file type for Flash to import is a **WMF** file (Windows Metafile). These files can be easily imported into Flash through the File ➤ Import ➤ Import to Stage (or Import to Library) menu. Because they are already vectors, they are easily manipulated after import.

WMFs are usually imported as groups, so when you want to edit them, you can either edit each group separately or highlight the whole group and use the Modify ➤ Ungroup option to convert them into lines and fills. There are sometimes lines and fills hidden behind others in clip art files, which can increase the file size. To prevent this, ungroup the whole image, deselect the object to let Flash merge the visible objects together, and then discard the hidden ones. Also, it's always a good idea to optimize clip art with Modify ➤ Shapes ➤ Optimize because clip art is made for print and is not designed to be compact for the web. Optimizing it ensures a lower file size.

Don't be afraid to use clip art in your Flash movies. Some people don't like the way clip art looks, but keep in mind that you can use it as a building block for your own art because you can edit it to the look and feel of your own website.

Images are not the only visual elements that Flash can handle. It can also use your system fonts and some modification tools to give your movies that extra personal zing.

Fonts and typefaces

It comes as a surprise to some people just how much of a difference a font can make. Fonts are so much more than just boring "clothes" for words. They can define a website—and a bad choice of font can easily put people off from viewing your movie or staying at your site. Building a font collection is a relatively easy task because the Internet holds many free font repositories, and there are hundreds of font collections on CDs that can be found lurking in computer store bargain bins.

Warning: You might not realize that fonts, like images, are usually copyrighted. If you find a font you like and want to use on your site or in your movies, check the copyright on the font and get the permission, or buy a license to use the font. If that seems like too much of a hassle, use system fonts that you know are copyright free or create your own, although this latter option is not as simple as it seems!

One of the advantages of Flash is that it's not as fussy as HTML when it comes to fonts. Although HTML supports the standard fonts—Arial, Times New Roman, and Courier (and a few others)—if you use a more exotic font in HTML, it will be replaced with one of the standard types. It is possible to *embed* a font in an HTML document, but Macs and PCs differ in the fonts they use, and embedding fonts make your files slower to download.

There are two ways to get over these obstacles in Flash. The first way is to convert the font to a graphic symbol, although this means that the text part of the object can no longer be edited or selected. The other method is to *embed the font within the movie.* Flash automatically includes embeddable fonts in your movies when you publish them from the FLA file.

Flash also works with TrueType, Open Type, PostScript Type 1, Bitmap fonts (Macintosh), and Device Fonts.

Working with device fonts

Of the four font types just mentioned, the first three are embedded into a Flash movie, bulking up its SWF file size. The fourth type, **device fonts**, is not embedded, so the file size is much smaller. When you use a device font, Flash searches the computer that your movie is being played on for a suitable font, and then use that to display your text.

As mentioned earlier, Flash comes with three device fonts, and you can identify a device font in your font list because the names start with _ (an underscore):

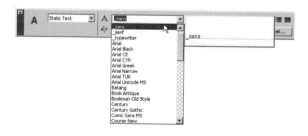

The standard device fonts are:

- _sans (appears similar to Arial or Helvetica)
- _serif (appears similar to Times New Roman)
- _typewriter (appears similar to Courier)

Be sure to either select the font from your font list when you first use it, or have Use Device Fonts checked in the bottom half of the Property inspector:

Working with text

In Flash, you have many of the same commands at your disposal that you find in a word processing program. We covered most of the text options in the Property inspector earlier, but there are a few more.

You can change text to any solid color and it remains editable, but if you want to make any more complicated effects, the text must be broken apart and converted to graphics. This will increase file size, but you can give your text some pretty interesting effects:

You'll see some more advanced use of text later in the book when you learn how to use text fields for user input and interaction.

Finally, let's work on your case study exercise.

Case study

In the last chapter, you set up your buttons and aligned your elements. Now you're going to import some images for your web portfolio and add a gradient to highlight your company name.

151

Adding a gradient to the website

The purpose of this gradient is to highlight the company logo and name. You'll do this with a custom gradient.

1. Open your saved case study document:

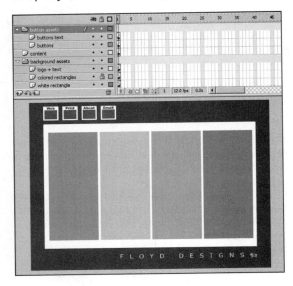

2. Open the Color Mixer panel (Window ➤ Design Panels ➤ Color Mixer) and select Linear from the Fill Style drop-down menu:

3. Click below the current gradient to add a new color:

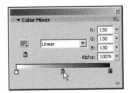

4. Change the color of the first bucket on the left to the current background color (#003366). Do the same with the last bucket. You're doing this because the gradient will consist of two colors, with a different color in the center.

5. Select a lighter blue for the center pot (#0033FF).

6. Move the buckets nearer to the left edge so they look like this:

7. Select Add Swatch from the Color Mixer menu at the top right of the panel. Now you can apply it.

8. Insert a new layer called gradient and place it at the very bottom of all the layers.

9. On the new layer, draw a rectangle covering the stage with your new linear gradient fill and no stroke. Use the Align tool (with the To Stage option switched on, and using the Match Width and Height Size modifier) to ensure that the rectangle is as big as the stage.

10. Select the Fill Transform tool and click the new rectangle.

11. Use the Rotate handle of the Fill Transform tool to rotate the gradient 90 degrees counter-clockwise.

 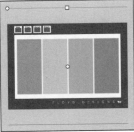

At the moment, you can't see the fill, so you'll have to use the Resize handle to bring the gradient stripe on stage.

12. Drag the Resize handle down to the top of the stage and release it.

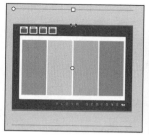

13. Not bad for a first try? Pull it down a little more until the stripe covers the text and doesn't affect your white rectangle:

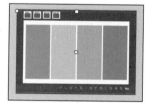

14. Lock the layer to ensure that it is not accidentally changed later. This gradient has lifted your logo off the page significantly.

Importing images

The last thing for this chapter is to import a few images for your web and print portfolio pages.

1. Select File ➤ Import ➤ Import to Library and download the following files from our site:

- fmc.gif
- friendsofed_website.gif
- hypertelia.gif
- nettle_wine.gif
- pinderkaas_website.gif
- qanik.gif
- gandhi.jpg
- einstein.jpg

Don't forget that you can use *CTRL*+Click or *SHIFT*+Click to make multiple selections on the PC.

2. Click OK to import them.

3. Create a new Library folder called imported images and place all the images in it:

This will keep your Library a little tidier, and make maintenance a cinch.

4. Save your case study file and close it.

You'll be returning to this case study at the end of the next chapter.

Summary

In this chapter, you examined some general Flash features, all of which are targeted at helping you make the objects in your movies more effective.

You saw that:

- You can use the palette of **web-safe** colors that render properly in any browser in the known universe.
- You can create your own **custom colors** and have great control over their constituent colors.
- You can use **hex** values to match and amend colors.
- You can use **gradients** to bring flat objects to life, and you can create, modify, and save your own customized gradients and color sets.

- You have infinite potential to manipulate **gradient fills** after you've applied them to an object.

- You can import, trace, and optimize **bitmap images** for use in your movies—but there can be a file size penalty you should be aware of.

- You can **import PDFs** and files from other Macromedia products easily, and doing so allows you to keep the imported assets editable within Flash.

In the next chapter, you're going to focus on **animation** through motion tweening.

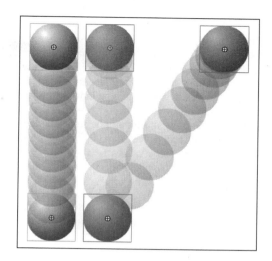

Chapter 6

MOTION TWEENING

What we'll cover in this chapter:

- Using **motion tweening** to move objects around in your movies and animate them convincingly
- Scaling, rotating, fading, and change objects' color as they move
- Making objects appear to accelerate and decelerate using **easing**
- Using **onion skinning** to view multiple frames simultaneously to make convincing animations
- Creating **motion paths** for your moving objects to follow

The first five chapters immersed you in a number of aspects of Macromedia Flash: its basic layout, its tools, and how it uses symbols and color. You're now going to start combining these different elements in some more sophisticated ways, giving you plenty of opportunity to test things out and—of course—practice, practice, practice. This is an important chapter—as well as learning about motion tweens, you'll apply a substantial amount of what you've learned so far in your case study exercise—you'll see the case study further take shape and begin to come to life.

Now you're going to return to the subject of animation, which was touched upon briefly in early chapters when you encountered an animatronics mushroom and a static-yet-moving car.

Animation revisited

As you no doubt recall, Flash animation is based on the simple principle of representing change over time. When Flash tweens, it creates the frames in between two significant moments of action, which are themselves defined by the contents of keyframes. The replayed sequence of "keyframe, in-between frames, keyframe" is the essence of a Flash animation.

There are two different types of animation in Flash: the **shape tween** you used to make your mushroom grow, and the **motion tween**. A shape tween is a morphing operation; the original object is transmogrified into a different object:

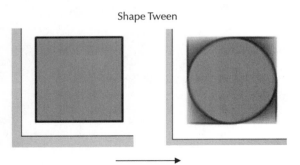

Shape Tween

Square morphs into circle over time

A motion tween is the representation of an object moving around the stage:

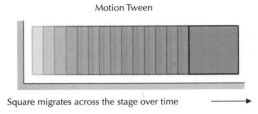

Motion Tween

Square migrates across the stage over time ⟶

In this chapter, you're going to focus on motion tweens, and in the next chapter, you'll look at shape tweening in more detail.

Motion tweens

Motion tweening, put simply, is moving an object around on the stage from Point A to Point B. Motion tweens will only work for **symbols** or **grouped shapes**.

Here's an example.

Creating movement with motion tweening

1. In a new Flash document, draw a square, select the fill and the outline together, and convert them into a symbol with the name square. Give it a graphic behavior and a center registration point. Then place the square symbol on the left side of the stage:

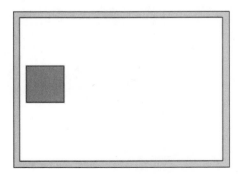

2. In the timeline, insert a keyframe at frame 30 (Insert ➤ Timeline ➤ Keyframe or *F6*).

3. In the new keyframe (click frame 30 in the timeline if it's not currently selected), move the square symbol to the far right side of the stage:

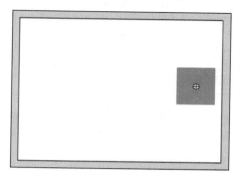

4. Click any frame between 1 and 29 in the timeline.

5. Open the Properties panel and select Motion from the Tween drop-down menu:

Notice that Flash has drawn an arrow-headed line from frame 1 to frame 29 and colored in the frames:

The arrow indicates the length of the tween from frame 1 through frame 29. The tweened frames are colored blue to indicate a motion tween.

If you see a dotted line instead of the arrow, it means that there is a motion tween between the frames, but it's not executing properly:

This indicates that there's something wrong with the events in the timeline and Flash can't construct the tween successfully.

You may, for example, be trying to motion tween ungrouped shapes, which cannot be tweened. Also, make sure you haven't added extra keyframes or objects that are disrupting the motion, and if you still can't see where you've gone wrong, don't be afraid to delete the whole layer and start over from scratch.

6. Test the movie and watch the object move from the left to the right.

You might want the objects in your animations to do more than just move from A to B. You might even think that this plain vanilla motion tween looks kind of wooden and mechanical. By using some of the more sophisticated features of motion tweening, you can make your objects change size, spin round, move in complex patterns, and move more convincingly. Let's look at these features now.

Scaling objects in motion tweens

The first thing you're going to do is scale your object—change its size—as it moves across the stage. Scaling an object using a motion tween is not the same as the shape tweening, or morphing, you did in the first chapter when you made your mushroom grow. In a scaled shape tween, the shape itself remains the same: only its size changes.

Tweening simultaneous motion and scaling

1. In the movie you've been working on, click frame 1 on the timeline.

2. If it's not already displayed on the screen, open the Properties panel.

Notice that the tween Scale field is already checked:

This is checked by default and there is no reason to uncheck it. **Tween scaling** allows you to change the size of your object over the duration of your animation. With tween scaling turned off in your current movie, the square would remain at its original size for 29 frames, and then suddenly jump to its new size in frame 30. This will look very abrupt, and that is not the staccato effect you want here.

You know that the tween scaling option is turned on, so let's scale your tweened square so that it'll make use of the default tween scaling feature.

3. Go back to the stage, and still in frame 1, ensure the square is selected.

4. Select the Free Transform tool and click the Scale button in the Tools panel options:

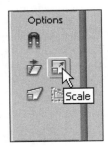

The selected object now has a dotted box around it with eight scaling selection handles:

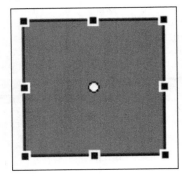

5. Grab the lower-right corner handle and use it to scale the object down to about half of its original size.

6. Click frame 30 on the timeline, where the motion-tweened square is located on the right side of the stage. This time scale the square up by about a half, using the bottom-left handle to do the scaling.

7. Test the movie, and you'll see the square gradually grow larger from frame 1 to 30 as it passes across the stage.

8. To see exactly what the tween Scale option does for your animation, go back to frame 1 and turn it off in the Properties panel by unchecking the box.

Now retest the movie and notice the migrating square's sudden change in size when the playhead hits frame 30. With the tween scaling option turned on, Flash is doing all the hard work of "connecting the dots" of the animation, creating a relatively smooth and gradual motion and growth effect.

Motion tweening also allows you to spin objects round and round as they move on their path. Again, this is fairly straightforward. Here's how.

Adding motion and rotation

1. Back in frame 1, turn tween scaling on in the Properties panel.

2. Click the arrow next to the Rotate box and look at the resulting menu:

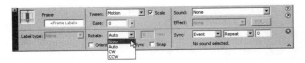

You can rotate an object clockwise, counterclockwise, or not at all. The value in the (currently grayed-out) box to the right of the Rotate menu controls how many times, if any, an object will rotate in the selected direction.

You'll see that you currently have no rotation selected—let's change that.

3. Click frame 1 in the timeline and then select CW (clockwise) in the Rotate drop-down menu. Change the number of times to be rotated from 0 to 3:

4. Test the movie again, and you'll see the object rotate clockwise three times during its movement across the stage.

This is OK for a start, but you can also customize the rotation to achieve a more interesting effect. For instance, you can change the center point around which the square rotates.

5. In the keyframe at frame 1, draw a box around the grouped square shape to select it, and then choose the Free Transform tool. As usual, you'll see a white dot in the center of the square. This is the center point:

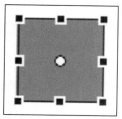

This shows you the position of the currently defined center point of the shape. This is the point that Flash will use as the center of rotation, and by default, Flash will always position the center point slap bang in the middle of the object. This applies both to symbols and to grouped shapes.

Click the center circle and drag it to a different position on the square—we put ours at the bottom middle.

6. Play the movie again, and notice the difference in the movement. This time, the square seems to have some weight that's governing the rotating motion. Experiment with the center point in different locations, and see the effect that this has on your square's style.

For further variation, you can try placing the center point *outside* the square:

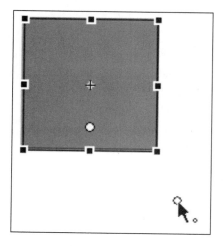

If you play your movie now, the square will rotate in bigger, weightier, arcs.

The ability to rotate objects around different center points helps you to imbue your objects with character and individuality—essentially, with characteristics that mimic how things move in the real world. This is one of the secrets of really convincing animation. Flash has other features to help you here. One of them is **easing**.

Easing

If you need another way to add a touch of real world physics to your Flash animation, you can use the **easing** feature on motion tweens to make an object move more naturally. Easing is essentially a way of controlling the apparent **acceleration** and **deceleration** of the motion-tweened object.

If you look just above the Rotation field in the Properties panel you'll see another field called **Ease**:

Easing is set to 0 by default. On this setting, motion-tweened objects will move at a constant speed—as they have in the motion tweens you've created so far. By entering a figure in the Ease box, you can make your tweened objects start slowly and accelerate (**easing in**), or start quickly and decelerate (**easing out**).

Easing runs on a scale of −100 to 0 for Easing In and from 0 to 100 for Easing Out. The number represents the amount of easing that's applied to the tween. The further away from 0 you get, the more pronounced the easing becomes:

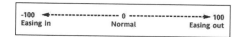

To illustrate how easing can be used effectively, you're going to create an animation of a bouncing ball.

Easing a bouncing ball

First, you need a ball.

1. Open a new Flash document. Rename its default layer Standard Ball.

2. Using the Oval tool and a suitable radial gradient fill, create a strokeless sphere on the Standard Ball layer, and then convert it to a graphic symbol called Bad Ball.

3. Place this ball at the top left of your stage:

4. Add keyframes at frames 10 and 20.

5. Click keyframe 10 and move the ball to the bottom of the stage (remember that by holding *Shift* you can ensure that the ball will drop in a straight line). If you click keyframe 20, you'll see the ball is still at the top of the stage. You now have three positions for the ball:

   ■ The top of the drop (frame 1)
   ■ The bottom of the drop (frame 10)
   ■ The top of the bounce (frame 20)

   The next step is to animate the bounce.

6. Add a motion tween between frames 1 to 10, and then another between frames 10 to 20. These two tweens animate the fall and the bounce of the ball respectively.

You can select both sections by clicking the timeline between frames 1 and 10, holding down the Shift key, and then clicking the timeline between frames 10 and 20. With both sets of frames selected, you can add both motion tweens at once using the Tween drop-down menu in the Properties panel.

Whichever way you add the two motion tweens, your timeline should now look like this:

7. Test your movie.

   You'll see that it drops and bounces—but the movement is too uniform to really resemble a bouncing ball, isn't it?

   Let's add another ball to your animation and try and make it act more realistically under the influence of gravity.

8. Add a new layer to your movie and rename it Eased Ball.

9. Create a new graphic symbol on this new layer consisting of another sphere that is a different color than the last one but about the same size. Call this symbol Good Ball.

10. On the new Eased Ball layer, repeat the steps you took with the Bad Ball: click keyframe 1 and place your new ball at the top of the stage next to the original ball; create keyframes at frames 10 and 20; move the new ball to the bottom of the stage at keyframe 10, and then add two motion tweens to make it bounce.

11. Test your movie and verify that both balls drop and bounce in identical fashion:

Now you can add some easing to the second ball.

12. Make sure you're working on the Eased Ball layer, select keyframe 1 and use the Ease box on the Properties panel to set the easing to -100 (that's negative 100). You can do this with the slider or by typing the value in. This easing value will only apply to the first motion tween on the timeline.

Remember, this is the most extreme "easing in" value: the ball will start slowly and accelerate as it approaches frame 10—the bottom of the stage position. This will make the ball appear to accelerate as it falls to the bottom of the stage.

13. At keyframe 10, set the easing (out) value to 100— the maximum. This will make the ball *accelerate* out of the bounce, and *slow down* as it reaches the top of the bounce.

14. Test your movie.

The Good Ball now looks more like a real ball— speeding up as it falls (easing in) and slowing down as it rises (easing out). This is a good way to mimic the effects of gravity on animated objects—you need to think how the object would behave in the real world, and add the appropriate easing to the motion tween.

> *Remember: ease in to speed up, ease out to slow down.*

It's also important to note that you can only specify easing values *once* on any single motion tween. To make an object speed up and slow down, as in the example above, *two* motion tweens are needed. Each motion tween has its own easing setting, so for every change of speed you want your object to have, you must create a separate motion tween.

> *Another thing to keep in mind when practicing your animations is if you want two or more objects to move simultaneously, they have to be on separate layers. For example, you can't have two circles in layer 1 with one moving from top to bottom and the other moving from bottom to top. To achieve this, each circle should be in its own layer with its own separate motion tween. Two objects can move on the same layer provided that each has its own tween at separate points on the timeline.*

Next, you're going to look at some editing options that can help you when you're creating tweens.

Options for editing your animations

When you want to make minor corrections to your animation or get a sense of the flow and direction of the animated frames, it can be a great help to view more than one frame at once. Flash's **Onion Skin** tool allows you to do just this. You can edit more than one frame at a time as well.

Using onion skins

Using onion skins allows you to work as though you were drawing each frame on a sheet of tracing paper and piling them on top of each other as you worked. The term "onion skin" comes from the days when traditional cel-based animators used transparent onion paper to ensure that the frame they were drawing followed correctly from the previous one. Being able to see the outlines of the previous drawing through the semi-transparent paper meant that they could better gauge changes of position, acceleration, and so on over time.

In Flash, however, instead of shuffling through a pile of paper sheets, you need only click couple of buttons in the bottom-left corner of your timeline:

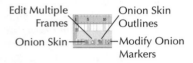

Edit Multiple Frames — Onion Skin Outlines

Onion Skin — Modify Onion Markers

You may never have used these buttons before, but they'll prove to be very useful as your Flash career develops.

So how is onion skinning used? Let's go back to your animation of the two bouncing balls. If you click the Onion Skin button, the transitional world of the motion tween starts to reveal itself:

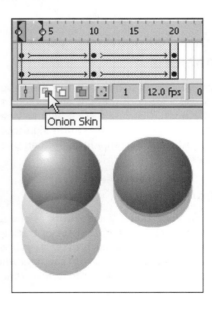

There are a couple of things to notice here.

First, because the playhead is on frame 1, you see both balls in all their glory, clearly defined at the top of the drop. You can also see a ghostly image of each of the balls at subsequent stages of the drop. Note that the appearance of each ball is slightly different in the ghosted frames—this is because one has easing and the other one does not.

The second thing to notice is the change on the timeline—two little markers have appeared, and they're spanning frames 1 to 3:

Onion Markers

The onion markers define the number of frames that will be ghosted in around the frame that the playhead is currently on.

If you click the right marker and drag it off to frame 20, you'll see that you now get a preview of all the movie's frames:

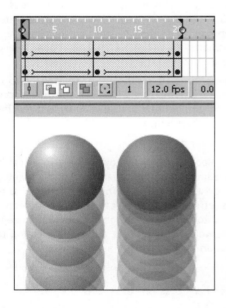

By clicking and dragging the markers, you can alter the range of onion skinned frames.

If you find that the density of ghosted frames in the onion skinned view makes it harder to see what is happening on the stage, you can view only the ghosted outlines of the animated frames. You can access this feature by clicking the Onion Skin Outlines button:

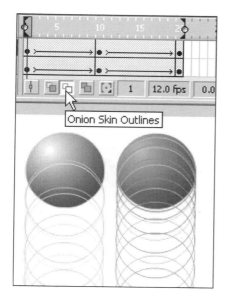

To give you an unobstructed view of the ball, a cluster of tightly packed frames appears at the top of the drop, and only a few at the bottom of the bounce. To see things even more clearly, turn off the Onion Skin Outlines option, and switch Onion Skin back on. Click frame 20 and drag the end position version of the Good Ball (remember this is the ball on the Eased Ball layer) to the right:

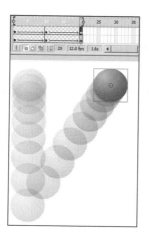

Now you can see the uninterrupted flight of the ball without the down and up legs superimposed on each other. Note also that Flash has automatically recalculated and rerendered all the in between frames. If you test the movie now, you'll see that moving the end position image results in a new flight path. Onion skinning is an excellent way to see the effect of your amendments on the finished movie.

Let's consider those clusters of frames again. The density of frames shown by the onion skinning is greater at the start of the drop and at the top of the bounce and smaller at the bottom of the bounce. This is because when you apply the easing option, Flash uses a tighter time-clustering of frames to simulate slow motion, and a looser clustering to represent high speed. This can be a little counter-intuitive until you realize that the apparent speed of an object is determined by a combination of the number of frames and the frame rate. The more frames it takes for an object to move, the slower the apparent motion will be on the screen. When your brain sees only a few images within a fixed timeframe, it fills in the blanks and figures that the object must be moving fast. If your brain gets the chance to register more images (frames) in that fixed timeframe, it assumes that because it is seeing a lot of intermediate images, the object is moving slowly.

Let's get an overview of the other onion skinning options.

The Modify Onion Markers button allows you to alter the way your markers and onion skins appear on the timeline and the stage.

If you want the markers to always be shown on the timeline (even when you aren't using onion skins), select Always Show Markers from the Modify Onion Markers menu:

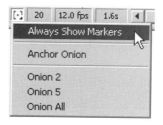

The Anchor Onion option, when checked, prevents your markers from moving as you move the playhead. This means that you see only the frames that are within the markers as you move the playhead. If this option is not checked and you move the playhead along the timeline, the markers move with the playhead to show you the onion skins in the section you are viewing.

Selecting the Onion 2, Onion 5, or Onion All options from the menu moves the markers to show varying numbers of onion skinned frames. For example, Onion 2 will show the current frame plus two onion skinned frames on either side.

It's important to note that the onion skin effect does not export with your movie and is never seen by the end user. If you want to create an onion skin effect for the user, you have to manually create it frame by frame (sorry about that).

Onion skinning allows you to view multiple frames simultaneously; let's see how to *edit* multiple frames.

Editing multiple frames

Being able to edit several frames at once can be extremely useful—provided that you are careful!

Suppose you decide that everything in your bouncing ball animation needs to be moved to the right to accommodate another graphical element on the left of the stage. Thanks to the **Edit Multiple Frames** feature, this can be done in once rather than having to alter every single frame.

In your bouncing balls movie, click the Edit Multiple Frames button:

Now adjust your onion skin markers so that all the frames in your animation are selected:

Make sure none of the objects on the stage are selected, and use the Edit ➤ Select All menu option to select everything on the stage.

Both balls, at all phases of their movement, are selected:

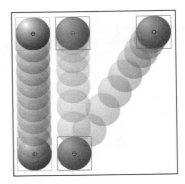

Note that if you'd chosen the Edit ➤ Select All menu option *without* having first chosen the Edit Multiple Frames tool, only the objects in the current keyframe would have been selected. Using Edit Multiple Frames, you pick up everything within the bounds of the onion markers.

Now you can drag all the selected content across the stage to its new position:

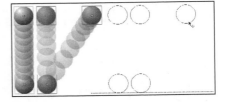

This option can be a real time saver because you don't have to worry about precisely repositioning everything frame by frame. Another great example of how Flash can do your work for you.

Motion tweening is not limited to controlling the movement of objects. It can also make them fade in, fade out, and change color. Let's see how.

Motion tween effects

There are two ways you can make an object slowly disappear and reappear in the motion tweening context: changing an object's **alpha** value, or changing its **tint**. *Alpha*, as we've mentioned before, is really transparency, and *tint* is part of an object's color characteristics.

Each of these two attributes possesses different qualities and you decide which one you use when. Let's work through examples of both of them, starting with alpha, and then you can decide for yourself.

Fading with alpha

1. In a new Flash document, create a new graphic symbol—we've used a simple filled square here. Make sure your movie's background color is set to white.

2. Place the graphic symbol on the stage in the default keyframe at frame 1, and then insert new keyframes at frame 15 and frame 30:

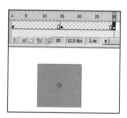

3. Click frame 15, select the symbol, and open the Color drop-down menu in the Properties panel.

   Hidden in this drop-down menu are the various effects that you can apply to your symbol:

4. Select Alpha from the drop-down menu, and then set the alpha slider to 0%. This setting will render the symbol totally transparent in the keyframe at frame 15:

5. Add two motion tweens from frames 1 to 15, and from frames 15 to 30, respectively:

When you test your movie you'll see the object fade in and fade out as you gradually increase and decreasing the square's level of transparency. When you get to frame 15 where the transparency is 100 percent (invisible), you can see through the square completely. The tween from frames 15 to 30 fades the square back in, gradually obscuring the movie background again.

Now you'll achieve the same end result again using the **Tint** approach.

Fading with tint

Use the Flash document you created in the previous exercise and retain the white background.

1. Insert a new layer.

2. Place a second instance of your graphic symbol on the stage at frame 1 in the new layer, and again insert keyframes at frame 15 and frame 30.

3. At keyframe 15, select the new symbol and open the Color drop-down menu in the Properties panel.

4. This time, select Tint from the drop-down menu.

   Unlike the Alpha effect, Tint has a percentage value and RGB values. With Tint, you place an opaque layer of color on top of the object's existing color. The parameters of the Tint effect control the color used and its opacity.

5. Set the Tint's opacity value to 100% and choose white from the Tint Color box.

   When you choose white, the RGB values are all set to equal 255, indicating that all the constituent colors of (electronic) white are present at full strength. Each of the three R, G, and B boxes has their own slider, which lets you control the amount of each base color in the tint color. If you prefer to use Hex values to select your colors, open the palette and type in the appropriate value in the Hex fields.

By setting your values to 100% and white, you're telling Flash to place an overlay of completely opaque pure white over the symbol:

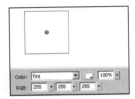

6. Add motion tweens from frames 1 to 15, and from frames 15 to 30.

7. Play the movie.

Again, you'll see the object fade in and out just as before, but this time the mechanism underlying this effect is different. The alpha effect literally makes the object disappear by decreasing its opacity and making it transparent, whereas the tint effect changes the color of the object itself. The great thing about alpha fades is that you don't have to make sure the color of your object changes to match the background—the background color shows through naturally. However, the trade off is that this process is more CPU intensive—it's harder for computers to process, and it's a bit slower. Using tint is a little more involved because you need to alter the color settings, which can be complicated if you have multi-colored objects and backgrounds.

Alpha is the easy way to fade, but tint also allows you to change the colors of your objects during your animation.

Color change animations

Let's look at how to change the color of an object during a motion tween.

In this example, you'll move an object across the stage and change its color as it moves.

1. In a new Flash document, create some text to apply the color effect to (check in the Properties panel that you are typing Static Text). You can use any font, but a large blocky sans serif font (we used Arial Black at 48 points) best illustrates the effect. Use black for the text color:

2. Select the text and convert it into a graphic symbol. Remember, only symbols (movie clips, buttons, and graphics) and grouped objects can be motion-tweened.

3. Place the symbol on the stage at frame 1 (if it isn't already there) and create three more keyframes at frames 10, 20, and 30.

4. At keyframe 10, select the symbol and open the Color drop-down menu in the Properties panel.

5. Select Tint from the Color drop-down menu and change the tint amount to 100%. Then use the color selection palette to change the color to red.

6. Repeat this procedure at keyframe 20 but select green as the tint, and again at keyframe 30, this time selecting blue as the color. Now your text should be red at keyframe 10, green at keyframe 20, and blue

at keyframe 30. If you test the movie now, you'd see it change color in jumps.

7. Add three motion tweens to the timeline between frames 1 and 10, 10 and 20, and 20 and 30:

8. Now if you test your movie you should see your text undergo a chameleon-like color-change.

Experiment with clicking each of the keyframes in succession and dragging each particular instance to a different position on the stage. (Doing this with onion skinning turned on will give you some groovy psychedelic effects). If you do this and then play the movie, you can see that the tint (and alpha) effects can be combined with actual motion around the stage.

There's something else of real significance here: although you had only one instance of the graphic symbol containing your text on the stage, you were able to change its color in three different keyframes, using the Tint option on the Color drop-down menu of the Properties panel. What's more, you were able to drag each of the different colored versions of the text around on the stage independently. You can do this because each different colored version of the text in the different keyframes is effectively treated as a separate instance of the graphic symbol. That is, all the instances have the original symbol as their base, but each instance has properties you can change independently of the underlying symbol.

You've already seen how you can change the tint and alpha of an individual instance, but you can also scale, skew, and rotate instances—all without affecting the underlying symbol. However, if you edit the underlying symbol in Edit Symbols mode, these changes will ripple through to all the instances although any instance properties you've set (tint, alpha, etc.) will be retained:

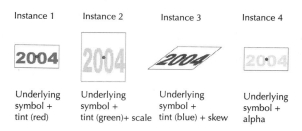

Instance 1	Instance 2	Instance 3	Instance 4
Underlying symbol + tint (red)	Underlying symbol + tint (green)+ scale	Underlying symbol + tint (blue) + skew	Underlying symbol + alpha

This facility gives you a tremendous amount of flexibility and power in the way that you use symbols.

You can now make your objects grow, shrink, spin round, speed up, slow down, disappear, and change color—but they're still moving in straight lines. You can also get your objects to move in complex patterns like curves, loops, and zigzags. To add these features to your animation, you need to learn to use **motion guides**.

Motion guides

A motion guide is a path you draw for an object to follow during a motion tween. The motion guide is invisible outside of the authoring environment, and it sits on a special layer underneath the object you're tweening. Let's create a motion guide and see how it works.

Using motion guides

In this exercise, you animate the boat you created in Chapter 2 and add a flying fish animated on a motion guide.

1. Check that the snap feature is on by selecting the View ➤ Snapping ➤ Snap to Objects menu option and making sure that the option is checked. You want your drawn object to snap crisply to an underlying motion guide.

2. Open the boat.fla file from Chapter 2. Let's animate the boat first.

3. Select all the boat graphics (including the text)—hide or lock all the other layers if necessary—and use *F8* or Modify ➤ Convert to Symbol to turn it into a graphic symbol. Give it a central registration point.

   You might have noticed that your boat symbol instance is on the text layer. This is because it was the highest layer in the order of the boat's selected components. Because the layer name text is a little counterintuitive, let's rename it.

4. Double-click the text layer name and rename it boat instance.

5. On the boat instance layer, insert keyframes at frames 10 and 20:

6. On frame 10 of the boat instance layer, move the boat down the stage about 10 pixels.

7. Use the Tween drop-down in the Properties panel to set a motion tween between frames 1–10 and 11–20:

8. Test the movie to watch the boat gently sway on the water. Pretty idyllic, but something is missing—the waves need motion.

9. Select the waves and convert them to a graphic symbol with a central registration point.

10. As with the boat instance layer, insert keyframes on frames 10 and 20.

11. On frame 10, shift the waves about 10 pixels to their left. This will create a gentle lapping movement.

12. Insert motion tweening between frames 1–10 and 11–20 as before, and test the movie. Ahoy there, matey! Don't get seasick! Now it's time to add the flying fish.

13. Use Insert ➤ New Symbol to create a new Graphic symbol called fish.

14. In the new symbol, draw a small fish:

15. Once you are happy with your little fishy, return to the main stage and create a new layer called fishy above the boat instance layer and beneath the waves layer:

16. Drag a copy of the fish symbol onto the fishy layer.

17. Lock the boat instance and the waves layers to prevent them from accidentally being modified.

18. Click the waves layer's Show Outline button to allow you to easily work behind it:

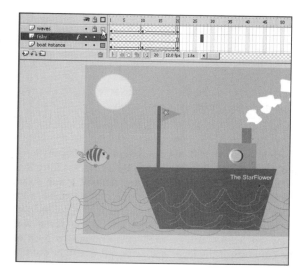

Now you are ready to animate the fish.

19. Select the fish and position it at the left side of the stage beneath the wave.

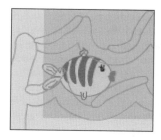

20. Insert a keyframe on frame 20 of the fishy layer.

21. On the second keyframe, place the fish at the right side of the stage:

22. Add a motion tween between the two keyframes. If you now run the movie, you'll notice that the fish is currently hidden beneath the waves. You need to make it jump! This is where the motion guide comes in.

23. Select the fishy layer and use the Insert ➤ Timeline ➤ Motion Guide menu option to create a **guide** layer. Alternatively, you can click the Add Motion Guide button below the layers:

The motion guide layer will automatically appear above the current layer, and it will inherit the name of the layer that it's a guide for, prefixing this with the word "Guide" and a tiny icon of a bouncing ball—the signifier for a guide layer:

The motion guide has its own layer, and it's on this layer that you will draw the **motion path** that you want your object to follow. **A motion path is simply a drawn line**.

24. Click the guide layer to select it, and then use the Pencil tool to draw the path that you want your object to follow. Draw the path at the location on the stage where the action will take place—you can always move it later if you want.

The motion path itself can be any length or shape you like: up, down, side to side, zigzag, curves, loops—just so long as it's a continuous line with no gaps. You don't have to use the Pencil tool—the Line tool, Pen tool, Brush tool, and even unfilled rectangles and circles can all act as motion guide shapes. The important thing is that you have a line on the guide layer.

25. Use the Pencil tool to draw a guide line from the far left of the stage to the far right. Include a couple of peaks at either side of the boat.

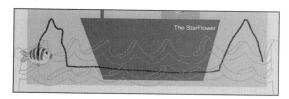

We used a black stroke at a thickness of 3 in this screenshot so you can see the guide clearly. Remember, you don't need to worry about the color of the path because it will not be seen in the final movie. Also, you can treat the line just like any other object: you can resize it, trim it, skew it, and so forth once you've selected it on the guide layer.

Now for the exciting part: making the object travel along the motion guide. To do this, you need to snap the object to the start and end points of the motion path—that's why you've got two keyframes: one for where the guided motion tween will start, and one at the end of the action.

26. Lock the guide layer so that you don't accidentally click the guide line.

27. On the first keyframe on the fishy layer, select the fish and move it to the start of the guide line. Once it snaps to it, release it. This is why you ensured that View ➤ Snapping ➤ Snap to Objects was switched on.

28. On frame 20, the second keyframe, pick up the fish and snap it to the end of the line.

29. Drag the playhead along the timeline to view the motion. Finally, select Control ➤ Test Movie to watch your flying fish attack! Our version is downloadable as boat_animated.fla.

30. Although motion guides are fairly simple to create, getting the object to snap correctly to the guide

takes time to get used to and not getting the object snapped properly is a common problem. So practice and don't get discouraged.

> *The motion guide must be the same length as the timeline for the object being guided.*

Keep in mind that if the animation is 30 frames long, the guide layer's timeline has to be 30 frames long too. In this exercise, you inserted a keyframe at frame 30 on the object layer and then added the motion guide layer. Flash automatically added 30 frames to the guide layer to match the fishy layer that the guide layer was spawned from. Flash is intelligent enough to look at the contents of the layer and work out where to put the keyframes in the guide layer—provided that you decide how long the actual animation will take and mark its boundaries first.

Adding keyframes to the fishy layer after creating the motion guide will alter the length of the animation. For example, if you create a new movie and draw an object on the stage in the default keyframe at frame 1, and then immediately add a motion guide layer, the guide layer will only be 1 frame long. If you added a keyframe at frame 30 on the object layer, that layer would be 30 frames long but the motion guide would remain a measly 1 frame long. The resulting problem is that the motion guide itself will not exist in frame 30!

You can get around this problem by adding frames to the guide layer, but it's much easier to plan things out, create the animation layer, and then let Flash create an appropriate guide layer when you ask it to.

> *Motion path effects can produce some really wild results, especially when combined with the other effects discussed earlier in the chapter. Once you've got the basic idea down, experiment with different color combinations, timeline lengths, and motion paths. The possibilities are endless.*

Case study

Now that you have your basic interface, you're going to add a little motion to spruce up the website when it first appears. You'll do this with a couple of simple motion tweens.

Animating an intro

The animation will be performed in the Content movie clip that you created in Chapter 4. The Content movie clip will contain all your website pages and, as you'll discover here, an intro sequence. The intro sequence will consist of a number of motion tweening text assets and a bouncing dog. The intro sequence will be played as soon as the viewer enters your website.

1. Open your saved case study file from the previous chapter.

2. Locate the Content movie clip on the center of the main stage—it's on the Content layer—and double-click it to enter Edit in Place mode. Editing it this way will allow you to work with the boundaries of the interface area.

As always, you know you are in Edit in Place mode because the rest of the screen is washed out:

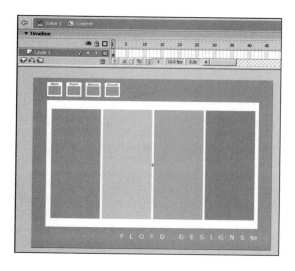

3. Rename the current layer animated rectangles. As mentioned in earlier chapters, it is always good practice to name your layers so they are easy to edit later.

4. Insert two new layers called welcome to text and floyd designs text above colored rectangles. These layers will house some simple text-based motion tweens.

5. On the welcome to text layer, use the Text tool to type Welcome to. Leave **two** spaces between the words. (These extra spaces will allow you to position the text over the white lines between the rectangles.) Use Arial at 24 pt, and don't worry about the text field's position, you'll move it in a moment.

6. Ensure that Snap Align is on (View ➤ Snapping ➤ Snap Align) and drag the Welcome to text to the top-left corner of the left rectangle. When it snaps to the top corner, release it:

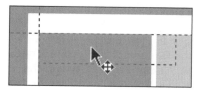

7. With the text still selected, hold down *SHIFT* and press the *DOWN ARROW* key to move the text down 5 pixels. Use the Selection tool to position the text horizontally so that the gap between the words is over the white line.

8. Set the text to the color of the orange rectangle. The best way to do this is to click the Color selector in the Properties panel and move the mouse pointer over the orange rectangle.

When you do this, the mouse pointer changes to the pipette mouse pointer, familiar from the Dropper tool.

Selecting a color this way is a nice shortcut and it saves you from having to use the Dropper tool directly:

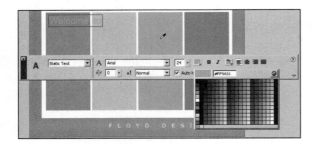

9. Make sure only the text is selected and select Modify ➤ Convert to Symbol. Give it a Graphic symbol behavior, the name welcome to text, and a central registration point.

10. Create a new layer called floyd designs text.

11. On this layer type Floyd Designs (this time use only a single space) in 28 pt Arial, and set its color to the light green of the second rectangle.

12. Position it at the bottom-right corner, 5 pixels from the bottom of the colored rectangles. As with the Welcome to text, ensure that the gap in the words is over the white line in between the two rectangles.

13. Select the Floyd Designs text and convert it to a Graphic symbol called floyd designs text.

The interface should now look like this:

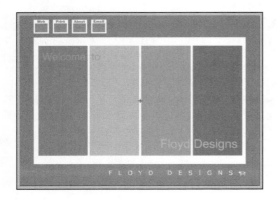

Now it's time to animate the text. Here's what you're going to do: First, the Welcome to text will tween in from off-stage left to its current position. Once it's in position, the Floyd Designs text will alpha tween in from an alpha of 0 percent to 100 percent.

14. Insert a keyframe on frame 15 of the welcome to text layer.

15. Return to the keyframe on frame 1 and move the Welcome to symbol off-stage left. This will be the starting position of the text. Its ending position is already set at frame 15:

16. Select a frame between 1 and 14 and select Motion from the Tween drop-down in the Properties panel.

17. Extend the frames on the animated rectangles layer to frame 15 using *F5*.

18. Test the movie to see the motion. It's all right, but it needs something.... A little alpha tweening action!

19. On the first keyframe, select the off-stage symbol instance and select Alpha from the Color drop-down in the Properties panel.

20. Change the Alpha value to 0% using the slider or by typing it into the text field to the right. This will make the starting instance completely transparent.

21. The Welcome to tween is now complete. Now it's time to tween the Floyd Designs text.

22. Click to select the keyframe on the floyd designs text layer. A rectangle is added to the mouse

pointer, indicating that you can move this keyframe:

23. Drag the keyframe to frame 15 in the timeline. This means that the tween, as the director has ordered, will take place once the Welcome to text is in place.

24. Insert a keyframe at frame 30 of this layer using the *F6* key.

25. Return to the first keyframe (at frame 15) and select the floyd designs text instance.

26. In the Properties panel, select Alpha from the drop-down and set it to 0%.

27. Click any frame from 15-29 and set a motion tween using the Properties panel.

28. Before you test it, use *F5* to insert additional frames on the other two layers so that they are all populated up to frame 30. Then test it using Control ➤ Test Movie.

So far, so good…but it's looping insanely! Don't worry about that, you'll fix it in a later chapter.

Animating with a motion guide

In this section, you're going to animate your little mascot, Floyd. He's going to scamper across the screen before settling above the Floyd Designs logo.

1. While still in the Content movie clip, insert a new layer above the others called dog tween.

2. Drag an instance of the dog movie clip to the bottom-left of the stage. Use the Free Transform tool to scale it until it is about the same height as the Floyd Designs text.

3. Select the keyframe on the new dog tween layer and drag it to frame 25. This animation will take place just before the end of the Floyd Designs tweening.

4. Insert a new keyframe at frame 65. This gives your dog a full 40 frames to sprint across the stage.

5. On keyframe 65, drag the instance of the dog to the bottom-right of the far right colored triangle.

6. Insert a motion tween between frames 25 and 64. This will make your dog travel in a straight line from one point to the next. Now for the guide.

7. Select the dog tween layer and click the Add Motion Guide button below the timeline:

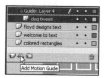

8. On the guide layer, use the Pencil tool to draw a squiggly line from the bottom left to just above the Floyd Designs text. Give Floyd the dog a little jump just before he reaches the text.

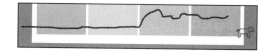

As before, we used a thick dark stroke here to make it easy for you to see.

9. Ensure that View ➤ Snapping ➤ Snap to Objects is on, and snap the dog to the end of the line on both keyframes.

10. Extend the frames on all the other layers to frame 65 using *F5*, and run the movie. If Floyd runs in a straight line, he isn't snapped properly. Go back and retry! When it's correct, you'll add the final touch.

Motion tween scaling for effect

Now you're going to scale and alpha some text to create a dramatic effect.

1. Still inside the Content movie clip, insert a new layer at the top called floyd designs grow.

2. Select the floyd designs text instance on frame 30 of the layer of the same name and copy it (Edit ➤ Copy or *Ctrl+C*).

3. Insert a blank keyframe (*F7*) on frame 65 of the floyd designs grow layer.

4. Use Edit ➤ Paste in Place (or *Ctrl+Shift+V*) to paste a copy of the floyd designs text in exactly the same spot.

5. Insert a keyframe (*F6*) on frame 75 of the same layer.

6. On this keyframe, select the text instance and open the Transform panel (Window ➤ Design Panels ➤ Transform or *Ctrl+T*).

7. In this panel, ensure that Constrain is checked, and type 150% into either of the boxes at the top.

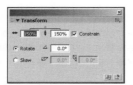

This will scale your instance to 150 percent of its original size.

8. With the instance still selected, change the Alpha value to 0% using the Color drop-down in the Properties panel. The text will now grow and disappear at the same time.

9. Select a frame from 65 to 74 and set a Motion tween.

10. Extend all the frames on the other layers to frame 75 using *F5*.

Your timeline and stage should look like this:

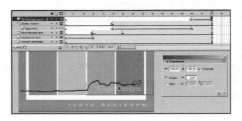

Run the animation to see the overall effect. A nice little intro for your website!

11. Save your case study movie and close it. You'll find the current version of the case study, case_study_ch6.fla, in the downloadable files for this book.

Summary

You've travelled quite a distance in this chapter, passing through the varied landscape of motion tweening.

In this chapter, you saw that:

- You can use **Motion tweening** to move objects around the stage, and you can use **motion paths** to guide the objects and **onion skins** to see multiple frames in the animation.

- You can alter objects as they move. You can **fade** them into the background, change their **tint**, and scale and rotate them.

- You can simulate **acceleration** and **deceleration** for more convincing animation using **easing**.

In the next chapter, you're going to have some fun with motion tweening's sibling: **shape tweening**.

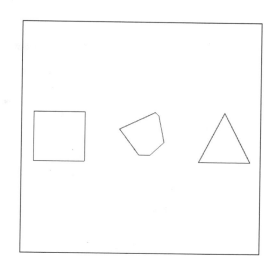

Chapter 7

SHAPE TWEENING

What we'll cover in this chapter:

- Using **shape tweening** to morph shapes into something new, rich, and strange
- **Morphing text** into shapes and vice-versa
- Using **shape hints** to overwrite Flash's default shape tweening behavior

Now that you've seen what motion tweening can do and you understand the power of Macromedia Flash as an animation workhorse, it's time to climb to the next rung on the ladder. So far, you can move a shape around the stage, but it is still the same shape at the end of the animation. By the close of this chapter, you'll be able to start the race with a tortoise and finish it with a hare, though Darwinians might not be too happy with what happens in between.

Shape tweens

Shape tweening is similar in concept to its motion tween counterpart and it's just as easy, but the results are often more impressive.

The basic idea is that at point A in time you have one object, and at a later point B you have another object. Between the two points, you have a gradual shape-shifting transformation from object A to object B. Like this, for example:

You already encountered shape tweening in the first chapter when you made a mushroom grow, and in this chapter you expand and add detail to that knowledge, fleshing out the whys and hows of shape tweening.

How shape tweens work

Shape tweens work just like motion tweens in the sense that you provide a starting point in one keyframe and an ending point in another, and Flash fills the intervening frames. And like motion tweens, it's advisable to have only one shape tween at any time on a layer—this way, you get more predictable results and less mayhem on the stage. Of course, if you want to shape tween multiple objects into one object at the same time, the objects will have to be on the same layer. It's really a question of necessity: If you need your tweens to interact with each other, they have to

be on the same layer, but if they don't interact, keep them on separate layers.

The most important thing to remember when creating shape tweens is that unlike motion tweens, shape tweens must involve **shapes** and not groups or symbols. For a shape tween to work, the basic attributes—the stroke and fill—must be able to change so that it can morph the original shape into something else. The simplest way to ensure that all the elements you want to shape tween are "shape tweenable" is to select all the objects and use the Modify ➤ Break Apart menu option to ensure they're broken down into their constituent elements.

Let's play.

Squaring the circle

First, you set up a basic shape tween and then play with it to understand the finer points of tweening. The simplest objects in Flash are squares and circles, so you use these in your first example.

1. Create a new Flash document, and draw a circle with a black line and fill in frame 1.

2. Click frame 15, and press *F6* to insert a keyframe. You now have 15 frames full of nothing but a circle.

3. In the keyframe at frame 15, draw a large, filled square (again with a black line and fill) over the top of the circle:

4. If you want to position the square more...*squarely* over the circle once you've drawn it, don't forget you can always turn on the Onion Skinning and View layer as outlines options in the Layer Properties window. You can bring up the Layer Properties window by right-clicking the layer name in the timeline and selecting Properties from the context-sensitive menu.

Now you have your beginning and end keyframes, so all you need to do is tell Flash to morph from one shape to the other over time by putting a shape tween between the two keyframes.

5. Click the timeline anywhere between the two keyframes, open the Properties panel, and select Shape from the Tween drop-down menu:

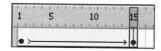

6. Select the Selection tool, and then click a blank part of the timeline to deselect your other frames. You can see that the frames are colored pale green and have a solid arrow on them:

7. If you click the Onion Skin Outlines button just below the timeline and arrange the onion skin markers to encompass all 15 frames, you'll see a rather beautiful rendering of the shape tween:

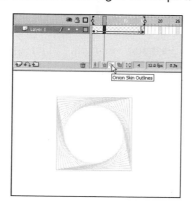

All this indicates that you've got a functional shape tween on your hands.

8. Select Control ➤ Test Movie to preview the movie. The circle transforms smoothly into a square. It's as easy as that.

At the moment, the animation loops back to the beginning when the playhead hits frame 15, meaning that your smoothly morphed square suddenly jumps back to being a circle again in a fraction of a second. Ugly. To correct this, you need to create some extra frames that will facilitate the smooth return of the square back to the circular starting image—this will make the animation loop much smoother.

9. Close the movie preview window and deselect the Onion Skin Outlines button for now.

10. Click frame 1; your circle should automatically be selected for you. Then choose Edit ➤ Copy (*CTRL*+C), and click frame 30.

11. Press *F7* to insert a blank keyframe. It's important that it's blank because you don't want this frame to inherit the image of the square from the previous keyframe.

12. Use Edit ➤ Paste in Place to put the copied circle in exactly the same place in frame 30 as it is in frame 1.

13. Click between frames 15 and 30 on the timeline to select them, and use the Properties panel to create a **shape** tween:

Now when you select Control ➤ Test Movie to preview your movie, you'll see a smooth transition from circle to square and back to a circle again. It's strangely mesmerizing to just sit and watch this simple shape beating out its regular morphing rhythm, but if you're going to get any further you'll just have to close that preview window and return to the Flash interface.

14. Click the keyframe in frame 15, and drag your square a little way off to the side. Preview your movie, and you'll see the circle move as it tweens into the square, and then move back as it returns to being a circle.

But if you can get motion effects on a shape using a *shape* tween, what's the point of a *motion* tween? The simple answer is computing power—it takes more power to perform a shape tween than it does to perform a motion tween. Running a lot of shape tweens will noticeably slow down the computer but the same number of motion tweens will run a lot smoother. Don't forget that you can have only one type of tween in the same frame on the same layer; you can't combine them. It's a question of judgment—use motion tweens whenever you're just *moving* an object, and use shape tweens whenever you want an object to change in some way as it moves.

Here's a simple table comparing when to use each type of tween:

Use shape tweens to	Use motion tweens to
Tween shapes into different shapes	Move groups or symbols without altering them
Change the color of objects	Change the transparency of objects as they animate
Move objects while altering them	Make a motion guide available

Now you have the basics of shape tweening under your belt, let's get a little more sophisticated. First you'll use the Free Transform tool to modify your shapes, and then you'll create some text-based tweens.

Irregular shapes

The Free Transform tool is essential for creating organic amorphous shape tweens. In this exercise, you tween a regular shape into an irregular one.

Here you'll use two more advanced modifiers of the Free Transform tool:

Distort
Envelope

Tweening shapes

This animation will start with a regular circle, and transmogrify into something that's really quite indescribable (in a good way, of course).

1. Open a new Flash document.
2. Change the frame rate of the movie to 30 fps in the Document Properties window (Modify ➤ Document).
3. Ensure that the Properties panel is open (Window ➤ Properties) and then select the Oval tool.
4. In the Oval tool options in the Properties panel, select a black fill color and a red stroke color.
5. Set the stroke thickness to 4:

This will allow you to see the outline tween clearly as well as the fill.

6. Use the Oval tool to draw a fairly big circle on screen.
7. Insert a keyframe on frame 20 of the timeline using *F6*.
8. With the circle still selected, click the Free Transform tool, and choose the Envelope modifier.
9. Drag the points around the shape and change the overall shape of the circle.

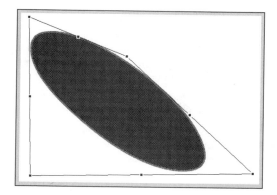

10. Click any frame between 1 and 19 and select Shape from the Tween drop-down menu in the Properties panel:

11. Test the movie to view your first morph. Pretty cool huh? Well, it does get better.

12. Insert a keyframe at frame 40.

13. Use the Distort modifier on the shape on frame 40 to create a new version of the shape. Don't try to mimic our shape, just go with the flow and experiment:

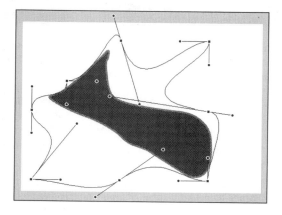

14. Select a keyframe between 20 and 39, and select Shape from the Tween drop-down menu. If you tested the movie now, it might show your fantastic manipulations, but it wouldn't quite create a breathing organism. To make this happen, you need to make the animation loop.

15. Select all the frames and choose Edit ➤ Timeline ➤ Copy Frames.

16. Insert a blank keyframe using *F7* on frame 41.

17. Paste the frames into the new keyframe using Edit ➤ Timeline ➤ Paste Frames.

18. Select all the frames from 41 to 80, and select Modify ➤ Timeline ➤ Reverse Frames. This will alter the direction of the animation, creating a loop of animation.

19. Test the movie using *CTRL+ENTER*. Your shape has an organic breathing motion. Using the Free Transform modifiers is essential for morphs and globular animation through shape tweens. The key to using these modifiers confidently is plenty of experimentation.

After that quick blast of amoeba-creation, let's look at a more common use for shape tweening text.

Common tweening text effects

In the following exercises, you tween pieces of text so they are transformed into different pieces of text, and then you morph shapes into text.

The main thing to bear in mind when working with text is that to be able to tween it, you must first break it apart to convert it into a graphic. This means that you can no longer edit it as if it were a text field, so ensure that the text is *exactly* how you want it to be before you break it apart.

First, the text-to-text tween.

Text to text tweening

This animation starts with one word and uses shape tweening to change it into a different word.

1. Create a new Flash document, and in frame 1, use the Text tool in conjunction with the Properties panel to write a big chunky This is my first, on the left side of the stage:

This is my first

We used Arial Black at 35 point.

2. Select frame 30 and create a new keyframe (*F6*).

3. Still on frame 30, highlight the text with the Text tool, delete it, and then type text 2 text tween… into the text field and move it to the right-hand side of the stage:

text 2 text tween…

4. Use the Selection tool to select the text field that that you just created (*don't* select the text by dragging while still inside the box), and use the Modify ➤ Break Apart menu option to break the text into separate letters:

Flash breaks the original text field into several smaller text fields—not exactly how you need it to be. It's worth remembering that Flash does this because it can be very useful for creating interesting text effects. Each letter is contained in its own text field, so each letter can be changed or moved individually.

5. Make sure you have all the text boxes and letters selected and select Modify ➤ Break Apart again to break them into graphics.

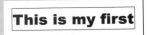

6. Do the same thing to the text in frame 1, remembering to break the text apart twice.

7. Click between the two keyframes on the timeline, and use the Properties panel to create a shape tween.

8. Preview your movie to see the first words morph into the second while moving across the stage.

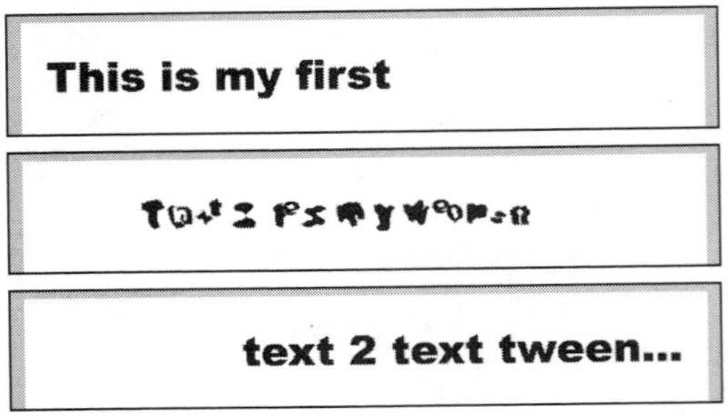

This is my first

ᛏᛟᛞᛏ ᛉ ᚠᛉᛒ�

text 2 text tween…

We said earlier that shape tweens would only work on shapes that have been reduced to their constituent lines and fills. If you've already created a symbol for your movie and you want to animate it, you can, providing that you first break it apart. Let's see how this works.

Shape to text tweening

In this example, you reproduce the shape to text tween we showed you at the start of the chapter—five squares morphing into the word Flash.

1. Open a new movie and draw a strokeless black square on the stage—make the square about three quarters of an inch (2 cm/60 pixels) across.

2. Convert your square to a graphic symbol called Square.

3. Drag four more instances of your square from the Library to make a total of five—one for each letter in the name of the world's greatest piece of software.

4. Align the squares neatly using Snap Align (switched on at View ➤ Snapping ➤ Snap Align) or the Align

panel (Window ➤ Design Panels ➤ Align). Either way, make sure that the squares are a small distance apart.

5. Use the Modify ➤ Break Apart menu option to convert your squares into their component fills.

6. Insert a keyframe in frame 20. This keyframe will inherit the broken-apart squares from the first keyframe.

Now you want to create the letters that spell out the word Flash—one letter to fit in each square.

There are two ways to fit the letters over the squares. The most precise way is to type the word as it is, break the one text field apart into five smaller text fields, position each individual text field correctly, and then break them all apart again. Phew. Another method is to write the word as one piece of text, and then modify its size and spacing to fit over the squares. Because you're using a simple tween, you can get away with using the second method. If you were designing a more complicated tween, it would probably be better to treat each letter individually.

7. Use the Text tool to write FLASH on the stage. Choose a text color that contrasts nicely with black.

8. Select the text field with the Selection tool and move it so that it's over of the squares, on the left side:

9. Use the Selection tool to select the text field again, and then use the Character Spacing slider in the Properties panel to adjust the text spacing so that the letters are positioned over the black boxes. The Character Spacing slider is directly below the Font menu (the one on the left with 40 in it in the screenshot):

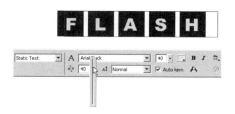

Don't worry about getting things too precise: just so long as the letters are roughly in the right place, things will be OK.

10. Click away from the text field to deselect it.

11. Still on frame 20, double-click each of the black boxes behind the letters and delete them:

12. This will leave you with just the word FLASH on the stage.

13. Now that the boxes are out of the way and you can see clearly, highlight the text and change its color to black.

You're finished working with the text *as text* now, and it's time to break it up.

14. Select the text with the Selection tool and use the Modify ➤ Break Apart menu option twice to convert it to a graphic. If you don't perform this action twice, your text will still be in text fields.

15. Everything is ready for tweening, so click between the keyframes on the timeline and use the Properties panel to add a shape tween. Your tween should now work perfectly when you preview your movie.

If some of the animations look a little odd to you—like the way that the A square transforms into the A—don't worry; you'll learn ways to tweak these little gremlins later in the chapter.

First though, you look at ways of making your shape tweened animations more enjoyable for your viewers. For the most control here, you really need to use some of the ActionScript that we don't cover until later in the book, but here are a few simple methods you can use right away.

Natural looking tweens

Whether you move a morphing object across the stage or keep it stationary as it changes from shape to shape, there's one slight drawback to using only two keyframes: the object immediately begins to tween in frame 1. This can be a problem. For instance, with a text tween, the user usually needs to see what the text says before it starts to change into the next word or shape.

In our previous example, the text was whole only in the final keyframe, which means that it was perfectly readable for only 1/12 of a second—not long enough for the average person to read. The way to change this is to add a "buffer zone" of frames that contain the tween-free text to the beginning or end of the tween. The static images in these frames will mean that Flash appears to pause over the static text.

Creating a more subtle shape tween

In the same example from the previous exercise, you make one small change before adding the buffer zone—you make it go backward.

1. Click the layer name in the timeline to highlight everything that's on that layer:

2. Use the Modify ➤ Timeline ➤ Reverse Frames menu option to reverse the order of the selected frames. Your movie starts with the word FLASH, and then tweens into the five squares. We've done this to make the changes that you're about to apply stand out more clearly.

3. Select all the frames again, but this time drag them across the timeline until the last frame is in frame 30, and then release them:

Notice that as you drag, a little rectangle is added to the mouse pointer indicating that you are dealing with a selection of frames. There will be ten empty frames at the beginning of your movie. Your animation will start at frame 11 and run through to frame 30:

4. Click the first keyframe of your movie (now in frame 11) to automatically select all the text that's in it.

5. Copy the text to your computer's clipboard by using Edit ➤ Copy (CTRL+C).

6. Click frame 1, and use the Edit ➤ Paste in Place menu option to paste your text into the frame in the exact position as it was in frame 11.

7. Preview your movie. The text will stay on screen for about a second, and then tween into the five squares. It's now easier to read the text before it starts to change into the shapes. Obviously, if you had more text, you'd want to have a longer buffer zone to allow people more time to read it.

Now that we have covered different shape tweens, let's spice things up a bit by looking at **changing color** while tweening.

Tweens with color

You used the Tint feature in motion tweens, and now you will add color to your shape tweens. In the previous chapter, you made text fade through different colors by using the Tint effect, and in the following example you expand your FLASH text animation to include color.

Coloring your shape tweens

1. Still using the movie from the last example, click the layer name again to select all the movie's frames.

2. Drag them so that the final frame is now at frame 50.

3. Click your first keyframe (now in frame 21) to select all the text, and Edit ➤ Copy it to the clipboard.

4. Click frame 1 of your movie, and use Edit ➤ Paste in Place to put the copied text on the stage:

5. Move the playhead to frame 10 and use *F7* to insert a blank keyframe. Then paste your text in place on this keyframe in the same way you did for frame 1.

You now have your basic structure set up and are ready to tween. The only thing left to add now is color.

6. Click back in frame 1, select the text shapes on the stage, and change the color in your fill color box to red. The text on your stage will change to reflect this.

7. Do the same for the keyframes in frames 10 and 21, but use the colors green and blue respectively.

8. Create shape tweens between all the keyframes to make your timeline a lean green tweening machine:

9. Preview your movie to see your text waltz through the spectrum before settling for black and tweening into the five squares.

10. As an added touch to show the power of Flash, click frame 50 to select your squares and change the fill color to yellow. When you preview your movie now you see the final animation changing shape and color at the same time.

So how do you get even tighter control? With **shape tween modifiers**, of course!

Shape tween modifiers

As with many other elements in Flash's expansive toolkit, shape morphing has modifiers and helpers that you can use to tweak your tween. The place to look, as always, is the Properties panel, in the Ease and Blend fields:

In shape tweens, **easing** acts exactly the same way as it does with motion tweens—it controls Flash's ability to speed up and slow down the action at the beginning or end of your animations. Here's a quick reminder on the effects of easing:

- **Easing In** to a value of **–100** makes the shape tween start slowly and **accelerate** as it progresses towards the end of the tween.

- **Easing Out** to a value of **100** makes the shape tween start quickly and **slow down** as it progresses to the end of the tween.

Unlike motion tweens, shape tweens also offer the option of playing around with the sharpness of lines in your tween—the values for this are set in the **Blend** drop-down menu.

- A **Distributive** shape tween creates an animation where the intermediate stages of the tween are smooth and irregular with no straight lines.

- An **Angular** shape tween creates an animation where the intermediate stages of the tween *preserve* corners and straight lines.

An **Angular** blend is used to shape tween shapes that have straight lines and corners, but if the shape has no corners, Flash will revert to a **Distributive** blend.

Now that you know how to create and work with basic shape tweens, you'll get those promised tweaking methods that'll bring them that little bit closer to perfection.

One of the best enhancers available to you is the **shape hints** feature.

Shape hints

Shape hints are used with shape tweening to give you a higher degree of control in the morphing process. To apply shape hints, you must select a frame that has

187

shape tweening already set on it. If it doesn't have shape tweening attached, Flash won't allow you to add hints.

When you create a shape tween, Flash automatically takes the "easiest" route to turn one shape into another, but that route doesn't always give the precise visual effect you're after. This is where shape hints come in. You can step in and override Flash's default tweening and finesse things to your taste. Shape hints can be a little complicated to implement in a complex movie, and they can give some spectacularly strange results when they go wrong, but with practice you can get a beautiful tween every time.

There's one other factor to note: shape hints demand a lot more processing power than straightforward tweening. If you can get away with not using them, it's best to avoid them rather than risk your movie slowing down when running on less powerful computers.

Shape hints work by highlighting particular points on a shape, and telling Flash explicitly where those points should move to on a subsequent frame after a motion tween. Suppose you created a movie that had a square in frame 1 and a triangle in the same location in frame 15, and you wanted to shape tween one into the other:

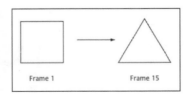

Frame 1   Frame 15

If you get Flash to make the tween, it does something slightly counter-intuitive: instead of pulling the top-left and top-right corners of the square into the middle to from the point of the triangle, it twists the square through some weird contortions to perform the tween—as shown in this sequence:

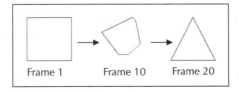

Frame 1   Frame 10   Frame 20

Using shape hints, you can force Flash to pull the two top corners of the square into the center, giving you a slightly more intuitive tween:

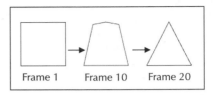

Frame 1   Frame 10   Frame 20

You mark the specific points that you want to "steer" in your initial shape, and you mark where you want them to end up in your final shape:

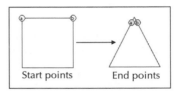

Start points   End points

Each hint is represented by a different letter so you know which matches up with which. The only drawback to this is that you can only have a maximum of 26 shape hints, but that should be plenty. If you need more, you should consider splitting your animation up onto different layers because it is probably too complicated anyway. Let's see this in action.

Using shape hints to control your tween

1. Start a Flash document, and draw a big yellow rectangle with a black outline on the stage. Use similar proportions to our rectangle here:

2. Use the Line tool to draw two lines forming a triangle on one side of the image, and fill it with the same yellow color:

3. Select the part of the line that acts as the base of the triangle where it meets the rectangle, and delete it, leaving a shape like this:

4. Draw a small blue circle inside the rectangle on the right side, just above the triangle:

This is the eye of your (admittedly basic) face.

5. Click frame 30 and press *F6* to insert a keyframe.

You're going to make an animation of the face turning from looking to the right to looking to the left, with the face looking straight at you in the middle of the tween. The first thing you need to do is make the image in the final frame look in the opposite direction.

6. In the new keyframe at frame 30, use the Modify ➤ Transform ➤ Flip Horizontal menu option to turn it around.

7. Insert a shape tween between the two keyframes and preview your movie in all its glory.

Of course, because this exercise is about fixing tweens that go wrong, you probably guessed something like this was going to happen. So now you have to go about fixing the tween.

8. Click the first keyframe, and use the Modify ➤ Shape ➤ Add Shape Hint menu option. A little red circle with an **a** in it will appear like a beauty spot in the middle of the face:

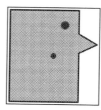

This is the first of your shape hints. Note that it's red at the moment.

Shape hints appear by default in the center of the shape that you are tweening. Remember that the center of the shape is defined by the invisible bounding box around it, and is not always where you might think it should be.

9. It's easier to work with shape hints with snapping turned on, so make sure Snap to Objects is checked in the View ➤ Snapping menu.

10. Click the shape hint and drag it to the top-left corner of the head:

It's still red.

Shape hints work best if you start with the top-left point and then work counter-clockwise around the shape. They can produce some beautiful but unexpected results if you get them in the wrong order.

11. Click the keyframe in frame 30, and you'll find a corresponding **a** shape hint (also red) there. Because you added a shape hint to the start image, Flash assumed that you want one for the end image too. Attach the shape hint in frame 30 to the top right corner of the face.

Notice that when you click away from the shape, the shape hint turns green. This indicates that it's properly attached to the shape and that its corresponding shape hint in the first frame is also attached properly. If you click back on the first frame, you'll see that it turns yellow. This green-yellow signal means that shape hint **a** is locked on and ready to fire.

12. If you preview your movie now, you'll find that it still doesn't look natural. A few more shape hints will sort this out, so go back to your first keyframe and add another **three** shape hints.

If you ever find that Add Shape Hint is not available in the menu, go back to your keyframe and make sure everything on it is selected. Shape hints can only be added when the object that you're tweening is selected. If you ever lose sight of your shape hints, make sure that the View ➤ Show Shape Hints menu option is checked.

When you add those three shape hints in succession, they're all added one on top of the other on the stage. This may seem a bit confusing at first, but you'll soon get used to it. The top hint will be **d** because that is the fourth one you created.

13. Drag the three new shape hints out to the other three corners of the rectangle, working counter-clockwise from the first point:

14. Go to your end keyframe and drag the hints out from their little cluster in the center, but this time, reverse the relative left/right positions of the shape hints. The shape hint that corresponds to the chin of the face in the first frame should still be on the chin in the last frame, but it is on the other side of the stage because the face is turned around. Your finished shape should look like this in the last frame:

15. Preview your movie, and the face should look as if it is turning from right to left. It's still not quite right though because the eye seems to float through an out of body experience before returning to normality in the last frame. Guess what? Time for some more shape hints.

16. Go back to the first frame and add another couple of shape hints. Place the hints on either side of the eye:

17. Go to the last frame and place the hints in the same relative (but horizontally flipped) positions on the final face:

18. If everything worked correctly, your face should turn when you preview your movie. If you want the eye to blink as the tween flows, just add another couple of hints to the eye, one at the top and one at the bottom, the same in both keyframes. The face should now flip perfectly and wink at you cheekily.

To remove shape hints, simply drag them off the stage, just as you would to get rid of a guide. Dragging the hint off the stage in any frame will affect both frames that contain the hints. The alternative method is to delete all the hints at once and start again. This can be achieved via the Modify ➤ Shape ➤ Remove All Hints menu option.

Shape hints can be confusing at first, but it's important to be aware of what they are, what they can do, and how you can use them to add more control to a shape tween. If you're dealing with a complex shape tween and no number of shape hints seems to help, you may want to try adding a "staging post" frame for your animation half way through, and include a keyframe containing an image of what the animation should look like at mid point. You can then add two tweens, one on either side, to link the three keyframes. This makes it a little easier for Flash to follow and should give better results. This is more time consuming, but it may wind up being easier than letting Flash decide how the tween will work, as well as saving you the hassle of adding and positioning multiple shape hints.

Case study

In this section you'll use shape tweens to add transitions for your case study website's pages.

Making the rectangles shape tween

Until now, the colored rectangles in your site interface have done little but glare back at you as you worked on the case study. In this section though, you will make each of them grow individually to cover the content area. The premise is that when a visitor clicks a page, a rectangle grows to fill the screen, and the content for that page is displayed in the newly revealed area.

Let's begin.

1. Open your saved case study document.

2. Double-click the Content movie clip instance to enter Edit in Place mode for that symbol:

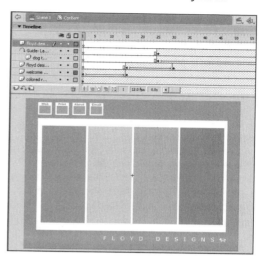

First things first, let's tidy up your scruffy looking layers!

3. Click to select the top layer and insert a new layer folder called intro.

4. Select all the layers except animated rectangles by clicking the top one and *SHIFT*-clicking the bottom one:

5. Drag all the selected layers into the intro layer folder and close it by clicking the small triangle to the left of it. Lock and hide the folder and drag it to the bottom of the layers order. This will put it out of the way for the moment.

6. Click the animated rectangles layer and insert a new layer called frame labels. This will be used to store frame label references to the activity you are about to create.

7. On frame 76 of the frame labels layer, insert a blank keyframe using *F7*.

8. Open the Properties panel (Window ➤ Properties) and click the new blank keyframe.

9. In the Frame label input field of the Properties panel, enter open web:

The reason you enter this as a frame label is quite simple. As we briefly explained earlier, each page has a transition—a shape tween—when it is clicked. The word "open" is used here within the context that each page also closes before the next one opens to create a smooth transition. You enter "web" to signify the name of the page.

> *You'll look at button clicking, frame control, and interactivity in detail in Chapter 9.*

10. Click frame 76 of the animated rectangles layer and press *F6* to insert a new keyframe. This will create a new keyframe with a copy of all the original colored shapes:

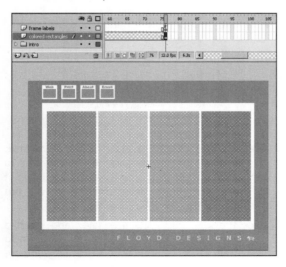

As you might have guessed, you don't need all the rectangles. Each transition consists of a single rectangle growing to fill the screen, and therefore, you only need one for each shape tween. Easy.

Uh. hold on a minute…if only one shape is growing, what happens to the other rectangles? Is the shape growing over the white rectangle alone?

Fear not, you've already taken a precaution for this in an earlier chapter! Remember the copy of the rectangles you left on the main stage? It is perfectly aligned to these shapes, so when each individual shape grows here, the rest of the shapes appear to stay as they are. This will—and you'll have to believe us for the moment—create the illusion of a rectangle growing and squashing the others.

> Before you delete the other rectangles, you need to measure all the rectangles' combined width. This will make sense in a moment!

11. Select all the colored rectangles and make a note of their width in the Properties panel. Write this down—you'll need it a number of times:

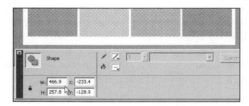

The width will be the combined width of all the rectangles, including the spaces between them.

12. On the keyframe on frame 76 of the animated rectangles layer, select the three rectangles on the right and delete them, leaving only the far left lawn green rectangle:

13. Now it's time to create the shape tween. Insert a new keyframe on frame 91 of the animated rectangles layer.

14. On this keyframe, select the rectangle and set its width to the value you previously noted (or copied) using the Properties panel:

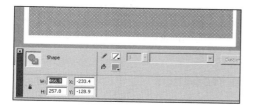

15. Select the rectangle and center it both vertically and horizontally using the Align panel.

16. Once you have the rectangle covering all the colored ones on the main stage, click a frame between 76 and 90 and set a shape tween using the Properties panel.

17. Drag the playhead over the frames to view the open shape tween:

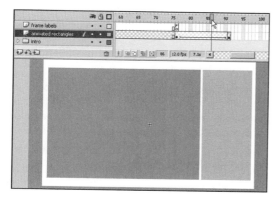

18. Next you'll create the close tween. Do this by copying the existing tween and reversing it. Insert a blank keyframe on frame 92 of the frame labels layer and add the frame label close web.

19. Select all the tween frames from 76–91 on the animated rectangles layer and select Edit ➤ Timeline ➤ Copy Frames.

20. Insert a blank keyframe at frame 92 of the same layer, select it, and choose the Edit ➤ Timeline ➤ Paste Frames menu option.

21. Now to reverse the direction of the frames to produce the close tween. Select all the newly added frames and select Modify ➤ Timeline ➤ Reverse Frames.

The last thing to do is to make the closing tween a little shorter. You are doing this to prevent any of your website users from having to wait too long. A closing tween looks far more professional than only having opening tweens and an immediate snap back on each user click. The opening and closing creates a fluidity.

22. Click to select the last keyframe on the animated rectangles layer, and drag it back to frame 100. This will make it just over half the length of the opening tween.

23. After you do this you'll notice that you have some dotted frames after the keyframe. Select these and delete them with Edit ➤ Timeline ➤ Remove Frames or *SHIFT + F5*.

You now have two transitions for your first page.

24. Before you test the movie, drag the intro layer folder above the others. You do this because the elements in this folder should be above the other layers.

25. Select Control ➤ Test Movie. The intro sequence runs, then your opening sequence plays, followed by your closing sequence.

In the final website, the timeline will halt after the intro and wait for the user to click the buttons, but for now, this will have to do until you know how to program the interactions.

Let's animate the other pages.

26. Insert a blank keyframe on frame 101 of the frame labels layer. Label it open print. This will be the start of your second set of transitions, for the print page.

27. Insert a blank keyframe on frame 101 of the animated rectangles layer. You now need to copy the second rectangle from the one of the previous frames.

28. Click the animated rectangles layer before frame 76 and select the second rectangle from the left. Select Edit ➤ Copy to copy it.

29. Return to the blank keyframe on the animated rectangles layer—frame 101—and use Edit ➤ Paste in Place to paste the copied rectangle in the same position. Now you should be on familiar ground.

30. Insert a keyframe on frame 116 of the animated rectangles layer—15 frames on from the last one.

31. On the new keyframe, as before, make the rectangle cover all four of the rectangles visible from the main stage by using your previous width reading. Once you have it scaled, center it.

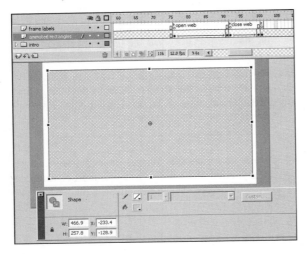

32. Select a frame between the two keyframes and set a shape tween in the Properties panel.

That completes your second "open" tween, now for the closing motion.

33. Insert a blank keyframe on frame 117 of the frame labels layer and label it close print.

34. Select frames 101–116 of the animated rectangles layer, and copy them with Edit ➤ Timeline ➤ Copy Frames.

35. Insert a blank keyframe using F7 on the same layer.

36. Paste the frames on this keyframe using Edit ➤ Timeline ➤ Paste Frames.

37. Select all the frames and reverse them using Modify ➤ Timeline ➤ Reverse Frames.

38. Select the keyframe on frame 132, and move it to frame 124 to shorten the closing tween.

39. Remove the excess frames (from frame 125 onward) by selecting them and choosing Edit ➤ Timeline ➤ Remove Frames (or SHIFT + F5).

40. Test the movie to watch the two sequences. It's certainly starting to come together! Now all that remains to do is to add the final two transitions for the remaining rectangles. Here are the steps for each rectangle.

Open sequence

1. Insert a new blank keyframe on the frame label layer (on the frame following the last keyframe) and name it (use open about first time, and open email the second time).

2. Copy the original rectangle from a frame before 75 on the animated rectangles layer and paste it to a new keyframe on the same layer.

3. Insert a keyframe 15 frames later and resize its width to the value you wrote down earlier.

4. Set a tween between the two keyframes.

Close Sequence

1. Copy the frame sequence, and paste it to a new keyframe following it.

2. Insert a blank keyframe on the frame labels layer (parallel to the last keyframe on the animated rectangles layer) and label the first on close about, and the second one close email.

3. Reverse the pasted frame sequence and shorten it to run for eight frames.

If you follow these steps twice, you should have a timeline something like this (give or take a few frames!):

Once you are done, test the movie, and you might get the feeling that you are being given a psychedelic sliding doors demonstration. Groovy man!

Summary

In this chapter, you took a gentle stroll around the world of shape tweening, thereby adding another tool to your increasingly powerful armory.

In the case study, you added the lion's share of your website's animation. In later chapters, you will control these opening and closing tweens with ActionScript, triggered by button-based interaction.

You saw that:

- **Shape tweening** complements motion tweening. It enables you to morph shapes into other shapes, morph shapes into text, and more.

- Shape tweens operate on **lines and fills** rather than the grouped shapes and symbols that motion tweens act upon.

- Shape tweening can be combined with color changes and movement.

- **Shape hints** give you a fine degree of control over the way a shape tween will work.

In the next chapter, you're going to look at a technique that can add engaging visual effects to your Flash movies, especially when used in conjunction with shape and motion tweens—**masking**.

Chapter 8

MASKS AND MASKING

What we'll cover in this chapter:

■ **Masks** are a powerful feature that allow you to selectively show and hide content. You can create a mask and apply it to a layer so that only content underneath the mask is visible. You'll explore their basic principles and see a range of different examples and applications.

This chapter introduces **masks** in Flash. Masks are used to selectively show and hide content in a Flash movie. Using masks, you can create great effects in your movies: illusions of depth, movement, illumination and more—as you'll see in this chapter.

We think you'll find masks indispensable once you grasp the techniques for using them. Some Flash designers don't seem to embrace the usefulness of masks, possibly because the effects you can create with them are more at home in animation than standard website design. But once you've seen the results that masks help you achieve, we think you may well be a convert.

What is a mask?

Very early in this book, we showed you how layers can be used to simulate depth. If you're animating a character—let's call her Jane Doe—walking across the stage and behind a house, you'd put the house on a layer at the front of the movie, and Jane on a layer behind the house:

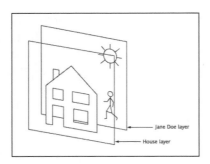

As Jane walks across the area occupied by the house symbol, Flash knows that you want the house to stay in front because of the layer order you assigned. This gives the appearance that Jane has walked behind the house and creates a sense of *depth* in the animation.

Suppose you want to show Jane walking around *inside* the house? That's more difficult, isn't it? You want Jane to be *visible* when she is behind a transparent part of

the house front—the windows—and *invisible* when she is behind an opaque object such as a solid wall:

Part of the front layer is opaque and part of it is transparent. To do this in Flash, you need a mask.

When you create a mask, it's as if you lay a piece of paper over the animation and block it all out. You then cut a hole in the paper and reveal a section of what's underneath. In Jane's case, you need to create a piece of paper shaped like a house, and then cut holes in the paper where the windows and door should be:

Once you've cut out the holes, you can place the mask in front of the background animation of Jane walking across the stage. You can then either move the mask around so that different sections of your animation are revealed or make the objects in the animation pass across the holes, appearing and disappearing as they do.

That's the basic principle of masking in Flash—you just use electronic layers to create your masks, rather than paper and scissors.

When would you need to use a mask in Flash? Here are a few examples:

- When you want to show text scrolling from left to right across a TV screen. You'd only want the text to be visible when it was behind the area corresponding to the *screen*.

- When you want to zoom into an area on a picture and keep the viewable area inside a constant-sized window. As the picture is magnified, you only want to show the zoomed area of the picture and hide all other areas.

- When you want to simulate text being typed on the screen so it appears letter by letter, from left to right.

None of these effects can be created using layers alone. In each case, you want to hide *part* of your object, and that's exactly what a mask will do.

To illustrate masking, let's create an animation based on the first example: text scrolling across a TV screen. You will find the completed FLA of this example in the download section of our website as maskTV.fla.

Putting on your mask

First, you need your TV set.

1. In a new Flash Document, rename the default layer TV.

2. In the default keyframe at frame 1, create your TV by drawing a shape that looks something like this:

3. Create the TV any way you like.

We made our (slightly retro) TV by drawing the basic shape with straight lines. Then we bent the straight lines using the Arrow tool to give the impression that the TV is a freehand drawing, and added the antenna and some chunky control knobs. If you want, you could use the Pen tool and the Subselect tool to create a Bezier-finessed masterpiece—it's really up to you. (Just make sure you end up with a TV that has a screen!)

A tip for drawing things in the cartoon style we've used here is to draw with thick black outlines, like Warner Brothers did in the psychedelic 60s.

4. Use the Paint Bucket tool to fill your drawing with color:

In your movie, you want your text to appear only on the TV's *screen*, so you need to create a mask that will show the text only when its position corresponds to an area inside the boundaries of the screen.

5. Add two new layers above the existing TV layer—Broadcast and Mask:

Mask will be your mask layer, and Broadcast will contain all the objects—the text—that you want to show on the TV screen. The order of the layers *must* be TV, Broadcast, and Mask from bottom to top.

Now for the clever part. Remember that the Mask layer is the piece of paper that you'll use to hide and reveal the underlying Broadcast layer. You're going to cut a hole in your paper that's the same shape as the screen of your TV so that whatever you put on the Broadcast layer will only be visible when it is inside the TV screen.

6. Select the filled screen area of the TV—not the stroke. (You haven't made the TV into a symbol yet; this is so you can select the screen on its own):

7. Copy the screen part into the clipboard with Edit ➤ Copy.

The next thing to do is use this screen shape to create the masked area on the Mask layer.

8. Select the Mask layer and paste the screen in place with Edit ➤ Paste in Place.

9. Hide all the layers except for the Mask layer, and you should just see the pasted screen as shown here:

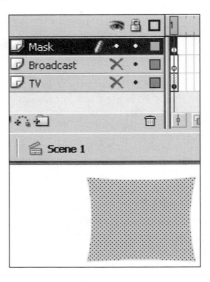

It's a good idea to make your mask areas a striking color so that you can easily differentiate them from other movie content. Using a color that you'd rarely use in your movie designs is a good way to help you make that differentiation. Let's choose a bright pink.

10. Select the Paint Bucket tool and fill the screen shape on the Mask layer with a bright pink:

There is one oddity of Flash masks—they are the inverse of real-life masks. The virtual Flash version of the house mask we talked about earlier has cut-out areas, such as the windows and door. In the current example, you want your virtual card to be in the gap area only—i.e. the screen.

Although it might seem counter-intuitive for a mask to be a solid filled color, trust us. Flash isn't constrained by the same laws of physics that stop light from passing freely through a piece of paper. So long as Flash knows the *shape* of the mask, you can make it any color you like—Flash just ignores the color and sees only the shape.

When this TV screen-shaped mask is being used, you'll be able to see anything on the underlying layer that falls *behind* the pink area, and nothing that's in the areas outside the mask.

11. Lock the Mask layer so that you don't select anything on it by accident, and unhide the TV and Broadcast layers.

12. On the TV layer, select the whole of the TV and convert it into a new graphic symbol called TV Symbol.

13. Lock the TV layer and unlock the Mask layer.

14. Select the screen-shaped mask on the Mask layer and convert it into a graphic symbol. Name it Screen Mask.

When you're working with masks on one layer, it's always a good idea to lock the layer containing the masked objects so that you can't inadvertently select both objects at once.

Now you're going to tell Flash that you want your floating TV screen shape to act as a mask.

15. With the Mask layer selected, choose the Modify ➤ Timeline ➤ Layer Properties menu option and click the Mask radio button in the Layer Properties window:

Mask radio button

16. Leave all the other values as the defaults, and click OK.

You've now converted the Mask layer so that it will act as a mask. Now, all Flash sees on this layer is the screen shape that you want to use as the mask.

Notice that the Mask layer's appearance has changed in the timeline:

The little checkered oval at the left identifies this layer as a mask layer.

Now you have to tell Flash which layer you want the mask to be *applied to*.

17. Select the Broadcast layer and choose the Modify
➤ Timeline ➤ Layer Properties menu option. This
time, select the Masked radio button to designate
the Broadcast layer as the one that you want the
TV screen shape to mask:

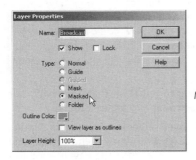

Masked radio button

18. Click OK.

Again, there's been a change with your layers in the
timeline:

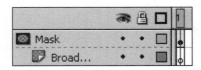

Note that the Broadcast layer now has an indented
icon that looks like a folded sheet of paper, indicating that this layer has a mask applied to it.

19. Unlock the TV layer and your layers should now
look like this:

The checkered oval icon on the Mask layer tells
you that you have created a mask. The indented
checkered icon in the Broadcast layer tells you
that *this* is the layer where you placed your mask.
The Broadcast layer is the one that the screen
shape on the Mask layer will apply to—hiding part
of it from view.

> *It's vital to note that the layer, or layers, that you
> want to be partially hidden must be placed below
> the mask you've created.*

You won't see the effects of the Mask layer yet
because the Broadcast layer currently has nothing
in it. Let's put a message on the TV.

The first thing you need to do is increase the
length of your movie to give you enough time to
read the text that will shimmy across the TV
screen.

20. Increase the movie length so that it lasts for a hundred frames. To do this, click frame 100 in the
Mask layer, and before you release the mouse button, drag the mouse pointer down to select all
three layers. When you release the mouse button,
press *F5* to will create a hundred frames in each
layer:

If you ever want to see more frames in the timeline
(as you can see in the previous screenshot), you
can click the Frame View button at the top right of
the timeline. Clicking the button brings up the
menu you see in the following screenshot. If you
click Small, **Flash will compress the frames that
are displayed horizontally, and you will see a
greater number of frames in the timeline.**

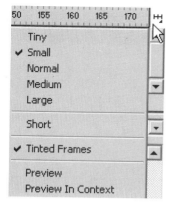

Frame View button

21. Now for the content. In frame 1 of the Broadcast layer, use the Text tool to add the text Stay tuned to this channel... to the right of the TV, and level with the center of the TV screen. We've used a black, 26 point Comic Sans font:

22. Convert the text into a graphic symbol called Text.

Now you'll make the text move across the screen.

23. In the Broadcast layer, add a keyframe in frame 100. With the new keyframe selected, move the text to the left of the TV to establish its end position after it has scrolled across the screen:

24. Click any frame in the middle of your timeline. Then use the Property inspector to add a motion tween between frames 1 and 100 of the Broadcast layer:

25. The last thing to do to make your mask work is to **lock** both the Mask layer and the Broadcast layer:

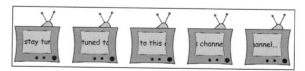

Flash will only show the effects of a mask in the authoring environment when all the affected layers are locked. If you want your masks to work in this way, always lock all affected layers. The mask will work in the final SWF file whether or not you lock them.

26. Press *F12* to preview your movie in a browser.

This is what you will see when you test your movie: the TV with the scrolling text appearing only on the screen where the mask is. With a little extra work, this would make a good loading page for someone's website.

You see how this can be a very powerful technique. The TV screen is a totally non-uniform shape, as is the rest of the TV. Simply by defining the area you want to display using a mask, you are able to achieve the complex effect you want with very little effort. The sequence of steps needs to be maintained, but after a little more practice and experimentation, you'll be turning out masked movies of your own.

Remember that when you create a mask, you have to specify the layer or layers that you want it to act upon. Only the sections of these layers that lie under the cut-out shape(s) you draw on the mask layer will be visible in the finished movie.

Another thing to be aware of is that all the mask effects that you create can be embedded inside movie clips and reused in all sorts of different ways. You can build great little animated masking effects, embed them in movie clips, and then use multiple copies of those movie clips to get all sorts of impressive action on the stage.

OK, you've created a mask and tweened some text across it to good effect. Let's see how to animate the *mask* and how to mask several layers at once.

Animated masks and masking multiple layers

You can also use masks and keep the background stationary while the mask itself is animated, selectively hiding and revealing different parts of your animation. You're going to learn how to do this now. You'll also see how one mask can be used to cover and reveal several layers at once.

Moving the mask

1. Create a new Flash Document.
2. Change the movie's background color to black using the Property inspector.
3. Using the Text tool, add the large bold white text shown here in the center of the stage and rename the layer Text:

4. Add a new layer and name it Spotlight. In this layer, draw a filled white circle that's a little bigger than the height of the text.
5. Convert the circle into a graphic symbol and name it Spot:

6. Make your animation 50 frames long in both layers by clicking, dragging, and pressing *F5* in the same way that you did in the last exercise.
7. Add a keyframe (*F6*) in frame 50 of the Spotlight layer. Your timeline should now look like this:

8. With the new keyframe selected, move your Spot symbol to the far end of the text, after the **u**, and create a motion tween between the two keyframes.

   The circle will now move over the text when you play your movie. Here's a preview of its motion with Onion Skin Outlines turned on:

9. Turn the Spotlight layer into a mask layer as you did earlier via the Modify ➤ Timeline ➤ Layer Properties menu option. Select the Mask radio button from the Layer Properties window for the Spotlight layer, and select the Masked radio button when you repeat the process for the Text layer.
10. Lock both the layers and test the movie—the layers in your timeline should look like this:

	🐦	🔒	🔲	1
Spotlight		•	🔒	◼
Text	✗	•	🔒	◼

There's a problem with the movie at the moment: you see the text revealed by the round shape of the spotlight as it travels along, but the circular shape of the spotlight doesn't really come across. That's because the background is totally black—a real spotlight would illuminate the background as well as the text. Let's remedy that.

What you need to do is make the spotlight illuminate the background slightly. To do this, you'll draw a gray area behind the text on a new layer. This will be lit up in contrast to the text as the spot passes across it.

You must do this exactly as shown; otherwise the Spotlight layer will not act as a mask to the new layer.

11. Select the Text layer and add a new layer. Name your new layer Gray:

You want your Gray layer to be *behind* the text, so you must move it to the bottom of the stack of layers.

12. With Gray still selected, drag the layer to the bottom, under Text. Your timeline should look like this:

Notice that both the layers Gray and Text have the indented icons next to them, signifying that *both* will be masked by Spotlight. Flash has automatically made your Gray layer a masked layer because of its adjacency to the mask layer when you created it.

13. Select Gray and draw a medium gray rectangle that covers the whole area that the circle will travel over. Unlock the Text layer to help you decipher exactly where your rectangle needs to go and how big it should be:

14. Lock all the layers again and test the movie.

You will now see what looks like an illuminated spotlight move from left to right, lighting up the darkness to reveal your text. This screenshot shows a graduated interpretation of the spotlight moving across the text in the movie you just created:

What's actually happening is that your circular "window" is moving across white text on a gray background—but the effect is quite striking. How about adding more keyframes to the mask layer and more motion tweens, creating a sweeping searchlight effect that moves up and down as well as from side to side. Or maybe a motion path that sweeps out in a spiral? Or a spotlight that starts small and grows bigger as the animation continues? Or...

We've only touched on the power of animated masks. The number of effects that you can create with these features in Flash is limited only by your imagination. So practice, practice, practice.

Now let's look at some more text/mask combinations.

Using masks with text

Masks can be used particularly well with text. Text can act as the mask itself, as you'll see later, and masks can simulate the effect of words appearing on the screen as if they were being typed. This is achieved by another method of animating the mask: instead of moving the mask around the stage, you *scale* it to make it grow—revealing more of the layer beneath it as it does so. Let's see how.

Simulating typed text

1. In a new Flash document, rename the default layer Text, and add a new layer above it called Mask. You now need to turn your layers into mask and masked layers, so here's a quick alternative to the Modify ➤ Timeline ➤ Layer Properties menu option method used in your last two exercises.

> *Now that you're getting good at masking, you can save some time by right-clicking (CTRL-clicking on a Mac) the Mask layer and selecting Mask. Much easier!*

2. With the Mask layer selected, right-click that layer and select Mask from the context-sensitive menu that pops up. Mask becomes a mask layer, and Text automatically becomes a masked layer. Note that both layers are locked:

3. Unlock both layers by clicking the topmost lock icon so that you can add some content to them.

4. Change the movie's background color to a hue of your choice, and then add some text in the Text layer:

We've used a pale green on a dark green background—just in case there are any of you out there who are nostalgic for the days of corporate dumb terminals.

5. You want to make the text look as if it's being typed in letter by letter. In the Mask layer, create a long white rectangle that completely covers the text, and then convert it into a graphic symbol with a **center left registration point**. Call the new symbol Mask:

We've given this shape a left registration point because we're going to make the text gradually appear by scaling the white rectangle—a little like a preloader bar. If you scale the rectangle with the registration point in the center, both ends are

going to get shorter or longer because scaling is done relevant to the registration point.

At this point, ensure the rectangle is positioned correctly, covering your text. Make any adjustments to its position until the text is fully obscured by it.

6. Make the movie 50 frames long in both layers and then add a keyframe to the Mask layer at frame **50**:

7. In frame 1 of the Mask layer, shorten the mask using the Free Transform tool and dragging the right side of the rectangle to the left so that it's too short to cover any of the text:

8. Click any of the frames between 1 and 50 and add a motion tween with the Property inspector. This will create an animated mask that slowly reveals more and more text as it gets bigger. Remember that only the text that's *covered* by the mask will show up in the final movie—the rectangle growing is like a cut-out window on paper gradually being torn open to reveal what's underneath.

9. Lock both layers and test your movie. Your text will gradually appear as the mask rectangle scales up out to the right.

Don't worry that the mask will show *parts* of letters: the transition is usually too fast for the viewer to see that it isn't actually typing a word at a time, but revealing the words bit by bit. If it starts to look too obvious when you test the movie, simply shorten the motion tween by ten frames or so by choosing the Edit ➤ Timeline ➤ Remove Frames menu option—making sure that the playhead is not on a keyframe. Alternatively, if you really want to emphasize words as they're created, rather than use a constant wipe, add some extra keyframes along your timeline, stop the motion tween for the desired time, and then pick up the tween again.

Now for another mean text-related masking technique.

A text-shaped mask

One of the easiest ways to create instant masks is to use text as the mask. When using text in this way, it's a good idea to use a simple, heavy, bold, and closely spaced font. Using this kind of font will mean that a larger proportion of the image behind your mask is shown. For this reason, **Impact** is a good choice, as is the **Haettenschweiler** font shown here:

Let's use this meaty-looking font as a mask in a practical example.

Masking with text

In this effect, you'll create a color gradient and mask it using a piece of text.

1. Open a new Flash document and rename the default layer Text.

2. Create a static text field in the center of the stage using a bold thick font, similar in length to this:

We used a black 65-point Haettenschweiler.

3. Create a new layer and call it Gradient. In this new layer, create a filled gradient that's taller and considerably wider than the text—like this:

We used a blue and gold color spectrum gradient, selected from the bottom of the color palette for the Fill color box in the Property inspector.

4. Make sure that the Gradient layer is underneath the Text layer by dragging it in the timeline:

5. You want to motion tween the rectangle, so convert it into a graphic symbol with a central registration point and name it Rectangle.

6. Make Text into a mask layer and Gradient into the layer that's being masked. Remember, the quick way to do this is by right-clicking the mask layer and selecting Mask from the context-sensitive menu.

7. Unlock both layers. Make your animation 50 frames long by clicking, dragging, and pressing *F5* in the now familiar way.

8. At frame 50 in the Gradient layer, add a keyframe. Move the Rectangle graphic symbol in this frame to the left:

9. Select any frame between 1 and 50 on the Gradient layer and add a motion tween from the Property inspector. Your timeline should now look like this:

10. Lock both layers and test your movie. You'll see the text cycle through several colors as the gradient moves past it:

There's an additional cool modification you can make to this effect, and that's to add a *border* to the text. This will improve the effect because, as it stands, the lighter colors in the spectrum can make the outline of the text difficult to see on some screens.

11. Select the Text layer and create a new layer above it. Call the new layer Text Outline.

12. Unlock the Text layer and then copy the text to the Text Outline layer using the Edit ➤ Copy and Edit ➤ Paste in Place menu options.

13. With the text field on the Text Outline layer still selected, break the text apart **twice** with the Modify ➤ Break Apart menu option. Hide the other layers.

14. Select the Ink Bottle tool and change the Stroke Color to black in the Tools panel:

15. Click all the outlines in the text. To do this for the word **spectrum**, you'll have to click the *interior* outlines inside the **p** and the **e**. You might want to zoom in to get a better view while you're using the Ink Bottle tool.

16. With the inner text still selected—*SHIFT*+click each letter to reselect them if they have become unselected—press *DELETE* or go to Edit ➤ Clear to delete filled areas of each letter so you only leave the outline:

17. Test your movie. You'll see the color of your text change again, but this time with a more clearly defined outline:

Notice that the Text Outline layer does not need to be locked for the mask effect to be seen, as it is not masking anything or being masked.

A really cool variant of this is to use a bitmap instead of a gradient. In a similar way to the computer typing you simulated earlier, you can even use a bitmap to gradually fill your mask and reveal your text. Here's how.

Filling your text with an image

You're now going to use a bitmap image called `sky-line.bmp` to slowly fill a text mask. This image is included in the downloadable files from our website—or you can use any image of your own choice, of course.

1. Set up a new Flash document. Rename the default layer Image and add a second layer called Text just above it.

2. Make Text into the mask layer and Image into the masked layer:

3. Unlock the layers by clicking the top lock icon, and in the Text layer, create a text field containing the word or words that you want to make appear, in the center of the stage:

4. Bring skyline.bmp (or your own image) onto the Image layer by selecting the layer and then using the File ➤ Import ➤ Import to Library menu option to navigate to the image in the dialog box. Pull the bitmap from the library onto the Image layer (you don't need to position it just yet, so drag it anywhere onto the stage).

5. Convert the imported image to a graphic symbol called Skyline Object and give it a center registration point.

6. Scale Skyline Object so that it's about the same height as your text, and place it on the stage so that its *right* edge is nearly at the *left* edge of your text:

7. Make your animation 50 frames long (both layers) and insert a keyframe at frame **50** on the Image layer:

8. With the new keyframe still selected, move Skyline Object so that it's behind the text. Then click anywhere on the Image layer between frames 1 and 50

and then assign a motion tween from the Property inspector.

9. Lock both layers and test your movie. Here's a simulation of the effect you will see:

Because your bitmap is moving, you can get away with quite a low-resolution quality so the download time can actually be surprisingly quick. Be aware that an effect like this, combined with a large bitmap, can become quite slow on older computers if your text fills the screen. Try applying text outlines to this example like you did in the previous one.

You can now create a layer that's a mask and apply this mask to a layer (or layers) that are labelled as masked. This is yet another powerful feature that you and your imagination can implement in conjunction with other techniques such as tweening, animated fades, and so on.

OK, that's it for the basic masking techniques. We think you'll agree that you can create some scintillating effects with them. The best way to learn more from here is to experiment and let your imagination run wild.

Later in the book you'll look at how to use movie clips as masks, using a little bit of ActionScript to create some interaction on them.

Case Study

In this section, you're going to begin creating some content for your pages, specifically the web page. The web portfolio page, in case you hadn't already guessed, will feature screenshots and text information on some websites that you've previously created.

1. Open your saved case study Flash file.

2. Locate and double-click the Content movie clip instance on the stage to edit it in place.

3. Within the Content symbol, insert a new layer called pages, and place it above the frame labels and animated rectangles layers. This is to make sure that the content appears above the rectangles so you can see it!

4. Insert a blank keyframe on frame 91 of the pages layer:

You've positioned a frame here to house the web page content. Its actual position is at the very end of the open web shape tween, meaning that your animation will have finished, and the rectangle will be fully grown.

5. Before you proceed, lock all the other layers except the pages layer to make sure that you don't accidentally alter any of them.

6. Select the Text tool and set the font to Arial 12pt, and the color to a dark blue (#003399). Type the following (or similar) and center it with the Align panel:

7. Use the Selection tool to select the text field, and convert it into a symbol with *F8* or Modify ➤ Convert to Symbol. Make it a movie clip symbol with a central registration point and give it the name web content.

8. Double-click the new web content movie clip instance on the stage to edit it in place.

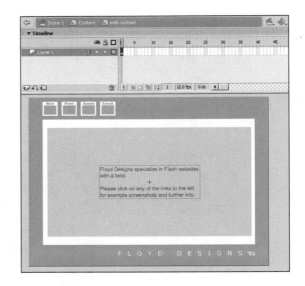

9. Rename the existing layer web examples and add three more layers below it called invisible buttons, buttons text, and thumbnails:

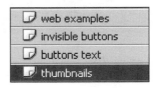

10. Switch on the rulers using View ➤ Rulers. This will enable you to position your elements a little more neatly.

11. Click the left ruler and drag a guide from it to the 250 pixel mark just left of the registration point. Then release it:

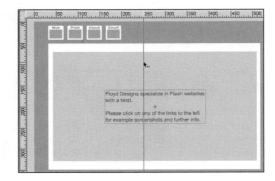

12. Lock the guide in place by clicking View ➤ Guides ➤ Lock Guides to prevent the guide from being moved.

13. Switch on Snap to Guides if it isn't already on by selecting View ➤ Snapping ➤ Snap to Guides.

14. Use the Selection tool to drag the text by its top-left corner to the left side of the guide. Release it when the small circle appears on the guide, and the text will snap to the guide:

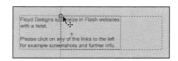

15. Center the text vertically using the Align panel.

16. Insert a blank keyframe on frame 2 of the web examples layer.

17. Open the Library (Window ➤ Library or *CTRL+L*), and drag a copy of the friendsofed_website.gif image out of it. Position the image in the top-right corner of the green rectangle, so that its left edge snaps to the guide:

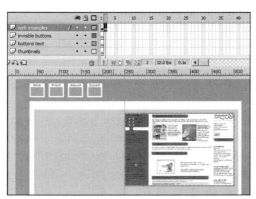

18. Select the text tool and type the following text anywhere on the stage with line-breaks as seen. Use the same font, size, and color as you set earlier (Arial 12pt, #003399).

friends of ed

A website created for the multimedia book

publishing company using HTML, Flash, and

ASP technologies.

19. Drag the text field below the image and snap its left edge to the guide:

20. For a little emphasis on the website name, select the text "friends of ed" and change it to bold in the Property inspector:

21. Add five more keyframes on this layer:

This is one for each of the examples. You're going to save a little arrangement time by swapping the bitmaps and simply editing the text field as required.

22. Select the keyframe on frame 3, and click the image to bring up the Property inspector information for it.

23. In the Property inspector, click the Swap button. This will allow you to replace this image with another from the Library:

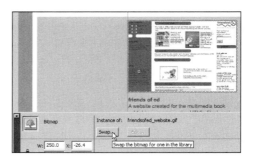

Once you've done this, you'll see the following window:

24. Select `pinderkaas_website.gif` and click OK:

The image on the stage is now replaced with the chosen image. Easy peasy eh? No aligning, dragging, or hassle, just an easy action. Editing the text isn't as easy, but it's nothing to panic about either.

25. Select the Selection tool, and double-click the text field. Then select all the text in the text field and delete it.

26. Enter the following text as seen (remembering to change the title to bold):

pinderkaas

A website created for the book flash math creativity. Created using Flash, HTML, and CGI.

Okay, that's two examples done pretty quickly. Rather than go through all the steps again for the others, just repeat these steps for keyframes 4 to 7:

■ Click next keyframe.

■ Select image and swap it using the Property inspector (follow the order of `nettle_wine.gif`, `qanik.gif`, `hypertelia.gif`, and `fmc.gif`).

■ Highlight all the text and delete it.

■ Replace it with a blurb. Here are the blurbs in order:

Frame 4:

nettlewine

Record label website. Created in HTML and PHP.

Frame 5:

qanik

Nostalgia site. Created in HTML and Flash.

Frame 6:

hypertelia

Creative site made with 3D, Flash, and PHP.

Frame 7:

flash math creativity

Friends of ED mini-site. Created using Flash and HTML.

Select the title in the text field and make it bold.

When you are done making the amendments, proceed with the next steps.

Creating the navigation elements

In this section, you're going to create buttons that will guide your viewers through the example pages.

1. Select the keyframe on the buttons text layer and select the Text tool.

2. Click the left side of the guide and type the following:

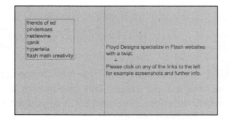

3. Extend the frames on this layer to frame 7 using *F5*. Doing this will allow you to easily position the text.

4. Ensure Snap Align is on using View ➤ Snapping ➤ Snap Align.

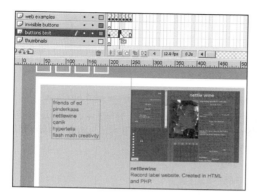

5. Pick up the text field you just created and drag it so that its top edge snap aligns to the top of the image to its right:

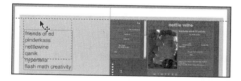

Now you're going to create some invisible buttons to put over these text fields. Hold on a minute...did we just say *invisible* buttons? We sure did!

Invisible buttons are one of the classic Flash tricks that carved its place in Flash history way back in Flash 4. The purpose of an invisible button is to allow user clicks and so forth while not having a physical presence on stage. In this instance, an invisible button will be placed over each website name so you still see the website name, but not the button covering it.

Creating an invisible button is quite simple. In fact, you already have the ability to do it. Once we show you how it is done you might kick yourself.

6. Extend the frames on the invisible buttons layer to frame 7 using *F5*.

7. Click the keyframe on frame 1 and select the Rectangle tool.

8. Draw a long thin rectangle, any fill color with no stroke, to cover the last line of text, "flash math creativity":

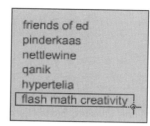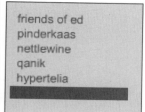

9. Select the rectangle and press *F8* to convert it into a symbol with the following details:

10. Double-click the newly created symbol instance to edit it in place:

11. Here's the magic bit (to send the rectangle to the Bermuda triangle). Drag the keyframe from the Up state to the Hit state:

Et voila! That's it! You now have an invisible button.

12. Go back one level to the web content symbol time-line, and you'll notice that the rectangle has been replaced by a pale blue aura. This is your invisible button:

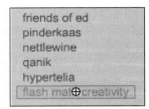

13. Create five duplicates of the invisible button and position them roughly over the text titles. Align them horizontally using the Snap Align:

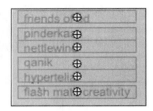

14. Select the top and bottom invisible buttons separately and center position them vertically as neatly as possible over their respective texts:

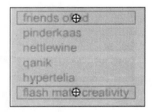

15. Select all the invisible buttons and use the Align panel's Space evenly vertically option:

This will align them neatly vertically:

16. Save your case study movie and close it.

Okay, that's it for this rather lengthy case study section. In the next installment, you'll add some of that interactivity we promised you.

Summary

You've seen that masks in Flash can help achieve a range of pretty snazzy effects. You can make masks as simple or complex as you want, and you can encapsulate masking functionality inside movie clip symbols.

You saw that:

■ **Masks** are created on a special mask layer.

■ The **mask layer** is applied to a **masked layer** (or layers).

■ The mask layer and all the layers it is applied to must be locked for the mask effect to be seen.

■ Masks can be static or animated.

■ Masks are useful for:

　■ Hiding and revealing selected parts of an animation.

　■ Achieving a sense of depth.

　■ Animating bitmap images as if they were vectors.

In the next chapter, you're going to examine **advanced animation and commands**.

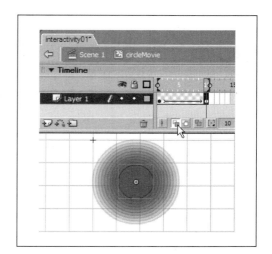

Chapter 9

ADVANCED ANIMATION AND COMMANDS

What we'll cover in this chapter:

- Adding cool automated tween driven effects with **timeline effects**
- Recording and reusing your workflow with **commands**
- Using **interactivity**—the fundamentals of **interaction**, **events**, and **event handlers** in Flash
- Creating interactive Flash sites with **behaviors**

In this chapter, you're going on an adventure. The purpose of this expedition is to advance your Flash skills even further. Until now you've been steadily trekking up the hill, and by the end of this chapter, you'll have reached a point where you can hoist your flag.

After this chapter you'll be a different kind of Flash user: a power user! Not only will you be able to automate the creation process using **commands**, but you will also be able to create **interactive** websites. On the way up the hill, you'll look at Flash's power user method of making complex animations, **timeline effects**.

Get your hiking boots on, and let's start trekking!

Timeline effects

When Macromedia made Flash MX 2004 and Flash MX Professional 2004, they were kind enough to invent **timeline effects** for Flash users who are in a hurry. To those of us in the know—that's you and me—timeline effects are basically automated motion tweens and graphic effects. The main benefit of timeline effects is the time gained from using them.

Imagine a situation in which you want some text to grow on the screen. Given your current knowledge, you would probably use a couple of keyframes, the Transform panel, and a motion tween. The same effect with timeline effects is only a couple of clicks away because the process has been automated.

Each timeline effect has a preview window where different parameters are set. The number of parameters depends on the depth and type of the effect. Here is a preview of the Blur effect:

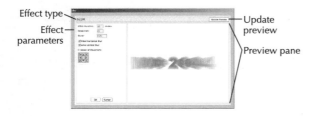

The existing list of timeline effects that comes with Flash is pretty minimal, but the beauty of timeline

effects is that you can download new effects so the list will be continually expanding. The current list of effects is separated into three categories, each with their own effects. The list includes:

- Assistants
  - Copy to Grid
  - Distribute Duplicates
- Effects
  - Blur
  - Drop Shadow
  - Expand
  - Explode
- Transform/Transition
  - Transform
  - Transition

You'll look at these a little later in the chapter.

In case you didn't already know, timeline effects are very easy to use. Timeline effects are applied by selecting an object on the stage and choosing the desired effect from the Insert ➤ Timeline Effects sub-menus.

Once an effect is selected, the Preview window appears, showing the parameters for the effect. Finally, once these parameters are set and confirmed, Flash will render the effect. Let's give it a shot.

Using timeline effects

In this exercise, you're going to create some movie-style titles using timeline effects.

1. Open a new blank Flash document.

2. Select the Text tool and type FOUNDATION FLASH MX 2004 or whatever you want. We've used Arial

Black at 26 pt. Center the text field horizontally and vertically on the stage using the Align panel:

3. Insert a keyframe at frame 10 of the existing layer. The reason you've done this is to give your viewers a chance to read the text before you apply a time-line effect that will render it virtually illegible.

4. Select the text on frame 10 if it isn't already selected, and select Insert ➤ Timeline Effects ➤ Effects ➤ Blur. You'll now see the preview and parameters window for the Blur effect:

As you can see here, Flash has automatically created a preview on the right of your text blurring. This current preview is rendered according to the parameters on the left.

> *Note that the Preview pane distorts the actual size of your timeline effects. Animations in the preview pane are scaled down or up so that the whole effect can be shown, so effects on the stage might be larger or smaller than you expected.*

The current parameters for this effect are in the left of this window. Changing the values of these parameters will alter the appearance of the effect:

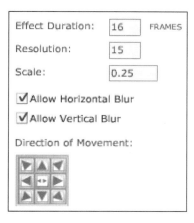

Let's briefly look at the parameters for the Blur effect:

- **Effect Duration**: This specifies the frame length of the timeline effect animation. After a little more investigation into timeline effects, you'll see that this is a common parameter for all the animation-based effects.

- **Resolution**: This specifies the quality of this particular effect. From an animation point-of-view, this denotes the number of copies of the text that are used to create the effect. A higher figure here will create a smoother and more seamless effect, but it will most likely demand more power from the computer processor. In most cases however, the default value is adequate.

- **Scale**: This represents the scaling value for the overall blur. The default setting of 0.25 makes the text blur to a quarter of the size of the original.

- **Allow Horizontal / Vertical Blur**: These settings specify the directions of blurring. The default, with both boxes checked, makes the object blur in both directions.

- **Direction of Movement**: This is the direction of the blurring and is specified from a matrix grid. As default, the object will scale from the center

219

outward. The options available here are dependant on the previous selection:

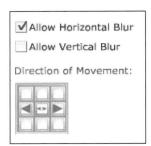

5. Change the Effect Duration value to 20 and the Direction of Movement to **North-West**.

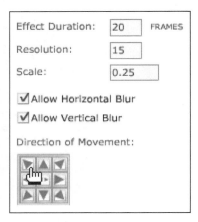

6. Click the Update Preview button in the top left of the window.

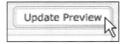

After a little while, the effect preview in the right pane will be updated. Both the direction of the blur movement and the length of the effect change (but you are pretty unlikely to notice the latter!). Whenever you make any changes to the parameters in this window—whatever the effect—you have to click this button the update the preview. Although the absence of a live update might seem peculiar, you'll soon get used to it.

We've chosen 20 frames as the duration here to nicely round up the length of the Foundation Flash MX 2004 text (including timeline effect) on the screen to 30 frames. However, you don't want the text to blur in this direction in the final effect. (We only did this to show you how the Preview pane works!)

7. Set the Direction of Movement back to the center selection and click Update Preview.

8. Click OK to render the effect. After a little computation, you'll be returned to the main stage where you might notice a few key things:

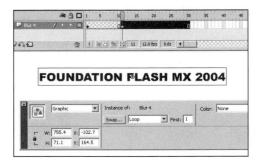

First, the frames have been extended beyond the second keyframe—a full 20 frames as you specified in the parameters. Second, the name of the layer has changed to that of your chosen effect, suffixed with a number. Last, the text has been changed into an instance of a symbol called Blur 4. This symbol represents the effect you just created. If you open the Library (Window ➤ Library or CTRL+L) you'll notice a few symbols new have been created:

Blur 4 is the symbol that features the effect, whereas the Effects folder contains elements required by this effect and others. In the event that you want to change the content of your timeline effect—for example, the actual text in the current example—you will most likely find the necessary modifiable symbols in this folder. You'll see how this is done a little later.

If you attempt to edit a timeline effect symbol like Blur 4, you'll be greeted with a slap on the wrist and a warning:

9. If you click OK, the timeline effect will no longer be modifiable (you'll see all about modifying effects in a moment). Unless you really want to edit the symbol, click Cancel.

10. Insert a new layer with a new keyframe on frame 31.

11. Use the Text tool to type SHAM BHANGAL or some text of your choice. Center the text using the Align panel:

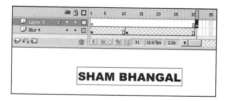

12. With the text selected, choose Insert ➤ Timeline Effects ➤ Transform / Transition ➤ Transition. As before the Effects window will appear:

This time we've selected the Transition effect. As you can see, this effect is like a video wipe.

Most of the parameters for this effect should already be familiar to you by now, with the exception of the Direction parameters:

- **In / Out**: This option specifies whether the selected object wipes in or out. If you want an object to appear, use In. If you want an object to disappear, use Out. By default, this is set to In.

- **Fade**: This option makes the object to alpha out or in.

- **Wipe**: This specifies whether the wipe effect is used or not. If this is disabled, the transition becomes a simple alpha tween.

- **Wipe Direction**: This sets the direction of the wipe. A down-pointing wipe, for instance, makes the object appear from the top:

13. Change the Direction to Out and click the down-pointing arrow in the grid. Then ensure that Fade and Wipe are checked.

14. Set the Effect Duration to 30 frames and click OK to render the effect.

15. As before, you'll notice the layer name has changed and the Library has a few more symbols. Let's finish your titles with one last effect.

16. Insert a new layer and place a keyframe at frame 61.

17. Use the text tool to type KRISTIAN BESLEY (or whatever you like).

221

18. Insert a new keyframe at frame 71. You're doing this for the same reason you did earlier—you want people to be able to read it before it transmogrifies!

19. Select the text on frame 71 and select Insert ➤ Timeline Effects ➤ Effects ➤ Explode. As you'd expect, you get the Effects window:

You might have noticed that there are quite a few parameters here! There isn't anything too complicated, but there is a lot of it to go through. Let's take a look at some of the important elements:

- **Arc Size** (**x** and **y**): This represents the arc in which the fragments move. At their defaults of 100 and 150 (x and y respectively), the fragments move up more than across. Experiment with these values significantly to see the different effects you can get.

- **Rotate Fragments by:** This parameter controls how much the fragments rotate over the course of the motion. The fragments will rotate incrementally to this set value over the whole of the animation sequence.

- **Change Fragments Size by:** This specifies the full size increase (or the final size) of each fragment over the course of the animation.

- **Final Alpha:** The final opacity of the fragments. As with the last two parameters, the alpha of the fragments will be steadily reduced over the course of the animation.

20. Set the Effect duration to 10 frames and change the Final Alpha to 50%. Click Update Preview and then click OK.

21. Test the movie using Control ➤ Test Movie. Pretty neat huh?

Unfortunately, you've intentionally put some mistakes in on the last effect (no cussing!), so you're going to have to rectify them. How do you do this? Simple.

22. Select the symbol on frame 71 and click the Edit button from the Effect section of the Property inspector. Alternatively, select Modify ➤ Timeline Effects ➤ Edit Effect:

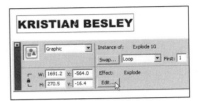

> To remove a timeline effect, select the effect symbol instance (such as Explode 10 in the screenshot) and choose Modify ➤ Timeline Effects ➤ Remove Effect or right-click it and select Timeline Effects ➤ Remove Effect from the context-sensitive menu.
>
> In either case, this will remove the effect and return your object to its original form.

The familiar effects window will now appear, allowing you to make the relevant changes to the effect.

23. Change the duration to 20 and the final alpha to 0%. Then click OK and test the movie again.

That's better! But it's still not quite cinematic enough, is it? Well, you can't give the viewer popcorn, but you can certainly get the colors right. As you are probably aware, the typical cinema titles scheme is white text on a black background.

Let's change the color of the text inside the effect to white. There are two ways to do this, and you're going to use both of them.

24. Open the Library and open the Effects Folder by double-clicking it:

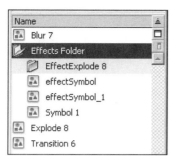

25. Locate your equivalents of the SHAM BHANGAL and FOUNDATION FLASH MX 2004 text symbols. In our Library these are effectSymbol and Symbol 1 respectively.

26. Double-click the first of them to enter edit mode and change the text color to white using the Property inspector.

27. Do the same for the next one, changing it to white too.

That's two out of three. The last one isn't so easy, and if you open up the EffectExplode folder, you'll see why:

True to its name, the Explode effect has broken your text into many tiny fragments, and changing the color of the text in each of these would be a long tedious job. Luckily, you can change its color in one fell swoop, via the symbol instance on the stage.

28. Select the symbol instance on frame 71, and use the Color drop-down of the Property panel to set a white tint to 100%:

29. Select the text elements on frames 1 and 61 and change their color to white in the same way.

30. Select Modify ➤ Document and change the background color to black. Test the movie and view your sophisticated titles created with almost zero effort:

It's not as easy as that in Hollywood!

As you've seen in this exercise, timeline effects can be used to create complex animations without the hard work normally involved in creating such intricacies. Even though some of the effects are almost as easily achieved with keyframes, effects like the Blur and Explode would take a great deal of time and effort to finesse, and even then they wouldn't be as easy to modify as the built-in timeline effects.

Other kinds of timeline effects

In the last exercise you saw a few key timeline effects, so let's run through the others before you move on. Even though you won't be using them practically here, we recommend that you experiment with them to see what…ahem…effects you can create. As you'll become aware as you experiment, the most convenient thing about timeline effects is the ability to change their parameters at will.

Let's look at the remaining timeline effects category. All these subcategories are located under the Insert ➤ Timeline Effects menu option.

223

Assistants

The Assistants effects are in place to help you with repetitive graphic tasks. The first of these, Copy to Grid, takes the selected object and creates a grid of copies using it. A single selected circle, for example, creates a grid of four using the default settings:

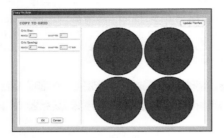

The second assistant, Distributed Duplicate, takes the object and duplicates it a given number of times. The parameters allow you to alter an almost infinite number of the duplicates' attributes, from color to rotation:

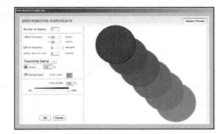

Effects

The Effects category concerns animation effects. The two effects that you've not seen are Drop Shadow and Expand.

The Drop Shadow effect allows you to instantly apply a drop shadow to any object:

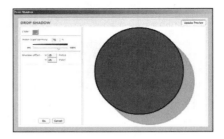

The parameters allow you to change the color and alpha of the shadow, as well as its offset position from the shadowed object.

The Expand effect is used to make shapes grow and move at the same time. One of the significant bonuses of using this (other than the Transform effect which you'll see in a moment) is the two-way animation it creates, allowing shapes to grow and contract. This effect only works on groups or symbol instances:

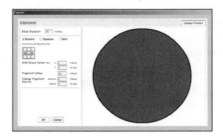

Transform/transition

The Transform effect is the most noteworthy of all the timeline effects simply because the motion that it produces is an important part of most Flashers' day-to-day Flash work. The parameters here range from scaling to positioning to coloring and so on. In fact, anything that can be done on a two-keyframe motion tween is performed here in one simple package:

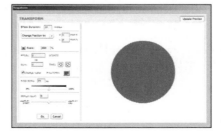

As you've seen in this section, timeline effects can save you a considerable amount of time. The chances are that you won't have a use for all of the timeline effects, but you'll find yourself returning to some key effects again and again. That said, if you have the time to put in some tweening graft, go ahead and do it because one of the limitations of timeline effects is the inability to carry on your motion sequences beyond the sequence of specified frames.

Let's continue your expedition.

Automated commands

If you've ever used Actions in Photoshop or Macros in Office packages, you'll know how you really can't live without them. For those of you not fortunate enough to have used them, it's time for another History lesson.

In a nutshell, commands in Flash are simply recorded actions that can be played back. The benefit of using them is that repetitive tasks can be repeated with a single click. Commands are created from History panel steps and are run from the Commands menu:

Creating a library of commands will allow you to save considerable time by automating tasks that you perform regularly. Once you are aware of what commands can do, you'll no doubt look to optimize your working practices by automating those little but time-consuming jobs. But before you tackle one of those jobs, here's a reminder of the amazing keeper of time, the History panel.

Reacquainting yourselves with the History panel

If you've forgotten the function of the History panel, your memory obviously isn't as good as its memory is.

In short, the History panel stores your movements and actions in the Flash environment. Any time you draw a square, move something, or make a new symbol, the History panel records it:

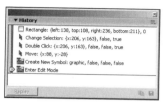

The History panel was originally discussed in Chapter 4. If you need a refresher, don't hesitate to turn back the pages, but don't panic too much because you'll revisit most of its functions in a moment.

Now that you recall the purpose and function of the History panel, how can it help you? The History panel is central to recording commands, so you'll have to use it if you want to create commands. This is because Flash, unlike Photoshop or Office packages, doesn't have the ability to record your actions "live." However, the History panel is just as good—if not better.

Once you've recorded a number of actions, you need to convert them into a command. Commands are created by highlighting or selecting a number of History panel entries and selecting the Disk icon in the bottom left of the panel:

The command is then given a name and is added to the Commands menu. Let's give it a go.

Creating your first command

1. Create a new Flash document and open the History panel. At this point, be careful not to click or do anything unnecessarily. (You don't want to fill the History panel with unwanted actions!)

> *If you accidentally perform some activity, fear not! Just select* Clear History *from the History panel menu.*

2. Open the History panel, if necessary, using Window ➤ Other Panels ➤ History. Then select View ➤ Arguments in Panel from the History panels menu. This will provide you with more detail in the panel.

3. Use the Oval tool to draw a simple circle in the top left of the stage. Don't worry too much about the colors:

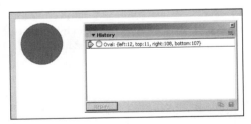

4. Double-click the circle to select its fill and outline.

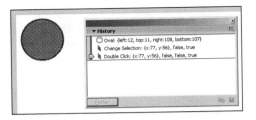

5. Use Edit ➤ Copy to copy the circle and Edit ➤ Paste in Place to paste the duplicate in the same location as the original. It will be selected by default.

Hold down *SHIFT* and use the *ARROW* keys to move the circle to the right, out of reach of the original:

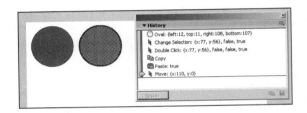

So far you have two rather dull looking circles on the stage. Nothing exciting, but you have some dynamite History entries to work with! In our screenshot, the last three entries are the ones that we're going to make into a command. Why? Let's explain.

The rather drab command that you're going to make will perform one simple function: it will copy whatever is selected (in this case a circle) and paste and position the copy over and to the right of the original. Now let's look at the three actions.

- *Copy*: This represents the copy you made of the selected object. Within the context of the command, this will copy whatever the user has selected. Remember that the only prerequisite of this command is to have something selected.

- *Paste: true:* This shows the Paste in Place that you performed. Within the command this will paste whatever is on the clipboard—conveniently what you have just copied—onto the stage. The word true specifies a Paste in Place.

■ *Move: {x:110, y:0}:* This action is a record of the movement of the circle 110 pixels to the right. The coordinate details stored here—x and y—are off-sets from the original position of the circle. These are not to be confused with (absolute) x and y screen-coordinates.

Each time this particular action is run, the newly pasted object will be positioned 100 pixels across from its original position.

Before you cast your command in stone, you can give it a trial run.

6. Highlight the three required actions in the History panel:

7. Click the Replay button at the bottom of the History panel. Once this is done, you should have another circle on stage, positioned across from the previous one:

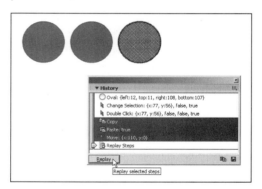

Success! Click Replay again to create another...Hurrah! It works. Finally, to save you from having to work in the History panel forever, you can attach the actions to a command.

8. With the three actions still selected, click the Save selected items as command (the Disk icon) at the bottom left of the panel.

In the dialog box that opens, give the new command a name. We've called ours copy paste move!:

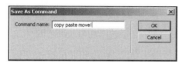

Now open the Commands menu to view the newly added command:

This allows you to run this command from within Flash at any time in any Flash document. Pretty fancy huh? Before you go on, let's quickly look at the other options on this menu.

■ Manage Saved Commands: This is where you can rename or delete any saved commands. Pretty use-ful for removing commands that you are only likely to use once.

■ Get More Commands: Selecting this option will dis-play a Macromedia web page where you can down-load various prebuilt commands.

■ Run Command: This allows you to run commands saved as external Javascript Flash (.jsfl) files. These might have been downloaded from the previous menu option—Get more commands.

Now to check that your command works.

9. Select the Rectangle tool and draw a small shape anywhere on the stage.

227

10. Select the shape and choose the newly created command from the Commands menu. As before, a copy of the selected shape is positioned to the right of the original.

Your command is functional. Before you revel in the glory, there is something important you should know.

11. Clear the contents of the History panel using Clear History from its menu.

12. Use the Pencil tool to draw a single squiggle of any description on the stage. If you now look in the History panel you'll notice a red x below the Pencil icon alongside the lone entry. True to symbolic form, the evil red x is informing you of something bad!

In fact, it indicates that this History entry cannot be replayed or added as part of a command. If this sounds disappointing, don't worry. The majority of actions that cannot be reused aren't the type of things that you'd want to re-create. To discover what actions can and cannot be used, leave the History panel open while you work and look for the red x.

Creating a reusable command

As we've already pointed out, one of the great things about creating commands is their reusability. Common actions are easily converted into commands and reused again and again. Even as you worked through this book, you have no doubt come across a number of recurring actions, which you could have condensed into reusable commands.

Reusable commands can be a major time saver if they are created correctly. For instance, in the last exercise you made a conscious decision to require a selection from the user. This decision is key because that command could be applied to any object on the stage.

In a situation where you aim to create a reusable command, assume the user (even if that is just you!) has

made a selection, and run the command from there. Let's see this in practice.

Creating a "center to stage" command

In this exercise you're going to create a simple command to automate one of the most common actions that you've used throughout the book—centering. Without any knowledge of commands, centering horizontally and vertically requires at least two actions, assuming you have the Align panel open and the To Stage modifier on.

You're now going to make these actions one click away.

1. Open a new Flash document.

2. Use the Rectangle tool to draw a square with any fill and stroke color.

3. Select the square and open the Align panel (Window ➤ Design Panels ➤ Align).

4. In the Align panel, switch on the To Stage modifier.

5. Click the Align horizontal center and Align vertical center buttons. This will center the square on the stage.

6. In the History panel, select the last two actions:

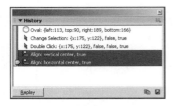

7. Click the Save selected steps as command button (represented by the disk icon).

8. Give it the name center to stage.

9. Move the circle away from the center, and with it selected, choose the new command from the Commands menu. The circle will now be centered on stage.

This simple command illustrates the ability (within the limits of possibility—remember the dreaded red x!) to create reusable commands. Even though this last command is incredibly minimal, the time you'll save from using it will make it worthwhile.

If this isn't impressive enough, remember that any commands you create in Flash including this one will be stored permanently on the Commands menu for any future Flash sessions. Commands library here you come.

You've still got a way to go in this chapter so grab a coffee, change the CD, and get ready to proceed. If you thought commands and timeline effects were good, you ain't seen nothing yet.

Behaviors

You're now going to start moving away from the predictable world of tweens and "animation on rails," toward something new—**interactive control of the timeline**. Instead of allowing the timeline to run sequentially, you will add features that allow the user to change its flow so that it can skip frames, start, or stop. That's a very powerful feature because it allows you to create *navigation* and *interactive animation*.

> *Behaviors work by automatically adding code instructions to your symbols, using Flash's scripting language, ActionScript.*
>
> *Behaviors create code that the developer will most likely never look at. They create code that is written in a format that is not conducive to update or enhancement. (It's actually written in an older dialect of ActionScript that was all the rage way back in Flash 5.) If you want to learn modern ActionScript, we strongly recommend you don't look at the code generated by behaviors. At least, not until you feel competent enough in ActionScript to explore alternative coding styles. You will be writing the modern dialect of ActionScript in Chapter 10.*

Although behaviors are simple drag-and-drop procedures, you do need to know the principles behind how they (and ActionScript in general) work. You will take a slight detour to learn about what interactivity actually is, and how it is implemented. You will also look at when you can (and can't) attach a behavior, an issue that can be confusing at first.

Interactivity

Interactivity in the world of Flash means that when your content is running in the user's browser, it *responds* to something that the user does or *reacts* to a predefined set of conditions. For example:

- Branching out of the movie's linear playback and playing a different movie clip when the user presses a button or when the playhead hits a particular frame
- Saving the user's name and e-mail address, which they've typed into a couple of text boxes
- Confirming the user's order when they've added things to their shopping cart in a Flash e-commerce site
- Playing different songs on a Flash jukebox
- Dragging around pieces of a puzzle in a Flash jigsaw
- Creating a game where the graphics move around in an intelligent fashion, reacting (but not being controlled by) the user's interaction. A good example of this might be a Space Invaders-type game.

All these examples rely on Flash's ability to respond to **events**.

An *event* is simply something that *happens as a result of something that is an input to Flash*. When you create an interactive movie, you plan the things that can happen, build an interface (buttons, text-entry boxes, etc.) that will allow the user to *make* those events happen, and create the ActionScript that will *handle* those events.

> *In advanced Flash content, Flash itself can generate some of its own input to modify its own responses, as would happen in the Space Invaders game. The way this is done is by coding with agents; self contained bits of code that control one thing (such as an alien) by talking or monitoring other agents and inputs.*

Events and event handlers

In order for interaction to take place, you need to have an **event** and an **event handler**. For example, when you visit a friend, you walk along the street until you reach his or her building. When the "reaching the building" event takes place, the "I've reached the building" event handler in your brain responds by turning your steps toward their door. Something of significance—an event—has occurred, and a piece of processing has been carried out to handle it.

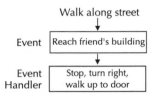

Now you push the doorbell or intercom button to let your friend know you've arrived. Your friend will then come to the door, look out of the window to see who's there, or grunt down the intercom.

Pressing that button is another event, and this time your friend responded to it—he handled it in that he *did something* when the buzzer sounded. From here you and your friend can discuss what you're going to do with your day—your extended interaction with your friend starts with the push of a button. If your friend had been out or hadn't answered the door, your "he's not home, I'll go to the mall" event handler would have kicked in. In the real world, events and event handling is complex—infinite, even. In Flash, you can control the environment, so in your interactive movies you can plan for an anticipated range of events and handle them all.

And that, more or less, is interaction.

Let's examine one of the primary and most intuitive of tools that Flash gives you for interaction with the user—the **button**.

Buttons as interactive elements

In an interactive Flash movie, an *event* is triggered by clicking the mouse button or dragging the pointer over something on the screen—typically a button. The event handler here will be a set of instructions that is attached to the button. These instructions tell Flash exactly what you want it to do when the user clicks that button and triggers the click event. These instructions can be created using **behaviors**, which are ready-made code sections for the most common interactivity building blocks. Although you don't need to create any code to use them, you do need to know the concept of the event-event handler pair because you have to specify (but not write) them.

It's important to realize the following two important points when using behaviors (or for that matter, raw ActionScript, covered in Chapter 10).

Symbols on their own do not create interactivity

A button on its own does not produce interaction. A button placed in a movie has its default states—Up, Over, Down, and Hit—but it won't actually *do* anything interesting unless you explicitly tell it to. You've already seen that you can add keyframes to the button's internal timeline and change its display in each state, which makes the button more interesting to look at. But the button is still essentially dumb—all it can do at the moment is *detect* events such as when it's rolled over or pressed. To boost the button's intelligence, you have to attach a behavior to one or more of its states: the ActionScript element, created for you behind the scenes by the behavior, creates the interaction:

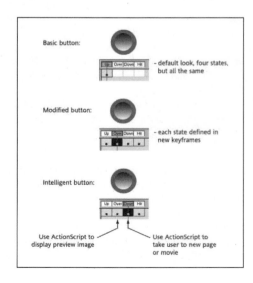

When you've attached the behavior to your button, the button waits for the user to interact with it.

In some programming languages—BASIC, for example—once your program starts, the program code is *always* running. In Flash, your program—the ActionScript (which is what behaviors end up as)—is attached to a button and will only run *when the button detects a particular action carried out by the user.* As your knowledge of Flash increases, you'll see why this is a much better way of creating user interfaces. One of the main features of advanced Flash sites is their use of buttons to start off lots of simple little sequences that, together, form a complex, fully animated, and interactive user experience.

As you progress in the next couple of chapters, you'll see that a button in Flash can be much more than just a switch. In addition to detecting simple things like mouse clicks to provide navigation, the button can be used to start whole *avalanches* of actions in motion.

Movie clips and buttons only behave on a timeline

You can only attach behaviors to symbols on a timeline. You should not attempt to attach a behavior to a symbol in the Library. You can however attach a behavior to a symbol that is on the timeline of a symbol in the Library.

Why? Because the library is simply a store; nothing in it is active and capable of doing much of anything until you place it on a keyframe. This is one of those things that is simple for experienced Flash users, but it totally confuses the beginner, so let's go through it slowly with an analogy.

Before you buy a CD player, it is kept in a stock room somewhere. It will most likely have a bit of plastic or a retaining screw somewhere in it that prevents the laser head inside it from moving or the spindle turning. This is to protect it from bumps and knocks during transit. The upshot of all this is that you can't play anything on it while it is set up for storage. Once you buy it and remove the packaging and all the protective bits of

plastic, you can start to use (or interact) with it. The same applies with symbols in the Library; they are not ready to be used when they are in the Library because something needs to be done to them first. This process is simpler than unpacking a CD; in the virtual world of Flash you simply drag the symbol onto the stage. This is the equivalent of unpacking the CD player and plugging it into a power supply. All the software connections are created to make the symbol work (a process called **instantiation**). That's the point when a symbol is ready to work with behaviors.

> Note that you can't attach behaviors or code to a graphic symbol. If you need to, make it into a movie clip first.

If you buy a car with a CD player, the situation is different. When the manufacturer built the car, someone had to test the CD player, so even though the vehicle may be in storage, the CD player will still be set up to work. The CD player is *embedded*; it is part of a larger product, and for that larger product to be built, the CD player has to be working when the product leaves the factory and goes into storage. A button inside a movie clip works in exactly the same way. The only thing that changes is the terminology. In this case, the button is *nested* (rather than embedded), but it works via attached behaviors for much the same reasons as the embedded CD player—it has already been wired to work inside its larger parent, even though the parent is in storage within the Library.

To further extend the analogy, the car factory also has a storeroom of CD players that haven't yet been fitted into a car. They will be the in the same state as the CD players in the first example—they are not embedded so you can't use them yet—they are still in storage. In the Flash world, an embedded button can have a behavior attached to it, but the version of the same button that is not embedded (and in the Library) cannot, again for the same reasons as the car CD player—it's only wired up to work (or instantiated) when it's inside the parent.

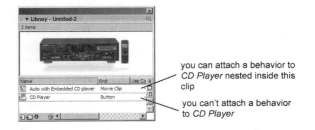

you can attach a behavior to *CD Player* nested inside this clip

you can't attach a behavior to *CD Player*

OK, that's all the theory. Let's start with a simple example—an FLA containing some interaction via buttons and behaviors.

Creating a simple button

To create an interactive element in your movie, you need a button on the stage waiting to be pressed—giving you an event—and some ActionScript attached to it to handle the event and tell Flash what to do.

Before you look at attaching behaviors that respond to mouse clicks, let's make sure you're getting the most out of your buttons by creating a simple button and slowly developing its abilities.

1. Create a new Flash document and rename the default layer buttons.

2. Go to View ➤ Grid ➤ Show Grid and then View ➤ Snapping ➤ Snap to Grid, and ensure that both are checked—this will help you position your symbols on the stage more accurately.

3. Create a new graphic symbol (*CTRL+F8*) and name it circle. Make it a red circle with a black outline. Don't put your new symbol on the stage just yet:

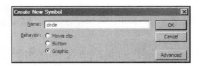

The reason you've created a graphic symbol before making it into a button is that you'll be using the circle many times within the button itself. By making the circle a symbol beforehand, you're allowing

Flash to reuse the circle symbol, thus saving time and space.

4. Click the New Symbol button in the bottom left of the Library window and create a new button symbol called button. Click OK.

Inside the button symbol, you'll see a blank stage with the button icon at the top. The timeline contains the four button symbol states: **Up**, **Over**, **Down**, and **Hit**.

Remember the definitions of the four states of the button symbol:

■ The **Up** state is how it looks in its original size and position

■ **Over** is how it will look when the user's mouse passes over it

■ **Down** is how it will look when it's clicked

■ **Hit** contains filled spaces that denote the areas the user must be over to press the button

5. With the playhead at the Up state, click the circle graphic symbol icon in the Library and drag an instance of it onto the stage inside the button:

You're going to need to know the *exact* position of your symbol in the Up state—this is so that you can make the different visual renderings of the button's other states consistent. To do this, you'll use the Align panel to place it in the exact center of the stage.

6. Click the To stage button in the Align panel. With your circle symbol selected inside the button

symbol, click both the Align horizontal center button and the Align vertical center button:

Only the Up frame of the button's timeline currently has a keyframe in it. To start bringing the other states to life, you need to add keyframes.

7. Add a keyframe (using *F6*) to each of the other three states. You have now put an instance of the graphic symbol circle into each state of your button symbol:

In the finished movie, you want to make this button get bigger when a visitor's mouse pointer rolls over it, and get smaller when it's pressed. You can do this by scaling the instance in each of the button's state keyframes. You're going to scale each one by a specific amount.

8. Display the **Transform** panel using Window ➤ Design Panels ➤ Transform, and select the Over state in the button timeline.

The Transform panel is useful for adding precise rotation, skewing, and scaling to symbols and shapes:

9. With the circle graphic selected, make sure that the Constrain box in the Transform panel is checked—this ensures the proportions of the circle

are maintained—then type 120 in either the horizontal or vertical scale fields and press the *ENTER* key to apply the scaling.

10. Make sure that the center position of the button stays in exactly the same place as in the Up state, otherwise the button will appear to move slightly when animated. You might need to drag the scaled version back to the central position—or you can use the Align panel again.

Also, don't make the Over state much bigger than the Hit state. You'll see why when you test the button: the parts of the Over state that are outside the Hit state won't respond to the mouse.

11. Select the Down state and scale the circle instance down to 80%.

Although it's not vital in this exercise, it's a good idea to make the Hit area a solid black object to avoid missing unfilled holes that, as explained earlier, could result in the button working erratically.

12. To do this, select the keyframe in the Hit state and then click the circle on the stage. From the Color drop-down menu in the Property panel, select Brightness and move the slider to -100%:

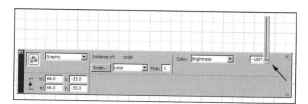

You can confirm that the Hit state circle has the same location and size as the Up state instance either by looking at all four states simultaneously using the Onion Skin Tool or by checking that the x and y values in the Property panel match for each state.

13. Click the Scene 1 text toward the top left of the timeline and put an instance of the button symbol at the center of the stage by dragging it out of the Library.

14. Test the movie. You'll notice that when the mouse rolls over your button, the mouse pointer changes

from an arrow to a hand icon and the button gets bigger. When you click and hold the mouse button, the button graphic gets smaller:

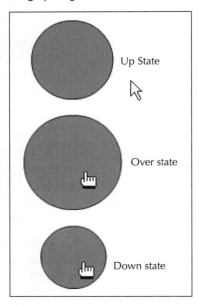

That's the basic button defined. Time to accelerate its evolution into a more intelligent species of button.

Creating animated buttons

Flash allows you to define a *movie* as one of the button states. This feature allows you to create buttons that have complete animations within them. Let's create a simple animation and add it to the Over state of your button.

Putting a movie into a button

1. Double-click the button symbol in the Library to edit it. Select the Over and Down states of the button from the previous exercise in turn, and press the Reset button in the Transform panel (or use Modify ➤ Transform ➤ Remove Transform). This will return both states' circle instances back to the same size as the Up state.

Now you'll create a simple movie that'll play when the user activates the button.

2. In the Library window, click the New Symbol button and create a new movie clip symbol called circleMovie.

3. In frame 1 of the new movie clip, place an instance of the circle symbol at the center of the stage—use the Align panel to correctly center this horizontally and vertically (or enter X and Y coordinates of (0,0) in the Property panel):

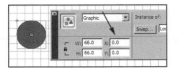

You could even use the center to stage command you created in the earlier exercise.

4. Add a keyframe at frame 10 and then use the Transform panel to reduce the size of the frame 10 circle instance to 40%:

5. Add a motion tween between frames 1 and 10. If you turn on onion skinning between frames 1 and 10, you should see the button make the vaguely psychedelic pattern shown in the following screenshot—simulating the way your button will shrink when its Over state is activated:

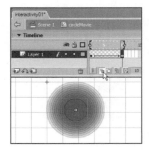

Once you've finished looking at the groovy pattern, click the Onion Skin Mode button again to turn it off.

You're now going to put your animated circleMovie symbol into the Over state of your button symbol—replacing the instance of the graphic symbol circle that's currently there.

6. To edit the button symbol, double click its icon in the Library, and then select the Over state.

7. Select the circle symbol instance in the Over state and use the Property Inspector to make a note of its X, Y, W, and H (x position, y position, width, and height) attributes.

Now you want to put an instance of your circleMovie animated movie clip in place of the circle symbol you just deleted.

8. With circle still selected, hit the Swap button on the Property Inspector. You will see the Swap Symbol window appear. Select circleMovie from the list by double-clicking it. This will cause circle to be replaced by circleMovie. Finally, in the Property Inspector drop-down menu (far left), change the setting from Graphic to Movie Clip.

> You could have also simply deleted circle and added circleMovie in its place, but this way, you learn about swapping symbols as well!

9. Select the circleMovie instance that is now on the stage, and in the Property Inspector, enter the attributes for X, Y, W, and H that you noted down from the graphic symbol circle before (ours is 66 pixels in diameter and at (x, y) position (-33, -33)—yours may be different).

10. Change the X and Y coordinates so they are (0,0): this way, you can ensure that it's in *exactly* the right place:

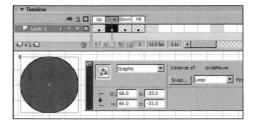

11. Test the movie with Control ➤ Test Movie.

12. Notice that when your mouse pointer goes over the button, you see a looping animation of a smoothly receding button.

Although the animation you chose here is not really *that* impressive, remember that you can have any number of animated effects embedded in a movie clip inside the button. Just make sure that the first frame of the animation is the same size as the rest of the button states—from there, your Over state button image could morph into a mushroom, a dog, a flying fish—anything you like. Also, note that **you should never animate the button's Hit state**.

Although you now have a button with visual feedback, the button is still silent. Real buttons tend to click or squeak or ring. Let's add a sound.

> Although Flash will allow you to add a movie clip for any button state, the Over and (occasionally) the Up states are the only ones you should consider doing it for. The Down state doesn't last long enough for anything to happen (it exists only for the time between the mouse click and release), and the Hit state represents the button's hit area, and you don't need to animate it—unless you want to confuse everyone!

Creating buttons that talk

The first thing you need is a sound file. You can use any kind of sound file you have on your computer or you can download one from the Internet. It's beyond the scope of this chapter to specify the ins and outs of sound issues, so instead let's simply use an appropriate sound.

Making your button buzz

The first thing to do is to get the sound into your movie's Library.

1. Download the file blip.wav (or search for a suitable sound on your hard drive—your operating system will most likely have a few button sounds). To import it into Flash, select File ➤ Import to Library. In the Import to Library window (shown as follows), select All Sound formats in the File of Type drop-down menu at the bottom, and then browse to your sound file.

2. Your Library window should now look something like this:

Ideally, you would now edit the sound to optimize it, but you'll leave all that until the dedicated sound chapter. Right now, what you need to do is attach the sound to the button.

3. Double-click the button symbol in the Library to go into Edit Symbols mode.

4. Create a new layer called sound—this layer will be used to hold the sound your button will make.

5. Add a blank keyframe to each of the button states using *F7*.

6. Select the Down state on the sound layer:

This is the button state that usually has a sound—putting your sound here will make the button sound off when it is pressed.

7. In the Property Inspector, click the Sound drop-down menu—this will show you all the currently available sounds. Unimpressively, only the one you just imported will be there. (Also ensure that the Sync drop-down is set to Event.)

8. Select your sound. The Property Inspector should now look something like the one shown here:

Look closely at the Down keyframe after you've done this. There's a tiny blue wave shown on the keyframe to signify that a sound has been attached there:

9. Test the movie. Hear your sound when you press the button? Yes? Then you're done!

10. Save your movie.

When you add sound to a button's Down state in the way that you've done here, you're adding sound to *all* instances of the button. This is a major advantage for adding sound to a previously silent website. If your website uses many instances of a single button symbol, you only need to add sound once for *all* your buttons to have sound.

The features of behaviors

Earlier, we likened clicking a Flash button to what happens when you ring someone's doorbell. Having a Flash button all by itself is like ringing the doorbell at a house where nobody's home, or where the wiring's been disconnected. The button you've just created looks pretty enough, but beyond the default state-related animations and sound that you've just explored, it doesn't trigger anything when you press it. It doesn't really *handle* the click event. When a user click a button, the sound or embedded animation that plays isn't what you're really concerned with—you're interested in where that button's going to take you, or what it's going to make happen. You need to *wire up the button*.

We also talked about the fact that behaviors can only be added to symbols once they are on a timeline (via our discussion about CD players). We called this process *instantiation*, and the copy created on the timeline is called an *instance*.

> *If you get into discussion with someone about the technical ins and outs of Flash, the word instance will crop up an awful lot because almost everything of consequence in a working site is one.*

By attaching a behavior to a button instance, you can make your buttons take you somewhere.

To start demonstrating the features of behaviors, you're going to create a simple movie in which Flash asks the user to pick one of two options, and then responds differently for each response. This implies a logical branching in your movie rather than a straightforward linear playback. You'll present the user with two colored buttons and the user will press one of them, causing Flash to go to one of two possible places. This ability to branch and make alternative choices is an important principle in creating interactive movies.

Before you can attach a behavior and make an interactive movie, you need to create a basic front end for the user to interact with. This will contain buttons that access the different places the user can go. You're going to set these up now.

Creating a basic front end

1. Continue working with the button movie from the previous exercise.

2. Drag another instance of your button symbol from the Library out onto the main stage—make sure you drag in the button symbol and *not* the graphic symbol.

3. Position the two button instances so they're next to each other in the center of the stage.

4. With one of your button instances highlighted, select Tint from the Color drop-down menu in the Property Inspector, and make the button blue using the color palette to the right of the Color drop-down menu.

5. You've just altered the properties of this specific instance of the button symbol: the underlying symbol has remained the same. Remember that each individual instance has a range of properties that you can change via the Property Inspector.

6. Repeat this Tint change for the other button, but make this one pink.

7. Create a new layer called text and use a static text box in which to type pick your favorite color above the two buttons.

Your stage should look like this:

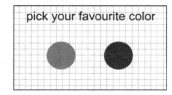

Here, you've used the same button symbol twice, but made them look different by changing the color of each instance. This is a timesaving trick used by many Flash web designers to help workflow when creating sites that have many different buttons on them. They just create one master button and then change the appearance of each *instance*.

Now you need to set up two areas of your site that Flash will display to when each button is pressed—one area for the pink button, and one for the blue button. You're going to put these areas in a separate layer called content. At the moment, your content will just be simple text messages, but it could be anything up to and including completely new pages within a Flash website.

8. Create a new layer, and call it content, and put it above the two existing layers.

9. Extend all layers up to Frame 30 by selecting frame 30 in each layer and pressing *F5*. Your timeline should now look like this:

10. In the content layer, add keyframes at frame 10 and 20.

11. Lock all layers except content. In frame 10 add a text message you clicked pink!' as shown in the following graphic. In frame 20, do the same, except change the text to read you clicked blue!

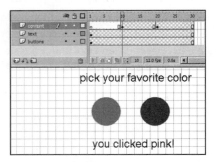

12. You now need a layer that will signal your jump points via **labels**. Add a new layer called actions as shown in the next screenshot, and add keyframes at frames 10 and 20. So that you don't inadvertently move your graphics around, lock all layers except actions.

You named the new layer actions and not behaviors because a behavior is pre-written ActionScript. When you add the behaviors, all you are really doing is adding code—you may not be writing it yet, but you will by next chapter.

When the user presses any of the buttons, you want Flash to jump to particular points in the timeline—specifically, the two keyframes you just added at frame 10 and 20, both of which will have content specific to the pink or blue choice.

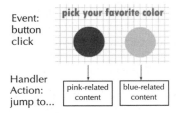

You'll now label these two keyframes so that they're properly labeled—which means that you can then use behaviors to jump straight to them.

13. Select frame 10 in the actions layer. Go to the Property Inspector and type pink in the Frame field:

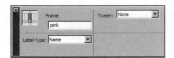

What you've done here is attach a label to frame 1 of the actions layer. This is a pointer or flag for the frame, and with it in place, you can use a behavior to jump directly to this frame from anywhere else in the movie on an event of your choosing. That's a pretty powerful thing to be able to do—bypass the linear tyranny of the timeline and jump around inside the movie.

You can also jump to a frame number, but the frame numbering will change every time you add a frame, so it isn't recommended—although it used to be the only way to do it in very early versions of Flash, and it took ages to create long animations because of it!

Notice that Flash has added a little flag in the timeline and is displaying the label name next to it:

You can use this label as a reference point for the pink button-related content that you want the user to be able to display.

Now you need to label the blue keyframe in the same way;

14. Click frame 20 in the same layer and add a new keyframe. In the Property Inspector use the Frame field again to label the new keyframe blue:

You've created two separate messages, each of which lives on its own separately labeled section of the timeline. You can use those labels as reference points that you can jump straight to using behaviors.

Attaching behaviors to frames and buttons

You now have a simple front end for the user to interact with and two alternate locations to move to from the two buttons. However, when you play the movie at the moment, the playhead will zip through the movie in a resolutely linear fashion: the frames will still play out as in a normal linear animation. You need to shout "STOP!" at frame 1 so that the front end

hangs around and gives the user time to ponder the alternatives and make their choice.

To do this you add a behavior **to a frame** in the timeline, telling the movie to halt at a particular point. This will give the user all the time in the world to choose a button. To react to a button click, you attach a behavior **to each button**. Once you've added your behaviors, you'll have a fully working interactive movie.

To summarize:

- You can add behaviors **to a frame** so that the associated ActionScript is triggered when the playhead reaches that frame. In this case, you will add something at frame 1 to tell Flash to stop at frame 1.

- You can attach a behavior **to a button** so that the ActionScript is only triggered when the user clicks the button. Here, the user triggers the event and the ActionScript handles it via the behavior code you will attach to the buttons.

Flash treats everything that happens as an event. Not only are non-periodic occurrences (such as the user clicking a button) events, but so are sequential or periodic occurrences, such as entering a new frame—an event is generated on every new frame. This means that although attaching to a frame and attaching to a button may seem like two different techniques, they are actually exactly the same; you are attaching a behavior to the thing that creates the event.

Adding behaviors to a frame

1. Select frame 1 in the *actions* layer. Display the Behaviors panel if it isn't already open (Window ➤ Development Panels ➤ Behaviors). Notice that the text at the top of the panel reminds you that you will attach your behavior to frame 1 of layer actions.

239

2. Using the plus sign (+), select Movie Clip ➤ Goto and Stop at frame or label. You will see the window shown in the following screenshot. The defaults are what you want (stop *this* timeline at frame 1), so you don't have to do anything other than make sure you are seeing what we say should be there. Also worth noting is the little "a" that appears above frame 1 when you click OK. This signifies that code (or actions) have been added to the frame.

If you test the movie now, you will see that the timeline doesn't play through anymore—it simply stops at the first frame, which is exactly what you want.

You used a behavior to achieve your first objective of keeping the buttons visible—and static—so that the viewer can choose their favorite color via the buttons.

What Flash needs to know next is where you want to take the users when they click one of those buttons. To do this, you're going to attach some ActionScript **to each button**. These pieces of ActionScript will hook up each button to its dedicated piece of content—you can use the labels to tell Flash and your behaviors where to go. But Flash also needs to know *when* to move to a new frame.

Remember the **events** and **event handlers** that set off your "visit a friend" interaction earlier in this chapter? You want your interaction in this movie to start with the user doing something with their mouse pointer on or near your button. What you're trying to detect here is called a **button event**. You can ask Flash (which acts as the event handler) to detect one or more types of button event. The most common ones are:

- A **Press** event occurs when the user *clicks* the button. You may think that this would be the event of choice to ask Flash to detect, but it actually causes Flash to race off and start doing new things as soon as the button is pressed. This doesn't leave any time for the user to see the button working—for instance, running the nice animation that you've built into the button.

- A **Release** is when the user *releases* the mouse button after a press, and it's what you use in many situations because it allows you to see the button in its Down state.

- A **Release Outside** event occurs when the user presses a button and then drags the mouse away from the button without releasing the mouse button. The event is triggered when the mouse button is finally released. Why would you use this event? If your buttons are very small, the user could inadvertently drag the mouse pointer outside the button area before they release it. In this situation, you could ask Flash to detect either Release *or* Release Outside.

- The **Roll Over** and **Roll Out** events are used to detect whether the mouse pointer is *over* a certain area. Buttons set up to detect only these two events don't usually look like buttons at all. For example, if you had a bitmap picture of the world and you wanted a bit of text at the bottom of the map to change to reflect which country the mouse pointer was over, you would add a lot of country-shaped buttons. Think of buttons asked to detect Roll Over and Roll Out events as "mouse position sensors" rather than true buttons, and this class of button event will start to make more sense.

> Note that in real life, the only event of consequence is "pressing the button." In the world of computers, things are much more tightly defined, and even in something simple like hitting a button, there are more events than you might have expected. This shouldn't put you off though, because in most cases, you only need one event—the Release event. You will only need the other ones once you start making all those cool and wacky interfaces that Flash is so famous for.

Adding a behavior to a button

1. You want to work with the buttons, so lock everything except the *buttons* layer. Click the pink button to select it. The Behaviors panel will change to show that you are about to attach a behavior to a button:

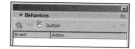

2. Click the plus sign (+) and select Movieclip ➤ Goto and Stop at frame or label. In the window that appears, change the bottom text entry box from 1 to pink as shown below:

> Note that the behavior for a button is called "Movieclip" instead of "Movieclips and Buttons." Obviously, space is a premium in drop-down menus!

The Behavior panel will now change to reflect what you just attached. The left column describes the *event* and the right column displays what the event handler will do. To change either, simply click them (although they are all set up as you want them by default):

If you test the movie now, you will see that the pink button works. Clicking it will send the timeline to the frame you labeled pink, and the content for that frame (the you clicked pink! text) will be shown:

3. All you now need to do to complete your example is to add the same behavior to the blue button. Repeat steps 1 and 2, but this time click the blue button and enter the label blue.

Now your buttons are functional and can be used to allow the user to hop from place to place at will. That's interactivity!

Case study

In the last case study, you began creating your web portfolio page. In this section you'll finish this page, and make it fully functional.

1. Open your saved case study document from the last chapter.

2. Open the Property inspector (if necessary), and click the content movie clip instance on the main timeline:

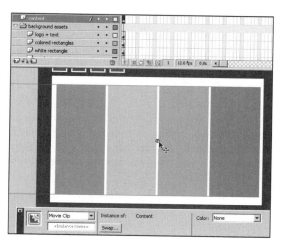

3. Type content_mc in the Instance Name text field in the Property inspector:

Giving it an instance name will allow you to control it with behaviors and ActionScript. You'll cover instance names in detail in the next chapter.

4. Double-click the content movie clip instance to enter Edit in Place mode.

5. Within the content movie clip, move the playhead to frame 91 and click the web content instance on the stage:

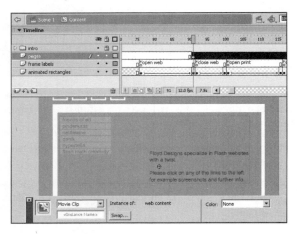

6. Type web_mc into the Instance Name text field in the Property inspector:

7. Double-click the web content symbol instance to edit it. You're now going to attach some behaviors to the buttons here to make them work. Before that though, you need to stop the playhead on the first frame here.

8. Insert a new layer above all the others and rename it actions.

9. Select the keyframe on the actions layer, and open the Behaviors panel (Window ➤ Development Panels ➤ Behaviors):

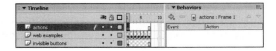

10. Click the plus sign (+) button in the Behaviors panel and select Movieclip ➤ Goto and Stop at frame or label.

11. In the dialog box that appears, select web_mc from within content_mc:

12. Click OK. That's your playhead halting done. Now onto the buttons.

Adding behaviors to the buttons

1. Select the invisible button covering the friends of ed text. The corresponding content for this button is on frame 2, so you need to send the playhead there.

2. Click the plus sign (+) in the Behaviors panel, and select Movieclip ➤ Goto and Stop at frame or label:

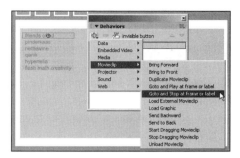

3. In the dialog box that appears, make sure the top text field reads this and change the bottom text field to read 2:

4. This refers to frame 2 within this movie clip timeline. Click OK to confirm this action, and the Behavior panel will have changed accordingly:

Now it's time to do the same for the rest of the buttons.

5. Click the invisible button covering the text pinderkaas.

6. Click the Add Behavior button (represented by a plus sign) in the Behavior panel. Select Movieclip ➤ Goto and Stop at frame or label.

7. In the dialog box, ensure the top field reads this, and the frame field is set to 3.

8. Repeat this process for the remaining buttons. Using the following details:

- nettle wine—frame 4
- qanik—frame 5
- hypertelia—frame 6
- flash math creativity—frame 7

Once you are done adding behaviors to all the buttons, you can give it a test. One useful way to test an individual piece of content alone, in this case a movie clip, is to use the Control ➤ Test Scene menu selection. This will preview the current scene (or timeline) that you are in. You can tell this as usual using the scene navigator above the timeline:

9. Select Control ➤ Test Scene to preview the movie.

Um....Who turned out the lights? Where has my text gone? Well, they are there, but they just happen to be the same color as the background so you can't see them. Let's switch the light on for a minute.

10. Close the preview and open the Document Properties (Modify ➤ Document).

11. Change the background color to white and then click OK.

12. Preview the scene again using Control ➤ Test Scene:

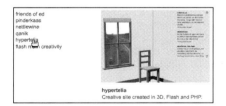

This time you can see the text, and better still, you can press the buttons to change the website preview on the right side. Before you change the background color back, there are a few more buttons to create. These new buttons will be thumbnails of the actual screenshots, arranged in a diagonal row.

13. Close the preview movie.

14. Select the blank keyframe on the thumbnails layer and drag a copy of the friendsofed_website.gif image from the library anywhere onto the stage.

15. Open the Transform panel (*CTRL+T* or Windows ➤ Design Panels ➤ Transform) and select the image.

16. Ensure that Constrain is ticked, and type 30% into either of the top two text fields. Then press Enter to render it:

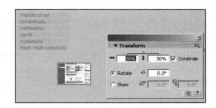

17. Ensure that Snap Align is switched on (View ➤ Snapping ➤ Snap Align), and move the image so that it snaps with the button text field and the main text to its right:

18. When it is in place, release it.

19. Select the image and duplicate it with Edit ➤ Duplicate or *CTRL+D*. This will place a duplicate down and to the right of the original. It will also instantly select the duplicate:

20. Select Edit ➤ Duplicate or press *CTRL+D* again. This will duplicate the duplicate, producing a duplicate of the duplicate down and to the right of the first duplicate!

21. Create duplicates in the same way until you have six images in all:

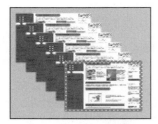

Flash has done you a great favor here because it has created a pretty pattern all on its own. (Okay you helped it out a little bit, but give it some credit please.) You're going to keep the images positioned as they are, all you need to do is to swap them with the required images.

22. Select the second image from the top and select Swap in the Property inspector:

23. In the dialog box that appears, select pinderkaas_website.gif.

24. Exchange the other images in the same way, in this order from top to bottom:

- nettle_wine.gif
- qanik.gif

- hypertelia.gif
- fmc.gif

It should then look like this:

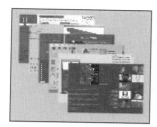

Now you need to add interactivity to these images, at the moment however, they are raw images. As you are already aware, to attach behaviors or ActionScript to objects, they have to be a button or movie clip symbol. You could convert them all by hand, but Flash can do this for you another way.

25. Select the top-left image and click the Add Behavior button (represented by the plus sign) in the Behavior panel. Choose Movieclip ➤ Goto and Stop at frame or label.

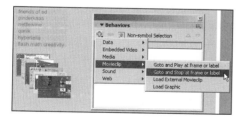

Immediately, Flash will see the error of your ways, and offer to convert the selected object into a symbol:

26. Click OK so Flash can do all the hard work for you.

27. As usual, the behaviors dialog will appear. Set it as seen here:

BehaviorObject1 here is the generic instance and symbol name that Flash has given your selected object. It's not particularly intuitive for future modifications, but you can live with it here.

28. Click OK to add the behavior. Now you need to do the same with the other images, linking to their corresponding frames.

29. Select the other images in the row, and repeat the process just outlined, specifying frames 3–7 as necessary. Remember each time to select the web_mc instance so the top text field reads this._parent. Here's the keyframe list:

- Frame 3: Pinderkaas
- Frame 4: nettlewine
- Frame 5: qanik
- Frame 6: hypertelia
- Frame 7: flash math creativity

30. Extend the frames on the thumbnails layer to frame 7 by pressing the *F5* key.

31. Select Control ➤ Test Scene to test the thumbnail buttons. Now your viewers have two forms of navigation.

Now you can see that it works, you can change the background color back to it's original setting.

32. Select Modify ➤ Document and change the background color back to dark blue (#003366).

Letting the user know where they are

In this section you're going to label each page to let the user know which page they are currently looking at.

1. From your current position within the web content movieclip, step back to the Content movieclip.

2. Click frame 92 of the pages layer and insert a blank keyframe by pressing the *F7* key. You've done this to prevent the web page from appearing where it shouldn't.

3. Click frame 91 of the pages layer and select the Text tool.

4. Type FLOYD DESIGNS : WEB in 15pt bold Verdana anywhere on the stage. Set the color as #003366:

5. With Snap Align still turned on, position the text field in the white area above the green rectangle. When it snaps vertically and horizontally to the green rectangle, release it:

6. Copy the text field using Edit ➤ Copy or *CTRL+C*.

7. Insert a blank keyframe (F7) on frame 116 of the pages layer.

8. Select Edit ➤ Paste to place a copy of the last text field on the stage.

9. Double-click the text field and change it to read FLOYD DESIGNS : PRINT.

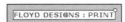

10. Drag the text field using the Selection tool to snap in the top-right corner as you did with the last one:

11. Click frame 117 of the pages layer and insert a blank keyframe to prevent the print page from appearing elsewhere in the movie. If you didn't do this, the print page would still be shown during the closing animation.

12. Insert a blank keyframe on frame 140 and paste another copy of the text. This time change it to read FLOYD DESIGNS : ABOUT and position it in the top right corner.

13. Insert a blank keyframe on frame 141 to stop the about page from running on for too long.

14. Insert a blank keyframe on frame 165, paste the text and change it to FLOYD DESIGNS : EMAIL.

15. Position it as before, and insert a blank keyframe on frame 166 to clear it.

That's it. Before you finish this chapter, there is one tiny thing left to do—add some sound!

Adding sound to the buttons

1. In the interests of safety, save the case study in it's current state.

2. Double-click the symbol generic button in the Library to edit it. This is how it looks at the moment:

3. Click the Down state frame, and press *F5* to extend the previous state onto it.

4. Insert a new layer and name it sound:

5. Insert a blank keyframe on the Down state of the sound layer. You're going to trigger a sound to play when a button has been released.

6. Select Window ➤ Other Panels ➤ Common Libraries ➤ Sounds to open the Sounds library.

7. Drag the Visor Hum Loop sound into your case study library.

8. Select the keyframe on the Down state of the sound layer, and choose the Visor Hum Loop sound from the Sound drop-down in the Property inspector:

9. Test the movie using Control ➤ Test Movie (or CTRL + ENTER) and click any of the buttons at the top left of the screen. Even though they don't actually control your navigation yet, the length of the sound will just about cover the opening shape tween of each page. Nice!

10. Finally! Save the case study file.

In the next chapter you'll use ActionScript to pull things together so that you can interact using the main buttons.

Summary

In this chapter, we introduced the important concept of interactivity, and you started to see how Flash implements this using behaviors.

This was an important chapter because the simple examples that you've seen here will be a foundation that you can build on, both in the next chapter specifically and in the rest of the book more generally because they establish the core idea of interactivity and the way it's implemented via events and event handlers.

You saw that:

- Timeline effects allow you to quickly create professional animations, the parameters of which can be customized and modified at any time.

- Frequently used sequences of actions within Flash can be saved as commands. These actions are selected from the History panel.

- Some History panel entries, denoted with a red x, cannot be saved as part of a command.

- Interactivity is about bringing the Flash movie to life and giving the user an interesting and satisfying experience.

- The principles of events and event handlers are at the heart of interactivity. Events—like a user clicking a button—happen, and you create actions or behavior that will respond and cope with these events.

- A powerful way of adding interaction in Flash is by using **buttons**. Buttons can have media—such as animation, sound, and movie clips—embedded in their default states, and they can be made even more intelligent by attaching **ActionScript** to the button events that buttons can detect.

- **ActionScript** is the string that ties together all the components of a Flash movie or website. In this chapter, you didn't write the code, but more importantly, you learned a lot about the principles that underpin ActionScript

- **Behaviors** can be attached to **frames** in the timeline, or to buttons and movie clip instances—that is, buttons and movie clips that are on a timeline.

- You can use behaviors to jump to specific areas inside your movies, and this stops your movies being fixed animations on rails, and turns them into interactive content, where the user decides where they want to go, and what they want to see.

In the next chapter, you'll explore the next stage in your journey toward Flash ActionScript. You will no longer use behaviors—you will write ActionScript directly. Sounds daunting, but you have already seen most of the theory, so don't worry!

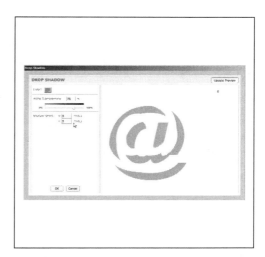

Chapter 10

ACTIONS AND INTERACTIONS

What we'll cover in this chapter:

- Introducing **ActionScript**, the programming language that makes Macromedia Flash so powerful
- Understanding syntax
- Looking at the ActionScript environment and how to write scripts in Flash (and how not to)
- Creating interactive Flash sites with buttons and your own hand-written ActionScript

This chapter moves you a significant way along in your Flash journey. You're coming to the crest of a hill, and a whole new vista of Flash possibilities is going to open up. There, bathed in sunlight, is the land of **ActionScript**. In the last chapter, you looked at behaviors, which are self-contained ActionScript building blocks that prevent you from getting your hands dirty with writing code yourselves. That's fine for basic sites, but to understand Flash properly (and to use all its advanced features effectively), you have to know at least basic ActionScript.

One thing we should say right at the beginning is that ActionScript is not for everyone. If, after dipping your toes into its waters for a while, you find it confusing and bewildering, that's fine. You may decide to use behaviors instead for now, and revisit ActionScript again later. Not knowing ActionScript well is not the same as not knowing Flash well: Flash is a very flexible tool and there are always at least two ways to do everything—so do it the way that feels right for you.

ActionScript vs. behaviors

In Chapter 9, we likened clicking a Flash button to what happens when you ring someone's doorbell. Having a Flash button all by itself is like ringing the doorbell at a house where nobody's home or where the wiring's been disconnected.

There are two ways to add wiring to a doorbell. One is to go out and buy a doorbell off the shelf. All you need to do is attach it to a wall, connect the wires, and plug it in. You don't have to do much else other than tighten a few wire terminals and drill a couple of holes in the wall. That's a cool way of doing it because all the electronics that control the chime are encased in the box, and you don't have to worry about it. That's also the problem though—you *don't get an understanding of how it works*. You can't fix it if it breaks, and more importantly, you can't upgrade it if you want it to, for example, control the back door as well as the front.

The harder way around is to learn enough about electronics to design your own doorbell. Once you do that, you realize that there wasn't that much in the box anyway! It's only a little circuit that drives a buzzer, with

the doorbell completing the circuit. Furthermore, when you look at the "off the shelf" doorbell, you might start to notice little oddities, like the transformer in there that is configured for USA voltage levels of 110V, or the 240V you see in some other countries, such as England. There may even be some sort of selector switch at the front of the box that allows you to choose between *Mission Impossible* theme tune, *Boys of Summer*, or *Jingle Bells*, so the bell plays your chosen tune whenever someone presses the button. The point is, if you design your own doorbell, you don't need to mess with these extra features; you simply design what you want, making the whole thing simpler. And Flash is the same:

- You can use a drag and drop behavior. It's fast and efficient, but at the expense of reducing your understanding of the problem, and it offers a solution that addresses problems that may not be part of your particular task. It's also a "one size fits all" solution—and how many times have you bought a one size fits all shirt and thought "Mmm fits perfectly, almost as if it was tailor-made for me?" Me neither.

- You can write your own code. It's a harder route, but it opens up a much wider vista than just creating button scripts. You can write other things that you can't use behaviors for; such as Flash games, advanced interfaces that no one else has even thought about (let alone wrote a behavior for), and so on. You can also create custom code that is exactly suited to your needs and fits the problem perfectly. A cool side-effect of writing your own code is that you can extend it later, so over time, your website will evolve from a simple button menu affair to one of those oh-so-fancy Flash sites where the whole thing is so integrated, you can't even *see* the buttons, never mind attach a behavior to them.

To start demonstrating ActionScript's features, you're going to revisit the example you created back in chapter 9, but this time you will not be using behaviors—you'll write the darn thing yourselves.

Before you can add some ActionScript, you need to see what ActionScript actually *is*.

Scripts, programs, and code—it's all Geek/Greek to me

That's what a lot of you are thinking so far, right? You have questions like "I thought code was written to create something called a computer program, so what's this 'script' thing?" and "Why am I programming inside a visual animation application?"

Programming and scripting

When you write a totally new standalone application (such as Flash itself, Microsoft Word, or Doom 3), you write in languages such as C++. This is a complex endeavor, requiring teams of highly skilled programmers.

When you just want to add some customizations to Microsoft Word for yourself, create a new level for Doom, or add a bit of intelligence to a web page, you don't need to create applications, you just need to tell the current application what to do. That is what a *scripting language* does. ActionScript is a scripting language—it tells the Flash player what to do, and it requires the Flash player to be present before it will work. Rather than a program or application, a scripting language is used to create, um...scripts. These are one or more short sections of code that tell the main application what to do. In Flash, you attach scripts to keyframes.

You can attach scripts to other things, such as directly to a button or movie clip, but a modern ActionScript coding style avoids this. As a beginner, attaching scripts to keyframes alone will give you the good habits needed to become an advanced ActionScripter much quicker, and also has the cool side effect of making your learning curve much simpler. Better all round!

The difference between a programming language and a scripting language is:

- Programming languages are meant for heavy-duty projects like creating PhotoShop from scratch. They require around a zillion years at college to learn, and most people don't bother trying because life is short enough as it is.

- Scripting languages are designed to create much simpler and shorter bits of code that specify how an application should run. Because they are designed to create simpler stuff than application building languages, you don't need that zillion years in college to understand them.

That's a real relief to the typical beginner Flash designer, who's likely thinking "Whuh? Programming? I'm a graphic/web designer...there must be some mistake!" In fact, scripting languages are designed on the premise that the people using them will *not* be trained programmers at all. Phew!

Scripting and animation

The stuff you've done so far in Flash has been cool, but (apart from behaviors) has been defined at authoring time. When you create a tween animation, it will do exactly the same thing every time you run it. Well, folks just *loved* all those wacky flash animations and spent hours watching them four years ago, but nowadays the novelty has lessened, and folks want to interact. They want animations that do things differently every time and provide things like challenging entertainment or efficient user interfaces. They want to be able to play a Flash version of Asteroids online, or they want to book a hotel room using an interactive Flash interface. ActionScript-based content can do all this, and has become more and more important in the last few years. Tweening, although still a big part of Flash, is becoming less frequently used.

Understanding scripting

Rather than go straight into animation, you will rework the navigation example you looked at in chapter 9, this time without behaviors—you will write the code yourselves. Before you do that though, you need to get deeper into ActionScript and cover a number of important concepts:

- ActionScript syntax
- The Flash scripting environment

251

Syntax

Syntax is something that is common to all languages, not just computer languages.

> *Syntax refers to the way you structure words into sentences. It doesn't refer to what the words mean, only to the structures that they are placed in to form readable text or intelligible conversation.*

In spoken English, you have a wide and varied syntax, full of special clauses and more than one way to say the same thing. There are very good reasons for all this variability and redundancy:

- The different ways of saying the same thing add to the *expressiveness* of English; you can add emphasis or a personal style to what you say or write.
- The redundancy in the spoken word means that you can understand what someone means even if you don't understand every word. You can usually understand what others are saying even if they use a different dialect or speak with an unfamiliar accent because the redundancy means you only have to pick up *most* of what was said.

The big difference between human syntax and computer syntax is that computers don't expect unfamiliar dialects or accents; computer language syntaxes are typically simple but very precise. This precision can seem totally alien to us; you don't usually expect someone to fail to understand you just because you don't speak or write in exactly the same accent as them…but that's the way computer languages work!

Luckily, ActionScript has very few syntax rules. In fact, it has only three that you need to think about when writing basic scripts:

Rule 1: End each line with a semicolon

Each line of script ends with a ';'
The following are both permissible;
line;
line;
line;

line; line; line;

If you press ENTER at the end of each line, Flash will be able to guess where all the semicolons need to go, so this is also OK.

line
line
line

The following, however, *is not* OK because Flash has no way of knowing where a new line starts:

line line line

Rule 2: The object, method, and argument

In English, you very often have three main types of word in most sentences: a noun (person, place, or thing); a verb (action); and an adjective or adverb (description).

Put together, you have sentences like "John runs quickly."

Flash is the same, except the syntax is *much* more precise, and also much simpler. Instead of a noun, you have an *instance* (also called an *object*); instead of a verb you have a *method;* and instead of an adjective/adverb, you have an *argument*. Each means something similar to your noun-verb-adjective in English syntax.

Computers are precise, so you can't use subjective terms like *quickly*. You and I have some idea of what quickly means, and the range of values that would be understood as quick movement if John was a toddler, an Olympic runner, or if he were running through waist-high molasses. Trouble is, a computer doesn't have the same subjective worldview we do because it doesn't know anything about our world. Instead, it understands only non-subjective or numerical terms, such as "John runs at 5 miles an hour." The 5 isn't subjective; it's a *value* that needs nothing else to describe it—it's *precise*. The argument is always enclosed in brackets, and the object and action are always separated by a dot (.). In ActionScript, this sentence would become *John.run(5)*.

Note that in some cases, the object.method(argument) structure is actually a single line, so from rule 1, you could say the following if the fact that John is running at 5 m/ph is all you wanted to say *John.run(5);*.

Some of you may have noticed that the computer version of your line has changed in its implication somewhat. "John runs quickly" is descriptive, whereas John.run(5); seems more like a directive. The computer version looks like you are telling John to do something, rather than describing what he is doing. This is not a mistranslation, it is a window into what code actually is—a set of instructions or commands that tell the computer what it should be doing. You will even sometimes catch programmers referring to code as instructions or commands because that is what code really is.

Rule 3: The code block

In the same way that English sentences can form paragraphs, ActionScript lines can form a *block*. A block encloses a number of lines, and begins with an opening curly bracket, also known as a brace ({) and ends with a closing curly bracket (}).

```
{
  line;
  line;
  line;
}
```

The block tells Flash the following:

- What it should do with the enclosed lines
- What the lines are

Here's an example of each in pseudo code (i.e. plain text that is not real code, but is formatted in the correct syntax):

```
Do this ten times {
  line;
  line;
  line;
}
```

A loop block lets Flash know that the lines within the block need to be repeated a number of times.

Loops are very useful in coding, because most things you get computers to do are repetitive or number crunching tasks that require the same set of instructions to be repeated many times.

A block is also used in event-event handlers; the start of the block denotes which event you are looking at, and the block contents are the event handler.

```
When you see a click{
  Do these lines;
  Do these lines;
  Do these lines;
}
```

The final rule (which you will look at later) has to do with building expressions. If you understand 4 = 3+1 then you're already a lot closer to understanding expressions than you might think!

And that's it! These are the core rules you need to know to write basic scripts. There are also a couple of other rules that, although not part of ActionScript, are part of good ActionScript style.

Camel case

When you name anything in ActionScript, it's common practice to use camel case. ActionScript doesn't like spaces (and when it does, they are there for your benefit—Flash actually removes them internally before running each line), so you have problems when you want to use an instance called John Doe instead of simply John. The way to get round this is to use camel case— John Doe becomes johnDoe, New Masters of Flash becomes newMastersOfFlash, and camel case becomes camelCase. The rule for creating camel case instance names is to start with lower case, and add an uppercase letter at the start of each new word.

It's called camel case because of the humps you create by adding capitals in the middle of a string of lowercase letters.

Indenting

If you look at Rule 3, you will notice that the script lines within a code block are indented. This makes reading a script much easier because it's easy to see which lines are in a block, and which are outside it. Indenting is such a good idea that Flash adds it automatically to your scripts as you write, as you shall see later.

Those are the basic syntax rules. What about actually entering code into Flash?

The Flash scripting environment

To create basic scripts in Flash, you use two panels: the Actions panel and the Property inspector. If you are using the vanilla panel settings (select Window ➤ Panel Sets ➤ Default Layout if you want to get back to them) the two panels appear in the lower middle docking area as shown in the following graphic.

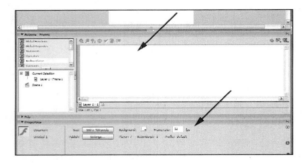

The Actions panel is used to enter scripts (from the default setup, you will have to open it to see it in its full glory). The big blank pane to the right of the panel is the text entry area for your scripting.

The Property inspector is used to add the link between ActionScript and the graphical interface: the *instance name*. This is the "John" in the example we talked about earlier.

First, a bit of set up. Scripts can get rather long and contain lots of lines, so it's a good idea to number them. To do this, select the Actions panel's drop-down menu (via the little pop-up menu at the top right of the panel) and select View Line Numbers.

Let's enter some code. You'll redo the button example in the last chapter, this time writing it all yourselves.

Writing your first script

You now know enough to do away with behaviors and write the code yourself, so that is exactly what you will do!

You'll start with the button symbols you created in the last chapter. You will find the FLA to start this exercise in the downloads for this chapter, called scriptStart.fla. It is the same as the example in the last chapter, minus the behaviors.

> *If you have grown attached your own version of the FLA, all you need to do is remove all the behaviors so you can replace them with your own code. To do this:*
>
> *1. Select frame 1 in layer actions (the keyframe with an a). In the Behaviors panel, select the one behavior that you see (it will have a* Goto and Stop at frame or label *action) by clicking its Action column. Click the minus (–) icon at the top left to delete it.*
>
> *2. Select each button in turn, and in the Behaviors panel, select the behavior and delete it with the hyphen icon as before.*
>
> *For the more lazy/cautious, you can also look at the completed FLA for this exercise,* scriptCompleted.fla.

If you test the movie as it stands, the timeline doesn't stop, so you first need to halt the timeline on frame 1.

1. Select frame 1 in the actions layer. The top-left pane in the Actions panel contains a set of icons that look like little books with arrows on the front. Scroll down until you see the book labeled Built-in

Classes. Click the icon. This opens the book. You will now see the book icon change to an open book, and a list of more books will appear below it. Click the one labeled Movie, the one labeled Movie Clip, and the one labeled Methods.

You should have opened a path of books that looks like this (expand the panel to get a better view). Icons in text are:

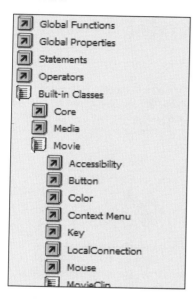

2. Below the open Methods book you'll see a list of circled arrows. These are ActionScript Methods of the MovieClip, which is a Flash Built in Class. You know this by looking at the trail of open books you have left. This is the method part of your *object.method(argument);* syntax we talked about earlier.

3. You're in the right ballpark, all you have to do is find the method that will do what you want—stop a timeline. It doesn't take much guesswork—you want to use the stop method (they are listed alphabetically). Double-click it. You will see the following appear in the right pane:

```
instanceName.stop();
```

This is your full *object.method(argument);* syntax. Notice that:

- Flash added this line automatically. The downside here is that it's a bit more involved than behaviors. This is because raw ActionScript's upsides gives you a lot of choices—just look at all the other stuff you could have selected!

- Flash added the semicolon at the end for you.

- Flash added color-coding. Your method part is in blue. Flash will always print all keywords or methods it recognizes in blue. If it doesn't do that for a method, chances are it has been misspelled and you need to correct it.

- Flash is using camel case. Instead of "Instance Name," it used "instanceName."

Flash added a *standard* stop method for you. You now need to customize it.

4. You need to decide on the object you want to stop. With movie clips, the instance is a timeline, and the only one you have at the moment is the one you are on. Flash has a special keyword that means "the timeline you are on at the moment." Flash calls it this or uses a blank. Because you are just beginning in ActionScript, you will go for the easier option, the blank. Click anywhere on the line. You will see a cursor appear. This is your text cursor. Using the keyboard arrow keys, position is so that it is just after the first dot, as shown in the following graphic:

```
instanceName.|stop();
```

You will talk about this at length later in this chapter when you look at scope, so don't worry, you will be covering everything in good time!

255

5. Press *DELETE* on your keyboard until you have deleted everything to the left of the method:

```
stop();
```

You need to specify an instance name of your own…or do you? As we just said, Flash assumes you are talking about the current timeline (the timeline the code is on) *unless* you specify an instance name. This means you can get away with having no instance name in this case because you actually *want* to stop the current timeline.

Finally, according to the rules discussed earlier, you need to add an argument. But you don't need to tell Flash *how* to stop ("stop" is precise enough as it is; you want Flash to stop now and do nothing). You don't therefore need an argument, so the line is complete.

> *Although all lines will contain the object.method (argument) structure, sometimes parts of it are implied by where the code is attached, or parts are not needed.*

Congratulations! You've just entered your first line of ActionScript. Some of you are thinking "Whoa! All that work just to type *that!?* I could have entered that by hand!" Well, exactly! As you learn ActionScript, you will realize that although there are many objects, methods, and arguments, 90 percent of your code will consist of about 5–10 percent of the available actions, and you will very soon *know them all by heart*. When you do, you will be writing stop(); as fast as you can type it, probably about a second slower than you just read it now!

If you test the movie now, you will see that the timeline stops at frame 1. Next stop, the buttons.

Getting back to the noun-verb-adjective vs. instance.method(argument) analogy, you know that it is John who is running in the sentence "John runs quickly" because you see his name. You do not yet have names for your two buttons, and you need these before you can add the instance part of your syntax. The first thing you need to do is give your two buttons *instance names*.

6. Select the pink button. In the Property inspector, you will see the following:

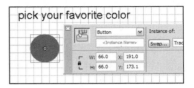

The text entry box currently with <Instance Name> in it is where you specify the name of the instance you want to attach your code to. Change the instance name by clicking anywhere inside the box and entering pinkButton.

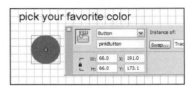

7. Do the same for the blue button, calling it blueButton.

> *ActionScript 2.0, which is what you are writing, is case sensitive. This means that pinkButton is a different name to pinkbutton and Pinkbutton. This has two implications:*
>
> *1. You have to type instance names exactly, or Flash will get it wrong by assuming you mean another name.*
>
> *2. You can have buttons called pinkbutton and pinkButton, and Flash will recognize them as two different buttons. Although you can do this, it is a recipe for confusion, and we strongly recommend that you use only camel case instance names throughout your ActionScript.*

Now that you have instance names, ActionScript can start referring to them, and you can create the code for the event-event handler pair for them.

8. Go back to the actions layer (you may have to scroll up the layer stack to find it), select frame 1, and view the attached code in the Actions panel. Add a few blank lines above the current line by placing the cursor at the start of line 1 and then pressing *ENTER* a few times.

9. You now need to add an on-release event for each button. Using the book and arrow icons in the left pane, go to Built-in Classes ➤ Movie ➤ Button ➤ Events ➤ onRelease and double-click it.

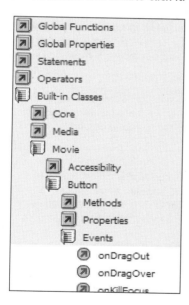

You will see `instanceName.onRelease` appear. Continue the line by adding `= function() {` (the word "function" will turn into blue text if you spell it correctly. Press *ENTER* twice, and then add a closing curly bracket. Finally, go back to line 2 so

that your Script pane looks as shown in the following graphic.

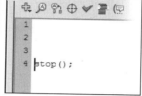

You just added a code block that defines a button onRelease event. The start of line 1 defines the instance you are defining your event for (it's currently the default name `instanceName`, which you will soon be changing), and the event (which is really just a special type of method) is onRelease. At the end of line 1, you have an opening curly bracket to define the start of the code block that will be the event handler, and line 3 is the closing curly bracket that ends the block. Your text cursor is at line 2—Flash is waiting for you to enter the event handler code in the block it has just created.

10. Using the books again, go to Built-in Classes ➤ Movie ➤ MovieClip ➤ Methods, and double-click gotoAndStop. You code will now look like this.

```
1  instanceName.onRelease = function() {
2      instanceName.gotoAndStop();
3
4  }
5
6
7  stop();
```

You will need two event handlers, one for the pink button and one for the blue button, so it would be a good idea to copy what you have so far before you start customizing the code for pinkButton and blueButton. Using the cursor, drag from the start of line 1 to line 4 so that all the text is selected (it will show up as inverse video: light text on a black background) as shown in the following graphic:

```
1  instanceName.onRelease = function() {
2      instanceName.gotoAndStop();
3
4  }
5
6
7  stop();
```

Right-click anywhere on the selection and select Copy from the menu that appears. Then right-click anywhere on line 5 and select Paste from the menu. You should now have two versions of the selection:

```
1  instanceName.onRelease = function() {
2      instanceName.gotoAndStop();
3
4  }
5  instanceName.onRelease = function() {
6      instanceName.gotoAndStop();
7
8  }
9
10 stop();
```

Before you start to customize your code, it would be a good idea to get rid of all those blank lines to tidy it all up. You can do this by clicking the **Auto Format** icon at the top of the panel. After you click this, your code should look like this:

```
1  instanceName.onRelease = function() {
2      instanceName.gotoAndStop();
3  };
4  instanceName.onRelease = function() {
5      instanceName.gotoAndStop();
6  };
7  stop();
8
```

If a window appears saying "This script contains syntax errors, so it cannot be formatted," you may have one or more typos. Click OK on the window and check that you have a closing curly bracket for every opening curly bracket (you cannot have an unclosed block) and that you have no spaces after the start of each line, except around the equal sign (=). Also, check that all the onRelease, function, gotoAndStop and stop text is all blue, and if it isn't, check your spelling. Then cross your fingers and try again.

If you get really stuck, click the Check Syntax icon. This will list all lines that Flash thinks have errors in them, allowing you to close in to the problem.

11. Using the text cursor as before, replace the first instanceName (line 1) with pinkButton, and the second one (line 4) with blueButton.

```
1  pinkButton.onRelease = function() {
2      instanceName.gotoAndStop();
3  };
4  blueButton.onRelease = function() {
5      instanceName.gotoAndStop();
6  };
7  stop();
8
```

The occurrences of instanceName on lines 2 and 5 are different than the two you just worked on; they are in code blocks that are already looking at pinkbutton and blueButton. By "looking at" we mean something called *scope*. Scope is very much like the way you understand the following paragraph:

John runs quickly—he is fast for his age. One day, he might even make the Olympics.

Who are you talking about when you say "he"? Easy question…you're talking about John. The funny thing is that *everyone* finds this easy when you talk about English, but difficult when you talk about Flash, but the concept is the same—if Flash already knows that a code block (which is Flash's version of a paragraph) is being written for a specific instance, you *don't have to tell it again,* for exactly the same reason that you know who John is "he" even if you don't always mention his name.

In short, Flash can determine what these instance names refer to because it understands the code context of the surrounding block.

In Flash, this concept is called *scope*. Lines 2 and 5 are within event handler code blocks, and Flash knows that the blocks are for pinkButton and blueButton because the head of each block tells it so.

Flash doesn't know about pronouns like those you would use to talk about things in real life when you already know what the subject in a sentence is. Code has much simpler syntax—you have to remember only one term: this. "This" refers to the same thing as "she," "he," and all the other terms used in the English language to represent the implied subject.

Another issue is what Flash does when you don't add any instance name at all (which is the same as adding no noun in English, so you would have "runs quickly"), or when you use it outside a code block:

- If you do not add any instance name at all, Flash assumes you actually mean the timeline your code is attached to *whether or not you are inside or outside a code block.*

> *If you have a this outside a code block, it doesn't matter whether you use it—the same subject will be implied either way (i.e. the current timeline). This is an important feature of ActionScript to remember, but it seems to trip up a lot of advanced users as well as beginners…worth remembering!*

That's a lot of very precise rules to take in, but hey, that's code! Don't worry if the issue of scope seems like it shouldn't really matter that much to you right now. As you continue your journey into ActionScript, you will refer back to this section time and time again, and you will soon know scope and its implications *very* well.

Back to the problem in hand.

Think about what you should be putting in front of the two gotoAndStop()s before reading on…no peeking!

12. You can have either gotoAndStop() or this.gotoAndStop() at lines 2 and 5. If you add the this, Flash will replace it with the implied subject, in this case, pinkButton and blueButton. If you omit it, Flash will assume you are referring to the timeline you are currently on. You want to move around the current timeline, so what you actually want is gotoAndStop(). Using the text cursor as before, delete the two instanceName bits and the dot immediately after them, as shown in the following graphic:

```
1 pinkButton.onRelease = function() {
2     gotoAndStop();
3 };
4 blueButton.onRelease = function() {
5     gotoAndStop();
6 };
7 stop();
8
```

> *You can get Flash to add gotoAndStop() instead of instanceName.gotoAndStop() by clicking the gotoAndStop in the Global functions ➤ Timeline Control book. Although this is easier for the here and now, it hides the issue of scope from you, something that was acceptable when learning previous versions of Flash, but you would be heading up a dead-end if you did the same in Flash MX 2004.*
>
> *Flash MX 2004 places more emphasis on structured ActionScript, and to write that, you need to know about a number of things such as scope from the start, so using the easier, non-instance-based methods (also called actions) is a very bad move. They may get you used to thinking in ways that do not address the instance.method(argument) structure, and you may have to unlearn some bad habits as you move forward to intermediate ActionScript.*

13. Unlike the stop(), which needs no argument, you have to specify where the gotoAndStop() should go to before it stops, and you do this by adding…you guessed it, an argument. Move the cursor so that it is between the () at the end of line 2:

```
1 pinkButton.onRelease = function() {
2     gotoAndStop();
3 };
```

14. For pinkbutton, you want to go to frame 'pink', so enter the text 'pink', including the single quotes. The new text should change to a bright blue as soon as you add the second single quotation mark. If it doesn't, check that you have used the same single quotes on either side of pink, and not a double quote and a single quote:

```
1 pinkButton.onRelease = function() {
2     gotoAndStop('pink');
3 };
```

15. For blueButton, you need to add 'blue' as the argument. When you have changed this, your code should look like this:

```
1  pinkButton.onRelease = function() {
2      gotoAndStop('pink');
3  };
4  blueButton.onRelease = function() {
5      gotoAndStop('blue');
6  };
7  stop();
8
```

That's the full script. Test the movie and you should see the same things happen as you saw in Chapter 9. If you don't, the following tips may help:

- Check that the instance names that show up in the Property inspector when you select each button are *exactly* the same as the ones you use in the code: pinkbutton and blueButton.
- The two frame labels are pink and blue.
- The code is exactly the same as the listing just shown.
- Compare your FLA with your finished one, scriptCompleted.fla.

What have you gained by writing your own script instead of using behaviors? Well, you gained a number of very cool features:

- You have all your code in one place—frame 1 of the main timeline. Behaviors are spread all over the place, and it is *very* easy to forget where they are in a large FLA. This way, you have a single script, which you can find easily, and even print out if you need to.
- The code is much shorter and more compact than the behavior code because you made it do *exactly* what you need and no more.
- You can customize or extend it later.

Actually, you're going to customize/extend it right now.

Linking your movie to a URL

In this exercise, you're going to use ActionScript to redirect the user to a web page with a specific URL,

depending upon which button they click. You're going to do this by adding more ActionScript.

Using ActionScript to jump to a URL

You're going to create two very simple drawings of a girl and a boy to display underneath the stereotypically color-gendered content in the goto keyframes (pink for a girl and blue for a boy, like your buttons). You're then going to put an **invisible button** behind each drawing and use ActionScript to link the drawing to a web page when it's clicked.

> The completed FLA for this part of the chapter is scriptURL.fla *if you get stuck.*

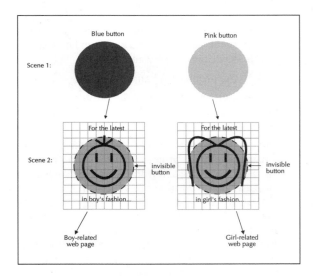

1. Continue using the same button-based movie you used in the previous exercise.

2. Create two new graphic symbols called girl and boy, and in each one, draw an image of a girl and a boy respectively.

Leave it to your own ingenuity and good taste to create your own boy and girl drawings, but make sure you include a line of text that'll entice the user to click the invisible buttons that you'll add soon:

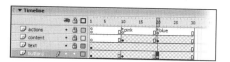

3. Lock all other layers except content. In the content *layer* select the keyframe pink. Drag an instance of girl out of the Library and position it under the you clicked pink! text. Do the same for the keyframe blue using the boy graphic symbol.

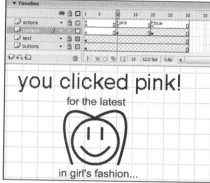

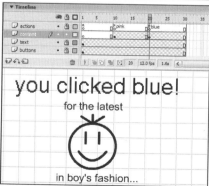

4. Lock all layers except buttons. Add new keyframes at frames 10 and 20 in this layer.

5. Select frame 10 in the buttons layer, click your button symbol in the Library, and drag it onto the stage behind the girl symbol.

6. Scale the button so that it completely surrounds girl. You should have something like this:

Now you want to take users to a new web page when they click the button behind girl.

The ActionScript you attach to this button will tell Flash to go to the web page specified when the user clicks and releases the mouse over this button. You do this using the getURL action.

7. Before you can control the new button, you need to give your new button an instance name. Select it, and in the Properties panel, give it a name girlLink:

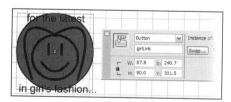

8. Repeat steps 5, 6, and 7, to add a button called boyLink on frame 20 of the Buttons layer:

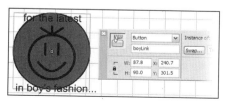

261

9. Select frame 10 in the actions layer (the one labeled pink). You will add your event handler for the girlLink button here. In the right pane of the Actions panel, select Built-in classes ➤ Movie ➤ Button ➤ Events and double-click onRelease. Your script pane will now look like this:

```
1  instanceName.onRelease = function() {
2
3  }
```

10. Click the blank area in line 2 to get the cursor at the start of this line. Then, from the left panel, select Built-in Classes ➤ Movie ➤ MovieClip ➤ Methods and double-click getURL. Your script will now look like this:

```
1  instanceName.onRelease = function() {
2      instanceName.getURL();
3
4  }
```

11. You now need to customize the script. Change the instanceName on line 1 to girlLink, and delete the instanceName on line 2. For the argument of the getURL, you can add any URL that takes your fancy, such as http://www.friendsofed.com—or a URL of your choice—it can even point to a file on your own machine if you like:

```
1  girlLink.onRelease = function() {
2      getURL("http://www.friendsofed.com");
3  };
4
```

Notice that you've added the whole URL here, including the http:// bit, making the address an *absolute* one. It's always a good idea to do this in Flash, otherwise the command may have strange effects on certain servers.

> *Why not add your script to that already on frame 1? Well, you can only define a script for an instance name if that instance name currently exists. As soon as Flash sees an instance name in a script it will look on the current frame. If it doesn't find it, it will not be able to do anything with the associated script lines because there is nothing to control with them. You can only define scripts for an instance name for your button when that button is actually on the timeline, and the first frame you can do this is frame 10.*

12. Select the keyframe labeled blue in the actions layer and repeat the process to create an event handler for boyLink, going to another URL of your choice.

```
1  boyLink.onRelease = function() {
2      getURL("http://www.futuremedia.org.uk");
3  };
```

You can test the movie now, and will find that when you click the boy and girl images, a new page will appear (assuming you are online or go online when requested to do so by your browser) corresponding to your URLs.

13. The red buttons behind the boy and girl icons are not really needed for your graphic design, so you can make them disappear (while still maintaining their button functionality) by making them *transparent*. To do this, select each of the two buttons on the pink and blue labeled keyframes, on the Buttons layer. Select the Color drop-down menu on the Properties panel and select Alpha. In the slider that appears to the left of the drop-down menu, change the value to 0%. The buttons will now be invisible, but they will continue to work, giving the impression that the boy/girl *icons* are the buttons. Sneaky, huh?

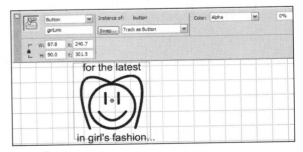

In this chapter, you learned how to give Flash instructions to jump to new parts of your movie when it detects the user clicking a button. More importantly, you created event-driven scripting yourselves, without using behaviors. There's probably more unanswered questions going through your mind about ActionScript, but you're already realizing its power. Some of you will want more of the same...don't worry, there's *much* more!

Case Study

In this section, you're going to create a simple e-mail page, and move toward finalizing your navigation.

Creating your e-mail and contact page

1. Open your saved case study document.

2. Select the content symbol instance on the main stage and double-click to edit it in place:

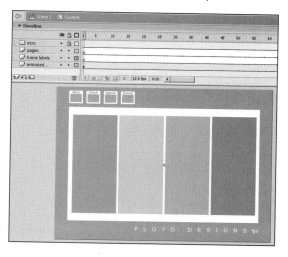

3. Scroll the timeline to frame 165. This is where your email page is located:

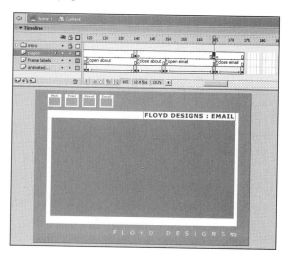

4. Lock all the layers except the pages layer, and select the keyframe on frame 165.

5. Select the Text tool. Set the color to #003366 and the font to Arial 15pt bold.

6. Use the Text tool to type the following as seen:

   Here at Floyd Designs,
   we welcome your comments,
   queries or praise!

7. Select the text field and open the Align panel (*CTRL* + *K*). Click the To Stage icon.

8. Center the text field vertically with Align vertical center, and align it to the left of the center point using Align left edge:

9. With the text field selected, select Modify ➤ Convert to Symbol (or *F8*). Give it the name email content, a movie clip behavior, a center left registration point. and then click OK.

10. Select the new instance on the stage and give it an instance name of email_mc.

11. Double-click the new instance to enter Edit in Place mode.

12. Within the email content movie clip, select the Text tool and type an @ symbol in the top-left corner of

263

the green rectangle area. Do this in 20pt Arial bold, in white.

13. Select the @ text field and select Insert ➤ Timeline Effects ➤ Assistants ➤ Drop Shadow.

14. In the Drop Shadow settings, change the x and y Shadow Offset values to 2 each. Click Update Preview to view the new effect:

One significant thing you might have spotted is that your white character is rendered invisible due to the white background, this is one of the flaws of timeline effects.

15. Click OK to render the timeline effect. This will have created a new layer called Drop Shadow followed by a number. Lock this layer:

16. Back on the stage, select the Text tool and set the Property panel as seen here:

17. Select the Layer 1 layer and type floyd@floyd-designs.inc or your own e-mail address below the @ text field.

18. Position the text field in line horizontally with the @ symbol (switch on Snap Align if necessary or use the Align panel), and a little below it:

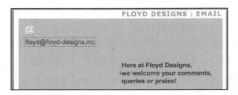

You'll modify this text a little later by turning it into a button and attaching appropriate ActionScript to it. Before that, contrary to the page name, you're going to put a postal address.

19. Zoom in to about 400 percent and use the Rectangle and Line tools to draw an envelope:

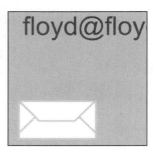

20. Select the envelope and group it (*CTRL* + *G*). Zoom back out to 100 percent.

21. Use the text tool with its current settings to type the following:

Floyd Designs,
Floyd Tower,
Main Avenue,
Floydsville,
94710

22. Align the text field to the envelope above it, leaving a little vertical gap. Your cosmetically complete email page looks like this:

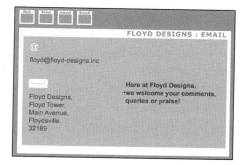

Now, as promised, you're going to put in an e-mail link.

Creating a mailto link

Even though you might not be aware of the term **mailto**, you will no doubt have used a countless number of them. A mailto is a hyperlink which opens up the users default email application and creates a new email to the given email address.

The following ActionScript opens your default mail application (if not already open).

```
myButton.onRelease = function () {
    getURL ("mailto:webmaster@friendsofed.com");
}
```

It then creates a new blank e-mail to the friends of ED webmaster (Don't all do this at once!):

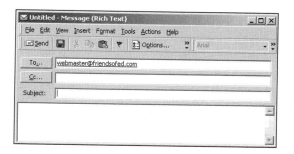

You're going to do a very similar thing in your case study website by creating a button with a mailto link to the given address.

1. Use the Selection tool to select the floyd@floyd-designs.inc text and press F8 to convert it into a symbol. Call it mailto button, with a button behavior and a central registration point.

2. With the new button instance still selected, give it an instance name of mailButton in the Property inspector.

3. Double-click the button instance on the stage to edit it in place.

4. Insert a new keyframe on the Over state by pressing on the *F6 KEY*.

5. Select the text field on the Over keyframe, and change its color to white:

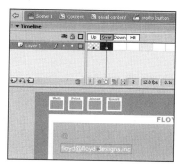

6. Insert a keyframe on the Hit state, and draw a square to cover all the text.

Click the Back button in the top left to return to the email content timeline:

Contrary to what we said earlier in the chapter, you're going to use behaviors just one more time. The reason for this is speed—you have a lot to get through in this chapter!

7. Select the button instance and open the Behaviors panel (Window ➤ Development Panels ➤ Behaviors).

8. Click the Add Behavior button (represented by the plus sign) in the Behaviors panel, and select Web ➤ Go to Web Page:

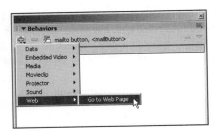

9. In the dialog box that appears, set the details as follows and click OK:

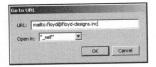

Once you are done, you've finished with your e-mail page. Nice and simple, but functional. Once the case study is done, you can spruce the pages up to your own taste. For now though, you're going to use some ActionScript to program your navigation.

Coding your navigation

You actually did all the hard work creating your opening and closing pages a very long time ago, and until now they've just opened and closed continually because of a lack of halts in the timeline. In this section you're going to make the website navigation functional, if not complete.

1. Click the Back button above the timeline to return to the Content movie clip timeline.

2. Insert a new layer above all the others called actions.

3. On the actions layer, insert a blank keyframe (using *F7*) on frame 75. This corresponds with the end of the intro sequence.

4. Insert a blank keyframe on each frame where a shape tween **ends**. You'll start off with frame 91:

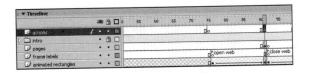

5. To try and help you further here, here are the frame numbers in your case study file (yours might be slightly different):

91, 100, 116, 124, 140, 149, 165, and 174.

Place a blank keyframe on each one.

6. Select the keyframe on frame 75 of the actions layer.

7. Open the Actions panel if it isn't already in view and type the following in the script pane:

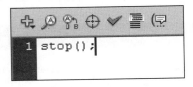

This will cause the movie to stop after the intro animation has played.

8. Select this line of ActionScript and copy it (*CTRL + C*). You're doing this because you are going to add this code to all of the previously added keyframes. Yes you are.

9. Click all the blank keyframes on the actions layer (as listed), click in the Actions panel each time, and paste the copied code (*CTRL + V*).

When you are done, all the keyframes should have a little a above them. For now, you're done with this timeline.

10. Return to the main timeline using the Back button.

11. Select the Web button on the top left of the stage, and give it an instance name of webButton in the Property inspector. Do the same for the others, giving them instance names of printButton, aboutButton, and emailButton respectively.

12. Insert a new layer called actions, and place it above all the others.

13. Select the keyframe on the actions layer and open the Actions panel.

14. In the left pane, open the reference books and browse to Built-in Classes ➤ Movie ➤ Button ➤ Events.

15. Double-click onRelease from within the Events book. As before, you'll see this:

```
1  instanceName.onRelease = function () {
2
3  }
```

16. Copy this code section and paste it three times below it. Leave a line break in-between each section:

```
1   instanceName.onRelease = function () {
2
3   }
4
5   instanceName.onRelease = function () {
6
7   }
8
9   instanceName.onRelease = function () {
10
11  }
12
13  instanceName.onRelease = function () {
14
15  }
```

17. Change the very first instanceName to read webButton:

```
1  webButton.onRelease = function () {
2
3  }
```

18. Click line 2 and select the Insert a target path button:

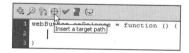

You'll learn about this option and others in detail in the next chapter.

19. In the dialog box that appears, select the content_mc tier, and click the Absolute radio button:

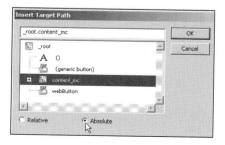

20. Click OK. This then leaves your code looking like this:

```
1  webButton.onRelease = function () {
2      _root.content_mc
3  }
```

21. Open the Built-in Classes ➤ Movie ➤ Movieclip ➤ Methods books in the left-hand pane of the Actions panel.

22. Double-click the gotoAndPlay entry. This will attach the gotoAndPlay method to the end of the previous code:

```
1  webButton.onRelease = function () {
2      _root.content_mc.gotoAndPlay ()
3  }
4
       MovieClip.gotoAndPlay( frame )
```

The cursor is also primed for input in-between the parenthesis.

23. Type "open web" in the parenthesis—remembering to add the double quotation marks—so it reads:

```
1  webButton.onRelease = function () {
2      _root.content_mc.gotoAndPlay("open web")
3  }
```

24. For good practice, add a semi-colon to the end of the line.

Okay, we know you've been dying to...test it with Control ➤ Test Movie. Click the web button and you'll be directed, opening tween and all, to the respective page. One thing to note here is that frequent clicks of the button will ruin the effect due to the same opening animation being played over and over...for the moment at least (you'll sort this out in the next chapter).

Right now though, you've got to add code for the other buttons. The quickest way to do this is to copy and paste line 2.

25. Select all the code on line 2 and copy it (CTRL + C).

26. Click line 6 and paste the code (CTRL + V):

```
1  webButton.onRelease = function () {
2      _root.content_mc.gotoAndPlay("open w
3  }
4
5  instanceName.onRelease = function () {
6      _root.content_mc.gotoAndPlay("open w
```

27. Change the instanceName text here to read printButton.

28. Change open web to read open print:

```
1  webButton.onRelease = function () {
2      _root.content_mc.gotoAndPlay("open web");
3  }
4
5  printButton.onRelease = function () {
6      _root.content_mc.gotoAndPlay("open print");
7  }
```

29. Change the remaining two sections of code, pasting where necessary. Change the button names to aboutButton and emailButton, and the destination frame labels as open about and open email:

```
1   webButton.onRelease = function () {
2       _root.content_mc.gotoAndPlay("open web");
3   }
4
5   printButton.onRelease = function () {
6       _root.content_mc.gotoAndPlay("open print");
7   }
8
9   aboutButton.onRelease = function () {
10      _root.content_mc.gotoAndPlay("open about");
11  }
12
13  emailButton.onRelease = function () {
14      _root.content_mc.gotoAndPlay("open email");
15  }
```

30. Test the movie again to see if all the links work. If they don't, check that you have given used the correct instance names, destination frame labels, and failing that, check that you have given them instance names.

If all has gone well, you should start to see the navigation coming together. There are no closing animations as of yet, but that will come in the next chapter when you have learned about variables.

Summary

In this chapter, we introduced the important concept of scripting your own interactivity, and you started to see how Flash implements this using ActionScript. This was an important chapter because the simple applications of ActionScripting you've seen here will be a foundation that you can build on, both in the next chapter specifically and in the rest of the book in general.

You saw that:

- **Interactivity** is about bringing the Flash movie to life, and giving the user an interesting and satisfying experience.

- At the heart of interactivity are the principles of scripting **events** and **event handlers**, and their relationship to **Instance Names** and **scope**. When things—events like a user clicking a button—happen, Flash looks for a code block that is denoted as to be run when that event occurs, and the event handler is executed.

- A powerful way of adding interaction to Flash is by using **buttons**. Buttons can have behavior such as animation, sound, and movie clips embedded in their default states, and they can be made even more intelligent by attaching **ActionScript** to the mouse events that buttons can detect.

- **ActionScript** creates the event handler and links it to the event. It is a *scripting* language for Flash, which means it is used to control the Flash player.

- ActionScript should only be attached to **frames** in the timeline if you want to maintain a good scripting style.

- You can use ActionScript to jump to specific areas inside your movies, and you can even jump to specified web pages and sites.

- You can don't have to keep creating new symbols for every new item you need in flash. Instead, you can customize existing symbols by changing their color, size, or even making them transparent.

In the next chapter, you'll explore ActionScript in more depth and see more ways that it can work for you.

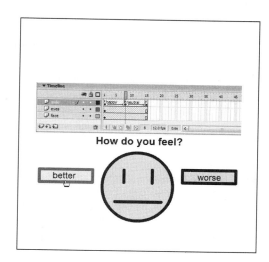

How do you feel?

better   worse

Chapter 11

INTELLIGENT ACTIONS

What we'll cover in this chapter:

- ActionScript
- Increasing interaction
- Giving instructions to specific objects on the stage
- Variables and conditional statements
- Storing values for later use within scripts
- Allowing Flash to make choices about what to do

In the previous chapter, you used ActionScript to make a multi-section interactive Flash movie that allowed the user to navigate through various routes. You may be a beginner, but you have already aced behaviors and are going it alone by creating your own code, something you will continue to do in this chapter.

ActionScript can be used to do much more, including supercharging frames and buttons so they are much more talented than their ordinary cousins. This is at the heart of why Flash is a much richer and more flexible environment for web page production than HTML, and the reason Flash can be used to produce sites that are more interactive and dynamic in the way they allow the user to move around. Some Flash sites even seem to think for themselves.

This chapter will show you how to start giving your Flash sites these qualities. In the last chapter, you simply controlled the main timeline, but you can get much more out of Flash if you use ActionScript to control symbols. You can make Flash throw movie clips around the screen in a dynamic, organic way, based on how the user is interacting via buttons or the mouse position, or something else more complicated, such as a fiendish plan you've coded in ActionScript for Flash to follow without any external interaction. You will also backtrack a little in this chapter because we introduced a few concepts in the last chapter without explaining them thoroughly, particularly *dot notation* and the importance of *instances*. If you are a little fazed by the last chapter, don't worry too much, we will be revisiting all the important concepts because they are so crucial to an understanding of ActionScript.

As with the previous chapters about ActionScript, you may find this chapter a little daunting at first, particularly because ActionScripting may be intimidating to those of you coming from a Photoshop/graphic design background. Bear in mind that ActionScript is one of the easiest scripting languages to learn, and a good way to learn programming in general.

The power of ActionScript

In the previous chapter, you saw that ActionScript is *event driven*. This means that the actions you told Flash to perform are carried out only when an event you

specified takes place—when the mouse pointer does something specific or when a frame containing some ActionScript is encountered on the timeline. This makes ActionScript easy to write. For example, once you've created a working button, all you have to do is add an ActionScript to it that tells Flash what the button should do. There's no long obscure program to write—you just decide what you want Flash to do, generate the appropriate bit of ActionScript, and then move on.

A designer wrote once: "Whenever I think of Flash scripts, I have this irrational mental image of a little superhero with a letter 'A' on their chest. Made up of normal Flash Frames, they have come to you from the planet Interactivity to free you from the clutches of their archenemy, a secret organization known only by the initials HTML. Ridding the world of boring, static web pages wherever they may exist, with powers that give one command the abilities of 100 lines of JavaScript...Is it a bird? Is it a plane? No. It's *ActionScript*."

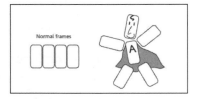

ActionScript is fundamentally much more dynamic than, for example, a button rollover or a linear animated movie. With ActionScript, you can control just about every attribute of just about everything on the stage. Surreal as it sounds, ActionScript enables individual elements of your movie to talk to each other. A button symbol can tell a movie symbol, "When instance X of me is clicked, you start playing from frame Y." Buttons no longer just control navigation as in plain old HTML; *they also control other objects,* such as movies and graphics. This is done using a type of ActionScripting known as **dot notation**.

Defining instances for dot notation

With dot notation, you can make one instance in your animation, a button for example, tell another instance what to do. Before we can demonstrate this concept, you need to create a couple of symbols so that one can tell the other what to do.

Let's create a little face...something you can tell to be happy or sad, depending on your mood.

> *Make sure you save the movie you work on throughout this chapter: you'll be enhancing its capabilities with ActionScript as you progress through the book.*
>
> *You can find the finished movie,* smilerMovie.fla, *on our website, in the download section for this chapter. This file has all the ActionScript you will be developing in this chapter already attached to it. If you want a version with just the graphics in it (so you can add the ActionScript yourself) use* smilerMovie2.fla.

1. In a fresh Flash document, create a new movie clip symbol called smiler.

2. Inside smiler, create two new layers. From the bottom up, rename your three layers face, eyes, and smile. These layers are to hold the separate parts that will make up your face.

3. Place a yellow circle with a black stroke 8pt thick in the center of the stage on the face layer:

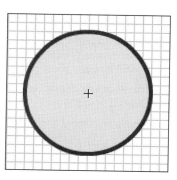

4. In eyes layer, use two lines with the same stroke width as your circle to add two eyes:

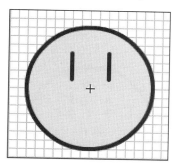

5. Select the smiler layer and add a horizontal line where the mouth should be:

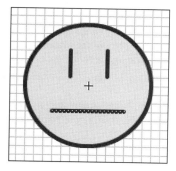

We know what you're thinking: your face should be smiling.

6. Make all the layers 15 frames long and add a keyframe in the smiler layer at frame 15:

Now you'll animate the mouth so that it goes from a smile to a frown, passing through all the intermediate expressions in between. To do this, you'll set up a shape tween from frame 1 (smiling) to frame 15 (frowning). For the next part to work, you must not have the mouth selected (if you have, simply click a blank part of the stage).

7. Choose the Selection tool and go to frame 1. Put the pointer on the mid-point of the mouth until the pointer displays the curve attachment and drag the center of the mouth down to make your face smile:

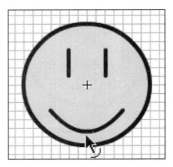

> You may find working on the smile easier by locking the *smile* and face *layers*.

Hmmm.... Not quite as enigmatic as the Mona Lisa, but if you're happy with it, we're happy....

8. Using the Property panel, add a label happy to this frame and select Shape from the **Tween** drop-down menu:

A light green shape tween will now extend from frame 1 to frame 15.

You'll notice that you have nothing else on the smiler layer. This is a requirement in *all* tween animation, as you'll remember from earlier in this book. You'll confuse Flash if you have more than one item in the layer, and your tween won't work. Also, note that the smile object is just a drawn shape and *not* a symbol—if it were, this would also prevent the shape tween from working.

9. Select frame 15 of the smile layer. Your face here is in its expressionless, neutral position. By using the pointer in the same way as before, make the face *frown*.

10. Use the Property panel to add a label called sad to the keyframe at frame 15. (You won't see this label on the timeline because there's not enough space to show it, but you will see a little flag in the frame to show that it's been labeled):

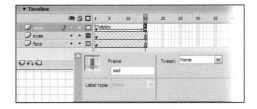

11. You can see the motion that smiler will perform by selecting it in the Library window and clicking the Play button, using the Onion Skin tool to see all the frames at once, or dragging your playhead through the timeline:

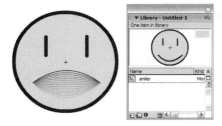

You also want to label the neutral facial expression. The exact position of this will depend on how you drew the mouth, but it should be somewhere near the middle of the movie.

12. Drag the playhead up and down the timeline until it is on the frame where the smile is closest to the straight horizontal line you drew originally.

13. Insert a keyframe at this frame. Use the Property inspector to label it neutral:

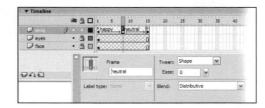

Each of these labels corresponds to a different expression: you want to be able to target the expression you want to see. To do this, you need a button to click.

14. Using Insert ➤ New Symbol, create a new graphic symbol and call it rectangle. This symbol will form the basis of your button.

15. Inside the graphic symbol, draw a yellow rectangle:

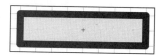

You're going to put text over the top of your button eventually, so make sure the body of your rectangle is big enough for some text.

16. Again using Insert ➤ New Symbol, create a button symbol called rectangle button.

17. Inside the button symbol, drag an instance of the rectangle symbol onto the stage. Open the Info panel (Window ➤ Design Panels ➤ Info), and click the center dot in the 3x3 matrix so it looks like this:

18. Enter 0 in both the X: and Y: boxes. This centers the rectangle exactly at the center of the button stage:

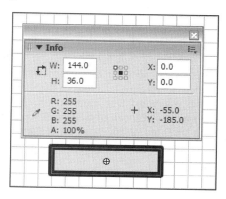

As we mentioned before, it's important that the graphics in a button's states all line up. For that reason, it's a good idea to **always center buttons**. Then, if a button ever starts to look wobbly when it's used in your final movie, you'll know all you have to do to correct the problem is set its position in all states to X:0.0; Y:0.0 with the Info Panel.

19. Add keyframes to the Over state and the Hit state.

We suggested earlier in the book that it was a good idea to make the shape in the Hit state a distinctive color. Here, however, because you know that the square is solid, you don't need to change the shape in the Hit state from yellow to a distinctive black by adjusting the brightness, but you may want to do so for practice.

You'll let the users know they're over the button's "click" area by making the button a lighter shade when it's in the Over state.

20. Select the Over state in the timeline, and then select the rectangle. Choose the Brightness option from the Property panel's Color drop-down menu and set it to 40% using the slider:

21. Go back to the main stage in Scene 1 and add two new layers. Rename your three layers, from the bottom up, face, buttons, and text:

22. Select the face layer and drag an instance of smiler onto the stage from the Library. Then, in the buttons layer, add two instances of the rectangle button symbol. Your stage should look like this one:

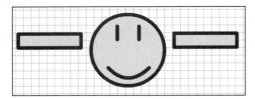

> If you find that you made your graphics too big to fit them all on the stage, use the Free transform tool to scale them down a little.

Now to give the user some hints about which buttons they might want to click.

23. In the text layer, use the Text tool and the Property inspector to add the words better and worse on top of the buttons as shown. Then at the top of the stage, type How do you feel?

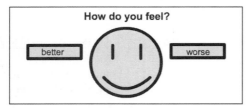

You can test the movie now if you like. When you go over the buttons, they should become lighter, and the face will continuously change from happy to sad, but nothing will happen when you click either button.

24. Save your Flash document for safekeeping.

The next step is to use the buttons to control what mood smiler is in, but before you begin adding the ActionScript, let's look at how dot notation works in theory.

Dot notation

It may not sound very exciting, but dot notation has incredible possibilities for your Flash movies.

Dot notation in Flash and ActionScript is a way of expressing a **path** through a movie. It gives you a way of targeting a particular object and telling it what to do, irrespective of its position in the movie's structure. If you want to direct a particular piece of ActionScript at a specific movie clip, or if you want to tell an instance of a square symbol to change its alpha value to 10, you can do that by specifying that object's location using dot notation.

A typical line of dot notation ActionScript would look like this:

```
square._x = 100
```

This line would move the square instance to an x (horizontal) position of 100 on the stage. Notice the dot before the _x? Perhaps this is what gives dot notation its name!

> You may recognize this as something you already used in the previous chapter. You used ActionScript lines like instanceName.gotoAndStop(); and instanceName.onRelease=function() earlier, although we didn't let on what it was called.

Dot notation enables you to reference any instance within the Flash movie, but for this chapter, we'll stick to one location for all your instances—we'll look at how to reference different locations in the movie using paths later in the book. Dot notation only works on individual, *named instances* of a symbol. Let's briefly refresh your memory about what an instance is and why you use them. We also want to make sure you are clear on the difference between an instance name that appears in the Property inspector and the symbol name that appears in the library.

The original "master" symbol that sits in the Library is the *template*, and any instances of it that you put on the stage will be replicas of this master symbol. Whereas the version in the Library is the original, think of the instance on the stage as a clone, permanently linked to its master. An instance will **always** look and behave like its original, and when the original changes, **all** its instances will change also. This characteristic is what differentiates an *instance* from a *copy*: If you simply draw a square on the stage, copy and paste it next to the original, and then go back to the original and change it, the copy would not be affected in any way because a copy has no link to its original.

When you create new symbols, you give each a symbol name that appears in the Library. In the FLA you are building at the moment, you used the names rectangle, rectangle button, and smiler. The symbol names are just descriptive labels that are attached to each symbol in the library so you know what each one is; Flash doesn't use them at all. Note that the symbol name can have spaces.

In the last chapter, you also used the instance names pinkButton and blueButton. The instance names *are* used by Flash. Unlike symbol names, instance names have very definite rules defined by Flash (or more correctly, *ActionScript*—the rules for defining instance names are part of ActionScript's rules for naming things):

- They must be typed the same way every time you use them (including case), and it's a good idea to stick to camel case

- They can't include spaces

The instance names are unique to each movie clip or button you put on stage, and if you don't give a name to a particular symbol, you cannot control it via ActionScript because Flash won't know which name to reference it with.

You can see the link between originals and instances for yourself by altering the rectangle symbol you created in the last exercise.

Symbol templates and instances

1. If you haven't done so already, save your FLA. In the Library window, double-click the rectangle symbol to go into Edit Symbols mode.

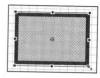

2. Select the yellow rectangle with the Selection tool and use the Free Transform tool to stretch it at the top and the bottom. Once you've changed the size of your rectangle, re-center it by entering 0 in the **X** and **Y** boxes of the Property inspector.

3. Click Scene 1 at the top of the timeline to go back to the main stage and notice that **both** instances of rectangle have mimicked the change made to their Library-housed template:

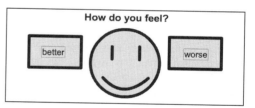

4. Exit the current FLA (don't save the changes) and reload the file you saved in step 1.

The instances of rectangle you put in each state of rectangle button have changed and consequently, the instances of rectangle button on the stage have changed as well. The changes you made to the original symbol have rippled through to all the instances associated with it. This is a big advantage for editing and changing your website—Flash can just follow the link to each instance of the original and make the necessary changes.

When you change a symbol, you alter its **primitive** attributes. These include things like the lines and fills that make up the symbol's appearance.

You can also make changes at a per instance level:

5. With the newly loaded FLA, select one of the buttons on the stage by clicking it, and then scale it. You will see that this time only one of the buttons changes:

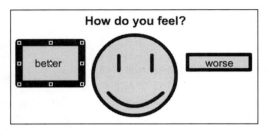

6. Press *CTRL+ Z* (undo) to make both buttons the same size again.

An instance has *properties,* and these are what you have just changed. There are two cool things about properties as opposed to primitive attributes:

■ Each instance has its own set of properties, which are created as soon as you drop a symbol onto the stage. There are a number of properties, such as the ones that control the position of your two button instances (and that is why you can place them at different positions on the stage). There are also other properties that control the scale of the buttons; you changed these for the left button.

■ ActionScript can control the properties of each instance, *as long as it has some way of identifying the instance.* As we discussed previously, that identification property is the instance name.

Let's see how this can work.

7. Select each button in turn (make sure that you do not select the text instead—lock the text layer if you need to). Using the Property inspector, give the left and right buttons the instance names leftButton and rightButton:

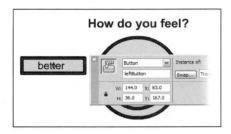

8. You can now control the properties of your two buttons via ActionScript. To do this, first add a new layer above the others called actions:

Select frame 1 of the new layer and open the Actions panel. Enter the following line of code by typing it directly into the Actions panel. Check your spelling after (noting the capital B in leftButton), and make sure _yscale appears blue (if it's not blue, you spelled it incorrectly).

```
1 leftButton._yscale = 200;
2
```

9. If you test the FLA now, you will see that your line of code has scaled the left button. This time, you didn't do the scaling, *ActionScript did it for you!*

This might seem like a fairly boring example, but consider this—what if you scaled every frame by a small amount or moved the button a little every frame. In both cases you would end up with animation created by ActionScript, something called scripted animation. The really cool thing about doing it this way is that your ActionScript can think before it animates; things move around as if they have a brain, rather than sticking to fixed tween railroad tracks…this is the basis of interactivity in Flash.

This is a fairly fundamental concept in Flash, so let's have a closer look at how you did it.

Our line still kind of looks like the instance.method(argument); syntax, but now you have something else. You have

```
instance.property = value;
```

You can change the instance's property by equating it to a new *value*. In this line of code:

- You can access properties as well as methods via dot notation: dot notation is a general "glue" used in ActionScript to form lines by adding stuff separated by the dots.

- You can *equate* one thing to another by using the equal sign (=) much as you do in math. This type of line is called an *expression;* it expresses something that has to be done by Flash. In this example, it expresses that the scaling of leftButton is 200%. This is a *literal value.* This is a value that never changes—you will scale by 200% every time.

There are lots of other properties you can play with before moving on. Here are a few you might want to try:

```
leftButton._rotation = 90;
leftButton._alpha = 50;
leftButton._x = 200;
```

You can even try all four lines at the same time. See if you can guess what will happen before you test it!

Dot notation has at least two forms; one to access methods, and one to access properties. It can also be used in expressions to change properties, which is the basis for scripted animation.

Phew! That's a lot to take in. Let's expand the idea a little by taking control of the smiler instance.

Changing properties with dot notation

1. Select Smiler on the stage and open the Properties panel. Give it an instance name of face:

At the moment, smiler plays continuously during your movie, but you want it to stay on the neutral expression until one of the buttons is clicked.

To do this, you're going to control the smiler instance's _currentframe property. This is a number that signifies which frame in the timeline the movie clip is on, starting with 1. Rather than changing it directly as you did above, you will use an old friend: the gotoAndStop method.

> *Using methods such as* **gotoAndStop** *hides the fact that you are still really only changing properties. Methods work by changing properties as well but the advantage of using them is that you don't have to worry about the underlying properties. Because Macromedia has written them for us, there are lots of features that make them easier than accessing properties directly. For example,* **gotoAndStop** *gives you additional features that you can use instead of raw frame numbers, such as frame labels. Hiding the properties of an instance by controlling it using methods is called abstraction.*

2. Select frame 1 of the actions **layer** and delete the code that you added earlier.

Before you begin your coding, let's take a closer look at some of the icons above the text box in the right pane to see what they do and what benefit you can gain from them (icons described from left-right):

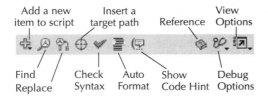

- **Add a new item to script**: Opens a list of all the ActionScript commands available for adding to your script. You can select a command from this menu and it will appear in the script, similar to the left pane you used in the last chapter.

- **Find**: Allows you to locate a piece of text within the active script pane.

- **Replace**: Locates a text string and replaces it with another string, (similar to the "Find & Replace" feature in most text-editing programs).

- **Insert a target path**: Locates instances in your Flash movie. You'll look at this in more detail in a moment.

- **Check Syntax**: Checks the validity of your code. If Flash locates a syntax error, an output box appears on screen, detailing the location and reason for the error(s). As you learn ActionScript, you'll begin to see the Output window more and more—don't worry—this is normal for anyone learning ActionScript (and even the masters from time to time!).

- **Auto Format**: Formats your ActionScript to look neat, tidy and correctly indented.

- **Show Code Hint**: Makes Expert mode a lot easier! Code hints appear to suggest the correct arguments required for ActionScript methods. Hints will appear whenever you type the open parentheses to begin the arguments section of an instance.*method*(arguments) structure:

You can hide the code hints by right-clicking the **Show Code Hint** button, but for now we recommend that you leave this on until you are fully familiar with ActionScript.

- **Reference**: Makes ActionScript guide appear in the Help panel. The full set of ActionScript actions and methods are listed alphabetically in the left pane. If you want to use the reference for a particular ActionScript keyword, highlight it in the Actions panel, and then click the reference icon. The Help panel will appear with the entry for your keyword displayed.

- **Debug Options**: Debugging is the process of checking your ActionScript and removing any glitches contained in it. The Debug Options icon displays a debug options menu.

- **View Options**: This allows you to view Escape shortcuts and line numbers and enable/disable word-wrap.

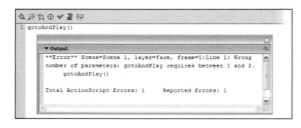

Now that you've looked at all the buttons in the Actions panel, let's give one of them a try.

3. Make sure that you have frame 1 of the actions layer selected, and that you deleted all scripts from the right code pane. Then click the Insert target Path icon.

This reveals all potential targets in the movie that you can control. You can control everything with an instance name beside it:

In this case, you see that _root, face, leftButton, and rightButton are the only things available. The A() represents the stage on the text, which you are not concerned with at the moment.

4. Click face to select it, and leave the rest of the window unchanged. Then click OK:

The right pane in the Actions panel now contains the dot path this.face.

5. You've now pointed Flash at the correct target. You may remember, however, that including this is only relevant in a code block. Because you are not in a code block, remove the this to leave you with just face.

What you want Flash to do is make the smile movie start on its neutral, expressionless face. You labeled

that frame neutral, so that will be your argument in the gotoAndStop().

Let's tell Flash exactly where to go...

6. Type a dot after face in the right pane of the Actions panel:

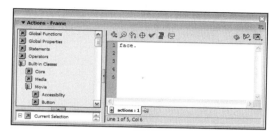

7. Type gotoAndStop(into the right-hand pane after the dot you just entered.

As soon as you type the open parentheses, Flash thinks you will add an argument in a moment, so it displays a hint:

If you can't see the hint, click the Show Code Hint icon in the Actions panel. Flash shows you the correct syntax for the gotoAndStop command. You already have the first two elements in place; the field that is required is shown in bold text: frame.

8. Complete this line of ActionScript by typing "neutral");

If you test the movie now, you will see that your face has stopped animating and is paused on the neutral frame:

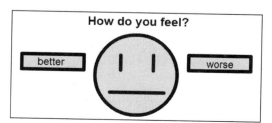

We now need to add some code to define your button events. The only difference is that you will be controlling the face timeline instead of the code timeline.

9. Because it is customary to place event handlers before other code, place the cursor at the start of line 1 and press *ENTER* on your keyboard a few times to create some space:

```
1
2
3
4  face.gotoAndStop("neutral");
5
```

Now you need to add ActionScript to the buttons. leftButton will make the face happier, and rightButton will make it sadder. To do this, you have to move one frame to the left or to the right in the timeline. Here's a reminder of what the timeline looks like:

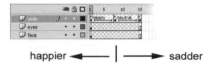

happier ◄——— | ———► sadder

10. Let's wire the buttons next. You will recall from last chapter that the basic code block to define a button click-release event handler is:

```
instanceName.onRelease = function(){
}
```

What you want to do is create such a block for each of the two buttons.

11. Type this code directly or use the left pane (as you did last chapter). Either way, make sure you end up with this:

```
1  leftButton.onRelease = function() {
2
3  };
4
5  rightButton.onRelease = function() {
6
7  };
8
9  face.gotoAndStop("neutral");
10
```

You've added the basic event handler blocks, now all you have to do is put some code in them to define the event handler code.

You want to create an ActionScript that tells Flash to make the face smile when leftButton is clicked, and make the face frown when rightButton is clicked. More accurately, the ActionScript will instruct Flash that when it detects a user clicking and releasing her mouse button over one of the two buttons, the face will jump to the happy or sad label on the timeline.

12. Now that you've used ActionScript for a while, you can probably create these commands a little more confidently. Add the lines shown here as lines 2 and 6:

```
1  leftButton.onRelease = function() {
2      face.gotoAndStop("happy")
3  };
4
5  rightButton.onRelease = function() {
6      face.gotoAndStop("sad");
7  };
8
9  face.gotoAndStop("neutral");
10
```

13. Click the Check Syntax and Auto Format buttons to check and format the code, and then test the movie.

You should see the face go from euphoria to abject sadness, all at the click of a button:

There are a few questions to answer here:

- Why didn't you add this in the event handlers so you had this.face.gotoAndStop()?

You don't use this because the code is already on the face timeline, so the assumed scope (the main timeline) is the one you want.

- Why is this any different from the pinkButton and blueButton stuff last chapter?

This chapter's exercise is fundamentally different because you are controlling a timeline *other than the main one*. This is the key to creating great sites and impressive interactive content with Flash. The interrelationships and control of timelines is what makes Flash designers stay up at night thinking "If I scaled that embedded timeline, but at the same time rotated the one it is in....Wow! It moves in a receding spiral!"

You now know how to use dot notation to control instances and enable bits of your animation to boss each other around. But you can also give Flash the power to make decisions for itself by using two more of ActionScript's special powers: **variables** and **conditional structures**.

Teaching your movie to think for itself

Using ActionScript to help Flash make structured decisions enables you to build very advanced Flash interfaces. This feature allows Flash to move beyond being merely a graphical interface for web pages and enter the domain of full-fledged web applications and games. By adding ActionScript to a Flash web page, you can do more than just make it interactive—you can give it a brain.

At the moment you only see the frames of the smiler movie that you labeled: happy, neutral, and sad. It would be nice if you could see all the intermediate frames and expressions as well.

Currently, clicking the better button displays the best expression and clicking the worse button displays the worst expression. You want to be able to click the better button to make the movie go one frame nearer to the happy label, or frame 1, and show you a *slightly* happier expression. Similarly, when you click the worse button, you want the movie to go one frame nearer the sad label at frame 15, and show you a *slightly* sadder expression. You want to give smiler a more nuanced range of expressions rather than just the two extremes.

Essentially, what you want to do is go to the previous frame when the better button is clicked, and to the next frame when the worse button is clicked:

To do this, you need an ActionScript that tells Flash to make face move back one frame when the better button is clicked and move forward one frame when the worse button is clicked.

But—and it's a big *but*—what happens when you reach the first or last frame of the movie?

If the better button is clicked when face is at frame one, or if the worse button is clicked when face is at frame 15, the actions you told Flash to carry out will be impossible and your instructions won't make any sense.

We need Flash to be able to decide what action it should take in these circumstances—whether it should move to another frame or stay where it is. To be able to do this, Flash must know what frame it's currently at. You can tell Flash where it's at by using variables.

Variables

A variable is a named container in which you store values or data that you want to use again and again while a program—or Flash movie—is running. A variable is essentially a bit of computer memory to which you give a name. You store information in this memory location, and when you give Flash the name of the variable, it knows where to find the information you stored.

There are two types of value in Flash you need to look at—**literals** and **expressions**.

A **literal** is a value that doesn't change: that is, whenever you use it, it will be something like a name, an address, or the color of your eyes. It's a value that you want to read as a fixed thing, something that you won't modify once you've set it.

If you want to tell Flash your eyes were blue, you would define this variable like so:

```
eyeColor = "blue";
```

The quotation marks ("") around the value denotes that it is a piece of text, or in programming terms, a *string*. It won't change until you change your eye color. Although your eyes could be any color at all, Flash will deduce that now they're blue, and they'll always be blue—until you tell Flash otherwise.

You could also tell Flash how many eyes you have:

```
numberOfEyes = 2;
```

In this case, you are telling Flash you have two eyes.

An **expression** is different from a literal variable. Its value is not fixed; you can change it.

For example, look at the following statement:

Number of dollars in my pocket + number of dollars in my pay check

This is an expression: it has two component parts, each of which needs to be evaluated and added together before a final figure can be calculated. If we worked through this expression last year and again today, we would get two different results, even though we used the same expression.

To tell Flash that the number of dollars in your pocket is 10, write:

```
dollars = 10;
```

The "10" here is a literal value. It will always be 10. Most things start off as literal values when you set their first value (or in programming terms *initialize* them). It's what happens to the values next that makes them interesting.

Having given Flash this information, you can now forget how much money you have and get Flash to keep track of your accounts. If you were to find a dollar on the floor and put it in your pocket, you could tell Flash that you now have one more dollar than you had before. You would write this:

```
dollars = dollars + 1;
```

Flash would then make the value of dollars equal to 11. If you found another dollar under the sofa, you would use the same expression again to give you 12.

> *By contrast, running:* numberOfEyes = 2; *more than once still yields 2 eyes, which is why it is a literal. You will never get value other than one on the left of your face and one on the right of your face.*

You can apply this knowledge to your movie and get Flash to keep track of what frame of face you're on. You can create a variable, call it `smilerFrame`, and store the current frame number inside this variable. Once Flash looks at this variable and knows which frame you're starting from, it can add or subtract one frame from this variable each time a button is pressed. The value of smilerFrame will change using an expression that essentially says:

```
smilerframe = smilerframe + 1
```

or

```
smilerframe = smilerframe−1
```

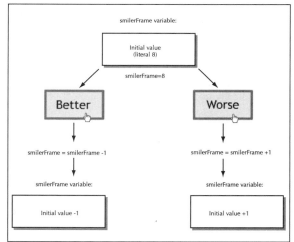

These expressions will create the new value of smilerFrame and store it in the variable. Let's put this into practice.

Using variables

Your first step is to find the frame number that corresponds to the neutral expression of face. You can then store this value in the smilerFrame variable and use it as the starting point for the frame-by-frame movement from happy to sad.

Earlier, you attached ActionScript to the first frame of the movie, which told Flash that at the start of the movie, face should be on the frame labeled neutral. This is the frame number that you'll use as the initial value for your smilerFrame variable.

1. Double-click the movie symbol icon of smiler in the Library to go into Edit Symbols mode.

2. Move the playhead to the frame containing the neutral label. You'll be able to see exactly what frame this is by looking in the frame-counter pane at the bottom of the timeline:

In our example, neutral is on frame 8, but in your movie it could be different depending on how you drew the mouth. You can now make your smilerFrame variable equal to 8 (or whatever the value is in your movie).

3. On the main stage, click frame1 on the actions layer.

4. You should now see your script again. Place the cursor at the end of the script and enter the following line:

```
smilerFrame = 8;
```

```
1  leftButton.onRelease = function() {
2      face.gotoAndStop("happy");
3  };
4  rightButton.onRelease = function() {
5      face.gotoAndStop("sad");
6  };
7  face.gotoAndStop("neutral");
8  smilerFrame = 8;
9
```

Because a movie clip also has a property called _currentframe, you could have also used the following as your last line:

```
smilerFrame = face._currentframe;
```

As soon as the playhead goes to label neutral, the _currentframe property (for instance, face) goes to a value of 8. The beauty of doing it this way is that you don't have to know what frame neutral is. This is another example of abstraction—if you use literal values, you have to know more about the code than if you use properties. If you use methods, you don't have to use properties or literals at all, which makes the line easier to understand and more general.

```
face.gotoAndStop("neutral");
```

That is actually the same as:

```
face._currentframe = 8;
```

The difference is that the latter looks, well... less than user friendly. It's difficult to understand what is going on unless you know what _currentframe is and what the significance of the literal value 8 is. Furthermore, if you happened to move the label neutral to frame 7, the second line would stop working, whereas the first would continue to work.

The logical conclusion of abstraction is something you will hear a lot about in Flash 2004; class-based programming, or Object Orientated Programming (OOP). Although it is beyond the scope of this book, this edition has been changed significantly (where ActionScript is concerned) from previous editions to make your crossover into the world of OOP as seamless as possible.

Your new line of code sets the smilerFrame variable to its initial value at the center of the happy/sad continuum as soon as the movie starts. It also directs the movie to the middle of the face instance's timeline, pausing the movie there with a neutral facial expression and waiting for the user's input.

Now you need to change the ActionScript instructions that are attached to each of the buttons. Instead of telling face to go all the way to the happy or sad labels of the smiler movie clip as soon as they're clicked, you

want them to tell face to move forward or back *one frame at a time*.

When you found a dollar, the new value the money in your pocket became dollars + 1. Similarly, when a button is clicked and the timeline moves one frame forward or one frame back, you want to *update* the value of smilerframe as either:

```
smilerframe = smilerframe + 1;
```

or

```
smilerframe = smilerframe-1;
```

You'll still be using the gotoAndStop action to make face move up and down the timeline, but you'll now tell it to go to the previous frame or the next frame. Fortunately, Flash has built-in facilities to help you do this.

However, you still have the problem of what Flash will do when you get to either end of the timeline and it can't physically *go* to the previous or next frame. How do you stop Flash going off the end of the movie?

You use a **conditional statement**.

Conditional statements

A conditional statement allows your Flash movie to make choices on which code block it decides to run, based on the situation it finds itself in. This means you can tell Flash to follow the instructions you've given it only if certain conditions apply. Helpfully, if is the name of the action you'll use to insert a conditional statement in your button.

If, in the dollars example, your pockets were only big enough to hold a hundred dollars, you'd add a conditional statement in your instructions to Flash. That statement would tell Flash that every time you find a dollar, put it in your pocket only if dollars (the variable) is less than one hundred. If dollars already equaled one hundred, Flash would know to ignore the rest of the instruction.

Let's define the conditions that must apply in your Smiler movie for Flash to follow your instructions.

When the better button is clicked, you want it to tell face to go to the previous frame of smiler if—and only if—Smiler is not *currently* on frame 1. If smiler is currently on frame 1, the smilerFrame variable will equal 1. If smiler is *not* on frame 1, smilerFrame will be greater than 1.

Flash will go to the previous frame if you're at a frame greater than 1 (smilerframe ➤ 1). If smilerframe equals 1, the movie will not move when the better button is clicked:

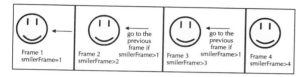

Let's add this instruction and conditional statement to the better button.

Updating the buttons with sexier ActionScript

We now need to change the code in the event handlers to use the smilerFrame variable.

1. Highlight the second line of code.

```
1  leftButton.onRelease = function() {
2      face.gotoAndStop("happy");
3  };
```

2. Press the *DELETE* key. This will leave you with the following:

```
1  leftButton.onRelease = function() {
2      |
3  };
```

Before you tell face to go to the previous frame of smiler when it's clicked, you need to add your conditional statement. Remember, you only want your instructions carried out if smilerframe ➤ 1.

3. Type the following:

```
if (smilerFrame ➤ 1) {
```

Be careful to get the spelling of smilerFrame exactly right, otherwise Flash will think you're talking about something else. In particular, make sure you stick to the camel case (uppercase at the start of every new word, lowercase everywhere else with no spaces).

```
1  leftButton.onRelease = function() {
2  if (smilerFrame > 1) {
3  };
```

As you typed the if command you probably noticed the code hint tool tip. Remember that this is Flash's way of helping you fill in the argument for the if, in this case a *condition*.

You now have to tell Flash that if smilerframe *is* greater than 1, it should decrease that value by 1 in preparation for the next time the button is clicked: you have to update the value of smilerframe to reflect the fact that the playhead has moved up one frame. By tracking the value of smilerframe in the same way as it would with your dollars, Flash will always know where face is on the smiler timeline.

4. Press the *ENTER* key to place the cursor on a new line:

```
1  leftButton.onRelease = function() {
2  if (smilerFrame > 1) {
3      |
4  };
```

Notice that the cursor has been indented because you are writing the code block associated with 'yes, smilerFrame *is* greater than 1.

5. Type the following and then press *ENTER* to place the cursor on a new line:

```
smilerframe = smilerframe -1;
```

You now need to tell Flash to move the playhead along the timeline.

6. Enter the following new line:

```
face.prevFrame();
```

```
1 leftButton.onRelease = function() {
2 if (smilerFrame > 1){
3     smilerFrame = smilerFrame-1
4     face.prevFrame();
5
6 };
```

Your code for the better button is almost complete. Like an on handler, an if statement must be closed with a curly bracket. Let's place one.

7. Type a closing curly bracket on the new line. It will immediately realign itself to be in line with the if statement:

```
1 leftButton.onRelease = function() {
2 if (smilerFrame > 1){
3     smilerFrame = smilerFrame-1
4     face.prevFrame();
5 }
6
7 };
8 rightButton.onRelease = function() {
9     face.gotoAndStop("sad");
10 };
```

8. Click the Auto Format button above the right pane to clean up your code.

The better button is now ready to use.

9. Test the movie. You'll see that face will get happier each time the better button is clicked, whereas it will go straight to its sad expression when you click the worse button. (Clicking the worse button may also stop the better button from working because it doesn't use smilerFrame yet.)

Notice that although your code has an error in it, Flash doesn't tell you about the error if you click the Check Syntax icon. Check Syntax icon does just that—it checks whether the code is using correct syntax. A bit of text like this is syntactically correct:

"All trees are covered in bark. Bark is created by dogs when they open their mouths and make a noise. It is then collected and glued onto trees at night by a special process involving pixies and a fertile imagination."

But it is not actually true. Code can be syntactically correct, but can still do something wrong, and syntax checks will not fix this for you.

Now to make the worse button fully functional. You need to repeat the same sequence of steps as you did for the better button, but with some significant changes to your conditional statement and to the instructions.

10. In the same way you added the new event handler code for leftButton, add the following code for rightButton, taking care to note the differences (which appear in bold so you don't miss them).

```
rightButton.onRelease = function() {
if (smilerFrame < 15){
  smilerFrame = smilerFrame+1;
  face.nextFrame();
}
```

```
1 leftButton.onRelease = function() {
2 if (smilerFrame > 1){
3     smilerFrame = smilerFrame-1
4     face.prevFrame();
5 }
6
7 };
```

11. When you are happy with the result, click the Auto Format icon so all the extra spaces are removed, giving you the final listing:

```
1 leftButton.onRelease = function() {
2     if (smilerFrame>1) {
3         smilerFrame = smilerFrame-1;
4         face.prevFrame();
5     }
6 };
7 rightButton.onRelease = function() {
8     if (smilerFrame<15) {
9         smilerFrame = smilerFrame+1;
10        face.nextFrame();
11    }
12 };
13 face.gotoAndStop("neutral");
14 smilerFrame = 8;
15
```

Notice that the if code is now double indented. This is because it is a nested code block; the if block is within an event handler block.

12. Test the movie again. Now both the buttons will make the mouth move incrementally. You'll see face change its expression smoothly from happy to neutral to sad and back again as the buttons are clicked.

13. Save the movie.

There has been a lot to take in through this chapter, but we've covered fundamental concepts for creating top quality Flash sites.

Understanding what instances are and how dot notation can be used to control them will enable you to give your sites a far greater degree of interaction for the user to enjoy and marvel at. In addition to navigating the site, your users will be able to do things like start or stop movies and affect the appearance and behavior of movie elements. You can do a whole lot more with dot notation, and the basic skills you've gained here will provide a solid footing for learning fancier stuff later in your Flash career. Indeed, you have two more advanced chapters on ActionScript later in the book, so we hope that this whet your appetite.

You've also been introduced to the use of variables and conditional statements. These are the features that give Flash the ability to think for itself. When used together, they give Flash some fairly powerful decision making abilities.

Finally, you have some understanding of instances, properties, methods and abstraction.

Case Study

In this case study you're going to add more ActionScript to enhance your navigation.

1. Open your saved case study document.

2. Select frame 1 of the actions layer, and open the Actions panel using *F9*. Here is how you left it in the last chapter:

```
1  webButton.onRelease = function() {
2      content_mc.gotoAndPlay("open web");
3  };
4
5  printButton.onRelease = function() {
6      content_mc.gotoAndPlay("open print");
7  };
8
9  aboutButton.onRelease = function() {
10     content_mc.gotoAndPlay("open about");
11 };
12
13 emailButton.onRelease = function() {
14     content_mc.gotoAndPlay("open email");
15 };
```

Now you're going to use variables to store information about which rectangle should open and which one should close. By doing this, you can play each closing sequence before the next opening one. Your sequence looks (or loops) like this:

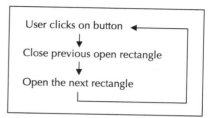

Let's break this down into ActionScript reasoning:

- The user clicks a button, and you store their selection (this is actually a frame label) in a variable.

- The closing sequence plays.

- Once the closing sequence has ended, the value saved from the user's click is retrieved, and the playhead is sent to this retrieved frame label.

- Once the opening sequence has ended, the playhead is halted with a stop frame.

The previous diagram and reasoning is all well and good, but you've actually skipped one key bit of information: Which came first, the chicken or the egg? Okay, it's not quite as mind-boggling as that, but it is a pretty important factor in your portfolio site.

The steps assume that you already have a sequence to close before your opening one, but in fact, you don't. If you were to dry run this sequence for the first time, you'd quickly realize that there is no closing sequence to run, and you'd be waiting forever...well, maybe.

Given this, the first time a user clicks a button in the movie, you show her an opening sequence. Every time after that, you show her a closing sequence first, followed by an opening sequence:

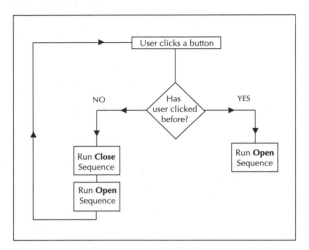

From a Flash ActionScript point-of-view, you can use a single variable to check whether the user has clicked anything. You'll see how in a moment.

3. Select all the code on line 2 of your code and delete it. It sounds drastic, but it isn't:

```
1 webButton.onRelease = function() {
2    |
3 };
```

4. Type the following code carefully, in between the curly brackets as seen here:

```
1 webButton.onRelease = function() {
2    toOpen = "open web";
3
4    if (userHasClicked == true) {
5        content_mc.play ();
6    } else {
7        content_mc.gotoAndPlay(toOpen);
8        userHasClicked = true;
9    }
10 };
```

In this code, note the following:

■ On line 2 you create a variable called toOpen to store, predictably, the frame label of the chosen open sequence.

■ Line 4 uses a conditional statement to check if the variable userHasClicked is positive. This variable is used to check if this is the first click. (A little later you will initialize it as false.) In this conditional, you are checking if this is anything but the first click. If this condition is met, you set the playhead moving with a simple play method on line 5.

■ The code on lines 7-8 is run in the event that this is the first click because userHasClicked is set to false. The code on line 7 sends the playhead in the content movie clip to the frame label value stored on line 2. The line 8 code changes the value of userHasClicked to true, meaning that any subsequent clicks will run the closing animation before the opening one.

This chunk of code is almost the same for each button, so you'll do all the buttons now.

5. Select the code from lines 2 to 9 and copy it using CTRL + C.

6. Highlight the handler code for the printButton onRelease event on line 13.

```
12 printButton.onRelease = function() {
13     content_mc.gotoAndPlay("open print");
14 };
```

7. Paste the previously copied code using CTRL + V.

8. Change the value of the toOpen variable to open print:

```
12 printButton.onRelease = function() {
13     toOpen = "open print";
```

9. Select the handler code within the aboutButton curly brackets, and paste lines 2 and 9 of the code over it.

10. Change the toOpen variable to open about.

11. Paste the code over the existing in the emailButton code, and change toOpen to open email.

12. Before you move on, add userHasClicked = false to the end of the code.

The code for the buttons is finished for this chapter. To make the code functional, you now have to add some code to the various frames in the content movie clip.

Adding frame code

13. Double-click the content movie clip instance on the stage to edit it in place.

14. Scroll along the timeline to frame 100.

15. Click frame 100 of the actions layer and look in the actions panel. At the moment it has a stop frame that you added last chapter.

16. Delete the stop code and replace it with this:

```
1  gotoAndPlay (_parent.toOpen);
```

The reason that you have added this code in this particular place is clearer by looking at the timeline:

Frame 100 is the last frame of the web closing sequence, and therefore, once the closing animation has played, this line of code instructs the timeline to move on to the selected opening sequence stored as toOpen.

17. Select this line of code and copy it.

18. Select frame 124 and replace the existing code with that on the clipboard.

19. Repeat this for frames 149 and 174.

When the playhead hits any of these frames, it reads your code and redirects the playhead to the relevant play sequence.

20. Save your case study document.

21. Test the movie and try any of the buttons out. Pretty impressive so far, but there is one significant bug that you'll sort out in the next chapter. If you'd like to figure it out for yourself, skip the next paragraph and go to the summary.

Too lazy to find out eh? Click any button twice in a row and see if anything strikes you as unusual....

Summary

This chapter has built further on the ActionScripting foundation you established in the previous chapter. You've taken an important step toward being able to create well-integrated, intelligent, responsive movies using ActionScript.

You saw that:

- **Labels** provide reference points for you to jump to using ActionScript.

- You can name specific instances of movie clip symbols on the stage using the Properties panel. Naming an instance—instantiating it—means that you can use that name in scripts and manipulate that instance using ActionScript commands.

- You can use actions to point at particular instances on the stage and pass them instructions about how they should behave.

- The goto action is used to jump to an individual frame number or label within a movie clip's timeline.

- You can add intelligence and decision-making to your movies using variables and conditional statements.

- **Variables** are memory locations where you can store values and information for later (re)use.

- **Conditional statements** let Flash decide what action to take, depending upon the conditions it finds.

If you want to do serious, industrial-strength work with Flash, you need to learn ActionScript. You'll be returning to explore ActionScript in much more detail later in the book.

In the next chapter—**sound and video**!

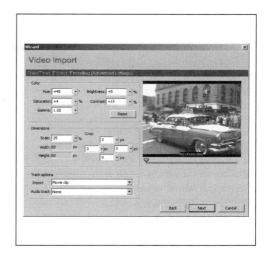

Chapter 12

MULTIMEDIA: SOUND AND VIDEO

What we'll cover in this chapter:

- **Creating sound**—creating or acquiring sounds and music to use in your movies
- **Importing and exporting sound and video**—the types of sound and video that Flash can handle, and the best ways to get sound into and out of Flash
- **Using sound and video in Flash**—manipulating sound and video inside of Flash once you've got it there
- **Flash sound issues**—tips on the particular issues related to sound implementation in Flash, such as potential pitfalls and strange effects
- **Flash video issues**—tips on when it's best to compress imported videos

This chapter will show you how to use sound and video to enhance your Flash movies. You've already attached sound to a button in a previous chapter, but here you'll be opening up the world of Flash multimedia and climbing right inside.

Non Flash multimedia websites have always separated the sound and video content from the rest of the site. For example, embedding a video into a separate, stand-alone, application was the norm with standard HTML websites. Although you don't have to do this in Flash, it is a good idea to separate large sound and video files from the main site.

The key to getting multimedia onto the Web without compromising loading times is *optimization*, so we'll go through all the things you'll need to consider when you finally are ready to export your movie. You'll look at sound and video elements separately, and consider the implications of each when you add them to your movies.

In this chapter, you'll construct a soundtrack that will play alongside your website's visual content. In this example, you'll separate the soundtrack and the visual content to minimize download time. By doing this, the website will load first, allowing people to begin navigating while the soundtrack loads in the background and starts playing when it's ready. There's another advantage to keeping the sound and visual components apart: if you want to change or replace your soundtrack, it's much easier to do if the soundtrack is separated from the rest of the content.

Before you look at sound in the first section, we recommend that you download the set of sounds from our website to get the most out of the examples in this chapter.

Plug in those speakers and let's rumble.

Sound on the Web

Sound on the Web used to be problematic, and then a little thing called MP3 came along and blew everything else out of the water. Before the advent of MP3, there were really only two options for the web designer: **MIDI** and **sampled sound files**.

MIDI (Music Instrument Digital Interface) is a format that's understood by all digital music instruments, all music cards, and most soundcards.

For most sound formats, the sound file contains a *digital representation* of the actual sounds, with the corollary that a higher quality representation of the sound implies a larger file. The advantage of MIDI is that it doesn't hold representations of the sounds themselves—it holds the instructions for *how to play them* on a specific instrument. This means that MIDI files are very small and compact compared to other formats. It's a bit like raster and vector graphics: a MIDI file is similar to a vector in that it's an *instruction* to do something, not a direct representation of the thing (the sound). MIDI can also be embedded in simple HTML.

A MIDI soundcard contains a bank of instruments that the MIDI file instructs the card to play at certain times, volumes, pitches, and so on. This can be a problem because only the instruments embedded in the card can be played. New instruments can sometimes be added to the card, but this means a loss of standardization because you can't guarantee that everyone will have the correct instrument, resulting in another instrument being substituted for it.

The problems with MIDI are that it's not a universal standard, and the final sound output depends on the quality of your MIDI-compatible synthesizer or music card. More importantly, MIDI is a music language only: it can't be used to create vocal sounds or non-musical effects such as a door slamming.

The other pre-MP3 option was to have sampled data in the various sound formats of the time—WAVs, SNDs, and AIFFs. These were big and bulky and tended to be a major headache during download. Waiting an extra thirty seconds for a voice to say "Hi there!" on a homepage did not really cut the mustard! Additionally, not all sound formats were understood by both PC and Mac platforms, causing further bugs and uncertainties.

Then along came MP3. This is a sound format that compresses sounds intelligently via several different filters to give a much smaller file size for a given quality than any other sound compression system (with the exception of MIDI, which as previously explained, is really an electronic music language for instruments).

MP3 is now *the* standard for music files on the Web, in the same way that Flash is the standard for high-impact, highly interactive websites. It therefore comes as no surprise that Flash supports MP3.

Flash and MP3

When using Flash and MP3, once the music is embedded into Flash, it can be heard on the Web but it can't be copied in the same way that regular MP3 data can be downloaded.

Although MP3 simplifies the sound export options available from Flash considerably, there's still the problem of getting the sound *into* Flash in the first place. In this section, you'll experiment with different ways of doing this.

Without further ado, let's start honing your Flash multimedia skills by using sound. Creating and manipulating sound is probably something novel to many new Flash users, so you have some separate tutorials in this chapter. The Sound Sampling appendix at the end of this book describes the fundamentals of digital sound. You might like to look at that too if you're totally new to digital sound.

Let's begin, logically enough, with how to create or source the sounds you want to use.

Creating sound

The first issue when getting sound into Flash is acquiring your sound files. There are generally only two options:

- Get them from a sound library CD or a website offering public domain sounds.
- Create the sound samples yourself.

There are a lot of sites out there that rip off their sounds from obscure dance or hip-hop records. The implications of this may not be too serious when you're starting out, but when you create sites commercially, a revelation that you are using material in violation of copyright can be both costly and embarrassing. The easy and safe option is to get your sounds and loops from a royalty-free website. For those who go for this

option, there's a list of useful sources in the Sound Sampling appendix, so just nip to the Web, download a couple of sounds, and fast-forward to the next section.

Now we'll briefly illustrate a typical route for *creating* sounds for Flash.

There are two main types of sound you'll want to capture: incidental sounds and music. Incidental sounds are things like doors slamming or cows mooing, which can easily be recorded with just a microphone, a handy cow, and the free sound recording software that comes with your computer (Sound Recorder on the PC or the Sound control panel on a Mac). You could record music in the same way, but the results would be huge files with poor quality. The best way to get high quality music onto a computer is to create it yourself.

One of the techniques that you'll learn later in this chapter is how to create a full sound score, optimized for the Web. One of the best ways to utilize sound on the Internet is by creating a **sound loop**. This means that you start and stop with exactly the same noise, so you can repeat the sound endlessly and smoothly without any obvious breaks in it. The advantage of this is that you only need to download one small file that can carry on playing for a long time. Because music loops are one of the hardest sounds to create well, you'll with the thought process that goes into them, before moving onto the creation itself.

To create music professionally, you'd use a sequencing program along with a battery of expensive synthesizers and instruments, but you can obtain simple (and relatively cheap) entry-level sequencers from the Web (see the Sound Sampling appendix for a few to try). Instead of using expensive "physical" instruments, you can use the sequencer to control your soundcard's *built-in* instruments via MIDI. The real advantage of this method is that all current soundcards support playback of sampled sound (as well as sound capture via a microphone). If you have a decent soundcard, you probably have a full synthesizer and sampler sitting in a slot in your computer right now. The sound quality of internal soundcards won't be a problem because you'll be compressing the sounds extensively for web transport, and in the end there won't be much difference between them. Once you've created your musical masterpiece, it's necessary to *export* it from your sequencer as audio.

We created this chapter's accompanying sound files by importing the sequencer/synthesizer output into Sound Forge—a popular sound editing program made by Sonic Foundry, with a cheaper, cut-down version available—at 44 KHz and 16 bit, which is the equivalent of CD quality. Using Sound Forge, you can also *normalize* the sounds. Normalization takes the loudest sound in the sample and increases/decreases the overall volume based on this level, setting it as the highest point in the possible range of sounds in your movie. This ensures that there's a much greater range available for the quieter sounds in your file, thus avoiding excessively loud quantization noise (hissing) during the sampling process (see the Sound Sampling appendix for an explanation of quantization). If you don't have any really quiet sounds in your file, this isn't really necessary.

After this Sound Forge-based processing, the sounds were passed through a package called ACID (from the same makers as Sound Forge) to create a seamless loop, and then saved on to the computer. If you're using a Mac, use Macromedia's SoundEdit to edit your sounds and the built-in Loop Tuner to perfect your loops. The most common formats for saving in are WAV files (PC) or AIFF files (Mac). We'll be using WAVs as the default file format for our sounds throughout this chapter, but if you're using a Mac just substitute this for AIFFs—all the processes remain the same.

The files are now ready for importing into Flash.

To allow you to use the individual sounds, we've included them with the files in the download section of our website. We've kept the sound files at CD quality throughout the sound capture process, for the following two reasons:

- The maximum (best) sound quality that Flash can export is limited by the sound quality at which you choose to *import*. The better your input, the more flexibility you have with the output. There's always the chance that you may want to use better quality sounds as Internet transmission speeds creep up and more people have faster connections. By keeping the files at CD quality, you're never in danger of having to re-record samples.

- You may want to create screensavers or other non-web applications, and these will be able to use CD quality sound because bandwidth won't be an issue. In this case, you wouldn't have to re-record the sounds because they would already be at the highest quality.

Of course, you may not have CD quality *output* available, particularly if you're using nonoptical connections and/or a soundcard as your synthesizer. In that case, keep your sounds at the highest quality your setup can manage—you may just save yourself from major hassle later on.

Importing and exporting sound with Flash

In the last section, we gave a brief overview of how to get audio onto your computer so that it's ready for importing into Flash. You'll now look at how to get it into Flash, and how to optimize it for *export* onto the Internet.

To import a sound, all you have to do is use the File ➤ Import menu.

Flash can import a number of sound formats: WAV, AIFF, and MP3 are probably the most popular. If you've created your own sounds, it's strongly recommended that you keep them as full quality WAV files because MP3 is what's called a **lossy** format. This means that to get the highest amount of compression, the computer intelligently discards sounds that it thinks you won't hear. The problem with this is that there's a drop in quality, and once the sound information is discarded, it's lost forever. Although you may not be able to hear the differences, you'll see them in programs like Sound Forge and ACID, and you may start to have trouble synchronizing the lower quality sounds as precisely. This is because the waveforms have started to "blur," making accurately locating the sound's start and stop positions much more difficult. This is much the same effect as when you use low quality JPEG images, and the image colors and edges start to look washed out and blocky.

Let's get your fingers busy and work with some real sounds.

If you haven't already visited our site and downloaded the sound files that accompany this section, do so now. Go to www.friendsofed.com, follow the links to the Code page, find the correct code download page for this book and download the relevant sounds file. We included both CD quality and Flash-optimized (and therefore smaller) versions of the files.

Bringing sound into the mix

1. Open a new Flash document and save it away as Soundtrack.fla.

2. Use the File ➤ Import ➤ Import To Library command to open the Import dialog box, and select All Sound Formats from the drop-down menu:

3. From here, navigate to where you saved your downloaded sound files, open them all, and add them to your Library (you can do multiple selections in the PC dialog box using *SHIFT*-click or *CTRL*-click, or simply select all files in a folder by pressing *CTRL*+A).

Once the sounds are imported (which may take a while on slower machines, and you may see a

progress bar as Flash imports the files), they'll appear in your Library:

The preview window will show a waveform representation of the selected sound. If you see *two* separate waveforms, the sound was imported in stereo. If you click the Play button in the preview window, Flash will play one loop of your *original* sound. It's important to remember this because Flash will play the sound as it was when you imported it, ignoring any compression you may have added inside of Flash since the original import.

4. Display the Sound Properties window for the MainDrumLoop sound either by double-clicking its speaker icon in the Library, or by selecting it and pressing the Properties icon at the bottom of the Library window:

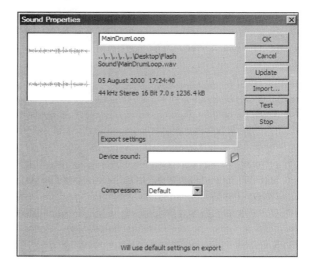

297

This window displays the basic information for the selected sound file including how the sound will be exported in the final movie. The form Flash will export the sound in is dependent on your selection in the Compression drop-down menu.

5. Click the Test button, and your sound will play in its original state. If you leave this set to Default, Flash will take the settings from your Publish Settings window's Flash Tab (this window is covered fully in Chapter 14). At the moment, the default compression settings are MP3 at 16 bit, but you won't *hear* this difference until your movie is published.

6. In the Compression drop-down menu of the Sound Properties window, change the setting to MP3:

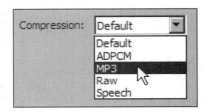

This will open up another list of options:

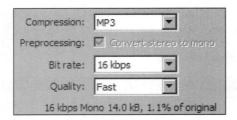

Note the text at the bottom of the window. This text tells you how big your file is and how much it has been compressed. For example, the original file was 1236.4 KB. Using MP3 compression, we got the size down to 14.0 KB, an amazing 1.1 percent of the original file size.

7. Click Test now to hear the compressed sound. Notice that it doesn't sound quite the same as your original sound.

You can juggle the file size against the quality by playing with the MP3 settings until you reach a happy medium. The Bit Rate is another way of expressing the sampling rate of the sound: it's found by multiplying the *sampling* rate (in Hz) by

the *number of bits* per sample. The Quality defines the conversion algorithm used. Leaving it at Fast means that Flash will convert to MP3 quickly at the expense of quality. Setting it to Best will give you the best conversion quality, but Flash will take slightly longer. This setting has no effect on file size, it's just an anachronism from the days when computers took ages to compress sound—if you have a modern computer, it will probably do the conversion in a blink of an eye no matter what setting you use, so go for Best.

8. When you've tweaked your sound to what you consider to be the best balance, click OK to confirm the settings. If you decide later that your sounds are taking up too much room, you can always go back and change the settings to give a smaller size.

9. Tweak the rest of the sounds to give the best results for you. You'll use these optimized sounds later.

10. Save the Flash document.

Sounds can be a major part of the download for the final movie. If you're using sounds, it's recommended that you do not simply accept the default sound settings or set the export options globally. Play around with the settings for each sound individually, and choose the most appropriate setting for each one by considering the sound quality you hear and offsetting this against the relative importance of the sound. Be fairly brutal in this because sound files may make your final website unviewable if they are large and uncompressed.

In particular, you might consider the following:

- Making button click sounds as small as the compression allows—the sounds will be a lot deeper and a bit muffled, but hey, what's the difference between one momentary click sound and another?

- Making less prominent sounds lower quality—if you have a big thumping bass line and percussion up front, do you really need all those background effects to be high quality?

■ The human ear is very poor at sensing the direction of deep sounds, so stereo is not really necessary for things like thumping bass lines. MP3 takes this into account during its compression, but other methods may not.

We'll end this section with a discussion of the different sound compression methods (called **codecs,** which stands for **Co**mpression—**DEC**ompression). In practice, the only way to be sure you've used the best settings is to keep tweaking and testing until you're happy with the audible result.

■ **ADPCM** is there mainly for compatibility with Flash 3. It can sometimes give good results for short sounds such as button clicks, but for longer sounds or musical samples it's best to stick with MP3. As always, the only way to be certain is to try them all and pick the one that's best for you.

■ **MP3** is the compression codec of choice for the Internet in general. You'll find that it gives the best sound for the smallest file size. It works by splitting the sound up into frequency bands and then applying numerous filters and tricks, based on which sounds the human ear would hear. This weeds out redundant information before recompiling the sound.

If you have a definite maximum file size, work your way down the **Bit Rate** menu until the desired file size is reached. MP3 also allows you to select stereo when going above 16KB per second, but because of the way MP3 compression works, this won't always make a huge difference. Often on a stereo track, most of the sounds in one channel are mirrored in the other: part of the MP3 compression cycle is to compare the two channels and delete all the mirrored information from one and just mark the differences in the other channel. When the track is played back, one channel plays in stereo until it comes across a marked difference and it plays that difference in the other channel. With this method, the size of the track is almost halved while still remaining true to the original. MP3 then performs a number of other more complicated routines to get the track size down even further.

■ **Raw** has no compression routine, and as its name suggests, it exports raw digitized sound. You can reduce the file size by specifying a lower quality, but your final file size will generally be much higher than using any of the other methods. You would only use this method if you were running the final movie from a hard drive in applications such as Flash screensavers. Raw does have the advantage that it is the fastest way to play sounds. When using something like MP3, a certain amount of the Flash player's time can be spent decompressing the sound, so if size is not an issue but speed is, you might be better off choosing this.

■ **Speech** is a form of compression that is best, predictably, when used on recorded voice tracks. Because voices record at a lower frequency than most sounds, including music, for example, this allows you to use a lower sample rate—5KHz or 11KHz are acceptable. Try this when you have a voice track for your Flash movies. Flash uses the Speech codec when it is performing real time compression (via the microphone object), and its selling point is speed rather than compression, so you may find that even for raw speech, MP3 is better.

> *In all the options just listed, it's important to note that putting the sound sampling settings higher than the original imported sound won't produce better quality sound (it can actually create worse quality in some cases!).*
>
> *Also worth noting is that it is a common trap when optimizing sounds to compare the optimized sound against the original. If you simply listen to the sound in its own right, you tend to go for lower compression rates, and this is closer to the real life—web listeners will not be comparing the sounds against the original either!*

Using sound in Flash

You saw how to attach sound to buttons in the Actions and Interactions chapter. Attaching sound to the timeline is almost identical in nature, but there are additional sound features Flash offers that we've not yet touched on. We'll repair that state of affairs right now.

Attaching sounds to the timeline

This is as easy as it sounds: you create a keyframe, and attach a sound to it. There are, however, several options that can be selected to make full use of the sound, and extra optimization facilities offered by Flash. Although the number of drop-down menus may seem a little daunting, it all fits together in a fluid movement when you're actually adding the sound. The best way to illustrate this is to try it.

Attaching sounds to the timeline

1. Continuing with the last exercise, change the name of the Soundtrack movie's default layer to Percussion1. Then insert a keyframe in frame 5. You should now have this basic setup:

2. Open the Properties panel if it's not already open. From here you can attach your sound and add effects and different timings to it. If the keyframe in frame 5 is not already highlighted, click it. Open the Sound drop-down menu from the Properties panel—all the sounds in your Library will appear in a list:

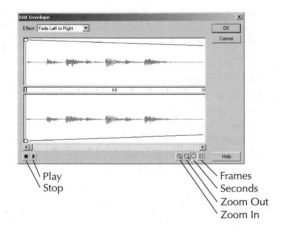

3. To attach a sound to your keyframe, select it from this list—scroll down the list and click Percussion1. Once you've selected your sound, a little waveform appears in the keyframe. Right now it just looks like a straight line because you can only see a small fragment of it.

4. To rectify this, add frames by pressing *F5* at frame 90 so that you can see the end of the waveform just poking into frame 89:

5. Test your movie. You should hear a short pause, and then the sound will begin playing at frame 5.

6. Click your sound in the timeline (the keyframe at frame 5) and return to the Properties panel. The next thing to look at is the Effect drop-down menu:

This option allows you to add audio effects via a **volume envelope**. The envelope allows you to see and control the volume in different parts of the sound.

7. For an example of this, select Fade Left to Right from the Effect drop-down menu, and then click Edit (next to the menu) to display the Edit Envelope window:

This window contains the Edit Envelope dialog, with Play/Stop buttons at bottom left and Frames, Seconds, Zoom Out, Zoom In buttons at bottom right.

Once the Edit Envelope window appears, use the Zoom buttons on the bottom right until you can see the full waveform.

Stereo sounds are split into two **channels**, one for the left speaker and one for the right. This window contains two panes, the top pane shows the waveforms for the left audio channel, and the bottom pane shows the waveforms for the right channel.

You'll always see two channels, even if the sound you're editing is mono—the one channel will just be repeated twice. The scale between the two panes represents time, which can be measured in seconds or in frames. You can toggle between the scales with the two buttons on the bottom right. You can test your sound at any time by using the Play button.

Superimposed on top of the waveforms are a couple of lines with little white squares on either end. These lines depict the volume envelope, and they can be used to control the volume of your sound. The top of the pane represents 100 percent volume, and the bottom is silence. Because you selected Fade Left to Right, the top pane (the left channel) will have a diagonal line running from the top at the beginning of the sound to the bottom at the end, whereas the bottom pane will show the opposite. This means the sound in the left speaker will start at full volume and drop to nothing, and the sound in the right speaker will start at nothing and rise to full volume, giving the effect of the sound panning from one side to the other.

8. Press the Play button to hear the effect.

9. The squares on the lines are control points, much like on Bezier curves, and they can be dragged to change the shape of the envelope—try it now.

10. Drag the control points higher and lower, and use the Play button to preview your changes. You can add up to eight control points by clicking anywhere on either the top or bottom pane. When you add a point in one pane, Flash adds an identical point in the other. You can easily make some pretty strange sound effects by playing with these settings:

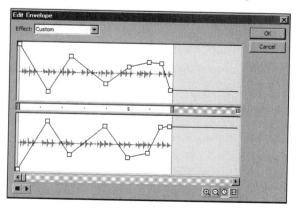

11. To get an idea of some basic effects, run through the Effect drop-down list at the top of the window, and notice how the envelope changes to reflect your selection.

Always play your sounds after you make an alteration to ensure you're achieving the effect you want. As with most things, the best way to appreciate how it works is to play with it and learn by listening to the effects you make. Notice that you can still zoom in and out using the magnifying glass icons while you're editing the envelope—this allows you to be more precise with the timing of the control points.

12. Click Cancel to close the window with no effects applied to your sound.

You want no effect because you want the sound to play as per the original (no fade or pan effects) but feel free to come back later and experiment.

As you may already have begun to realize, the volume envelope can be very powerful when creating sound effects. For example, the sound of an approaching car can easily be simulated by importing a basic engine noise, and using the envelope controls to make it slowly increase in volume. The same engine noise could also be used to simulate the car moving from left to right across the screen by using the Fade Left to Right effect. By clever use of the envelope controls, you could even incorporate both of these effects into the same sound. Many more complicated effects are possible with these controls, but they are beyond the scope of this book. For now, just knowing these basics will stand you in good stead.

13. Open the **Sync** drop-down menu in the Properties panel. This will give you a list of four options— Event, Start, Stop, and Stream:

The most important of these options are Event and Stream. Although the selection of these Sync types will have little effect on your movie while you're testing it in Flash, they have a profound effect on

301

how Flash loads the sounds during Internet playback.

14. Leave this selection set to *Event*.

15. Save the Flash document once again.

Sounds in Flash take precedence over animations and videos, and follow their own separate "lifetimes." For example, imagine you have an animation that's 10 seconds long, and a sound that also lasts for 10 seconds. You could tell Flash to *start* them both at the same time and expect them both to *finish* at the same time. In reality though, if someone runs your movie on a slow computer, your sounds can easily get out of sync, especially if you're streaming sounds (sending the file down bit by bit as it plays). If you ran the 10-second animation/sound example on a slow computer, it might get half way through the sound and animation without a problem, but then have to pause the animation as it waited to load the next part of the sound as it arrived down the wire. If it were the other way and the animation was the problem, Flash would try to skip frames to allow the sound to play smoothly.

- The Event option tells Flash to treat the sound the same way it treats movie symbols. It will only load one version of the sound into its Library when the movie is first played, and will reuse the sound if it has to play it more than once. Event sounds are not played until the whole sound has been loaded, and they are not locked to the timeline. If you have an event sound lasting 10 seconds but the user's computer is too slow to maintain the frame rate, the sound may not end on the frame you would have expected. The problem with this is that your movie may take longer to begin playing because Flash is loading all of the sounds before it starts.

- Stream tells Flash to start loading the sound directly from the Internet as a constant sound stream. Flash starts playing the sound as soon as it has approximately five seconds of the sound loaded. If you repeat the same sound several times, Flash will reload the sound each time because it's not kept in the computer's memory. When you have several sounds all streaming at the same time and stopping at the same time, Flash will mix them all together when it creates the SWF file for Internet playback, and will stream back only one channel. Additionally, Flash will lock the sound to

the timeline. This means that if the sound gets ahead or behind of the main timeline, Flash will stop or skip frames to make sure the sound stops at the right instant. This can cause choppy animations as Flash tries to keep the frame rate up with the sound, but does ensure your animation keeps in sync with your soundtrack.

> *A good analogy between event and streaming sounds is the difference between owning a song on CD (event sound), and listening to it on the radio (streaming sound). To own it, you first have to go out and buy it, but after that you can play it as often as you like, and pause it if you want to do something else for a while. If you listen to it on the radio, you can listen to it once all the way through every time it is played but if you want to do something else for a moment, you can't pause it, and if you turn the radio off, you have to wait for the song to be broadcast again before you can hear it again. The good thing about the CD is flexibility, but you have a larger initial outlay (you have to buy it). The good thing about the radio is that you don't have any initial outlay, but you loose flexibility in its use.*

Having said all that, the choice between Event and Stream is usually easy. If the sound is relatively short and will be played more than once or looped, select Event. If your sound is a long, non-repeating, introductory tune that has to start playing immediately, select Stream. It's usually more economical to build tailored sounds from scratch for your movies, which can be easily looped if they need to be. In this case, you'll rarely have to use the Stream option, and will therefore save your sounds from having to be reloaded when you want to reuse them.

The Start option is almost identical to Event except that it won't allow more than one version of the same sound to play at the same time. For example, if you have a long sound attached to a button, it will usually replay every time the button is pressed, and rather than stopping the first sound if the button is pressed again, Flash will just start playing the new sound over the top of the original one. As you can imagine, this can make a mess of your carefully constructed sounds!

The Stop option does just what it says it does—it stops the sound attached to the keyframe, and all other versions of the same sound file that are already playing.

The final sound option in the Properties panel is Loop. Flash plays the sound from end to end as many times as you specify. If you leave this set to zero, the sound won't loop—it will play once and then stop. There are numerous tricks you can perform with this option: for instance, if you set Loop to a huge number like 9,999, and then put a Stop action in the keyframe containing the start of the sound, you could create a sound that will effectively play forever—certainly longer than anyone is likely to listen to it. When you have a looping sound, the volume envelope will extend across all of the loops, allowing you to apply fades and effects across the whole sound, not just each individual loop. This is useful for repetitive sounds like car engines and helicopter whirrs.

Now let's examine some of quirks of sound in Flash.

Flash sound issues

There are a fair number of unexpected things that can happen when you're using sound in Flash. These surprises have put off many otherwise competent Flash web designers from dabbling much further than adding sound to the odd button click in Flash. It's important that you're aware of these from the beginning so that you won't have too much trouble with them later.

> *These unexpected results have been with Flash for a number of revisions, and look set to stay, so don't treat the methods listed below as workarounds for the current revision, but rather as the way you have to do it every time in Flash.*

- The Flash Player sometimes gets its synchronization wrong when all the sounds start on the first frame of your movie or the first frame of any scene. For this reason, it's a good idea to start all sounds at about frame 5. It's also worth noting that if you have a sound on a gotoAndPlay action in a movie with a long timeline and high frame rate, it's a

good idea to put the sound a few frames after the destination frame.

- From time to time, Event synchronized sounds may not last as long as they should, or may not sound as if they start on the same frame, even though they are set to do so on the timeline. There's a little trick that you can use to correct this: In addition to starting your sounds at frame 5, try adding a new layer with a one-frame sound in frame 4 and setting it to Stream. We call this a "kicker" layer, because it seems to kick the Flash Player into action and make it behave like it should. It doesn't matter which sound you use, but remember to set its volume envelope to nothing, so you won't hear anything when it plays. You'll need to do this for every new scene you have that contains any Event sounds attached to a timeline that are supposed to start at the same instant. Alternatively, you can create a very short sound sample specifically for use as the kicker in all your projects. A potential danger with this technique is that if you have a movie with very intense animation, the streamed kicker will force frames to be skipped, including the possibility of skipping other code and sound keyframes.

- Event sounds are only synchronized to the timeline when they're started. If, for some reason, the computer fails to keep up with the frame rate, your carefully triggered sounds can start to play too late, leaving gaps and—worse—becoming unsynchronized. There are three ways around this:

  - When you are ready to publish your movie (more on this in the **Publishing** chapter—Chapter 15), set your movie playback to Auto High. If you've set your movie to High quality, Flash will try to maintain the picture quality of your animations at a maximum and won't be too bothered about maintaining a constant frame rate. This may result in your sounds being triggered too late because the timeline itself is "getting behind." You can lower the quality to Auto High from the HTML tab of the File ➤ Publish Settings menu. This tells Flash to maintain a high quality until it's in danger of becoming too slow, at which point Flash will drop the picture quality to keep up. Flash can therefore compensate intelligently.

  - Drop the frame rate.

- Use advanced ActionScript. Rather than attaching your sounds to frames, you can create a code based sequencer that uses the `Sound.onSoundComplete()` method. Unfortunately, this process is a little beyond the scope of this book, but it is covered in the book **Foundation ActionScript for Macromedia Flash MX 2004** (Apress, 2003).

- Whether you're producing a professional website or one for personal use, it's still best to test it out on a minimum spec computer. Although this used to be a major issue, it's becoming increasingly less so as the average computer becomes faster. The other option is to forget the issue completely unless someone reports a problem, which is less likely to happen as time goes on, but it still can stop that person from ever returning to your site.

Now that you know about how to acquire or create sound loops, and avoid some of the pitfalls associated with sound, it's time to do something a bit more useful than attaching the odd click to a button or a few low-quality sound effects to the timeline.

Integrating sound

In this section, you'll create a full soundtrack. There are few websites that actually have such a thing, possibly because of all the problems that have been encountered with Flash's **Event** sound type, so you're now beginning to walk a trail less trodden, one that many before you have been afraid to follow. You may be a beginner, but that's no excuse for being afraid. Enjoy.

Creating a movie soundtrack

A feature of Flash that we've not talked about yet is the loadMovie action. This action allows Flash to run *more than one movie at the same time*. One of these movies could be your website's visual content, and the other one could be the soundtrack.

In this chapter, you'll create a soundtrack movie, and we'll show you how to add it to a website movie when we talk about publishing later in Chapter 14. Your soundtrack will not be a traditional Flash movie because it'll have a blank stage—the timeline in the soundtrack movie will control sound only. Don't be put off by this; it will all begin to blend together when you get to the **Publishing** chapter. For now, let's paste together the loops you imported earlier and make a polished soundtrack.

In your Soundtrack.fla Flash document, you should already have a full, optimized Library, and one layer containing a percussion sound:

These sounds have been specially selected to allow the creation of a number of different compositions, or in the more modern parlance, they allow different remixes of the same tune. You can bring certain elements to the fore or delete others to give completely different styles. For example, you can use strings and melodies for an ambient sound or focus on percussion for a more insistent dub sound.

As you saw earlier, the sounds were created for looping and reuse, so you'll use Event syncing throughout. Taking into account the problems that can occur with Event sounds, the first thing you must do is add a kicker.

1. Create a new layer and name it kicker.

2. Insert a keyframe in frame 4 of the kicker layer, and then attach the BassLine sound (although you can use any sound) to the keyframe:

3. In the Properties panel, set the Sync drop-down menu to Stream.

4. Insert a blank keyframe in frame 5 of the kicker layer. Because you set the sound to Stream, you want to make sure that the sound plays for only one frame before stopping.

5. Click back to frame 4, and then click the Edit button in the Properties panel to open the Edit Envelope window for the BassLine sound. Drag the control points to the bottom to set the volume to zero for both channels, then close the window:

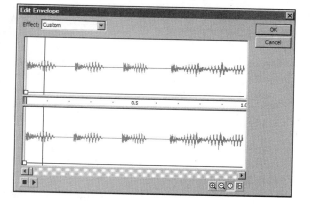

There's no need to change the Loop option in the Properties panel because you want your sound to play only once.

6. Because it's imperative to know where in the timeline you are at all times (you'll have to count beats and frames to sync everything up just right), you'll add a comments layer to hold labels. Add a new layer above your Kicker layer, and name it Comments.

The layer will automatically match the length of your longest layer—in this case, the Percussion1 layer. If it needs to be any longer at any stage, you can always lengthen it. You could also make this layer a guide layer so that it doesn't get exported into the final movie, but because it contains nothing but labels, it won't make much difference.

7. Insert a keyframe in frame 4 of the Comments layer, above your kicker sound. Use the Frame field on the left of the Properties panel to put a comment in this keyframe that reads //Kicker and Percussion1. Don't worry if the label is too long for the text field. The labels on this layer will let you quickly see what's happening, and when, in your soundtrack:

> Adding two forward slashes (//) in front of a frame label makes it a comment—Flash will not include it in the final SWF, and it exists only in the FLA for your benefit.

8. Make sure that your percussion sound is set to be an Event sound that doesn't loop. Unless otherwise stated, this will be the setting for all the other sounds, too. Don't forget!

As a safety check, let's make sure that this sample looks how you expect it to. In Sonic Foundry's ACID program, the samples were 7 seconds long each. The movie is playing at 12 frames per second, which for 7 seconds equates to 84 frames. The sample starts at frame 5 and ends at 89, which seems about right.

The percussion sound is two bars long, and so are all of the other samples. You're writing a dance track, so the pattern you must follow is to create four bars before inserting a change. This is the standard pattern for all dance and most pop music, so it's one to remember. This means that you need another two bars before you can have a new pattern, so you must repeat this pattern once more.

9. Insert a keyframe in frame 89 of the percussion1 layer, and attach another Percussion1 sound using the Sound drop-down menu in the Properties panel.

10. Play your sound through to make sure there are no glitches in it. Insert frames as you did before, until you can see the whole sound wave on the time-line—this will allow you to easily sync other sounds to the end of it. If your sounds are a little out of sync, try moving their starting keyframe forward or backward until you find where they sound best.

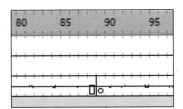

You may be wondering why you didn't just repeat the first sample for two loops using the Properties panel. You could have done that, but remember that Event sounds are only synchronized to the timeline *when they're started*. The longer the event sound lasts before you attach a new version to the timeline, the more chance there is of your sound getting slightly out of sync with the timeline.

Next, you'll add a new loop, Percussion2, which is a slightly fuller rhythm with more bass.

11. Add a new layer called Percussion2 to put the sound in, and move this layer to the bottom of the list. This means that your layer order follows the order of the samples in the soundtrack. If you need to see all your layers at once, click the bottom of the timeline and drag it down until they are all in view.

12. Add a keyframe in this layer at the frame immediately after the first percussion loop finishes, and attach the Percussion2 sound to it:

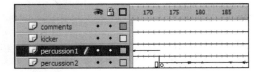

If you are having trouble finding the end of the sounds, you can set the frames to a longer size by clicking the icon at the top right of the Timeline panel and selecting Large from the drop-down menu.

13. Add a keyframe to your Comments layer above where you started the new sound, and label it Percussion2. (You can also extend the timeline a few frames after the keyframe so that you can see the full comment text, as shown in the following graphic.)

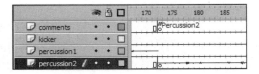

This label reminds you that you're now in the second set of four bars, and that you're using the second percussion sample. Documentation of music files is pretty much a necessity. You may recognize all the individual waveforms now, but in six months time when you want to spruce up your website and decide on a celebratory remix, it may take you some time to find where each new sound comes in on the composition.

14. In accordance with the four bar rule, repeat the Percussion2 sound at the frame after it ends, in the same way as you did for Percussion1 (in our example, this is at frame 257).

The four bar rule is there for the main loops that shape your composition, but you can have sounds that start and finish before and after a four bar interval. Some samples do this in the final file, soundtrack.fla.

15. Next you'll add two sounds that will start at the same time in the third set of four bars. Prepare

the timeline by adding two new layers to the bottom, calling them Percussion3 and BigBang:

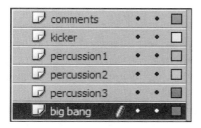

Extend your timeline until you see the end of the last sound (if you haven't already). Insert your new sounds in their respective layers immediately after the end of the second Percussion2 sound. In our example, this occurs at frame 341:

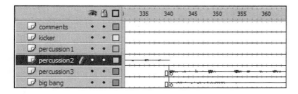

16. Update your Comments layer to include the new sounds:

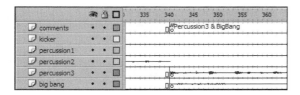

17. Preview your movie to hear your soundtrack. Now that you have more than one sound playing at the same time, one sound will start to overshadow the other. This can be corrected by messing with the relative volume of each track to make for a more pleasing composition.

18. You want to bring the BigBang sound to the fore, so open up the Edit Envelope window for the

Percussion3 sound, and lower its volume by dragging the control points down a bit. Then return to your movie and play it again. If the volume needs to be adjusted again, go back and drag the points a little lower. Repeat this until you're happy with the results:

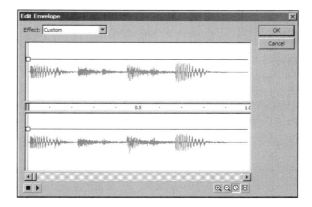

You can also easily bring the volume back up to 100 percent after the BigBang effect has played. By doing this, you can insert another Percussion3 track afterward at full volume without having a noticeable jump in the sound.

19. Look on your timeline, and note which frame the BigBang sound finishes in (it will be around frame 355):

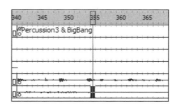

20. Go back into the Edit Envelope window for Percussion3 and change the timer to frames (click the button next to Help and you'll see the frame numbers of your movie appear in the Edit Envelope window).

307

21. Move along the sound until you come to the frame where you noted as the BigBang sound's end point (around frame 355), and put in another control point:

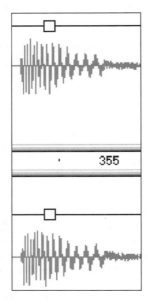

22. Move about 10 frames forward to give a gradual volume increase, and put in another control point at 100 percent in both panes, and then press OK.

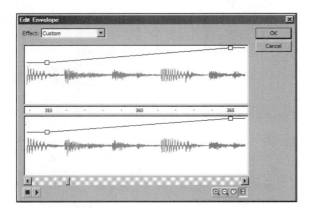

23. Play back your soundtrack. It should play smoothly all the way through, and you probably won't even notice the change in volume at the end.

To sum up, the process for adding new sounds is:

1. Create a new layer and name it after the sound.
2. Insert a keyframe in the new layer where you want the sound to start.
3. Attach the sound to the keyframe using the Properties panel.
4. Add a label to your Comments layer so you can track what's happening.
5. Add frames to the layer until you can see the end of the waveform.
6. Play the soundtrack and decide if you want to make any volume or synchronization changes.
7. Make any changes you need to, and play the sound again to make sure you're happy with it.
8. Either add another copy of the sound afterward, or start a new sound on its own layer.

24. Use the other sounds we've provided you with—or ones you've created yourself—and put them together to create your own complete soundtrack. Don't worry if it ends up quite long; that's what the soundtrack is for—to provide a backdrop while the visitor is at your site.

At the end of the soundtrack, you're going to put in a loop so that a section of it will carry on playing forever.

25. Add a label in your Comments layer at the end of your last sound and call it End Loop.

26. At (or around) the end loop frame, add sounds as you did before. Note that in our example, the sounds no longer start at the same frame—the longer your timeline, the more likely this becomes.

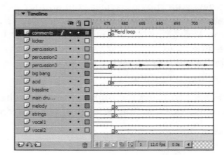

27. Using the Sound section of the Properties panel, set all the sounds in your final loop to play more than once. For sounds that you want to continuously loop, make them repeat 999 times, which should be longer than even the most avid fan of your music will remain. To do this, select the keyframe(s) below the end loop comment and set the Loop value to 999:

Because the sounds start at around the same time, they're synchronized to each other and won't fall out of time with one another. They may fall out of time with the *timeline*, but that doesn't really matter anymore because no new sounds will be started that need to be synchronized to any particular event.

28. The final thing to do is to put a Stop action in the End Loop keyframe in the Comments layer. If you want to have a number of separate soundtracks, say, for different sections of your movie, you could keep them all as different scenes in your main soundtrack movie and call them when required. By putting a Stop action in here, you're making sure that Flash won't start playing them when it gets to the end of your first soundtrack. Just select Stop from the Sync drop-down menu in the Properties panel.

That's it; your musical masterpiece is finished. Now just crank up the volume, press play, kick back, and enjoy—until you get sick of it and turn it off.

29. Save your movie.

And that's more or less all there is to the basics of putting music in Flash. Simply add or subtract sounds every 4 bars and you're on your way. The only thing we haven't talked about sound-wise is how to integrate something like this into a website. The problem with sound files is that they can be one of the largest things in your site, so it's a good idea to load them only when you are sure the user wants to listen to them. Let's see how to do that.

Assuming that you created a soundtrack called sound-track.fla using the steps just outlined, make sure that you have a file called soundtrack.swf in the same folder. (You will have this if you have tested the soundtrack at least once.)

> *Although the* soundtrack.fla *is on the download page for this chapter, it is a little on the large side (around 13Mb). To carry out the next exercise you need only a folder with* soundtrack.swf *in it, which is a much more reasonable 200k.*

Integrating the soundtrack into a website

1. Create a new FLA, and save it in the same folder as soundtrack.swf. Call this new file soundLoader.fla.

2. In soundLoader.fla, add two layers and rename the three layers you now have as (from the top) actions, text, and buttons.

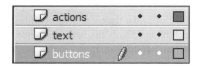

3. On the stage, create two buttons and give them instance names of sound_btn and noSound_btn.

309

4. In the text layer, next to sound_btn, add a static text field with the words "sound on" in it. Add another text field with the words "sound off" in it next to noSound_btn.

5. Add the following script on frame 1 of layer actions:

```
sound_btn.onRelease = function() {
    loadMovieNum("soundtrack.swf", 100);
};
noSound_btn.onRelease = function() {
    unloadMovieNum(100);
};
```

A Flash presentation can consist of *levels*. Flash SWF files can be arranged in a stack (much like layers), and this occurs at *runtime*. The lowest level is called _level0, and this has levels _level0, and _level1, all the way up to approximately _level16000. The advantage of using levels is that you can allow the user to decide whether they want to load them, which can save a lot of downloading.

In our example, we load the soundtrack.swf file into level 100 if the user presses the top button, and unload it again when the user presses the bottom button. Simple, easy, just the way it should be!

Well-designed sounds that can be seamlessly looped are gold dust to the Flash designer because they make the production of optimized soundtracks to go with your website just a matter of dragging and dropping sounds onto the timeline. Also, an understanding of how and how not to lay down sound in Flash will prevent you from falling into the traps that befall many Flash beginners. The use of sound in Flash for soundtracks and incidental effects will hopefully help lift your website designs above its mute contemporaries.

Next, let's have a look at how you can enhance your Flash movies using video.

Video on the Web

Video on the Web is primarily served through three players—QuickTime, RealOne Player, and Windows Media Player. The most common problem with these formats within a website is their lack of integration with the site interface. However, you now have the ability to embed video into Flash movies, eradicating the worry about issues such as integration. Now that Flash has this capability, the only real concern is whether the user has Flash Player 6 or above.

Flash uses the Sorenson Spark codec to embed video into Flash movies. Other Sorenson codecs are commonly used to create streaming content for QuickTime, among others. The Sorenson Spark codec works by encoding the video data on import and embedding the encoded video within the Flash movie. When you import a video file from an external source, Flash embeds it directly with its Library.

Let's talk about how to make video content before you worry about importing it into Flash.

Creating video

If you have a Mac with FireWire or have upgraded to Windows XP, you already have your own resources for generating video content. For several years now, Macs have come with a free version of iMovie, and more recently, Movie Maker was bundled with all copies of Windows XP, meaning that there is an increasing pool of computer owners with the resources to carry out non-linear video editing on their machines.

Non-linear video editing means that your video is on a storyboard that you can edit any part of. Traditional linear video editing dictated that you had to start at the beginning and work your way through the video. If you got to the end and wanted to go back to edit a few frames near the beginning, the likelihood was that you'd destroy anything after those frames.

Digital video (DV) cameras now regularly come with desktop editing software. This was made a lot easier by Apple and Sony's recommendation and development of the FireWire interface (also known as iLink on Sony products), along with powerful yet affordable software like Apple's Final Cut Express and Adobe Premiere. This means that creating movies with excellent picture quality at home is possible, and that is somewhat of a revolution. The revolution, which has taken Hollywood by storm, allows anyone to shoot and edit their own features without the expense of reels of film and edit time.

The uses of these technologies are not exclusive to the amateur filmmaker. Many Hollywood productions have embraced the DV format, including director Mike Figgis on the film *Time Code*. If all this talk of DV and FireWire doesn't apply to you though, don't worry—there are still many options available to you.

- **Windows users**—If you don't have a system with FireWire ports, there are many cheap capture cards available that work with analog and DV cameras. Most of these come with some basic editing software to get you going and will enable you to export in a format suitable for importing into Flash. Alternatively, you can buy a cheap FireWire expansion card and join the DV revolution!

- **Mac users**—There's a good chance that if you're reading this, you have built-in FireWire capability and a copy of iMovie. If you don't have FireWire, you'll need a capture card or FireWire expansion card to bring in video content. You can then get the latest version of iMovie free from the Apple website.

With all import options considered, you'll benefit greatly if your footage is shot on a DV camera using miniDV format tapes. The ability to shoot high quality videos is increasing as the price of DV cameras drops and higher quality cameras are released onto the market.

As a cheap investment, FireWire is also worth considering. It is fast enough to comfortably import video, and also allows the application to take control of DV cameras for reviewing rushes—removing the need to fiddle with the tiny play, rewind, and stop buttons on the camera!

Flash-friendly formats

Making video suitable for use in Flash is easy. Most (if not all) video editing applications will enable you to export your footage to a suitable format, such as MOV or AVI files. In all cases, try to export the content with little compression and at a reasonable size because Flash will take care of any scaling or compression on import. Just for the record, the following is a list of all the footage formats that Flash can import on both platforms:

- If QuickTime 4 (or higher) is installed on Macintosh or Windows:

  AVI, DV, MPG, and MOV

- If DirectX 7 (or higher) is installed on Windows:

  AVI, MPG, WMV, and ASF

There are occasions when Flash has issues with importing sound with video clips. To save yourself any problems, it's best to keep your footage saved in its original format wherever possible. That way, you can export the footage in a suitable format so that Flash can import the sound with the clip.

Before you begin, make sure you have some video clips handy, or have downloaded the video files that are available on our website.

Using video with Flash

Now that you know which formats you need, let's import a video clip into Flash.

Importing video

In this exercise you're going to import a video in the quickest way possible. The video, `redcar.mov`, is available for download from our website. This video was shot on a DV camera.

1. Open a new Flash document.
2. Use File ➤ Import ➤ Import to Stage to open the Import dialog box, and select All Video Formats from the drop-down menu.

3. Navigate to where you have saved the download files and select redcar.mov, or locate another clip from your hard disk. Select the clip you want to import and click Open.

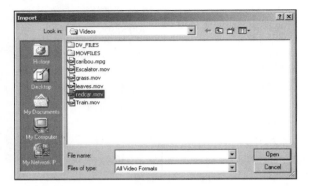

4. The Video Import Wizard appears. On the first page of the wizard, select Embed video in Macromedia Flash document, and click Next.

The other option is used when exporting a Flash movie as a QuickTime document.

5. The next page of the wizard appears, asking if you want to edit the video or import it as a whole. For now, select Import the entire video and click Next.

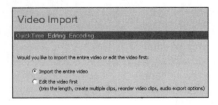

In this exercise, you'll concentrate on importing a video at the most basic level. You'll look at the editing options available to you in a moment.

6. On the final screen of the wizard, select 56 kbps modem on the Compression Profile drop-down menu. This is a preset set of values created with modem users in mind, so the compression will be pretty severe. Leave the Advanced Settings option set as the dotted line. Once you're done, click Finish to import the video:

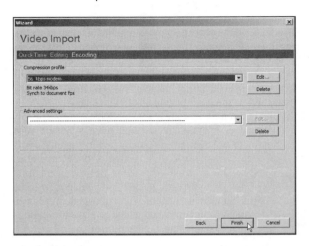

7. You should now see a progress bar which might take a while, depending on the file size of the clip you imported:

Once this is done, another dialog box appears:

Flash is offering to save you a little time by expanding the timeline to cover the whole contents of the movie—how considerate!

8. Click Yes to allow Flash to extend the timeline. You'll now see that the frames in Layer 1 are extended (up to frame 47 if you've imported the `redcar.mov`) and the movie is placed on your stage:

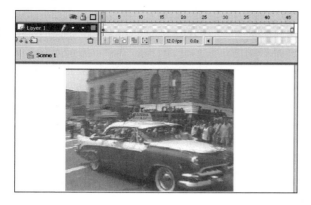

9. Drag the playhead along the top of the timeline and you'll see that the content of the movie changes according to where you are in the timeline:

10. Test the movie with Control ➤ Test Movie. It's worth comparing your compressed movie's file size to the original uncompressed MOV file. You can preview file sizes with the **Bandwidth Profiler**, which you'll have a more detailed look at in the next chapter.

11. With the test movie still open, select View ➤ Bandwidth Profiler:

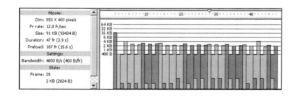

If you look at the left pane of the top part of the screen, you'll see that the file size, shown under the Movie category, is listed as 91KB. The size of the original MOV file is 1174KB, so this is an incredible saving, but the loss of quality is considerable.

Later on you'll learn a little bit about how to find a happy medium—good quality with a smaller file size—through optimizing. Now though, it's time to enter the cutting room.

Editing video clips in Flash

A great addition to Flash MX 2004 is the ability to edit and modify the appearance of imported video clips. As if the ability to import video wasn't impressive enough, the mini editing application built into Flash really takes it to another level. Even though the editing abilities here don't compare to Premiere, Final Cut, or even iMovie, their presence alone means that your workflow can be greatly enhanced, and it makes video even more accessible to all Flashers.

Let's get in the zone...

Editing a clip

In this exercise, you're going to clean up a single clip with a little editing. The clip used here was shot on a digital stills camera using the built-in movie capture at 10 frames-per-second. It was imported via USB from the cameras memory card.

1. Open a new Flash document.

2. Select Modify ➤ Document and change the frame rate to 10 fps. This will allow you to match the Flash document frame rate with that of the video.

3. Select File ➤ Import ➤ Import to Stage. Locate and select `bella_the_cat.mov` and click Open.

4. On the first wizard screen, click Embed video in Macromedia Flash document as before. Then click Next.

5. On the next screen, Editing, select Edit the video first and click Next:

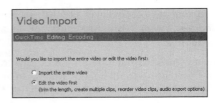

The Editing (Customize) screen (and a massive cat named Bella) appears. This is where all your video editing is done.

Clip Library   Preview pane

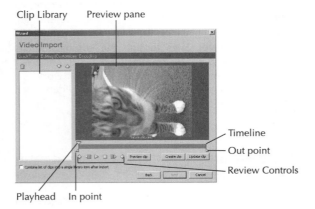

Playhead   In point

6. Press the Play button (the right-pointing arrow) to view the clip:

Play   Stop

Step back   Step forward
one frame   one frame

As you can see, the video is the wrong way up (a problem you can rectify later), and the clip consists of two shots, one filmed close-up and one shot from above:

Unfortunately, the transition from the first shot to the second is far from seamless. With a little editing though, you trick the eye into making it look one feline movement, shot with two cameras. The most logical way to do this is to match the prowling motion from the first clip to the second. In plain English, this means you have to trim a little off the end of the first shot, and some off the start of the second shot.

7. Experiment with dragging the playhead around. This allows you to review the clip in the same way as Flash's timeline playhead. When you first click the playhead, notice that it turns yellow, this shows it is selected.

8. Using the playhead, locate the frame where Bella is in full stride but not yet turning her head. For those of you without the patience required for frame-level detail work, drag the playhead so the timer shows 00:00:09.631:

For precision frame-by-frame placement, use the Step forward / back one frame buttons, or the left and right arrow keys on the keyboard. Either way, make sure that the playhead is selected first.

9. Once you have this frame location, click the Set out point to current position button:

This will move the "out" point (represented by the little triangle on the right below the timeline) to the same position as the playhead. The area shown in blue is your specified clip area. When you "make the cut" and create the clip, the area in blue will be converted into a discrete clip.

10. Before you use the scalpel, click the Preview clip button to view the current state of your clip-to-be. If you aren't happy with the selection, click the out point—it will turn blue to show it is selected—and move it to where you think it should be by dragging it, using the frame forward/back buttons or using the arrow keys.

11. Once you are satisfied with the clip, click the Create clip button. This will take the selection and make a new clip with it. The new clip is added to the pane on the left. This area is where all the created clips are stored:

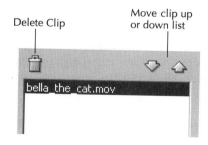

Delete Clip

Move clip up or down list

The currently selected frames have been rendered as a new clip and given the same name as the original clip. You're not going to be working with many clips, so

there is no need to rename it here. However, clips can be renamed by double-clicking them.

Now that you have the start clip, it's time to make the second clip, using a different selection.

12. Drag the out point all the way to the end of the timeline. This represents the end of your second clip:

13. Locate the frame in the second shot where Bella is in full stride. Again, we'll save you the frustration by telling you where to drag the playhead or in point—00:00:14.885:

14. View the clip using the Preview clip button. If all is good, render the selection as a clip using the Create clip button. This clip is now appended to the end of the clip list:

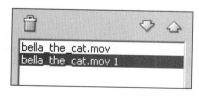

To re-edit any created clips, click them in the list. When you do this, the in and out points of the chosen clip will re-appear. Move these as necessary and then click Update clip to re-render it.

315

You now have two individual clips for import. If you were to proceed now, you'd have two video clips in the Library.

What you want, however, is for both clips to be exported together as one video sequence. Thanks to those nice guys and gals at Macromedia, you can do this with one click.

15. Click the Combine list of clips into a single library item after import **option below the clip list:**

☑ Combine list of clips into a single library item after import

To alter the order of your clips, use the up and down arrows at the top of the clip list.

16. Click the Next button. In case you haven't noticed, you're done editing! However, you always have the option of returning to the Editing screen using the Back button.

It's now time to see what options Flash has for modifying video clip appearances.

Modifying a video's appearance

In this section, you're going to see how to modify the color, contrast, and general appearance of your clip.

1. On the current screen, Encoding, select Create New Profile from the Advanced settings drop-down menu:

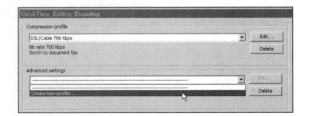

You're now directed to the Encoding (Advanced Settings**)** screen where you can specify a number of details about the video:

The various options here allow you to modify the appearance of the clip in a variety of different ways. Let's run through the available options in the Color section:

- **Brightness**—This specifies the lightness or darkness of the clip. This range runs from –100 (very dark) to +100 (very light). Default is 0.

- **Contrast**—The amount of contrast in the clip, from –100 (little contrast) to +100 (great contrast). The default is 0.

- **Hue**—This represents the amount of Red, Green, or Blue in the clip. At the default of 0, the clip retains its original appearance. This setting is useful for modifying the balance of colors in your clip for dramatic or subtle effect.

- **Saturation**—This specifies the strength of the color in the clip. A positive value here will make the colors in the clip stronger, whereas a negative value will remove color from the clip and will move toward a greyscale palette. Default is 0.

- **Gamma**—This option modifies the lightness of all the parts of the clip. When this value is increased, all the tones of the clip will become lighter. Darker parts of the clip will require a higher gamma setting to lighten. The default gamma value is 1.

2. Experiment with the Color settings to see what kinds of effects you can achieve.

3. Once you are done playing, press the Reset button to restore the original settings.

4. Alter the color settings to the following:

These settings will spruce up the color and general appearance of your clip.

5. Drag the playhead to preview the clip. One thing you will notice is that the preview window features the original unedited clip. This doesn't mean that your clip has unedited itself, it is just the way Flash does it. The beauty of the preview pane is its ability to display your settings effect on different parts of the movie.

Now that you've looked at the Color options, let's look at the other settings on this screen:

- The Dimensions settings allow you to modify the physical size or dimensions of the clip.

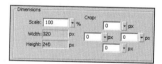

- The Scale slider allows you to scale down the clip. Reducing the size of a clip can shave many kilobytes off your file size because larger movies mean larger file sizes.

> *For an idea of file size guidelines for different bandwidths, use the following common pixel sizes: Modem users: 240 x 180; ISDN: 320 x 240; Broadband: 480 x 360.*

- The Crop settings let you mask off unwanted areas of the movie using the four directional sliders. The masked off areas are then removed from the imported video. A widescreen movie (ignoring your movie's current orientation!) might look like this:

In this example, top and bottom sliders are used to mask off the unwanted areas.

6. If you've altered the Dimensions settings, reset them to 100% scale with no cropping.

The Track Options settings relate to how the imported video clip(s) are treated. A video clip, for instance, can be embedded in its own movie clip on import from the **Import** drop-down menu. This is a highly recommendable option for many reasons:

The Current timeline selection imports the video onto the main timeline as you did in the last exercise using the `redcar.mov` video clip.

The Audio track drop-down menu provides three options: Separate, Integrated and None. The default selection, Integrated, forces the sound to be imported with the video. The Separate option will split the sound from the video and place them both as individual entities in the Library:

The soundtrack on this particular clip is little more than white noise. (There are some finger clicks and cat-attention grabbing tactics, but nothing that you really want to keep.)

7. Select Movie clip for the Import option and None for the Audio track.

8. The options for this screen should now look like this:

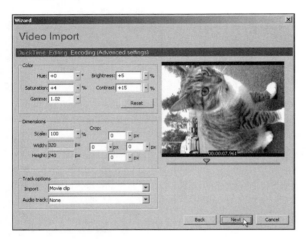

9. Click Next.

10. On the next screen, you are asked for a Name and Description of the specified settings. This is because you created a new profile on the last screen.

11. Enter the name Bella setting, and enter a little descriptive text outlining what you've done. Once you are done, click Next:

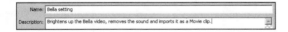

12. The Encoding page of the wizard appears. The new setting profile is selected, and the description is shown below it.

Any profiles that you create in Flash are retained here for use at any time.

Before you import the video, you have to compress it don't you?

Compressing video in Flash

So far you've edited and enhanced your video considerably. The last step in the process is compression. As you saw when you imported the redcar.mov file, there are already a number of presets in Flash for different user bandwidths, but sometimes these just aren't adequate. In this exercise, we'll see how to create a custom setting.

1. On the **Encoding** page, select Create New Profile on the Compression Profile drop-down menu. This will display the following window:

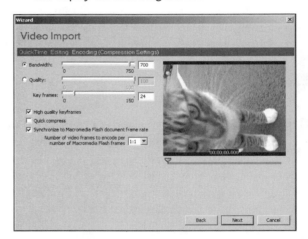

There are a number of modifiable options, so let's run through them:

- **Bandwidth**—This value specifies the approximate required download speed in kbps (kilobytes per second). The amount of compression applied to the clip is based on this setting. For instance, if the intended audience is 56 kbps-modem users, a value below 56 kbps is required. Typically, a lower value is required to take connection speeds and fluctuation into consideration. The higher this value, the less compression is applied and the greater the quality of the clip.

■ **Quality**—This is the required quality of the clip after importing and applying compression. If you set this to 0, the compression will be high but the image quality will be very bad. The more compression you apply to the clip, the smaller it will become—at a sacrifice to the image quality. It is best to try changing these settings for different clips because you might find that some clips will look better than others following the same amount of compression. The project you are working on might also be restricted by file size, so you need to take that into account too.

■ **Keyframes**—This is used to control the frequency of complete frames, or keyframes, in the clip. The number you choose determines the number of frames before the *next* keyframe. In between keyframes, only parts of the image that change are stored, meaning that the file size is smaller. If this is set to a low number, such as 1, a complete frame is stored for each frame of the clip, resulting in a larger file size, but this enables the movie to run much better on slower machines.

■ **High quality keyframes**—When using the Bandwidth compression method, having this option checked will ensure that all the keyframes are a good quality. If this is unchecked, the quality of the keyframes will be poor.

■ **Quick Compress**—Checking this will increase the encoding speed of the video, but it will subsequently reduce the quality of the image.

■ **Synchronize video to Macromedia Flash document frame rate**—This option allows you to synchronize the video clip's frame rate to that of the Flash movie. When synchronizing, if the frame rate of your Flash movie is slower than the video clip, some frames are lost on import. This will also reduce the file size as frames are spaced out to replace those that have been removed. If you have synchronized your clip, and choose later to change the frame rate of your Flash movie, you will need to re-import the clip—you'll look at how to do that in a moment. You can get some wacky effects by experimenting with this option!

■ **Number of Video Frames to Encode Per Number of Macromedia Flash frames**—This is the ratio of video frames to encode for each Flash frame. With this option, Flash will space your frames out, making the clip run less smoothly, but saving you a few kilobytes.

Flash caps the maximum frame rate at the frame rate of the movie, so if your clip has a high frame rate that you intend to keep on import, be sure to increase the frame rate of your Flash movie beforehand.

2. Set the compression settings for the clip as shown in the following graphic:

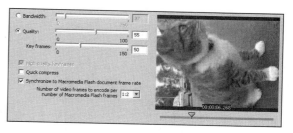

What have you changed here? You chose a moderate quality of 55, set a new keyframe every 50 frames, and specified that one video frame will appear for every two Flash frames. The last setting will reduce the fluidity of the video, but it will halve the overall file size.

3. Click Next to proceed. On the next screen, you'll be asked for a name and description of the new profile. Set these and click Next. The Encoding page will now look like this:

Video Import

QuickTime Editing Encoding

Compression profile

Lo-quality

Quality 55, Frame Ratio 1:2, Keyframe interval 50

Edit...
Delete

Advanced settings

Bella setting

Brightens up the Bella video, removes the sound and imports it as a Movie clip.

Edit...
Delete

4. Click Finish to import the video. As before, you'll now see the import progress bar, and after some processing, you'll see the following dialog box:

5. Click Yes to extend the video to show the whole timeline. You'll now see the video clip on the stage, with only one keyframe in the timeline:

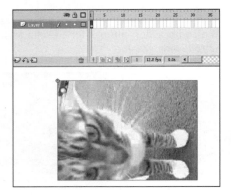

This is because the video has been embedded within a movie clip. If you look in the Library you can see both the imported video and the movie clip:

6. Double-click the movie clip icon in the Library to edit it. Now if you scan the timeline with the playhead, you can see where the video is. It is spanning the timeline:

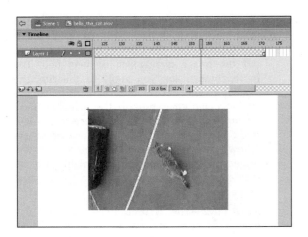

7. Return to the main timeline and select the movie clip instance on the stage.

8. Open the Transform panel (*CTRL+T*) and enter 90 in the Rotate text field. This will straighten the video up.

9. Select Control ➤ Test Movie to view the video. Select View ➤ Bandwidth Profiler to see how big the SWF is:

The size is 420Kb, compared to the original of 3470Kb. This is a significant saving due to the compression settings. Even though you might be able to squeeze more kbs out of this movie, the quality would be sacrificed considerably.

As we mentioned previously, different videos will all compress differently in Flash and it's best to experiment with each one individually to establish compression settings that best suit the clip you are working with.

Video with lots of motion does not compress well in Flash because there is little to reproduce and carry forward from the previous frame. Videos that have a similar background to reproduce on each frame will compress well, such as a newsreader, for example—the only changing parts of the image will be the newsreader's motion, while all the things around them will remain static (unless they're doing an outside broadcast at a speedway competition).

10. Save the Flash document as `cat_video.fla`, and leave it open.

OK—that's enough about compression. Let's see what you can do with the video clips and have a bit of fun.

Treating video clips like any other Flash symbol

If you thought being able to import video into Flash was enough—you don't know the half of it. The real power of using video in Flash is that when it is embedded in a symbol, it can be used like any other symbol instance. Let's quickly see what you can do with it to make your videos a little more fun.

1. Make sure that the Flash document from the last exercise, `cat_video.fla` is open.

2. Select the video movie clip on stage and duplicate it using CTRL+D.

3. Select one of the movie clips and flip it using Modify ➤ Transform ➤ Flip Horizontal.

4. Place both movie clips alongside each other on the stage, ensuring that Snap Align is on (View ➤ Snapping ➤ Snap Align), so you can position them next to each other at the same vertical level:

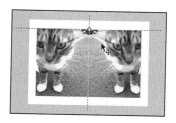

5. Test the movie using Control ➤ Test Movie. Eek…It's twins!

As you can see here, you have a very simple mirrored effect created with minimum effort. You can create some truly remarkable effects using a little flipping and some masking. Now for a little coloring.

6. Select the movie clip on the right and open the Properties panel (Window ➤ Properties).

7. From the Color drop-down menu in the Properties panel, select Tint.

8. Choose Advanced from the Color drop-down menu in the Properties panel.

9. Click the Settings button and set the colors as shown in the following screenshot to invert the colors of the movie clip:

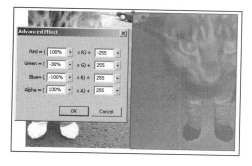

10. Test the movie and witness good cat vs. evil cat.

You've only just scratched the surface when it comes to using video in Flash. As with other aspects of Flash, video comes alive when you start using ActionScript to manipulate it. Combined with the effects you can achieve by simply adjusting color settings, using the Free Transform tool, or adding masks, you can easily achieve great-looking results.

321

The best thing you can do now is experiment, but don't forget about the rest of the book—there's lots more for you to learn that can help enhance what you've already discovered so far!

Case Study

In this section, you're going to create a nice and simple about page using a little video to spruce it up.

1. Open your case study movie.

2. Double-click the Content movie clip instance on the stage to enter Edit in Place mode for it:

3. Move the playhead along to frame 140 in the timeline:

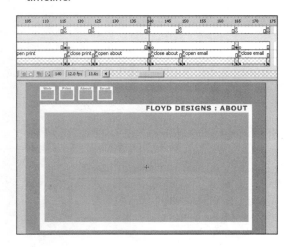

This is the location of the about page.

4. Select the keyframe on the pages layer. This is where you will add your about content.

5. Use the Text tool to type the following text in 15pt Arial dark blue (#003366):

   Floyd Designs is a multimedia company based in Floydsville.

   We create websites, CD-Roms, kiosks, and web applications using Macromedia Flash.

To join your list of satisifed clients, get in touch with us via the email page.

6. Center the text field using the Align panel.

7. With the text field still selected, press *F8* to convert it into a movie clip symbol. Call it about content and give it a center registration point.

8. Double-click the about content instance on the stage to edit it in place:

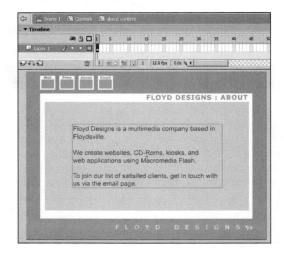

9. Rename the existing layer text, and move the text field near to the left edge. Hold down the *SHIFT* key to ensure that its vertical position does not change.

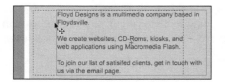

You're doing this to create space on the right edge for your videos. *Videos*? Well, yes and no. You're going to use one video three times....

Importing and placing the videos

Because of the usual traumas of videos bumping up file size drastically, you're going to use a nice small compressed video a few times to create a nice visual effect.

1. Within the about content movie clip's timeline, insert a new layer called video 1.

2. Select the keyframe on the new layer and choose File ➤ Import ➤ Import to Stage.

3. In the file dialog box that opens, locate the red-car.mov file from earlier in the chapter. Then click OK. Now you'll select the import options as usual.

4. On the Quicktime page, select Embed video in Macromedia Flash document. Then click Next.

5. On the Editing screen, select Import the entire video and click Next.

6. When the Encoding page appears, select the 56 kbps preset on the Compression profile drop-down menu:

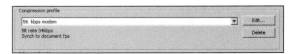

7. In the Advanced Settings, select Create new Profile.

8. On the new profile screen, set the details as seen here:

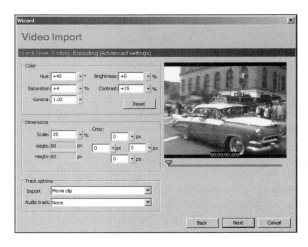

The most noteworthy changes here are the Hue (to +45) and the Scale (to 25%). The first change will give you an orangey car to fit in with your orange about page.

9. After you have selected the appropriate settings, click Next.

10. On the next screen, give the new profile a quick name and description, followed by Next:

11. In the Encoding screen, click Finish.

12. After you see the import progress bar, click Yes:

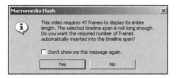

You'll now see a mini-copy of the video that you saw earlier, with an orangey twang to match the page it is on.

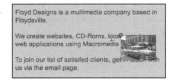

13. Use the Selection tool to move the video movie clip to the top right of the orange rectangle.

14. Select the video movie clip and copy it (CTRL + C).

15. Insert a new layer called video 2, and insert a blank keyframe (by clicking F7) on frame 5 of it.

16. Select the keyframe, and press CTRL + V to paste a copy of the video movie clip:

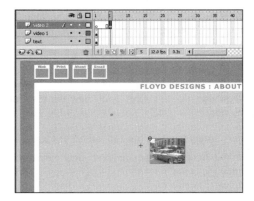

17. Insert another new layer called video 3, and place a keyframe on frame 10.

18. Select the new keyframe and paste a copy of the video.

19. Extend all the frames on each of the layers to frame 15 with *F5*:

20. Arrange the video movie clips in line along the right side of the orange rectangle, with the video 1 layer instance at the top, the video 2 instance in the middle, and so on. Use the Align panel to make sure they are in line, and there is even spacing between them:

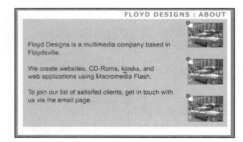

21. Test the movie with Control ➤ Test Movie. The videos never really get a chance to play right through, do they? As soon as the car is in full flow, it skips back to square 1.

What is actually happening here is what happens to all movie clip timelines—they loop. The playhead in this instance is running from frame 1 to 15 and back to the start over and over again.

The solution to get around this is to stop the playhead on the last frame to prevent the looping. This will then loop the movies over and over, without removing them. You can do this with your new bestest friend, ActionScript.

22. Insert a new layer at the top called actions.

23. On the actions layer, insert a new keyframe on frame 15.

24. Select the keyframe, and open the Actions panel (*F9*).

25. Type stop (); in the Actions panel:

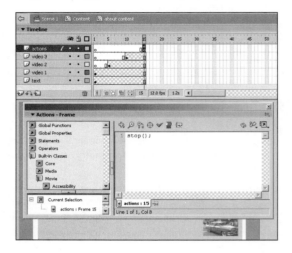

26. Test the movie again and click the about page. This time, your videos are smooth, running at a 5 frame offset. Simple, but effective:

27. Save your case study movie.

Summary

If used well, sound and video can add an extra dimension to your Flash movies and websites. You already knew that you could attach sounds to buttons, and in this chapter you also learned how to incorporate multiple sound elements onto the Flash timeline.

You saw that:

- You can import generic or purpose-built sounds and videos into your Flash movie.

- You can process and optimize the **properties** for a sound or video once you've imported it into the Flash Library.

- You can attach sounds to keyframes in the main timeline (or inside a movie clip's timeline) using the Properties panel, which gives you access to an extensive range of panning, volume, syncing, and looping effects.

- You can create a complete, independent, soundtrack movie that will play alongside your visual movie—you'll see how to integrate these two components in the Publishing chapter.

- You can edit and clean-up the appearance of video clips imported into Flash.

- You can import video clips as symbols into your Flash Library.

- You can modify video clips instances just like any other symbol instance.

- You can affect the visual appearance of your video clips through your old friend, the Property inspector.

- You can import video clips into your Flash Library and how to manage them on the timeline.

- You can re-import videos to optimize their compression settings in the **Import Video Settings** window.

- You can affect the visual appearance of your video clips through your old friend, the Properties panel.

We have briefly discussed optimizing movie settings in this chapter—in the next chapter we'll examine this aspect of creating Flash movies in a little more detail.

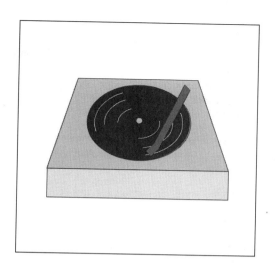

Chapter 13

OPTIMIZING

What we'll cover in this chapter:

- The nature of the Internet, and how this affects your Flash movie
- How to attract your target audience
- How Flash can transmit content across the Internet effectively using **streaming**
- How Flash's tools for optimizing your movies download and display on the Internet
- Techniques for designing optimized Flash movies:
    - Loading content on demand
    - Organizing the space on the stage efficiently

Picture the scene: you finish your Flash website and it looks great. Excitedly, you put it up on the server that's hosting your site, replacing that boring old HTML site you've had for years. You're sure to get more visitors as word spreads about the multimedia extravaganza your site has become.

Two days later, you check the number of visitors, anticipating a massive surge. But wait...surely not! The number of visitors has actually gone *down*.

There's a very good reason for this, and one that the first-time Flash designer needs to take careful note of. The site may look great when it's running from your hard drive, but once it's up on the Internet, the rules are very different. All those multimedia bells and whistles have made for a bigger and fatter site—and one with a longer download time. The average web surfer has a very short attention span, and while she's waiting for your site to appear, the rest of the Internet is trying to entice her away from your sluggish download and onto *their* web pages.

Once you've discovered all the exciting features that Flash MX 2004 has to offer, the next lesson is always the hard reality of download time. It's something that you must **always** bear in mind when designing Flash sites that'll be accessed over the net.

Flash and the Internet

Now that we've broken your dream a little, we'll use the rest of this chapter to do what the US Army does: build you back up and give you some insights into the practicalities and disciplines you're going to need to turn your Flash dreams into reality.

Before you look at how your Flash files behave on the Internet, let's recap what the Internet and World Wide Web are, and revisit some other terms you'll have heard but perhaps never really understood.

The Internet

The Internet's existence was instigated by the US Department of Defense, who needed a fault-tolerant system that provided basic communications services between computers: file transfer, e-mail, remote logon, and remote control of computers—all of which had to work, irrespective of different computer types or operating systems. The solution was designed to be able to take the hits a communications system would get in battlefield use. To achieve this, the system had to be able to carry on even if parts of it were knocked out, and it had to be accessible by a number of different computers (from hand held laptops to big dirty mainframes, and everything in between).

The technology that achieves this, and which makes the Internet work the way it does, is a **transmission protocol**, something that goes by the catchy title of **TCP/IP**. This transmission protocol is the universal "vehicle" that everyone uses on their networks to move data between remote computers. As the slash in TCP/IP suggests, this vehicle comes in two parts.

IP (Internet Protocol) is the tractor that shunts data around across the network, based on a destination address called the *IP number*. The IP number is a unique numeric code used to identify any computer on the Internet. It's a four-byte value expressed by converting each byte into a decimal number from 0 to 255, and then separating each byte with a period, so an example IP could be: 245.239.99.34, or 22.254.0.128. The Internet Protocol is a technology that takes the thing that you want to send—a file, an e-mail, whatever—and encodes it as a series of little data packets that can be sent down the wires that connect up the different IP numbers.

The data that's passed between different IP numbers is directed across the Internet by special communications computers called **routers**. Routers are like switching stations that direct data to its target destination. Each router passes the data that it receives on to the next closest *working* router to the target address. The routers are arranged to be intelligent enough to pick the fastest available route for the data to take. Because the network is in a constant state of flux, your data might be directed via an infinite number of possible routes—but the router will do its best to pick the best route for you.

TCP (Transmission Control Protocol) is the technology that *verifies* that the data got to its destination. IP doesn't care if the packets of data are sent out of order, or even not sent at all. It's up to its big brother TCP to make sure that all the data eventually gets to where its sender intended.

In terms of *hardware*, the Internet looks like a lot of nodes (or computers) all connected together. Although it may seem rather anarchic and organic, there is actually a broad structure.

Nodes tend to be grouped together in clusters, and these have a large, high-bandwidth transmission point called a **hub** at their centers. Such hubs are sometimes connected together by very large bandwidth links called **backbones**, which connect large population areas or continents.

The World Wide Web

The Internet, therefore, is a network of physical networks across which you can send, receive, and view text files using the transport methods of TCP/IP. The World Wide Web is a more recent development that came about because there was a need to access multimedia files containing music, pictures, and video across the network of machines.

The Web consists of two parts: **browsers**—software that allows the computers that are part of the Internet to read and view multimedia files; and **servers**—computers that can host and disseminate these documents.

It's the universally agreed upon components of the Web, coupled with the expandability and versatility of the underlying TCP/IP and communications hardware that have made the Internet such a success. One of the key web components is **Uniform Resource Locators**, or URLs. You use these in the same way you use file names, but a URL designates a file that can exist on any computer within a network, such as the Internet. Another component is **HyperText Markup Language**—or HTML for short—which is a system-independent way of telling a browser how to render information.

Now when a client asks you what the Internet is, you can tell them. But one of the key things you need to know about before you put your work out on the net is **bandwidth**.

Bandwidth

Bandwidth denotes how much data will travel along a given path in a given time, or how much information a modem can download and how quickly.

Bandwidth is measured in bits or bytes per second—a bit being the smallest individual morsel of computerized data: a 0 or a 1. The higher the bandwidth, the faster things get to and from your computer. Different types of content demand different amounts of bandwidth to be used effectively—for example, it takes more bandwidth to download an animation in one second than it does to download a static text page in the same time. Because the size of the "pipe" you send the data down to a user's computer is fixed by the capacity of his or her modem, you need to think about the size of your movie and how long it's going to take to get down the pipe and onto the user's screen. Photographs, sound files, and video clips all add to the bandwidth required to quickly download a file.

Data sent over the Internet will usually get to its destination, but neither the sender nor the receiver knows *when* this will occur or the *route* that will be taken. Over time, the average transmission rate becomes fairly constant, but because of the nature of TCP/IP and the way that it parcels data into little packets as they're transmitted, it's unwise to assume a given transmission rate over a short period. Again, there are implications here for the way you design your movies—as you'll see when we discuss *streaming* later.

A full Internet connection is only as fast as the *slowest* node, meaning that slow sections will tend to drag down the average transmission time across the whole network—the difference between a 33.6K modem and a 56K modem in download times was not that great until the transmission lines across the Internet began to be upgraded. Although this "lowest common denominator" factor is not so much of a problem now, it can still rear its ugly head during peak times when it's the Internet itself that's the slowest component in the system. Here's an example.

A large number of people are trying to access the same server or web page. The closer a router is to the target server, the number of available alternative routes drops but the amount of data being shuttled goes *up*, creating a bottleneck of queuing information. So what can the poor routers do? They give up and throw your data away! You, and everyone else, try again, and the repeat attempts generate even more traffic, grinding the whole thing to a standstill.

These problems show up sometimes as numerous repeat attempts and connection losses when trying to connect to popular pages or a sudden drop in bandwidth, most likely due to the loss of a route, causing traffic to be suddenly shoveled on your local routers!

This is far less of a problem than it was a few years ago for most sites—the overcapacity created by the dotcom era has left many out of pocket, but also created a lot of web infrastructure. As any designer will tell you, business is now picking up as the Web matures, but the client has changed—from trendy young companies with strange business models to existing large companies that are finally taking the Web seriously because it is now making them money—so expect this overcapacity to quickly disappear.

The important thing to remember is that the time it will take your potential viewer to download your Flash site file depends on what's in your file and (within the constraints of the Internet we've just discussed) how quickly their computer can read it. This means that when you make a Flash site you not only have to consider *what* you put in your Flash movie file, but *who* you want to be able to see it. Who is your audience, and what assumptions do you make about their computer equipment?

The end user—your audience

If you're coding your site on a super fast G5 Mac, what happens if the user has a slow PC? There have been all sorts of discussions about this on the Flash newsgroups for some years, leading to accusations of elitism and/or Flash snobbery on the one hand, to the "take no chances" corporate Flash designers on the other.

The following are some general rules to keep in mind before putting your site on the Web:

- No user will wait more than fifteen seconds for your site to download if nothing *interesting* is happening at the same time (now read that again) unless you're a cool enough Flash designer to warrant the wait. Times have changed, and to be blunt, pointless-but-pretty just doesn't cut the mustard anymore, so even the real guru designers have to live with the 15 seconds rule these days.

- A cutting-edge, designer Flash website should be viewable using a two-year-old computer's standard hardware configuration.

- A commercial Flash site should be viewable on a standard three-year-old computer.

- The speed of connection you can assume is largely dependent on two things:

  - Whether your target is a business or design audience (assume they have a connection that was "cutting-edge" 18 months ago) or a domestic user (assume the worst!).

  - The relative affluence of your target audience. Although there are always accusations of web elitism, this is a rule that actually works—people who want to buy an expensive car will expect a high-end site to sell it to them.

Now that you've absorbed all this techno-jargon, you'll be aware just how easy it is to lose your movie file in the digital jungle that is the Internet. To ensure your file survives, it's essential to understand the concept of **streaming**, and to consider how to use it when designing Flash movies for the Internet.

Streaming

As we said, the bits of your Flash file that will make your site stand out from the crowd—your movies, sound effects, and so on—are the bits that will take a long time to download. If you have them all at frame 1 of the timeline, your user's modem will be unable to download your movie right away and the user will have to sit and look at nothing until the download is complete. You visitors will most likely get bored and take their business elsewhere.

However, when **streaming** is used, your Flash presentation starts playing before all of it has loaded into the user's browser. By starting the Flash page as soon as there is enough information to show *something* rather than waiting until the whole thing has loaded, the user waits much less time before viewing part of the website. This means that you can hold the user's attention while the cast of your all-singing, all-dancing, interactive masterpiece is downloaded.

> Well thought-out Flash sites often have a specific scene at the beginning that loads up immediately, allowing the viewer to watch it as the rest of the movie is downloaded. This type of scene is called a **preloader**. We'll look at preloaders more thoroughly later in the chapter.

Streaming, as you saw when using sound in your movies, is a very good thing. Although it doesn't make things load faster down the user's pipe, it intelligently organizes what's needed in the movie and when, so that everything is loaded in the best order. Used efficiently, streaming can ensure that everything in your movie is downloaded *before* it's needed on the stage, meaning that the movie will play smoothly without any pauses to wait for an image or a movie clip to appear.

When a user requests a Flash web page across the Internet, Flash has to send the user two things:

- The Flash movie's timeline, including attached ActionScripts and "non-instanced" components (things that aren't stored as symbols) such as text and drawn shapes that haven't been converted into symbols
- The Flash Library, including the sounds, symbols, and bitmaps used in the movie

When Flash sends this data across the net, it will send the movie timeline *in frame order*. If the movie is split into separate scenes, it will send the scenes in the order they appear in the Scene panel. Flash will also arrange the transmission of Library symbols so that they're sent in the sequence in which they appear in the timeline.

You can think of your web-bound movie as having two markers traveling along its timeline. The first one is the *streamer*, which tracks how much of the movie has been downloaded and is ready to play. The second is the *player*—which points to the current frame being played:

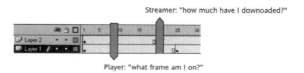

For streaming to work, the *streamer* always has to be in front of the *player*. If the *player* catches the *streamer* the movie will pause because the next frame of animation has not yet been loaded. To avoid the player constantly playing tag with the streamer and causing a pause every time it catches up, it's a good idea to give the streamer a head start. We call this head start a **streaming buffer**. A streaming buffer operates by starting off the streaming process before the playback starts, giving Flash a chance to download some of the movie onto the user's computer in advance of the playback starting.

To illustrate this, imagine a movie that has a movie clip symbol called **A** in frames 10 and 30, a graphic symbol **B** at frame 20, and a drawing on frame 40 that isn't a symbol, like this:

Flash would follow this sequence during streaming:

- Start the **streamer**, sending the timeline data beginning with frame 1. As it sends each frame, Flash also sends all timeline ActionScripts. If the streamer reaches frame 10 before the player, movie clip A will start to load. If, during this process, the player catches up to the streamer, the movie will pause as it waits for the movie clip to load.

- Once the movie clip A has loaded, the streamer will race toward frame 20, leaving the player plodding along the timeline, playing back the content that's been downloaded so far. Hopefully, the graphic symbol **B** will have loaded by the time the player reaches frame 20.

- At frame 30, the streamer sees a new instance of the movie clip symbol **A**, which it's used before. It doesn't have to load it again because the information is already in the Library. It just adds the instance name (and any other instance-specific information on the timeline) to the symbol template in the Library and re-creates the instance without having to download it again.

- At frame 40, the streaming marker sees a drawing on the stage that has not been converted to a symbol. The information for this drawing is not in the Library—instead, it's attached to the frame in which it was drawn. The streamer will load the information as part of the frame data, but because the data is not in the Library, the drawing cannot be reused in the same way as in frame 30, and it will have to be loaded again if it is encountered in another keyframe.

The idea of streamers and players may be a little hard to visualize, but Flash has something that lets you see these two markers in action and work out how Internet download times will affect your Flash presentation's delivery to the user's browser. That's what we're going to look at next—the **Bandwidth Profiler**.

The Bandwidth Profiler

The Bandwidth Profiler lets you preview how your movie will behave as it downloads in the real (bandwidth-limited) world.

The first thing to be aware of is that Flash's Bandwidth Profiler assumes *constant* transfer rates. Having read the introduction to what the Internet is, you'll realize that the Bandwidth Profiler graph is a close approximation at best, and a downright fiction at peak traffic times. However, you can use the Profiler to get a good idea of which stages of your movie are going to be problematic for a user to download, even if you can't get *exact* precision for all times.

Using the Bandwidth Profiler

1. Create a new Flash document and make it 20 frames long by clicking the timeline at frame 20, and pressing *F5*:

2. In frame 1, type the following into a static text box: This is a test to see how I can optimize this movie using the Bandwidth Profiler in the center of the stage in 24 point Times New Roman:

> This is a test to see how I can optimize this movie using the Bandwidth Profiler

3. Convert the text into a graphic symbol with *F8* or by choosing the Insert ➤ Convert to Symbol menu option. Call the symbol text1.

4. At frame 1, under the text you've already placed on the stage, add a new static text box containing this text: Flash will be made to load two pieces of text in different fonts, and we'll use the Bandwidth Profiler to optimize the movie. Use 16 point Arial for this text.

5. Make the text a graphic symbol as before, and call it text2. Your stage will look something like this:

> This is a test to see how I can optimize this movie using the Bandwidth Profiler
>
> Flash will be made to load two pieces of text in different fonts, and we'll use the Bandwidth Profiler to optimize the movie

6. Save your FLA as bandwidthTest.fla, and then test your movie by pressing *CTRL+ENTER*.

7. While the movie's playing, go to the View ➤ Bandwidth Profiler menu option or press *CTRL+B*. A graph will appear:

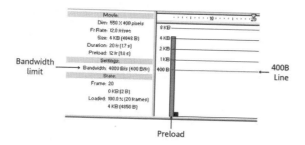

At the far left of the graph, there's lots of useful looking information under the headings Movie, Settings, and State. To the right is a little bar graph that tells you how much data is downloaded during each frame. Under Settings, you'll see something like Bandwidth: 4800B/s (400 B/fr). This tells you the amount of information, in bytes, that can be read per second and per frame. The red line at the 400B point on the graph also shows this. This is the **Bandwidth Limit** and it represents the maximum throughput a particular modem can handle.

Your Bandwidth and Bandwidth Limit figures may differ from those shown in the screenshot: there are five different values it can have, as you'll see now.

8. Look in the View ➤ Download Settings sub-menu:

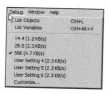

You'll see the numbers **14.4**, **28.8** and **56K** listed on this menu, and one of them will be checked. Do those numbers and acronyms sound familiar? They're modem speeds, and these options represent the download rates that the Bandwidth Profiler can simulate.

9. Our Bandwidth Profiler is currently simulating download using a 56K modem—set yours to the same.

If you look under the Movie heading in the left of the Profiler window, you can see Size 5KB and Preload: 12fr (1.0s), or figures that are close to this, depending on the exact fonts your machine has installed. This tells you that the movie is a 5KB download in total. Because everything appears in frame 1 of your movie, Flash has to preload everything *before* frame 1 can be played. This preload time, the time the user will wait to see the movie, is 1 second.

Try changing to simulate a 28.8 modem, and if you really want to see how we used to live, try out the 14.4 modem as well. As you can see from the Size and Preload figures at these different settings, some people are going to have to wait longer than others to see this movie. Now you have a feel for how different modems have different download times, let's see what we can do about it.

If you look toward the top of the Profiler, you can see a little marker that whizzes back and forth while the movie is running. This is the player we described earlier. What a help it would be to see the streamer as well. You can…

10. Select View ➤ Simulate Download. Did you catch that? Let's see it again in slo-mo.

11. Choose the 14.4 modem setting from the View ➤ Download settings sub-menu and select the View ➤ Simulate Download menu option again.

Nothing happens for a second or so except some frantic activity going on under the State heading at the bottom left of the Profiler (you may have to increase the height of the Profiler window by dragging the lower edge of it to see the new stuff). Then you'll suddenly see a green band along the top of the Profiler. The data in the frames covered by the green band is what has already been loaded.

The leading edge of this band is the streamer and the distance the green band is ahead of the player is your streaming buffer.

In this movie, you have no streaming buffer at all. The player catches the streamer at frame 1 as it waits for your symbols to load. You need to go back and redesign your movie to allow streaming to take place so you can spare your user that second of waiting. As we're sure you'll appreciate, this wait can be a lot longer for more complex movies—but the method needed to avoid it is the same one we're about to use.

12. Close the Test Movie window (by hitting the lower of the two X icons to the top right of the bandwidth Profiler) and go back to the main stage.

13. Delete all the text from frame 1 and add two new blank keyframes at frames 5 and 15:

14. With the keyframe at frame 5 selected, drag an instance of the text1 graphic symbol onto the center of the stage. At frame 15, do the same with text2.

15. Test the movie—making sure the Bandwidth Profiler is still running (*CTRL+B*)—and use the View ➤ Download Settings sub-menu to set the modem speed to 14.4.

16. To see the streamer again, go to View ➤ Simulate Download.

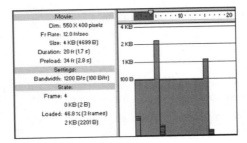

You will see something like this graph to start. The green bar, or streamer, will race ahead to frame 4 almost immediately—even on the 14.4 modem—because these are blank frames. These blank frames are your streaming buffer—the time you have to start streaming before the player starts trying to play back the movie in the user's browser. The player will move along at its usual "one frame every twelfth of a second" pace until it catches the streamer at frame 4, where the streamer has been delayed by the first peak in the data graph.

Frame 4 is the *end* of the streaming buffer. The player will now have to wait while the extra data that's needed for frame 5 (the text1 symbol) is loaded before it can play that frame.

When you test the movie with Simulate Download turned off, the extended pause at frame 4 is not shown. By using Simulate Download, we're simulating what the movie would look like during transfer and playback across the Internet.

However, you can see that there will be a pause before frame 5 just by using the graph. The first download spike on the graph tells you that the modem can't preload all the data needed before the frame is due to be played:

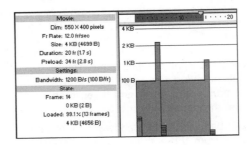

This is perhaps not surprising for a 14.4 modem because the bandwidth limit allows only 100 bytes per frame to be downloaded.

The spike on the graph also tells you how much you've exceeded the bandwidth limit by, enabling you to judge how long the pause in playback will be.

Notice that the profile scale is not linear. This scale, from the 1KB line upward is an exponential function of 2. Don't worry if you never paid attention in math when you did exponential functions, all it means is that every value on the scale is double the value below it. Flash will create an appropriate scale for whatever amounts of data it needs to display.

You can see that the data contained in frame 5 is over 2KB more than can be downloaded in one frame. The modem we're currently simulating takes a second to download 1200 bytes, so the movie will pause for almost two seconds. To give the modem enough time to download the data for frame 5 we'd need to add over 20 blank frames to the start of your movie—keeping the viewer waiting for playback to start and giving them a very dull first impression of your site.

Even then, your movie will pause once more at the second spike on the graph when text2 is being loaded, and fixing this will require further lengthening of your already protracted movie.

On a 14.4 modem it's still very difficult to avoid pauses due to the very low bandwidth limit. In this case, you may have to accept that even streaming can't solve the problem. You can easily switch to something more current by selecting the 56K modem from the View ➤ Download settings sub-menu.

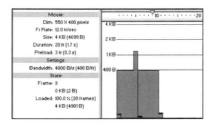

As you can see above, the use of a 56K modem makes the second spike disappear, but you're still stuck with the first one at frame 5 when the data required for text1 again takes you over your bandwidth limit.

17. Go back to the movie and add three blank frames (*F5*) before the first keyframe:

18. If you test the movie now, you'll get a bandwidth profile like this:

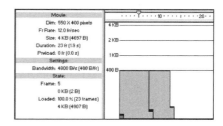

Notice that the bars *never* go above the bandwidth limit. This means that when downloaded by a 56K modem, the movie will run smoothly with no pauses.

> *How did we know that we had to add three frames? The spike was about 1k over the 400B line, and three frames at 400B/s would remove it.*

The streamer will always be ahead of the player because all the data needed for each frame is loaded before it needs to be played—you gave your movie a sufficient streaming buffer.

In short, the movie will look and behave the same whether it is viewed from your hard drive or over the Internet with a 56K modem.

The movie you just created is fairly simplistic, but the theory you applied is the same for much bigger sites. Here's a bandwidth profile for a real commercial site:

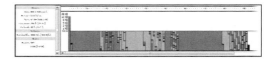

There's an initial preload at frame 1, but after that, the site is always inside the bandwidth requirements of a 56K modem. Why did its designer choose a 56K modem? This particular site is for a nightclub. Its designer considered two of the guidelines mentioned earlier: the target audience, in this case 18 to 26 year olds; and the relative

335

affluence of this audience. Thinking about these factors allowed the designer to reason that the people coming to view the site would have at *least* a 56K modem at the time the site was going out. The designer reasoned correctly—the hit rate for the nightclub site jumped when this Flash site was used!

> If you see a peak on the Bandwidth Profiler for one of your movies and want to know which frame is causing it, click the peak and the movie will go directly to the offending movie frame. Remember though, the bar graph is arranged in the order that streaming will take place, and the bar you click will rarely represent the frame that the numbering along the top of the graph (which is the current frame being played) suggests it should. You can see which frame you clicked by looking under State to the bottom left of the screen.

As you can see, the Bandwidth Profiler is a vital tool. With it, you can tailor your movie to meet the bandwidth constraints of your target user. With the Simulate Download option activated, you can actually see how bandwidth will affect your movie in real time, and alter things accordingly.

There are some sites that don't use streaming at all. Instead, they load the whole movie in one go. For example, Flash animations that lip-sync to sound don't use streaming because even a slight slowing down of playback would greatly affect the movie. However, the designers judge that their viewers will be prepared to wait for this spectacle.

A lot of unstreamed sites are Flash showcase sites where Flash designers show off to other Flash designers or potential clients. As fledgling Flash users, you're unlikely to be aiming your sites at these people and consequently your audience is unlikely to have the same level of technical equipment to view sites as these people do.

For most web audiences, long waits for websites are a real turnoff. Although the Internet is getting faster all the time, low bandwidths are still with you for a sizeable section of the web audience, so you must learn to overcome them. The Bandwidth Profiler is a powerful weapon to have in your armory in this respect.

> The issue of low bandwidth may become more rather than less important as time goes by. Although most tech-savvy folks have high speed connections for their desktop machine, they may well have also bought into mobile Internet access for their cell phone or palm top…and guess what, we're back to 56k!

You may not be aware of it, but content created for the Flash Player 6 and 7 is compressed by default when published. Vector objects, text, and ActionScript are all compressed. But be aware—if you are authoring for the Flash Player 5, you'll need to switch this compression off. You can do this by going to File ➤ Publish Settings and un-checking the Compress Movie option on the Flash tab.

> The Bandwidth Profiler takes into account any file compression during SWF compilation—the SWF will be compressed if there is a check against Compress Movie in the Publish Settings Window. Previous versions of Flash did not take compression into account.
>
> The only reason you might want to turn compression off when publishing for the Flash 7 player is when your SWF content is already compressed by other means. This would occur if you have a lot of video in your SWF. Video is already compressed via the video compression routine, so compressing the SWF again gives no real advantage. The disadvantage is that every compression requires a decompression when the user views your content, so you may want to decline the unneeded compression of the SWF.

Optimizing and fine-tuning Flash movies

There are a number of things you can do to make your movies more lean and compact for Internet download. In this section, we'll summarize all the Flash methods that allow you to achieve responsive sites before looking at how to optimize space for content on the stage. First, we'll look at what to consider when planning your site.

Structure

Perhaps the most important aspect to get right for a responsive site is a well-defined structure and download flow. You need to sit down and think about which major keyframes the user will see, and in what order, before you jump into Flash and start creating the movie. For example, an MP3 site would probably consist of the following keyframes (each of which would be the start of a new area of the site).

- Preloader
- Intro
- Main
- About
- Downloads
- Links

When visiting the site, the viewer would most likely:

- See the *preloader*, and be taken to the *intro* keyframe, where the timeline will stop.
- From there, the user would click a button and be sent to the *main* keyframe.
- Because he or she has come here looking for MP3 files, the user would go straight to *downloads*.
- Once he or she has set off a music file download, the viewer will probably browse the *about* section to find out more about the music.
- The viewer will most likely exit from *about* or via your *links* section.

This analysis of the way your site will be used dictates that you want *preloader*, *intro*, and *main* content to be loaded in that order, and this is therefore the order content related to them should be arranged on the timeline. By second-guessing what your audience will do and streaming content in the appropriate order, you'll make your site more responsive for most visitors. In this case, your preference would be to make *downloads* the next block of content on the timeline, followed by *about*, and then by *links*. If you arrange your content in a random order, you have no way of ensuring that it will be loaded in any useful order, and will therefore have to preload the *whole* site before any of it can be viewed. Although even many professional sites do this, it should be considered bad practice.

In a slightly more subtle vein, the average user in this example will spend little time in the *main* section because it is just a route to the *downloads* section. You can design that into the site by making the *main* content easy for the user's modem to download, thus buying time for the *downloads* section to be loaded more quickly as well. Structuring your Flash site in this strategic way is the hallmark of a good web designer. It will come with practice, and all designers will always be somewhere on that particular learning curve, struggling with the same problem as you face as a beginner!

Use the right components in your movie

Choosing the correct basic pieces to build up your site with is another area where forethought is required.

It's wise to use symbols wherever possible because symbols possess two very desirable properties that make them bandwidth friendly. These are the following:

- The attributes of a symbol (size, color, etc.) can be changed for an individual instance via the Properties panel.
- Flash downloads each symbol only once, and bases all instances of the symbol on the single downloaded version in the Library.

This means that instead of building a blue button and a red button separately, you can have a single gray button that Flash will download once but will use to produce two tinted instances. If you don't make an object a symbol, Flash will not store it in the Library after download, and will have to download it again the next time a copy of it appears in the movie.

One part of your site is an exception to this rule: a "starting credits" movie that you want the user to see first. If this is the case, and you make your starting credits a movie clip symbol, Flash will not begin playing it until it has completely loaded. If, however, you created the starting credits as animations that are placed directly on the main timeline of your movie, Flash would begin to play the content as soon as the first frame streams in.

The way you use fonts in your final movie will also affect the download time. If your movie contains text written in a sans serif font such as Helvetica, a serif font such as Times, and a typewriter style font such as Courier, all three font files will need to be downloaded before the movie can be viewed. If, however, you use the generic _sans, _serif, or _typewriter styles to write your text in your original file, the text in the downloaded version will be written using fonts on the user's hard drive that match these styles. No font files will have to be downloaded as part of the Flash file, and the download time will be reduced.

In general, every time you use a new font, Flash will have to download the font shapes you've used. If you're designing a site that contains a lot of text, make sure that you use the same font throughout. Because some fonts look very similar on the screen, you may not notice you're using two different fonts and are inadvertently adding to the download time of your movie. Be wary, also, of using complex fonts:

THIS FONT REALLY FITS IN WITH THE STYLE I AM GOING FOR BUT HOW BIG A DOWNLOAD OVERHEAD IS IT. . .

Before you use such fonts, look to see how big the font files are. They may really look cool, but some complex fonts can take up to 32K just for ten or so characters, leading to unnecessary download delays...try before you buy!

Optimizing elements

It's important to do everything possible to keep the file size of your Flash movie as low as you can. Let's look at the tools Flash provides for lowering the amount of data taken up by the individual elements of a movie.

Reducing the memory used by vector shapes

1. Create a new Flash document and add three blank keyframes to the timeline so that there are four in total:

2. Use the Pencil tool in the Ink mode to draw an abstract shape at frame 1. Make your shape very curvy, like ours:

3. Select your shape and copy it. Then select frame 2 and use the Edit ➤ Paste in Place menu option to copy your shape onto the stage in this frame. Do the same at frames 3 and 4.

4. Select the shape in frame 2 and go to Modify ➤ Shape ➤ Smooth.

5. Select the shape in frame 3 and go to Modify ➤ Shape ➤ Straighten.

6. Select the shape in frame 4 and go to Modify ➤ Shape ➤ Optimize and drag the slider to maximum.

The Smooth option will make your shape more rounded, in the way that shapes drawn with the smoothed Pencil tool appear, and Straighten, as you've no doubt surmised, will make your shape more angular in the way shapes drawn with the straightened Pencil tool appear. These commands can be repeated over and over again to make the shape more rounded or more angular.

The Optimize option will reduce the number of curves that make up the shape. Like the previous two commands, it can be applied multiple times—but only until Flash reaches a point where no more curves can be removed.

7. Test your movie, and make sure the Bandwidth Profiler is turned on (View ➤ Bandwidth Profiler):

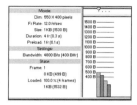

The graph will be the same shape whichever modem setting you use. It shows you that the modified versions of your shape will download more quickly than the original drawing. As designers, we must decide how much we're prepared to alter the appearance of our movie components in our quest for a lower download time.

One designing eye also needs to be kept on the size of any sound clips or bitmap images you use because the bigger they are, the longer they'll take to download. You discovered how to optimize bitmaps and sound files earlier in the book—you need to weigh how much they add to the movie's appeal against how long the user has to wait to see them.

Optimizing tricks and tips

Here are a few ideas that'll get you started on the route to efficient and responsive sites.

As we said earlier in the chapter, the key to good design is structuring your site so the elements load in the order they're needed. Make sure you load up all the functional and informative components first, such as the buttons that enable the site to be navigated, and let the eye candy that you put in to show off appear later because not everyone will want to wait for it.

One question that sometimes pops up is how to make Flash load symbols *before* they're needed. You would need to do this if, for example, you wanted a responsive site and were prepared for Flash to pause at the beginning while essential symbols were loaded. This is done using a **preloader**. A preloader is a scene created solely to occupy the user's attention while the symbols your site requires for later use are downloaded.

Remember, once they're in the Library, Flash doesn't need to reload them every time they appear.

In order to load the symbols without the user seeing them, you tell Flash they're appearing in the frame that's playing, but place them in the work area *outside* the visible stage. However, you want the viewers to look at something so they don't get bored and lose patience with your downloading site.

What a good preloader needs is a simple animation that plays as the download takes place, and some informative text to let users know they won't have to wait too long. You can see a good example this at http://www.2advanced.com/perspectives:

If you don't want to detail specific items that are in the process of being loaded, you could use a loading bar (like the progress bar used here, at http://www.iwantmyflashtv.com):

At this site, while the preloader is displayed, an initial Flash animation trailer is being loaded that will play immediately. The trailer introduces the site and simultaneously allows large amounts of content to be loaded to the user's computer in the background:

To give the viewer a "percentage loaded" figure, you would arrange all the objects you need to download among ten frames of the preloader so that each contained 10 percent of the total download (the Bandwidth Profiler could be used to fine-tune this).

These two methods, however, can be seen as overkill! If you have to give "percentage loaded figures as your site is downloading, your download may be too long! Be warned—while Flash designers expecting a fantastic Flash interactive experiment may be prepared to wait for this content, the average web surfer will leave the site before it is completely loaded. As always, the decisions whether to use a preloader or how you organize the loading of your site's content should always be determined by the user's hardware and motivation for visiting the site.

Loading multimedia on demand

A great tactic for optimizing your website is to load the content required on demand. Using the loadMovie and loadSound commands from your base Flash file, you can call in another SWF, MP3, or JPEG file. The bonus of doing this is that you only have to call content when the user requires it, meaning that the initial download overhead is much lower.

The loadMovie command works by loading content into a level above the main movie or into a movie clip target. Here's an example of how the ActionScript command would look when loading a SWF file into a movie clip:

```
mymovieclip.loadMovie ("myfile.swf");
```

It's worth mentioning that content loaded with the loadMovie command does not replace any of the content stored in the base SWF. Let's try this out to get a better idea of what options it gives you.

1. Open a new Flash document and save it as `record_base.fla`.

2. Rename the default layer record player. Create another two layers called blank and actions so that you end up with actions being the top layer, and record player being the lowest.

3. Draw a simple record player on the record player layer. Our attempt is a lovely orange and yellow, with a red arm:

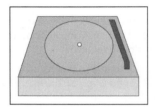

You're going to give the record player a record to play by loading an external SWF file. Until then, it's a sad and lonely record player.

4. On the blank layer, create a new movie clip symbol (Insert ➤ New Symbol) called blankClip. This movie clip will be used in its current form—totally empty. The reason for this is that you will load the external SWF file into this movie clip.

5. Without editing or adding anything to the movie clip's timeline, click the Back button to return to the main timeline. Drag a copy of the blankClip symbol from the Library and place it on the stage:

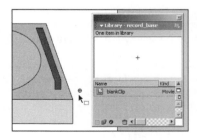

You'll notice that because the symbol is empty and it is selected, it's represented on the stage by a circle and a cross. If you deselect the movie clip by clicking elsewhere (such as on the record player graphic), it is represented by just an unfilled circle:

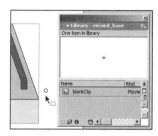

6. Place the blankClip at the top left of the stage (0,0) by selecting it and entering the coordinates in the X: and Y: input boxes of the Info panel. Note that the height and width of the movie clip is also 0 (because of course there is nothing in it!). With it still selected, give it an instance name of target via the Properties panel:

This will be used to load in the external SWF file. Let's add the code to load into your (as yet, uncreated) SWF file.

7. Insert a keyframe (F6) on frame 25 of the actions layer. Select frame 25 of your record player layer and extend your frames up to frame 25 by pressing F5. Do the same with the blank layer.

8. Select the keyframe back on frame 25 of the actions layer and open the Actions panel (F9).

9. Type the following into the Script pane:

```
target.loadMovie("record_on.swf");
stop();
```

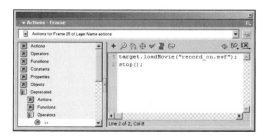

The code here might look similar to the dot notation you looked at in Chapter 11. The target instance of blankClip will load a movie clip over itself. This is much the same as if you swapped blankClip for another movie clip in the library during author time except that here you are getting Flash to do it for you at *runtime*, and you are asking it to load an *external* file (both of which make for a much more powerful way of doing things). The main timeline is then stopped.

If you test the movie now, nothing will happen—at frame 25 the Output window will open with the following—or similar!—message:

Let's give your record player something to play—a nice tune.

10. Save the current record_base.fla but leave it open.

11. Open a new Flash document and save it as record_on.fla. If the name sounds familiar, that's because it's the same as you entered in the code earlier.

The first thing you need to do is match the record player from the record_base file with the new file.

12. Return to the record_base document using the Window menu and select the record player graphic.

13. Select all the shapes' fills and lines that form your record player, and copy them (if you're using the graphic from the download FLA, you'll need to ungroup the graphic using CTRL+SHIFT+G):

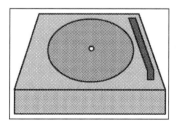

14. Return to the record_on Flash document and use the Edit ➤ Paste in Place menu option to position them in the same location as in the other movie.

15. Draw in the rest of the scene, placing a record on the turntable and moving the needle on to the record:

You may find it easiest to construct the "playing" record player by drawing each shape or fill on separate layers.

16. Save the movie in the same location as record_base.fla–this is very important because otherwise the loadMovie command will not work. Use Control ➤ Test Movie to publish the record_on file.

You might not be aware that Test Movie actually produces a SWF file. This is all that you need.

17. Return to the record_base Flash document and use Control ➤ Test Movie again. If all has been done correctly, the record player will be lonely for a short while, and will then be given a lovely record to play. If this hasn't worked, make sure that you gave the blankClip an instance name and that both your files are saved in the same folder—these are the most common places to go wrong.

Your turntable movie is finished. It could do with a little sound and a button to start the record, but now you know how to load in external SWFs, we'll leave this for you to play and experiment with.

Loading video files, MP3s, and JPGs

Now that you've seen how to use the loadMovie command using an external SWF file as an example, it's worth knowing how to work with other file formats so that you are able to call these on demand too.

Video

A typical system for working with video files on popular sites such as http://www.quicktime.com is to provide the user with a number of different files for their relevant bandwidth. QuickTime in particular has movie trailers for users with 56k, 100k, and 300k bandwidths. The files for the different users have been specifically sized and compressed so that the user gets the best possible experience without the long download time.

This technique can also work for you. By creating a number of different sized SWF files from the same video clip, you can use the loadMovie command to simply load the required file size content on demand. This means that lower-end users will not have to wait, and higher-end users can view the content in full-blown, luscious quality. Neat, huh?

JPG

Flash MX 2004 has support for importing JPGs on the fly, meaning that—as with the video tip—you can load content that specifically caters to the user's bandwidth (and patience!). JPG files can be imported directly using the loadMovie command, for example:

```
movieclip.loadMovie ("mypicture.jpg");
```

If you are new to Flash, this will make your work a lot easier!

A new feature of Flash MX 2004 is the ability to load JPGs into a text field. Text fields can be made to render HTML, and the <IMG> tag is finally supported. To display a JPG file in a text field:

1. Find or create a JPG image, and place it in a folder of your choosing.

2. Create a new FLA and save it in the same folder as the image.

3. On the stage of your FLA, create a **dynamic** text field big enough to show your image on frame 1 of a new FLA. Name the layer html.

4. Select the text field and give it an instance name (for example, htmlField). Make sure that the icon on the Properties panel is pressed. This enables the text field's ability to display HTML formatting.

5. Create a new layer called actions. In frame 1 of this layer, add the following code, substituting myjpg.jpg with your image name. Also, note the different quotation marks you are using—double quotes (") around the whole string and single quotes (') around the image name.

```
htmlField.htmlText = "my image -  <img
➥src='myjpg.jpg'>";
```

Test the Movie. You should see the image appear in the text field as soon as Flash sees the line of code. Loading images (and even other content, such as SWFs) using the <img> tag is cool because the content will act just like true HTML text—it will load only when it needs to be displayed. This is different from traditional Flash sites, which tend to load lots of content that may not be seen at all and can contribute to a larger than expected download time.

The downside of the implementation of the <img> tag is that it is a little temperamental about where it places text around it, and whether it works at all—placing the caption after the <img> causes the <img> to stop working altogether!

MP3

As with JPGs, the ability to import MP3 files is also available. This is the basic command format to load a streaming sound (denoted by the true in the loadSound). Use the Vocal2.mp3 file from the downloads section for chapter 11 to set this up, saving the FLA with this code in the same folder as the mp3.

```
target = new Sound (this);
target.loadSound ("Vocal2.mp3", true);
```

When using your own MP3s, note that Flash is very picky about loading MP3s, and you should test this before running your code. In most cases, if the authoring environment is happy loading the MP3, the Flash player will be happy during runtime as well. If in doubt, look at the MP3 files you use in chapter 12—looking at their MP3 file attributes via your MP3 conversion software will give you the clues you need.

Now that you've seen how to load content only when it is required, you have a valuable insight into how many websites are created with multiple SWF movies and loaded content. The code to load a sound (or image) could be placed within a Button script so that it only loads when the user clicks a button that requests the content.

```
myButton.onRelease = function(){
   target = new Sound (this);
   target.loadSound ("Vocal2.mp3", true);
};
```

The procedure to load an event sound is complicated a little by the fact that if you try to play a streaming sound before it is totally loaded, you won't hear anything. The following code fixes this by loading the sound when the button is pressed, but not playing it until the sound is completely loaded, as defined by the onLoad event:

```
myButton.onRelease = function() {
   target = new Sound(this);
   target.loadSound("Vocal2.mp3", false);
   target.onLoad = function() {
     target.start();
   };
};
```

Last minute checks

Armed with the information in this chapter, you're now able to ensure that your Flash sites will be suitable for exposure on the web. When you complete authoring a Flash movie, view it with Show Streaming on and ask yourself the following questions:

- Does the movie run smoothly when using the modem my target audience is most likely to have?
- Does it ever pause at inappropriate times because of streaming?
- Is the user made aware that they'll have to wait (and for how long) whenever a preload is required?
- If my site is running slow because of high bandwidth, what can I get rid of—is the tune that plays every time a button is pressed *really* necessary?

- Would it be better to load my content on demand?
- Am I making the most of the space available on the stage—and how can I utilize the space better?

Case study

In this section, you're going to create the print page and display some illustrations. Given what you've learned in this chapter about using loadMovie to load content on demand, you're going to show thumbnail versions of the images which, when clicked, load the full size jpegs.

For this exercise, you will need the image files gandhi.jpg, gandhi_thumbnail.jpg, einstein.jpg, and einstein_thumbnail.jpg from the code files for this book.

1. Open your saved case study document.

2. Double-click the Content movie clip instance to edit it in place.

3. Within the content movie clip's timeline, scroll the playhead along to frame 116:

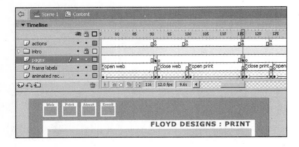

4. Select the keyframe on the pages layer and type the following text in 14pt Arial in #003366 as seen:

Floyd Designs specializes in cover designs and illustrations. Please click any of the thumbnails above to see example screenshots.

5. Center the text field and with it still selected, press *F8* to convert it into a symbol. Name it print content, and give it movie clip behavior and a center registration point:

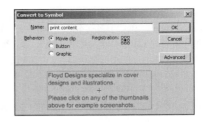

This new movie clip will contain the print page of the website.

6. Double-click the text field to enter edit in place mode for the print content movie clip:

7. Use the Selection tool to move the text field to the bottom left corner of the green rectangle.

   Now to import the thumbnail images.

8. Select File ➤ Import ➤ Import to Library and locate einstein_thumbnail.jpg and gandhi_thumbnail.jpg in the file dialog box, and import them.

9. Open the Library (*CTRL + L*) and drag a copy of both newly imported images onto the stage.

10. Position them in the top left corner and align them neatly:

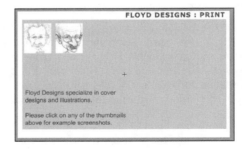

We used the left half of the screen purposely because the other half will be the display area of the full-sized images. Before you get to the other half, let's finish this one.

11. Drag a copy of the invisible button symbol from the Library onto the stage. You're going to reuse

this symbol to make simple buttons for your historical figures. To do this, you need to use good old Free Transform tool or the Properties panel.

12. Select the invisible button instance and use the Free Transform tool to modify the shape to cover the thumbnails only.

13. With the invisible button instance still selected, press CTRL + D to duplicate it.

14. Position both invisible buttons in the same position as the thumbnail images.

15. Select each button instance in turn and give them instance names of einsteinButton and gandiButton respectively:

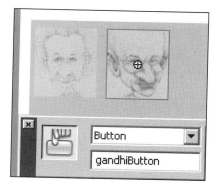

Before you write any button code, create the target instance for your images to load into. This is done with a blank movie clip instance.

16. Select Insert ➤ New Symbol. In the dialog box that appears, give it the name blank mc and a movie clip behavior:

The symbol will be in Edit Symbol mode, which is the usual behavior, but it is not where you want to be at all.

17. Return to the main stage and double-click the content movie clip instance.

18. Scroll to frame 162.

19. Open the Library if it isn't already open, and drag an instance of blank mc onto the stage.

20. Select the blank mc instance and drag it to just below the "F" of Floyd Designs. If you have Snap Align on, it should snap to the same vertical position as the thumbnails and the side of the text field like so:

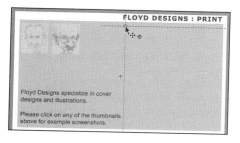

21. The last thing to do here is to give it an instance name. Select the blank mc instance and give it the name jpegLoad_mc in the Property inspector.

Adding the ActionScript

In this section we're going to add the required code to the invisible buttons. When either button is pressed the corresponding full size image will be loaded into the blank mc instance.

1. Select frame 116 of the actions layer, and open the Actions panel (F9).

2. Add the following code:

```
stop();
einsteinButton.onRelease = function () {
    jpegLoad_mc.loadMovie ("einstein.jpg");
}
```

Simple enough isn't it? When einsteinButton is clicked, the full-size image is loaded into the specified movie clip instance target. The benefit of doing this, as opposed to how you created the web page, is that the images are loaded on demand only.

3. Copy code lines 2 – 4 and paste the code into line 5.

4. On line 5 of the code, change einsteinButton to gandhiButton and on line 6, change einstein.jpg to gandhi.jpg.

Both your buttons are now functional. All you need now is the full-size images.

5. Place the full-size images, `gandhi.jpg` and `einstein.jpg`, in the same folder as the case study FLA and the SWF.

6. Test the movie and click the Print button, followed by a click or couple of clicks on their original images to show the full-size image:

Easily done, and extremely beneficial for your users. This means that they won't have to wait until the whole website loads before seeing any images. Cool!

7. If Gandhi is scaring you a little too much, save the case study document and close it.

Summary

You've now seen the technicalities of how you make sure your Flash movie gets where you want it to go in the form you intended, and in a manner that's satisfactory for the user.

You saw that:

- The **Bandwidth Profiler** lets you see:
  - How your movie will play on the Internet.
  - Where any pauses in playback will occur.

- **Streaming** is used to smoothly download the components of your movie before they are needed on the stage.

- A **preloader** can buy you time to download your entire movie in one go.

In the next chapter, you're going to look at the issues involved in preparing your movie for publishing on the web.

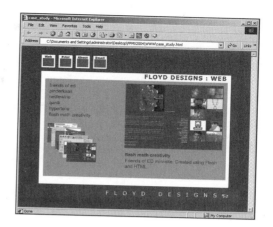

Chapter 14

PUBLISHING

What we'll cover in this chapter:

- The formats available for publishing, and when to use them
- How to create the necessary files to get your movie ready for the Internet
- The principles of putting your files on the Internet
- How to use **anchors** to enhance the user's navigation options

You've spent days—weeks, maybe—creating the perfect movie, and you're bursting to show it to the world, but so far only your dog and a few bewildered family members have been able to see it. Relax—the waiting is over—this chapter is here to help you and your movie make the transition from the cozy world of the local hard drive to the hustle and bustle of the Internet. It's time to go public.

The essential process is this: when you're happy with your movie, you use Flash's **File ➤ Publish** menu option to create a viewable file that you can share with the world. This file can then be put on your website.

When you're preparing your movie for display on the Web, there are a number of output formats you can choose from when you finally publish the movie.

Web formats

One of the things that makes Flash so successful on the Web is its small file size, and this is where publishing comes in. Up until now you've been working only with FLAs—the files in which your movies are created. When you publish your movie, Flash compresses the FLA, removes all the redundant information, and leaves just the instructions for a sleek, streamlined, multimedia presentation. The default output file from the Flash publishing process is a SWF (pronounced "swiff"). Associated with the SWF file is the HTML file. The HTML file has an embedded link to the SWF, plus information on how the browser should display it.

> *All web content is usually based on an HTML file that is loaded and decoded (or "parsed") by the browser. The parsed information then tells the browser what else it needs to load to build the final web page. Although some browsers can display a SWF without the HTML file, it is always a good idea to include the HTML because it is the standard way of defining any normal web page, and is thus likely to work on all browsers.*

Including SWF and HTML, the more common file types and their usual file extensions are:

- Flash—.swf
- HTML—.html
- Animated GIFs—.gif
- QuickTime—.mov

You can make your files as simple or as complicated as you want. Flash's publishing process means that you simply select the output options you want, and Flash does the rest for you, producing files that can be migrated straight onto your website and put into the public domain.

Let's look at each of the common output formats.

Flash

The full name for the standard Flash file format is **Shockwave for Flash**, hence SWF. The Flash Player is the software that plays the SWF files on the user's browser. The Flash player is now a standard across the Internet, and you can more or less assume that anyone who wants to watch Flash movies already has the Flash Player installed on his or her machine. In the transition from Macromedia Flash MX to Flash MX 2004, however, there's a slight hitch—new movies built in Flash MX 2004 are compatible with only the last version of Flash Player 6, so anyone with an older version will have to download the new Flash Player 7 to be able to see your movies. There *is* an option to export your movie in older Flash formats when you publish it, but doing this means that the viewer won't be able to see some of the new features in Flash MX 2004. For most of the things we've covered so far in the book, this won't be a problem, but if you intend to stream video or use some of the more advanced ActionScript techniques, you'll have to export your movie in the Flash Player 7 format. It's a trade-off: if you want to reach the widest audience, you'll be advised to always put a Flash MX (Flash 6) compatible movie onto the Internet, at least until Flash MX 2004 has been around for a few more months. However, if you want to show off some of the new Flash MX 2004 features (such as using ActionScript 2.0 Classes or streaming MP3 download) your viewers will have to use Flash 7 player.

The Flash 7 player is more optimized than the Flash 6 player, and it will run content up to three or four times faster. It's actually a big step up from the Flash 6 player as far as the end user is concerned, so the switch to the Flash 7 player is expected to be faster than previous versions

The Shockwave for Flash format is part of a larger standard called Shockwave. This standard is used in Macromedia's Director software, and it means you can incorporate your Flash movie seamlessly into Director. Director is a general multimedia-authoring tool that is designed to produce multimedia presentations for applications such as CD-ROMs and screensavers, as well as web applications and interactive 3D environments. The main difference between Flash and Director is that Director has been designed for general multimedia, and not just small, size-optimized, web graphics. Director can do many things that Flash is not designed to do, such as use real 3D (using 3D models and cameras) and provide greater synchronization between multimedia streams.

If you ever want to create more heavy-duty multimedia presentations, Director is a good place to start.

HTML

HTML stands for HyperText Markup Language. HTML is not a language in the same way that ActionScript is—HTML is a **formatting** language whereas ActionScript is a **scripting** language. This means that HTML consists of special instructions that tell the browser how to format the text and graphics on a web page. It's these instructions or *tags* that are the heart of HTML, and they are also its major weakness. HTML was only designed to present simple text data and static images. At its inception, this was enough, but as the Internet expanded, HTML became more and more old-fashioned and heavy. On the plus side, HTML is an integral, universal feature of the World Wide Web. Its ease of use and total compatibility make it a good choice if you want

simple information to be readable by absolutely everyone. One of its main features—links from one page to any other—was a defining feature that led to the current popularity of the Web as a tool for quickly acquiring information. Additionally of course, you don't need a plug-in or player for HTML to work.

The real problems with HTML start when you try to add multimedia elements to a web page. Because HTML wasn't designed for this, you have to use JavaScript (the scripting language that ActionScript is based on) on top of HTML, which moves away from 100 percent compatibility with all browsers. There are new versions of HTML and other supporting languages for multimedia and wireless devices in the works, but for the time being at least, there will be much less support for them on the Web than there is for the Flash player.

As a Flash designer, you have to know a bit about HTML because it's what carries your movie on the Web. To make your movie accessible over the Web, your movie file will be hosted inside an HTML file. Luckily, it's easy to publish your movie embedded in an HTML file, which you can then simply integrate into your website. As you'll see later in this chapter, all you have to do is tell Flash a few simple things about how you want the final movie to behave in the browser window, and Flash will generate the appropriate HTML file. You still may need to do other things with this Flash-generated HTML, however, because parts of your HTML document can perform tasks that Flash can't, like making descriptions and keywords for the web page available to search engines.

Furthermore, most Flash web pages don't just consist of a Flash movie on its own—they're usually made up of many separate elements. Things like hit counters and advertising banners must integrate seamlessly with the Flash portion of your site. In this chapter, you'll look at Flash's HTML publishing controls, but not the HTML site design and creation side of things: that's a whole subject of its own. We've included a couple of good HTML resource sites in Appendix B, and there are many books dedicated to HTML if you want a more thorough understanding.

Animated GIFs

Animated GIFs were an early attempt at animated content on the Web. We touched on them briefly when you imported them into Flash in an earlier chapter, but you can also export your Flash movie as a GIF. Why would you want to do this? For the simple reason that you don't need a special plug-in to view them. You can guarantee that everyone who can view images on the Web (and that really is just about everyone) will be able to view your movie. This is the reason why many banner ads are created as animated GIFs—they're universally viewable, and thus reach the maximum number of eyeballs. You can harness this accessibility in your own sites by having a Flash version and an animated GIF/HTML version of your site on the Internet, allowing people to visit either depending on their preferences. It's possible to export some or all your Flash movie as animated GIFs via the export options, which we'll cover later in this chapter.

QuickTime

QuickTime is Apple's Internet multimedia technology. The advantage of using it rather than Flash is that it can be integrated with other QuickTime technologies, it can be set up to run with QuickTime server-streaming content, and it has a large user base. You can embed a Flash SWF file in QuickTime as a multimedia channel, but at the time of this writing, Flash MX is not supported—QuickTime 6 (the latest version), only supports up to Flash 5 content. You can also export your Flash presentation as a QuickTime MOV file via the publish options.

So, how do you publish the movie?

Putting on the show

Once you've produced your movie, you have to create the necessary files for people to view it outside the Flash authoring environment. The way this happens is controlled by the settings in the **File ➤ Publish Settings** window:

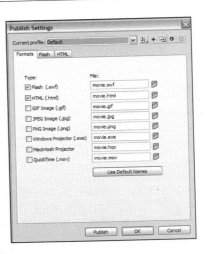

Each of the formats listed earlier is for playing your movie in a different environment, such as the Internet, a QuickTime movie, a standalone file that can be run on a computer without the Flash Player installed, or even as a static picture. It's important to realize that the file you've been creating won't be the file that's finally used in any of those applications. The "work in progress" FLA file will be converted to one or more new files that can be read by the target software.

The general method is as follows:

1. Select the way you want to publish your movie via the **Publish Settings** window.
2. Preview the movie.
3. Once you're happy with your publish settings, publish the movie. The requested files are placed in the same folder as the source FLA file by default, although you can change this by clicking the folder icons and selecting a new location for any of the created files.
4. Upload the published movie onto your server.

Let's walk through the publishing process.

Creating and publishing a basic movie

To start, you'll concentrate on the simplest and easily the most popular option: publishing a Flash movie in a form that can be viewed by anyone who's got a browser with the Flash Player installed. First, you'll create a simple movie to publish.

1. Start a new movie and place a static text box on the stage. In the text box, write This is a test movie in a big, bold font:

This is a test movie

2. Use the Align panel to make sure your text is in the exact center of the stage. To do this, display the Align panel (Window ➤ Design Panels ➤ Align), click the to Stage icon, then click the Align Horizontal Center and Align Vertical Center icons.

3. Press **F8** to convert the text into a graphic symbol called **text graphic** with a central registration point. To make the registration point central, remember that you have to click the central square in the 3x3 grid that appears in the Convert to Symbol window.

4. Insert a keyframe at frame 20 of your main timeline.

5. Using the Properties panel, add a motion tween between the keyframes at frame 1 and 20, and set it to rotate clockwise one time:

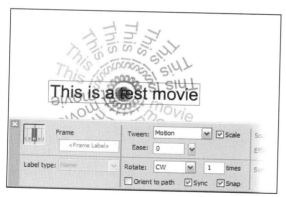

6. Test your movie (CTRL+ENTER). It's a simple movie, but it'll be effective for our purposes here.

7. Create a new folder on your desktop, and save your movie in it as movie.fla.

   If you look in your folder, there will be one file in it—the FLA that you just saved. When you publish your movie, Flash will automatically put all its

output files in this same folder, so if you're building a big project, it's a good idea to keep everything in a dedicated folder.

8. Go back into Flash and select File ➤ Publish Preview. A sub-menu will appear listing the publishing options:

   If you haven't altered the default settings, you'll see three options available: **Default**, **Flash**, and **HTML**. When you publish your movie via **File ➤ Publish**, Flash creates output files in all the formats that are in bold letters on the **Publish Preview** menu—in this case, SWF and HTML. When you select **File> Publish Preview** instead, Flash will do the same, except this time it allows you to view one of the output files.

9. Select the **Flash** option: this will take you to the familiar Test Movie screen.

   On this screen, Flash shows you what the movie will look like on its own. It has compiled your source FLA file and produced a SWF file, which is what is played.

10. Go back to the **Publish Preview** menu and select the **HTML** option. You'll see the same movie, except this time it's being played in your default browser. When you select this option, Flash creates an HTML file and embeds the SWF into it.

11. Look at the folder you stored **movie.fla** in. You'll see that there are now three files in it:

The SWF is the Flash movie file that's playable in the Flash player. The HTML file (actually, Flash creates a file containing a more recent dialect of HTML, xHTML) is just a text HTML document containing the formatting tags needed to display the page in a browser, plus a link to the SWF (on the fifteenth line of this text):

```
<HTML>
<HEAD>
<TITLE>movie</TITLE>
</HEAD>
<BODY bgcolor="#FFFFFF">
<!-- URL's used in the movie-->
<!-- text used in the movie-->
<!--This is a test movie--><OBJECT classid="clsid:D27CDB6E-AE6D-11cf-96B8-444553540000"
  codebase="http://download.macromedia.com/pub/shockwave/cabs/flash/swflash.cab#version=6,0,0,0"
  WIDTH="550" HEIGHT="400" id="movie" ALIGN="">
  <PARAM NAME=movie VALUE="movie.swf"> <PARAM NAME=quality VALUE=high> <PARAM NAME=bgcolor VALUE=#FFFFFF>
  <EMBED src="movie.swf" quality=high bgcolor=#FFFFFF WIDTH="550" HEIGHT="400" NAME="movie" ALIGN=""
  TYPE="application/x-shockwave-flash" PLUGINSPACE="http://www.macromedia.com/go/getflashplayer"></EMBED>
  </OBJECT>
</BODY>
</HTML>
```

SWF file link

When this HTML file is previewed in the browser, it will give you this result:

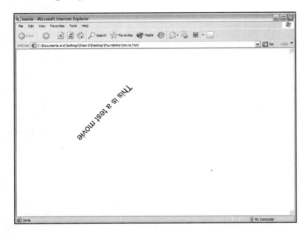

There's a slight problem with the way your movie is shown in the browser. The size is right—its dimensions are the same as we set in the **Document Properties** dialog box—but it appears in the top-left corner of the screen. You can change all that by giving Flash different publishing settings to work with.

12. Select the **File ➤ Publish Settings** menu option and display the Publish Settings window again.

On the **Formats** tab of the Publish Settings window, you can select the file formats in which your movie will be published. You'll see that at the moment there are check marks in the boxes for **Flash** and **HTML**—these correspond to the options that were available to you on the **Publish Preview** menu. At the top of the window there are tabs corresponding to these two selected options.

13. Click the **GIF Image** check box, and a new **GIF** tab will appear at the top of the window:

14. Uncheck the box, and the tab disappears. The tabs contain the individual settings for each of the file types that are checked in the **Type** list.

15. Click the **HTML** tab to display the **HTML Publish Settings** window:

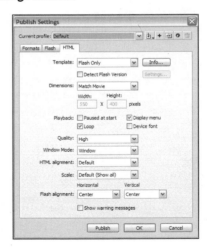

We'll be covering all these options in detail later in the chapter, but for now, let's just get your movie to play how you want it to.

16. You want the movie to take up the *whole* of the screen when it plays, and this is done through the **Dimensions** drop-down menu:

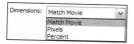

At the moment, **Match Movie** is selected so your browser will always keep the movie at the size set in the Document Properties window—in this case, the default 550 x 400 pixels. If you resize your browser window, your Flash movie will stay the same size and will begin to be cut off when the window gets too small:

The other problem with defining a stage size in pixels is that if someone is using a different screen resolution than you, the movie will be a different size on his or her screen. If you design your movie to be the perfect size on your 1280 x 960 pixel monitor and your viewer is viewing it on an 800 x 600 screen, she won't see quite what you intended. You can stop this from happening by changing the **Dimensions** setting to **Percent**. The **Percent** option refers to the size in the browser window, not the pixel size of the movie, so 100 percent will always fill the entire browser window, no matter what size or resolution it is. Neat.

17. Change the settings to **Percent**, ensure the **Width** and **Height** boxes both read 100, and use **File ➤ Publish Preview** (*F12*) to preview your movie again.

These settings are good because you know your movie will always stay central and fill the window.

Which **Dimensions** option you chose is a matter of preference. If you want your movie to be in an exact area on your web page and remain in the same proportions, choose the **Match Movie** settings. If you want it to play at a certain percentage of the screen size on any computer at any resolution, choose the **Percent** setting.

The most common settings used in commercial sites are shown in the following graphic. The SWF does not scale and always stays in the middle of the Browser window.

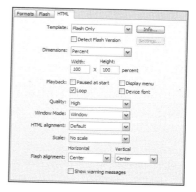

You can also save publishing options as templates, and this is very handy. Click the Import/Export Profile icon to the top right of the Publish Settings window, and select Export from the menu that appears. To import it to a new FLA, use the Import option. You can also save *profiles* as part of the current template by hitting the plus sign (+) icon. This saves the current publishing configuration as a new option in the Template drop-down menu.

18. Go back to the Publish Settings window and click the **Formats** tab.

Notice that each of the file formats has a box next to it that displays the name of your movie. These boxes show what your movie will be called when you publish it in that format. It's vital to be able to see which file corresponds to which format. If the extensions are not visible on your computer, it can be a problem telling them apart at a glance.

Change the names of your two selected file types to movie_flash.swf and movie_html.html respectively. Also check GIF Image and JPEG Image and change the file names to movie_gif.gif and movie_jpg.jpg.

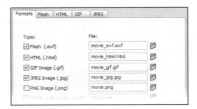

19. Click the **Publish** button. If you look in the folder where you originally saved your movie, you'll see a whole host of files there now. You added the file type to the name because many operating systems don't show file extensions in many views. Furthermore, as you can see in the following graphic, without the file type added to the name, there would be no way to distinguish between the GIF and JPG version.

20. Double-click the **movie_swf.swf** file in your folder, and your movie will play in the standalone player (provided you installed the Flash player when you loaded Flash onto your machine, of course!):

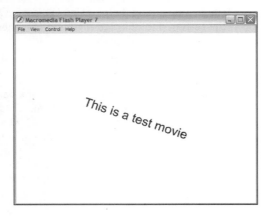

21. Close the player and double-click the **movie_html.html** file, and your movie will now start playing in your web browser.

> These two files—the SWF and the HTML file—are all that you need to put your movie on the Internet.

You could delete your FLA file now and still be able to display your work on the Web. This isn't recommended, though, because if you ever wanted to go back and edit your movie, you'd need the FLA. You should try to keep all your project files in one folder so you can easily find them again if you need to. It's also always a good idea to archive your FLAs onto CD or some other backup media.

Now that you've gone through the process once, let's take a more detailed look at the publishing options and how and why you'd use each one.

The many faces of Flash

Flash can do a lot of things, but it can't do *everything*. For this reason, there are many different publishing options that allow you to do much more with your Flash movie than create a SWF.

1. Open the Publish Settings window, and check *all* the **Type** boxes. A tab will appear for each type.

2. For ease of reference later, change the name of each file to include its format as you did before. The **projector** files are standalone executable files that are used if your movies will be viewed off-line, such as screen-savers, or if you want to e-mail your movie to a friend who doesn't have the Flash Player. The projector files contain a miniaturized Flash player inside them anyone can view your movie. A projector file is also useful when you want to create content for non-web applications (such as on a CD-ROM).

3. When you've finished, you'll have a screen like this:

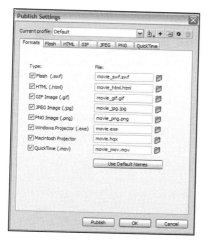

The two most important and most used tabs are **Flash** and **HTML**, so let's focus on these two.

At the time of this writing, there is no version of QuickTime that can handle the Flash 2004 SWF. If you need to publish QuickTime, you will have to export your movie as Flash 6 or even Flash 5 via the Flash tab.

Flash file publishing options

The **Flash** tab is where you specify exactly how the SWF file will be created:

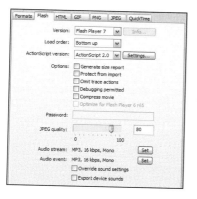

This tab contains the following options:

- **Version**—Use the Version drop-down menu to select the version of the Flash player for which you want your movie published. Flash Player 6 (or Flash Player 6r65, as explained in the Options section) is recommended until the Flash Player 7 has time to become more common across the Internet. The only time you should definitely use Flash Player 7 is when you need to include some of Flash MX 2004's extra functionality, such as the advanced ActionScript commands. These commands are highlighted in yellow in the Actions panel when you set the version to less than Flash Player 7. Note that Flash 7 components *may* work with Flash Play 6r65, but if in doubt, choose Flash Player 7.

- **Load Order**—This specifies the order in which Flash will load the layers for the first frame of your movie. It can load from the bottom layer up or from the top layer down. This option only has an effect when your movie is viewed over a slow connection, when the failure to load layers that are critical—such as the layer containing the navigation buttons—could result in a degraded user experience. In files that include ActionScript, make sure that the layer with ActionScript in it is the *last* to be loaded because the code usually expects everything else to be loaded before it (and may not work if it is not). If you follow this book and always put the ActionScript in it the top layer called *actions*, you should *always* keep this setting at Bottom up.

- **Options**—Select from the following options:

  - **Generate size report**—creates a text file that tells you about the final SWF file. The file can be useful when you're optimizing your movie because it gives you a frame-by-frame breakdown of the movie's size, and useful information about any symbols, sounds, pictures, and text that are in there. The exact content of this file is a bit beyond the scope of this book, but it's fairly straightforward when you view the file.

  - **Protect from import**—stops anyone from importing your SWF file back into Flash and copying all of your hard work. There are applications that allow a malicious user to break this protection, but you are still advised to use it for your final site.

357

- **Omit Trace actions**—makes Flash ignore any **Trace** actions you might have included in your movie. **Trace** actions are commands that allow you to track the value of a variable in your movie and display it in the Output window while the movie is running. This is very helpful for you when you're debugging your movie, but you don't want it popping up when someone else plays your file.

- **Debugging Permitted**—allows you to use the Debugger panel on the final presentation, which can be selected from the Flash player pop-up menu. This is useful when you're trying to track any bugs in your final movie, but again, it's not something that you want other people to be able to use. It's also possible to protect this option by entering a password in the **Password** box. This permits only those who know the password to use the debugging options.

- **Compress Movie**—allows Flash to compress the Flash movie when publishing. As mentioned earlier, ActionScript code, video, and text benefit most from this, but vector shapes are also compressed. This option cannot be used for movies intended for use with player versions earlier than Flash Player 6.

- **Optimize for Flash Player 6r65**—optimizes content when exporting for Flash player 6 and below. The rev65 version of the Flash player is essentially the same as Flash player 7, but it has been available for much longer. This option is greyed out for the Flash player, because Flash player content is always optimized.

- **Quality**—These are global settings for imported artwork and sounds, and they will only affect the movie components that you did not optimize separately. As you discovered in earlier chapters, it's always best to optimize all aspects of your movie separately because this provides the best compression to quality ratio. There's an **Override sound settings** option, but you should never need to do this. The **Export Device Sounds** option will only appear in Flash 2004 Professional and allows you to work with sound in certain handheld devices that do not support the full range of sound files that a desktop machine does.

HTML file publishing options

The **HTML** tab specifies how to configure the HTML file that will be published. For those of you who want to fine-tune the default Flash-generated HTML by hand, the appendix on HTML and Flash at the back of this book explains the key issues and expands on the use of Macromedia Dreamweaver with Flash.

- **Template**—This specifies the type of HTML file you want the SWF to be embedded into. Each different template includes specific types of HTML tags that allow you to extend the HTML file's functionality. There are more options in Flash 2004 Professional than Flash 2004 The **Info** button will give you a brief description of the selected template, and which file it is. The HTML template files are kept in the Flash MX 2004/en/First Run/HTML folder (or the equivalent folder if you are using an international version), so if you're an HTML/XHTML whiz and want to change them, back up the originals and have a go. In most cases, the Flash Only option will be fine.

- **Dimensions**—As you've already seen, this allows you to change how your movie is displayed on the screen. You can use your movie dimensions, specify another movie size, or scale your movie to a percentage of the user's browser dimensions.

- **Playback**—Options include the following:

  - **Paused At Start**—means the user has to tell the movie to play before it will do anything.

  - **Display Menu**—displays a menu when a user right-clicks your movie. This menu allows the user to control the playback of the movie, change the movie quality, and zoom in to see all that lovely vector detail. Switch this off if you don't want your users to have these options. Many commercial sites switch this **off** so users don't try to switch to low quality settings or zoom into the graphics to have a close look at how it was all put together.

  - Loop—plays your movie continuously if selected, or only once if it's not. This option is overridden by any stop actions you have, and can also be overridden by the user.

  - Device Font—replaces any static text in your movie with a system font, which can cut down on file size, although you have less control over which font is used. Flash uses the closest one it finds on the users machine, but these days it's usually very close as long as you use the generic fonts—_sans, _serif, and _typewriter).

- **Quality**—This option allows you to set the rendering quality that your movie will play at—the lower the quality setting, the faster it will run on a slower

computer. We recommended you set this to **Auto High** to allow Flash to drop the quality to maintain frame rate and synchronization if it needs to. It's not worth worrying about setting this to a low quality—if users are having problems with the quality, they can change it themselves at their end.

- **Window Mode**—These options affect how some advanced Dynamic HTML commands can interact with your movie in certain browsers. Most of the time, you'll want to leave this set to **Window**.

- **HTML Alignment**—This allows you to specify the position of your movie window inside the browser window. **Default** will center the movie, and the other options will align it along the desired edge.

- **Scale**—If you've changed the size of your movie with the **Dimensions** option earlier, you can use this option to define how your movie is scaled to fit into the browser window.

- **Flash Alignment**—These two options allow you to set the vertical and horizontal alignment of your movie inside its window, and how it will be cropped if it needs to be.

- **Show Warning Message**—When this box is checked, any errors discovered when the HTML file is played—for example, images that aren't where they say they are—are displayed as messages on the browser when the user views your site.

Until you become more familiar with the intricacies of HTML/XHTML coding, you won't need to alter many—if any—of these options. The **Dimensions** are the most important things to be aware of at this stage, and you can experiment with the rest when you become more experienced.

Using anchors in Flash

In earlier versions of Flash 5, there were a few usability issues, one of which was the Flash movie's ignorance of the browser's Back and Forward buttons.

Often, visitors to HTML websites became accustomed to pressing the Back button frequently during a session, and this was not necessarily conducive to easy navigation in some websites constructed entirely in Flash.

This issue is overcome by using **anchors**. Given that the lack of Back button functionality was seen as a major issue in earlier versions of Flash, let's look at how it was fixed.

Placing anchors in your Flash file

Anchors are created by adding a frame label and selecting Anchor from the Label type's drop-down menu.

Anchors can be placed only on the main timeline of your Flash movie.

Let's make a quick example to see how anchors work and how the Flash file is published:

1. Create a new FLA and save it as `anchors.fla`. Create three graphic symbols called pear, orange and apple, as shown.

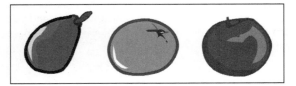

Also, create a simple button symbol called click button. It doesn't have to be animated, so you can have a single keyframe at the Up state, as shown.

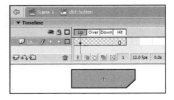

Add five layers to the existing **Layer 1**. From the top down, name your layers: actions, anchors, fruit, text, button text, and buttons.

2. On frame 1 of the **buttons** layer, drag four instances of **click button** onto the stage, toward the bottom. Give them instance names main_btn, apple_btn, orange_btn, and pear_btn respectively. On frame 1 of layer **button text**, add four static text fields above the buttons, containing the text main, apple, orange, and pear.

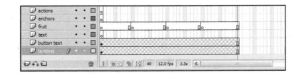

3. On the **fruit** layer, insert keyframes at frames 10, 20, and 30. Extend layers **fruit**, **buttons**, and **button text** to frame 40.

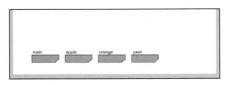

4. At frame 10 of the **fruit** layer, drag the **apple** symbol to the stage, resizing it as necessary to get the general proportions shown in the following graphic.

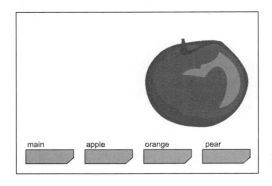

Add an **orange** to frame 20 in the same way.

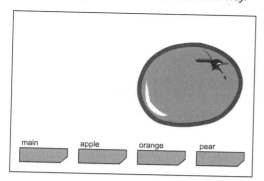

Add a **pear** on frame 30:

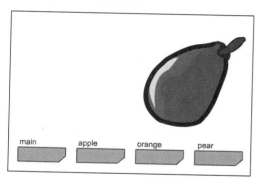

Your timeline should now look like this:

The keyframes at frames 10, 20, and 30 will signify different parts of your movie's timeline as you move between them. To be extra sure that you know where you are when the SWF is running, you'll add some text to the keyframes.

5. On the **text** layer, insert keyframes at the same frames as the **fruit** layer (frames 10, 20, and 30).

6. In each of the four keyframes in the **text** layer (1, 10, 20, and 30), in the bottom-left corner of the stage, add some static text describing the frame number and the name of the page, for example:

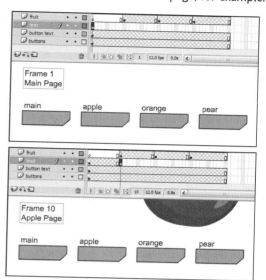

Now you need to add some anchors to your movie.

7. On the **anchors** layer, insert keyframes at frames 10, 20, and 30.

8. Label frame 1 main and select **Anchor** from the drop-down menu in the Properties panel.

You've just created your first Flash anchor. Congratulations. It wasn't so difficult was it? No time to bask in the glory; let's add the other anchors.

You might notice that the little red flag in the timeline (which denoted a frame label) has gone all sea-worthy and changed to an anchor shape now that you've made it an anchor.

361

9. Insert the following anchors at the appropriate frames:
   - **apple** at frame 10
   - **orange** at frame 20
   - **pear** at **frame** 30

10. Click frame 40 of the actions layer and drag your mouse pointer down to the Text layer. Press *F5* to extend your timeline so that you can see the pear anchor label completely.

    Your timeline should now look like this:

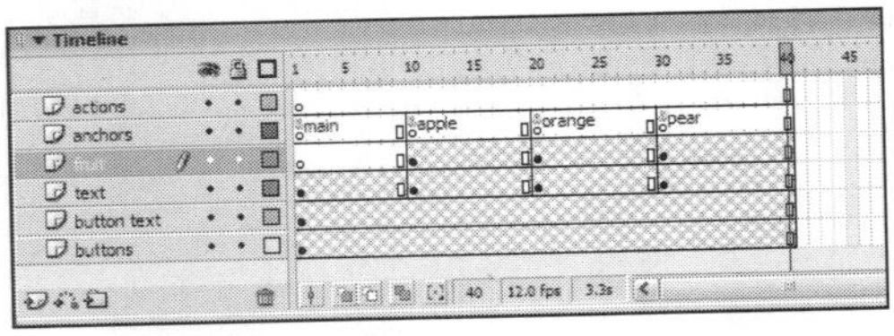

Now let's add some actions to your movie.

11. Add keyframes at frames 10, 20, and 30 of the **actions** layer.

12. Select all the new keyframes in this layer individually and add a stop(); action to each one. Leave frame 1 out for a moment, you will add the button scripts to that almost immediately.

    This will stop the timeline from running on to the next fruit before you are finished with the current one.

    Let's now add some simple ActionScript to the buttons you made earlier.

13. Attach this code on frame 1 of the actions layer:

```
main_btn.onRelease = function() {
  gotoAndPlay("main");
};
```

14. Add the same code to the other buttons, substituting the main_btn anchor name for the individual fruits' anchor names and using each button's instance name. Make sure you get these right. You should end up with the following listing on frame 1 of the actions layer:

```
main_btn.onRelease = function() {
  gotoAndPlay("main");
};
apple_btn.onRelease = function() {
  gotoAndPlay("apple");
};
orange_btn.onRelease = function() {
  gotoAndPlay("orange");
};
pear_btn.onRelease = function() {
  gotoAndPlay("pear");
};
```

The quickest way to do this is to cut and paste the code from the main **button** and make the minor anchor name and instance name change for each of the other buttons.

Finally, add a stop(); at the end of the listing to give you the following:

```
main_btn.onRelease = function() {
    gotoAndPlay("main");
};
apple_btn.onRelease = function() {
    gotoAndPlay("apple");
};
orange_btn.onRelease = function() {
    gotoAndPlay("orange");
};
pear_btn.onRelease = function() {
    gotoAndPlay("pear");
};
stop();
```

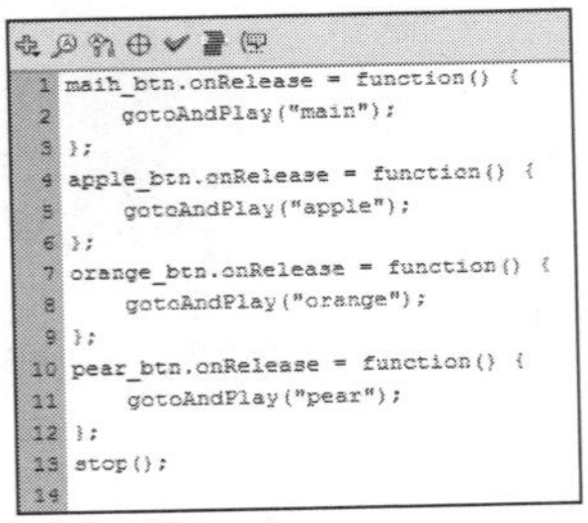

Once you've done this, your movie is finished—the only thing left to do is publish your page correctly. Earlier on in the chapter, you looked at the Publish Settings window, where the HTML template for publishing **Flash with Named Anchors** is located.

> *Testing that the anchors in your movie work must be done in a browser environment such as Netscape Communicator or Internet Explorer. If you were to test this movie within Flash, the anchors wouldn't function because there are no Back and Forward buttons.*

15. Open the Publish Settings window using **File ➤ Publish Settings**.

16. On the **Formats** tab, make sure that both the **Flash** and **HTML** boxes are checked.

17. Go to the **HTML** tab and select **Flash with Named Anchors** from the **Template** drop-down menu. You may not have as many options available to you from this menu as we have (the screenshot is from Flash MX Pro 2004).

This means that when you publish your movie, an HTML document will be created with code included to make the anchors functional.

18. Click **OK**. Select **File ➤ Publish Preview ➤ HTML** to open the Flash movie in a browser.

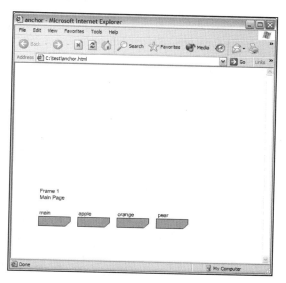

Test the anchors. From the main page, click the Pear button to open the Pear page and then press the

browser's Back button to redisplay the main page. Pretty neat, huh? This will save your visitors and yourself a lot of headaches and make the whole navigation experience a lot more intuitive.

19. Save your file and close it.

Most web users don't care what application the page is created in as long as they can use the features familiar to them. This new anchors feature also enables users to add the Flash page to their Favorites or bookmark it.

> At the time of this writing, anchors inside Flash files do not work correctly in IE 6 browsers. Hitting the Back button in IE 6 simply displays the previous anchor on the timeline (rather than the previous anchor you visited). So evaluate whether you want to include anchors in your Flash site, and then assess the proportion of your potential visitors who will be accessing your site using IE 6.

The remaining publishing formats in the Publish Settings window are fairly self-explanatory. We'll give you a brief run down of them and highlight the most important options.

GIF, JPG, and PNG

These bitmap export options are of particular interest to the Flash designer because they allow the easy creation of both a Flash *and* an HTML version of your website. All these formats will publish the first frame of your movie as a static image. The exception to this is GIFs, which can also be animated. You can specify an individual frame for Flash to publish by putting **#Static** as a label on that frame:

GIF seems to be the best option for publishing a static image because its compression routines are well suited to Flash's solid colors. If you use a lot of gradients in your movie, though, these can come out horribly dithered—it's worth checking the **Remove Gradients** box and replacing the gradients with solid colors to achieve a better quality image.

GIF files also have the option to be animated. When you publish your movie as an animated GIF, Flash saves each frame of your movie as a GIF frame that'll be played through in a flipbook manner to give the appearance of animation. This is best for HTML versions of sites or for doing small animations such as advertising banners that you want to be viewable on all computers.

Note that ActionScript is ignored when creating an animated GIF; the timeline will simply run from end to end.

If the image you're exporting contains a lot of gradients or imported artwork, the best option is to publish it as a JPG file. As you move the **Quality** slider to the left, the file size gets smaller but the quality of the image deteriorates—and vice versa:

It's worth playing with this option in conjunction with the **Publish Preview** option to find the best balance for your image. There's also an option to set the image as a **Progressive** JPG. This is a method for loading images on slower computers: the computer will load an interlaced version of the file (for example, every fifth line), and then fill in the image one set of lines at a time.

PNG is the only image format supported by Flash that includes an alpha channel for transparency. Remember that a transparent GIF can be fully transparent or fully opaque, but a PNG image can contain degrees of transparency. To use this option, you must have the **Bit Depth** set to **24-bit with Alpha**:

A PNG-24 image will be very large and is not really designed for the Web, so don't be tempted to use it as such. Select 8-bit if you want to use the PNG in a web page. The file size should be comparable (or less) than a GIF.

QuickTime movies

Publishing your movies in QuickTime format allows you to use them with other QuickTime files. The Flash movie will be published on its own track inside the QuickTime file, which can then be edited from inside QuickTime Pro—a program from Apple for the creation and editing of QuickTime files. The options control how the Flash track will interact with other tracks inside the movie, and which type of QuickTime controller to use to play the movie. It's a good idea to select the **Flatten** box because it tells Flash to build all the external files (such as graphics or movies) into the final QuickTime file, allowing it to be played as a stand-alone file on any computer. If this box is *not* checked, the final file will be smaller, but it will depend on links to the external files. If these files are moved or renamed, the movie won't be displayed correctly.

Now you've got your files together, the final hurdle is getting them up to the server and onto the Internet.

Uploading your files to the host server

To finally make your movies available to the viewer, you need to upload them onto your hosting server so that people can access them over the Internet. This task is always fraught with danger the first time you do it, but like riding a bike, after you get it right once, it'll just seems to come naturally. The options available to you when you upload your files depend on the web hosting company you're using, and it would be impractical to provide you with instructions on how to do it all in detail. We'll cover some of the basic principles here, but always check with your ISP to make sure you know all of its distinctive ins and outs.

The key stages in the process are as follows:

1. Choose your ISP and establish how much space they'll give you for your website and what features they'll support.

2. Find out the specific upload locations and procedures for your ISP.

3. Transfer your movie files up to the host site based on these procedures.

> *Most modern browsers have upload abilities built into them, so once you have all the information just outlined, it's only a matter of entering the correct address in the browser and dragging files into the browser window to upload them.*

The first issue you come across when you're getting your web page up and running is deciding exactly which files you need to upload. The only files that you need are your SWF and HTML files. Remember, the FLA file is just the authoring file; it isn't required once you've published your movie. Also, you don't need to upload any fonts, images or other external files (unless you are using features that allow external assets,) because Flash will embed these into your final SWF movie.

The second issue you'll come across is deciding what to *call* your HTML file. If the file is going to be a page inside your website, you can call it whatever you like as long as you include a link to that file name from another web page. If, however, your movie is going to be the *first* page of your website, you'll need to name it according to the protocols of your web server Typically, the first HTML page of a site is called index.html, but you'll need to check this with your web hosting company. When you type a web address into your browser, you usually just type the URL, for example www.apress.com, and the browser automatically searches for the web page called **www.apress.com/index.html**. It's just a convention designed to save people from having to type **/index.html** at the end of every web address. If you did not rename your file, the user would have to know to type **www.friendsofed.com/movie_html.html** into their browser to get to your movie.

The final hurdle is actually getting the files up onto the server. To perform file transfers to the server, you use a special protocol called **ftp**, which stands for **file transfer protocol**. You can either use a shareware program to do this (see Appendix B for some web resources), or one of the many site creation programs, such as Microsoft FrontPage or Macromedia Dreamweaver, which contain built-in features to help you upload your files. As mentioned before, though, your browser probably already supports ftp if it is a recent version, so there is now much less need for specialized programs

From here, you pass beyond the bounds of Flash, and out into the brave new world of the Internet.

Case Study

You're almost home free with your case study website. In this chapter you're going to publish the movie and set up the necessary files on your hard drive that you'll need to upload your website onto the Internet.

1. Open your case study document.

2. With the Flash document open, go to File ➤ Publish Settings to display the Publish Settings window. On the Formats tab, select the Flash and

HTML boxes (the File field may be different than the following screenshot—it'll be whatever you saved your case study movie as):

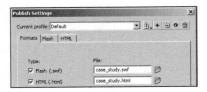

3. On the Flash tab, set the JPEG Quality to 80%. This will shear off a bit from the file size, but not so much that it will degrade the quality of the images you imported:

4. On the HTML tab, uncheck the Display Menu box so that the menu does not appear when users right-click the movie.

5. You want the Flash movie to scale in the user's browser without losing its original proportions. To do this, select Percent from the Dimensions drop-down menu and leave the Scale selection as Default (Show all):

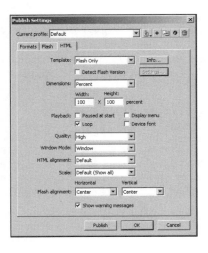

6. That's it! Click the Publish button, click OK and look in the folder on your hard drive where you've stored the files for this case study:

Open the HTML file to test how your SWF looks in a browser:

7. Save your case study document and close it.

When you upload your website to the Internet, don't forget that you need to include the einstein.jpg and gandhi.jpg files because these are external files that the Flash movie calls on with the loadMovie method.

Summary

In this chapter, we've given a brief survey of the issues related to getting your finished movies ready for viewing up on the Web.

You saw that:

- Flash has **publishing options** that will build all the output files you need to get your movie online.

- The most common publishing option for Flash is to embed a **SWF** file inside an **HTML** page.

- Flash will create the HTML file that hosts your movie, and you can tweak the HTML if you like.

- You can adjust the way your movie displays in the user's browser—and other attributes, too—by manipulating the values in the Publish Settings window.

- Flash MX includes the option to add **anchors** to your movie, enabling users to navigate your site using the Back and Forward buttons in their browsers.

- Once you've created the viewable files, you need to consult with your Web hosting company about getting your files up on your website.

In the next two chapters, we're going to delve deep into the heart of ActionScript and give you a taste of the future.

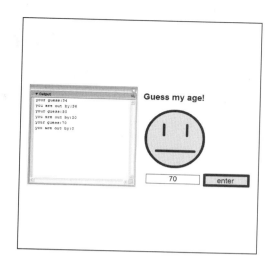

Chapter 15

INTERMEDIATE ACTIONSCRIPT PART 1

What you'll cover in this chapter:

- The first steps of intermediate ActionScripting:
  - Planning larger scale ActionScripts
  - Basic input and output
- Taking ActionScript further:
  - The logic of a Flash movie's internal structure, and why dot notation is a major advance
  - Getting movies to talk to each other using dot notation and code scope in ActionScript
  - Animating objects dynamically with ActionScript and user input

So far, you've gained enough Flash know-how to earn the grade of beginner—you're not a novice anymore, that's for sure. However, the rest of the book is going to take you further and enable you to earn your wings as an intermediate Flash user. The impressive effects on cutting-edge Flash sites will no longer baffle you—after the next two chapters you'll have insight into the methods that top Flash designers use to create those cool-looking sites.

This is the starting point of your road toward mastering Flash. This chapter and the next will teach you the three main programming techniques you need to get going on your journey. They are:

- Intelligently breaking down a problem and forming a structured plan to resolve it
- Treating a movie clip symbol as an object and understanding its relationship to the main timeline *and* to other movie clips
- Structured Programming

We'll cover the first two points in this chapter, and introduce the basics of the third so you can hit the ground running when you get to Chapter 16.

The rest of this book has a much steeper learning curve than in the previous chapters, and assumes you know how to perform basic actions (which were covered in Chapters 9 and 10) without being shown all the steps explicitly. However, you want as many readers as possible to get their wings, so if after reading the relevant section, you feel you haven't mastered one of these skills, go back and practice a little until you get the hang of it. The things you'll discuss in this chapter will make the difference between a plain vanilla Flash site and one that's packed with interesting and engaging features.

Planning your complex ActionScript: practical overview

This chapter's author worked in several "software-heavy" environments before going into multimedia and web design. These were at a different end of the spectrum—industrial display systems and safety-critical computer-control systems at nuclear plants. Working with this intense level of coding teaches two things about effective programming that are applicable to complex ActionScripting—which is really programming by another name:

- You must start by looking at the *problem* and not the solution, and then refine the problem until you have a collection of simpler problems to solve.
- You must treat these individual problems as small, self-contained tasks, and be able to code and test each small solution as you go along to make sure it's working properly. Once the discrete components are tested and working, you can integrate them and test again.

You're going to put these ideas into practice by modifying the Smiler movie you created in Chapter 11.

Some people are very sensitive about their age, so when someone asks, "How old do you think I am?" you need to reply with care. If your guess is close to the correct age, you'll please them. But if you're a long way off in either direction, you're likely to offend, and may need to retreat quickly.

You're going to make your Smiler equally sensitive about its age. Fishing for a compliment, it'll invite you to guess its age. If your guess is way wrong, it'll put on a big frown, but as your guesses get closer to its actual age, the happier Smiler will get. When you guess exactly right, you'll see Smiler's biggest possible smile.

This is going to involve quite a big change to the existing Smiler code. Following the advice above, the first question you need to ask is, "What exactly is the problem you're trying to address with your complex ActionScript?'"

Defining a problem

Is "guessing Smiler's age" the ActionScripting problem? No—that's the *user's* problem. You're creating the code for Flash to *respond to* the user's guess. Let's think about exactly what you want Flash to do by walking through the user's typical interaction with

Smiler—this will help you identify the contours of the problem and the sub-problems that it's composed of:

1. You want to define a number that the user doesn't know—Smiler's age—and you want to constantly check this number against the user's guess.

2. You want to detect when the user is wrong and, if so, by how much, and then convert the size of the user's error into an expression on Smiler's face.

3. The more wrong the guess is, the more Smiler will move toward its biggest frown, at the "sad" frame.

4. As the user's guesses get nearer to Smiler's age, the happier it'll get—moving toward the "happy" frame When the user guesses the exact value of Smiler's age, Smiler will put on its biggest smile and the game is finished.

How do you check that you've defined the problem correctly? By thinking it through and ensuring there's nothing else you want your program to do. If necessary, you talk to your client to confirm that you've analyzed the problem correctly.

> *At this stage, it's important to think only in terms of what you want Flash to do—now isn't the time to think about exactly how you're going to make Flash do it. You need to keep your minds untainted by solutions until you've got a clear idea of the problem and its sub-problems.*

You'll find that most problems can be stated in a similar form to the one just shown, even if they're very complex. A programmer would call the list of things that the ActionScript needs to do a list of **requirements**. This list doesn't state the solution; it just states *what needs to be done*. Because these are the only requirements you have for the interaction of Smiler and the user, you can be reasonably confident that your list is a general statement of the *whole* problem. A programmer would call these the **high-level requirements**, and would break each requirement down into a list of smaller, more detailed requirements for the program. This list is called a **requirements specification**.

The multi-billion dollar super-computer programs that refuse to work don't usually fail because they've been coded incorrectly. They fail—almost without exception—because the *wrong problem* was defined at the planning stage, so the programming solution that was built based on that definition didn't fulfil the requirements of the *actual* problem! This can mean that the programmers are not all working toward the same clearly defined goal. Although all the sections of the program work in isolation, when they're put together, the different chunks can't be integrated properly and nothing works. This emphasizes the importance of planning, and it's why you're not going to jump straight into creating the ActionScript for the new, improved Smiler. Instead, you're going to take things stage by stage, and guarantee that you come up with an effective solution.

Breaking down the Smiler problem

You now need to break down, or *decompose*, your high-level requirements into more detailed basic requirements. You keep breaking things down in repeated iterations until you have the simplest list possible—things that can't be broken down any further.

A first iteration has sub-points of each original point (1.1, 1.2; 2.1, 2.2…) and a second iteration has sub-points of each of these (1.1.1, 1.1.2, 1.1.3…).

Let's work out Smiler's detailed requirements specification, based on the high level requirement you've already specified:

1. Define a number representing Smiler's *age*.

2. Acquire a number—let's call it *guess* from the user, and check it against *age*.

3. Compare the difference between *age* and *guess* and apply this value to the Smiler movie in order to make it go to a particular frame to indicate how close the guess is.

4. If the difference is *zero*, make Smiler to go to the "happy" label on the timeline—Smiler's biggest smile—and stop. If the difference is *not* zero, repeat from point 2.

You can now break this down further in your first iteration by asking more questions about the nature of the problem. For example:

- How big a number can *age* be? Can it be 450? Can it be 6.124569081?

- Can *guess* be the word "five" or does it have to be number 5?

- How many frames should Smiler have?

This is what your first iteration might look like:

- 1.1—Define a variable—*age*—which is between 1 and 99.

- 2.1—Elicit a text entry from the user that's numeric.

- 2.2—Assign this text entry to a variable, *guess*.

- 3.1—Create a new variable, *difference*, which is equal to *age* minus *guess*.

- 3.2—If *difference* is a negative number, convert it to a positive number of equal magnitude.

- 3.3—In the Smiler movie clip, go to a frame number that's equal to *difference* to represent how far out the user's guess is.

- 4.1—If *difference* is zero, stop. Otherwise repeat from 2.1.

Through refining your problem you've almost written yourselves a set of instructions to solve it with.

If you put 1.1 to 4.1 in order, you end up with a list of what you need to do to reach a solution to the overall Smiler ActionScripting problem. This powerful technique goes by the name of top-down design: you've defined the high-level problem—the top—and then worked down into the problem by splitting up the requirements into their simplest forms. By the end of the process you have a problem that's so well defined it has become the answer itself—and the path to the final specification is traceable all the way back to the top-level problem you're trying to solve.

The converse coding style, bottom-up design, looks at the problem from the other way round—by starting at the bottom and asking questions like "What are the basic building blocks of this problem?" It then builds these blocks as software entities called objects, each of which is based on templates called classes that are used to define what objects are. The first set of classes (called superclasses) is then extended to form more precise classes, and thus a more precise solution. This coding system is called object-oriented design. You need to know structured programming to be able to use it well, so that is what you will concentrate on in your foundation, although, because Flash is itself object oriented, we have shown you how to follow the object oriented hierarchy of properties and methods that ActionScript is arranged around.

The Smiler example is a fairly simple problem, and you probably could have worked out the answer in your heads without listing your requirements. However, when you're working on a bigger coding project, you won't have that luxury. The top-down method of planning and problem definition will save a lot of time and brainpower when solving more complex problems, and it will help ensure that you're solving the right problem in the right way.

By giving your problem a defined structure, you are forcing your ActionScript to follow a similar, structured, form. You will write ActionScript that is well thought out and that addresses each requirement in turn.

For the beginner, thinking of the task in terms of the *problem* rather than the ActionScript has yet another, rather more subtle, advantage If you think only in terms of the code solution, you'll only ever use the Flash skills you've already got a handle on. However, if you define the problem properly before thinking about the code, you may well hit upon the requirement for tasks you can't yet do. You'll be forced to try new methods to achieve this—instead of repeating the tasks you already know how to do and allowing your Flash programs to become stale. By looking at what you need to solve a problem, rather than what problems you can solve with the skills you already have, you'll constantly improve your skills and upgrade your Flash technique.

You now know what you need to change in the old Smiler to create a new, age-sensitive, version. However, before you can solve the problem defined by your requirement specification, there're one or two pieces of Flash know-how you need to acquire. For instance, point 2 asks you to get the user to guess Smiler's age: so you need to know how to allow the user to *input* text and how to get Flash to *use* that input.

Basic input and output

So far, you've seen that ActionScript allows you to create *variables* that you can store values in, and that Flash uses these variables in the background without the user being aware of them.

Sometimes, as in the Smiler movie, you want to have these variables visible on the screen so that you, and the user, can see what they are. In Flash, getting and displaying variables—whose values can change, remember—is done with **input text** fields and **dynamic text** fields. Although we touched on using input text fields, most of the text fields you've used up to now contained **static text**, which, as its name suggests, doesn't do anything but sit in its box (even if the box itself is animated). Before we explain the two new types of text, there's something about the text fields themselves that needs to be explained.

If you just click once on the stage with the Text Tool while you have Static Text selected in the Text type drop-down menu on the far left of the Properties panel, you'll create a text field that will extend indefinitely as you type into it. The text field will only move to a new line when you press the *ENTER* key. This text field, with undefined width, has a circle in the top-right corner:

If, however, you *click and drag* on the stage with the Text Tool and make your text field a wide rectangle, this field will have a width defined by the size of the field you dragged out. The text you type into it will wrap onto the line below as the text reaches the edge of the field. This text field, with a *defined* width, has a square in the top-right corner:

An undefined text field will become a defined text field if you alter the width of it at any time. Additionally, you can revert a defined text field to undefined by placing your cursor over the little square and double-clicking.

Now to use text fields for input and update them dynamically.

Input text and dynamic text

Let's try an experiment.

1. Create a new movie and use the Text Tool to drag out a text field on the stage. Make it about two inches wide. Change the current Layer name (Layer 1) to Text.

2. In the Properties panel, use the Text type drop-down menu to change the text from Static Text to Input Text.

3. Notice that the square at the top right of the text box has moved to the bottom right, and that there are new fields visible in the bottom half of the Properties panel:

This text field is now enabled as an input field in the finished movie. The additional fields in the bottom section of the Properties panel allow you to control the behavior of that input field.

Let's use these fields to tell Flash that you want to store the user's input in a variable.

4. In the **Instance Name** field, enter inText. Change the Maximum characters field to 10, set the line type to Single Line and click the Show Border Around Text button. Also click the Left/Top Justify button and your panel will now look like this:

Selecting the Show Border Around Text option means that the outline of the text field will appear in the movie—this can be very helpful for the user because they don't want to have to search too hard for the text input area.

5. Test the movie.

6. Click inside the text field box and enter some text. You can enter up to 10 characters, the maximum you specified.

You've created a text input area for the user on the stage, and the text typed into here will be used later to set the value of a variable.

You can now also create an *output* text area that'll keep you informed about the current value of the variable.

7. Paste a copy of the text field you just created underneath the original.

8. Working with the new text field, change the Text type in the drop-down menu in the Properties panel to Dynamic Text. Also, change the instance name to outText.

9. Deselect the Show Border Around Text button and the Selectable button.

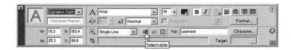

10. Insert a layer above the text layer in the timeline and name this new layer button. Add a button-sized circle to the stage in the new layer. With the circle (and any stroke it may have) selected, press F8 to make it a symbol. Make it a button, and call it input button. With the button still selected, give it an instance name of inButton using the Properties panel.

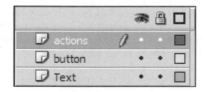

11. You now need to add an event handler for your button. Insert a new layer named actions above the button layer.

12. Select frame 1 of the new layer and add the following code in the Actions panel.

```
1  inButton.onRelease = function() {
2      outText.text = inText.text;
3  };
4
```

13. Test the movie.

You can enter text in the upper (input) text field, and as soon as you click the button, the value you entered appears in the lower (dynamic) text field. What's happening here? The text property of a text field allows ActionScript to access the text currently in a text field. By equating outText.text to inText.text, you copy whatever you just placed in inText to outText. The top text field is set up to allow user input, and the lower text field is set up to allow display that input.

Rather than tell the user what he or she already knows, as you're doing here, you can instead make Flash do something useful to the data you input before it displays it or outputs it for your viewing.

14. Select the lower text field again and change it so that it's an Input Text type field. Click the Show Border Around Text button, and enter 10 in the Maximum Characters field. In the Properties panel, change the instance name to inText2.

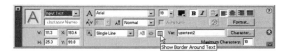

You're going to get Flash to add the input to inText and inText2 together and display the result in a third text area. You need to define this third text area next.

15. Draw a third text box in the text layer to the right of the button and make it a Dynamic Text field.

16. Make sure the Selectable button is unselected, and the Show Border Around Text button remains selected.

17. Give the new text field an instance name of outText.

Now you need to let the user do something new—when he or she clicks the button, you want the

values in the two text fields on the left to be added and displayed in the right one.

18. Select frame 1 of layer actions, and modify the code as shown.

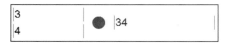

```
1  inButton.onRelease = function() {
2      outText.text = inText.text+inText2.text;
3  };
```

Remember that the code is case sensitive, so make sure yours look like our example, that all your variable names are in camel case, and the method and action names onRelease, function, and text are all in a dark blue.

19. Test the movie. Enter a number in both of the left hand fields, and then click the button to see the result of the addition.

```
3
4                    ●    |34
```

Um…you have a problem…

What went wrong? When you enter anything in a text field, Flash assumes that the values you enter are *text* (or to use the correct term, *string literals*). When you tell Flash to add the two text values, Flash does a string addition, which is called *concatenation,* that is, an action that puts the second bit of text after the other to make a single string. That's *not* what you want. You want Flash to assume the two inputs are *numbers* and to do an *arithmetic* addition. To do this you use Number(). This will turn your inputs into numbers, and thus Flash will be forced to do an arithmetic add. We've changed our circular button to a + here to better show what happens to our inputs when the button is clicked.

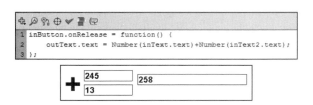

```
1  inButton.onRelease = function() {
2      outText.text = Number(inText.text)+Number(inText2.text);
3  };
```

It works! And you can even add decimals.

20. Try typing letters into one or both of the fields and clicking the button. The dynamic text field to the right shows NaN, or "Not a Number."

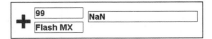

An informal rule in programming states: "If you're taking input from the user, assume that the user is a monkey." This isn't a reference to the monkey with a keyboard whose random typing produced, by chance, *Hamlet*. This is in reference to the billion other monkeys that *didn't*. Your input fields have to cater to all the *wrong* inputs as well as the *right* one, and you should write code that expects the wrong answers and can handle them. Your code has to be able to cope if the user types 89g6!trc instead of 896. Let's see how to add an intelligence filter (or should that be stupidity filter?!) to an input field.

Select one of the input text fields and click the Character button in the Properties panel to display the Character Options window. This window lets you specify what can be typed into or displayed in this input or dynamic text field. Flash assumes you want to allow input of *all* the standard English text characters, unless you select any of the options. You will see the window shown on the left of the following graphic.

21. Select the **Specify Ranges** radio button. You only want *numbers* to be entered in the input fields, so select Only from the window, and select Numerals [0-9] (11 glyphs) from the list, to give you the window shown on the right of the following graphic.

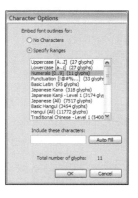

22. This allows you to enter any number that contains the numerals 0 to 9, plus the decimal point. The user might also enter a negative number, so you should add that as well. In the Include these characters text entry box, enter a hyphen (-).

23. Test your movie again. Now you can monkey about all you want: Flash will only allow you to type in text up to 10 characters in length, and it must be integers from 0 to 9, a decimal, or a hyphen.

> *It is still possible to add incorrect entries such as 98-9 instead of 98.9 or 9.9.9 instead of 99.9.*

ActionScript possesses a math library that contains functions such as sin, cos, tan, and so on, that allow you to develop this simple movie into a working calculator program.

Remember the Smiler specification you were planning before? You've just discovered an important building block that allows you to code it up in Flash. Now you've got the hang of input and output, getting the user to guess Smiler's age later in the chapter will be no problem at all.

First though, you need to learn a little more about **dot notation** and how to use it with paths in ActionScript.

Referencing paths with dot notation

As you discovered earlier, dot notation in ActionScript is a way of expressing the *instance.method(argument)* or *instance.property* code structures, enabling you to build your lines of ActionScript. The thing we haven't discussed is that the instance name does not just have to be a name, it can also incorporate a *path* to the instance.

If this name and path-plus-name stuff seems a little strange, this analogy might help.

John lives down my street. If I need to leave him a quick letter or note, I will write it on a piece of paper and deliver it to his house, addressed simply to "John."

Jake lives in a different city than me. When I want to send him a letter, I have to put "Jake" plus his full address on the letter because I need to specify which (of many) Jakes I want to receive my letter.

This address is just the same as a path. Whether I use a path depends on whether the person I need to communicate with can be identified with just a first name, or a longer address. If you want to reference something on the same timeline, you don't have to add a path. Otherwise you have to specify the path to the new location. The reason why you got away with not using dot notation so far is because everything you have done up to now involves stuff that is always on the same timeline.

Remember the structured planning you went through at the beginning of this chapter? You broke the Smiler problem down into manageable chunks or sub-problems. If you now structure your movie correctly, you can address each of your requirements *in a separate movie clip*. You can then use dot notation to make these movie clips converse with each other and control the movie as a whole.

What does the path consist of? Here's another analogy: on your computer, you have a hard drive with various folders and sub-folders—often nested several layers deep. To get to a particular folder, you use Windows Explorer, or you click the drive's icon on the Mac to open the folders you want to look at.

On my computer, the path for the folder of this text file (the one that I'm writing now, and that will eventually be made into the book you are reading), is based on its position in the folder hierarchy:

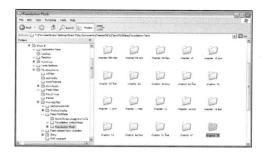

The actual path for this file is: C:\Documents and Settings\Sham B\My Documents\FriendsOfEd\ Flash2000Beta\Foundation Flash\chapter 15.

This path tells you how to get to this text file starting from the hard drive, C:\, which is the lowest level, or **root level**. (You'll note the tree-like nature of the way these networks are linked.) What we're saying here is that to get to the file, I have to go into a folder called *Foundation Flash*, where I'll find another folder called *chapter 15*, and if I open that folder, the file I want will be there. This path through the folder hierarchy gives me the entire journey, starting from the lowest level— the hard drive. If I specify the path in this way, starting from the hard drive level, it's referred to as the total or *absolute* path.

If I were *already* at C:\Documents and Settings\Sham B \My Documents\FriendsOfEd\Flash2000Beta\Foundation Flash, I could express the route to the document *relative* to where I'm starting from—I don't have to go back via the hard drive level. The path from here would be simply chapter 15\.

This is saying: "starting from where you are, open the folder *chapter 15*, and you'll find the file you want."

Flash uses a similar structure, except that instead of seeing levels of hard drives and folders, it refers to SWF files and movie clips, or to be more accurate, it refers to their *timelines* and *sub-timelines*.

Consider a Flash movie that has the following:

- A main timeline (or *root* timeline, called _root in Flash) that has one scene—Scene 1
- A movie clip called FoED on frame 27 of Scene 1

- A movie clip called FoundationFlash on FoED's timeline at frame 20

To access an object or frame on FoundationFlash's timeline, you could use the following *absolute* path in my ActionScript: _root.FoED.FoundationFlash.

Because the path just shown is an absolute path, starting at the _root and working its way through the nested timelines, I can safely issue it from anywhere and know that Flash will be able to find its way, down the path, to the FoundationFlash movie clip's timeline.

Note that each of the levels in this hierarchy is separated by a dot—hence the term dot notation. You can use this notation to specify the path that you want Flash to follow—and you can use it to point to any object, anywhere in the movie.

What if you want to access something in FoundationFlash's timeline from within the FoED movie clip? You *could* use the full, absolute path defined earlier, but because you're *almost* where you want to be; you can just give a shorter *relative* path in ActionScript as follows: FoundationFlash.

This path will start from where you are, and look for the next level of the path inside of the FoED movie clip:

And there's a special ActionScript command if you want to go *back* a level, for example—from FoundationFlash *back* up to the FoED clip): _parent.

You can also string these commands together to go back *more* than one level: _parent._parent.

Going back to your hard drive, you'll notice that you actually have more than just a C:\ drive. There are also A and D drives on most computers:

You can navigate to those drives by specifying their paths—such as A:\.

Similarly, you can include *external* movies in the paths you use in ActionScript. To access a separate SWF using dot notation, just replace _root with a reference to the external SWF's *level*, _level0 for the SWF at level 0, _level1 for the SWF at level 1, all the way up to level 16000 (which is the maximum number of levels you can have). In fact, 16,000 is the maximum number of symbols you can have in the Library, and 16,000 is the limit for just about everything in Flash.

378

In terms of the original analogy of your hard drive:

- SWF files—movies—are the equivalent of your separate hard drives.

- A movie's main timeline is the equivalent of the root path of each hard drive.

- Individual movie clips are the equivalent of folders and sub-folders.

On your hard drives, you use paths to access *files*. Flash allows you to access *instances and variables*.

To specify a variable at the end of a path, as with other dot notation, just precede it by a period (.). The full path for a variable called userinput in the FoundationFlash movie clip would be _root.FoED.FoundationFlash.userinput or _level0.FoED.FoundationFlash.userinput.

In your Flash movies, you'll find the root level displayed as level 0.

Many movie clips, many variables

Lets extend this discussion and think more about variables, the way they can be on different timelines, and how the same variable has to be referred to from different places in different ways.

Let's look at how this works in a brief exercise.

Movie clip-specific variables

1. Create a new FLA.

2. In the root timeline (that's the timeline on the main stage—you're going to be speaking in this new terminology from now on) add three layers: actions, text, and clips:

3. In frame 1 of the actions layer, open your Actions panel and type a=3;.

4. Select frame 1 of the text layer and insert a dynamic text field. Using the Properties panel, make the text non-selectable by switching the Selectable button to off, and give it a border by clicking the Show Border Around Text button.

   You want the variable displayed in this box to be called a, so type a in the Var field (make sure the text font color you've selected is *not* the same as the background color):

> *Using the* Var *field in a text field is a quick and easy way to link a variable to a text field. You are using it now for the sake of this example but you should avoid using it for all but the simplest stuff. This is because most advanced code structures (such as those found in components) expect you to use the* TextField.text *property instead, and won't work if you use the* Var *field. This field is a legacy feature left over from previous versions of flash that did not use components or object-oriented coding techniques.*

When you run this single frame movie, you'll see a text box with the number 3 in it. Not the most exciting movie you've made in this book. Bear with it, though, because the point this example illustrates will open your eyes to a wealth of exciting possible movies.

5. Back in the main movie, create a new movie clip called Mclip. Add new actions and text layers to it as you did for the root timeline.

6. Create a similar non-selectable dynamic text field on the text layer and click the Show Border Around

Text button, but this time set it to display the variable b:

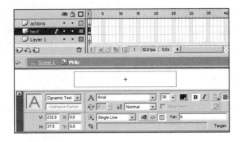

7. To help you remember that this text field shows a variable that's *inside* Mclip, you're going to label it. Draw a static text field next to the dynamic one and type This is inside Mclip into it (select a different text color from the text in the dynamic text field):

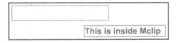

8. In frame 1 of the Mclip movie clip's actions layer, use the Actions panel and add the following line B=10;.

9. Go back to the root timeline. Place an instance of the finished Mclip on the clips layer, and give it the instance name mClip_mc using the Properties panel.

10. Test the movie:

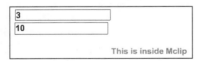

Now you have a variable in the root called a, which is equal to 3, and a variable in the movie clip instance mClip_mc called b, which is equal to 10. Here's the current variable/text field relationship:

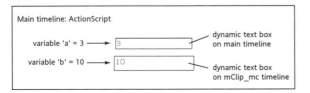

Now you're going to see how it's possible to have a variable name that has more than one value.

11. Inside mClip_mc, change the ActionScript in frame 1 from b=10; to a=10;.

12. Select the dynamic text field in mClip_mc and change the Var field on the Properties panel from b to a.

You've now set two variables, both called a, to two different values in two different places. The a=10; ActionScript inside mClip_mc is initializing a *new* variable called a, inside mClip_mc. This mClip_mc-specific variable is a *different variable* from the variable a that's being initialized on the main timeline, _root. You can think of them as the following:

- _root.a
- _root.mClip_mc.a

These are *absolute* references. They will work wherever you are in the timeline hierarchy, because they start from the lowest level, _root. This is much the same as starting at C:/ when specifying a file path on your hard drive.

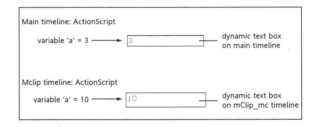

Each variable is associated with the timeline on which it was initialized.

13. Test the movie to see how Flash implements this:

Both text fields will show the same values as they did before. Although both text areas appear an a variable, one is showing 10 and the other is showing 3 because the two different variables have different *scope*. The a variable spawned from the main timeline applies to the main timeline, and the a variable spawned inside mClip_mc applies to the movie clip only.

Another way to think of this is that the absolute path is actually part of the variable name. So you have two different variables named _root.a and _root.mClip_mc.a. This is how Flash handles the situation internally, and closer to the way Flash actually thinks.

14. Try running the movie again, but this time select the Control ➤ Debug Movie menu option instead of Control ➤ Test Movie and take a look in the Debugger window:

Once again, Flash is showing you the path to each of your movie components: the path for the main stage/timeline is _level0, and the path to the movie clip is _level0.mClip_mc, showing you that mClip_mc is inside _level0.

Treat _level0 as the same as _root. There are one or two subtle differences, but let's not get bogged down by them right now.

As the icons suggest, the main or root timeline is just another movie clip: _level0 is represented by the same kind of icon as mClip_mc. This is something worth remembering as you advance further into Flash because all the things you learn to do with movie clips can also be applied to the root movie itself.

15. If you click the Variables tab on the left side of the Debugger window, and have one of the paths selected, Flash will display the values you've assigned to your variables.

With _level0.mClip_mc selected you'll see that the value of a is 10, and then select _level0, you'll see that here it has a value of 3. (You'll also see a variable that represents the version of the Flash Player that is running. This can be ignored because it doesn't affect your programming.)

Although you have two variables called a, one is called _root.a and the other is called _root.mClip_mc.a. Each variable is defined on a separate timeline, and exists in only one place. The version of a inside mClip_mc only applies to that movie clip.

The way Flash handles variables per timeline ("timeline variables") are exceptionally useful because they allow you to reuse a movie clip. For example, imagine you built a movie clip that controlled a single space invader using the internal, movie clip-specific, variables—invaderPos, invaderDead, and firePhotonTorpedo. If you then put another ten alien movie clips onto the stage, you would have ten space invaders with ten sets of discrete, internal, timeline variables, *all* being individually controlled.

Accessing variables from different code scopes

Just as variables have scope, code blocks have their own scope as well. Let's look at this a little deeper before you try it out.

Recall that scope in code applies to a code block in the same way the subject of a paragraph as the first thing that is mentioned. The following is a spoken language equivalent of scope:

John is a fast runner. Someday he might make the Olympics.

You define the scope of the paragraph ("John") so you can later refer to it in general terms such as "him" or "he."

In ActionScript syntax (noting that ActionScript doesn't have "he" but instead uses the much more general term "this"), the same thing would be:

```
John is a fast runner {
  Someday this might make the Olympics;
}
```

John and this are two ways of saying the same thing. Let's look at how you would refer to subjects *other* than John if you wanted to refer to them in a block that was scoping John.

John is a fast runner. Someday he might make the Olympics. Paul is good at swimming, so they better start clearing the mantle for all that gold.

Paul is not the subject of the paragraph, so you can't use "he" in the same way to represent Paul instead of John.

If you are referring to the person named Paul, who is here with you in the conversation, you just say "Paul." In Flash, this is the same as the subject being on the same timeline as the code. You don't need to specify where the subject is because by referencing it in this way it is understood that it is on the same timeline as the code.

So you would have:

```
John is a fast runner {
  Someday this might make the Olympics;
  Paul is good at swimming;
}
```

If the subject weren't on the same timeline as the code, you would have to specify which subject you mean.

```
John is a fast runner {
  Someday this might make the Olympics;
  Paul (the one who is in your presence) is
➥good at swimming;
  Paul who lives at number 32 down the road
➥is not into organized sports, but prefers
➥treking.
}
```

So how does that convert to Flash programming? When you write code that is in a code block that can cause the code to have a different scope to code outside the block (i.e. event handlers) you have to take into account *where the code is scoped*.

Add the following code (lines 2 onward) to frame 1 of the root timeline.

```
a = 3;
trace("-from _root-");
trace(this.a);
trace(a);
trace(_root.a);
trace(mClip_mc.a);
trace(this.mClip_mc.a);
trace(_root.mClip_mc.a);
```

The trace() action allows you to ask Flash to show you some of its variable values during Test Movie. You are asking it to tell you the values it sees for code that is not within a code block, so it will look at where the code is: _root. Even if you understand scope completely, you will be a little surprised at the result.

Whether you use this.a, _root.a, or a doesn't matter in this case because you are already at _root, so this becomes _root and anything with no dot path is taken to be in the code scope, which is _root again.

However, the code can't find the variable a in mClip_mc. The three attempts to read the version of a in mClip_mc all give undefined, which is Flash's way of saying "either it doesn't exist or it doesn't have a value" but it **must** have a value because you set it to 10 on the first frame of mClip_mc! The reason it does not equal 10 has nothing to do with scope. You may think Flash runs code concurrently, but it doesn't. The code attached to _root is run first, the code in any timelines on _root runs next, and any code on timelines nested in those clips is run after that. When this code first runs, there *is no* variable a in mClip_mc because the code to set it up hasn't run yet! To fix this:

1. Go into mClip_mc and delete the code layer. This deletes the a = 10; code.

2. Add the line myClip_mc.a = 10; as part of the current script as shown.

```
a = 3
mClip_mc.a = 10;
trace("–from _root–");
trace(this.a);
trace(a);
trace(_root.a);
trace(mClip_mc.a);
trace(this.mClip_mc.a);
trace(_root.mClip_mc.a);
```

Putting as much of your code in one place as possible means you do not get caught out by order-of-execution problems, which are very difficult errors to find and fix in large projects because they occur at the start of a frame but are corrected by the end of the frame. (In fact, the error conditions only exist for a few milliseconds!)

This time, you define everything before the trace() actions run and you will see:

The three versions of your path to a on the timeline mClip_mc also all work. Note that adding this.a and a is the same thing if you are already at this (which is always the case for code that is not within a code block). You *never* have to add this outside a code block.

Now let's see how a change of *code* scope will affect this.

The preceding bit was tricky, and the next one is trickier still. If you don't understand all of it, come back later when you have finished the chapter and re-read it. Don't worry if it takes time to sink in…knowing this bit well is something that until recently would have been considered part of an advanced Flash users repertoire.

3. Change the script as follows:

```
mClip_mc.onEnterFrame = function() {
    trace("–from mClip_mc's event handler
➥block–");
    trace(this.a);
    trace(a);
    trace(_root.a);
    trace(this._parent.a);
    trace(_parent.a);
    delete (this.onEnterFrame);
};
a = 3;
mClip_mc.a = 10;
trace("–from _root–");
trace(this.a);
trace(a);
trace(_root.a);
trace(mClip_mc.a);
trace(this.mClip_mc.a);
trace(_root.mClip_mc.a);
```

The scope of the code within the block is changed from _root to mClip_mc in the same way our athletic friend becomes the subject of a paragraph. This time this actually does something because the code scope and where it is are two different things.

```
▼ Output
--from _root--
3
3
3
10
10
10
--from mClip's event handler block--
10
3
3
3
undefined
```

In particular, note the following:

- Using a and this.a allows you to look at the two versions of a on the two different timelines. Although this is a cool way to quickly access different variables, it is also a quick and easy way to access the *wrong* variable!

- The last pair of dot paths refer to this._parent and _parent. The parent timeline is the timeline a movie clip is on, and the first version tries to access mClip_mc's parent, _root. The second dot path attempts to access the root timeline's parent, but given that _root is the lowest level, it has *no parent,* so you get no value or undefined.

Before you put this into practice, let's think about the dynamic animation we promised you at the start of the chapter.

Dynamic animation

For dynamic animation to work, you have to be able to target a movie clip and alter some aspects of its appearance or action. To do that, you work with a movie's properties. You can view these properties by looking at the movie in Debug mode.

Viewing a movie clip's properties

1. Open one of your movies—preferably one with a movie clip attached to the main timeline.

2. Choose the Control ➤ Debug Movie menu option to display the Debugger window with the movie in test mode.

3. Click the Properties tab (about half way down on the left side of the Debugger window) and extend the size of the Properties pane if necessary.

   When you get the Debugger window up, you'll see something like this, though you may have to adjust the size of the window. (If the Call Stack is covering it, drag the call stack title bar downward.)

The top-left pane shows you the hierarchy of movie clips in the movie. It also gives you the path for each nested movie clip, starting at the root with the main timeline, and down to the movie clip inside Scene 1. Note the dot separating the nested clip from the timeline:

Movie clips have more aspects than just the variables that you define and set. The names and values shown in the bottom pane of the Debugger window when you click the different movie clips are the properties of the movie clip. All movie clips will have this same set of properties, but the values for the properties in an individual movie clip will differ.

Essentially, properties are just like variables except that they relate to a particular aspect of the movie clip such as its size, rotation, position on the stage, or whether all its frames have streamed in yet. There's one difference between variables and properties that you may already have guessed. If you change a property of your movie clip at any stage, you'll alter its appearance on the screen—it'll be animated, because animation is just that: creating change. You're going to do this in a moment with dot notation and event handlers, but first let's try doing it *manually*.

Actually, a variable is also an instance, much like a movie clip, but it has only one property called value. Because a variable has only one property, you don't need to tell Flash which property to access. This makes it look like a variable doesn't have any properties and is somehow different.

If you go to the Properties tab on the Debugger while the movie is being tested, you can directly see the effects of changing properties. For example, click the box in the table to the right of the _x property. You will see it turn into a text entry box. Enter the value 10.

_visible	true
_width	25
_x	10

You should see the movie clip suddenly move to somewhere near the left side of the stage (you may have to move the Debugger window to find it). Do this several more times, but add 5 to the value every time, so you enter 15, 20, 25, and 30.

See that? Rather than a sudden change of position, you are changing the _x property by small values, so the change in position is regulated and looks as if the movie clip is *moving* from left to right. This is the basis of ActionScript-based animation. Spend a moment trying to change other properties, but don't change them too far from their original values. (You might make the clip shoot off the edge of the screen and you'll never find it again!) This is by far the best way to get an idea of what properties allow you to do. Notice also the effects of reducing _x (clip moves to the left), increasing _y (clip moves down) and decreasing _y (clip moves up).

The Flash coordinates are based on print conventions rather than math conventions, so the origin is at the top-left corner (the start position of line 1 in a print based page), and not in the bottom left. You will see this if you set both _x and _y to zero—the clip will jump to the top left corner of the stage. This is of course why the _y property seems to act the wrong way round to anyone with a math background—in a print based layout, the y axis points downward.

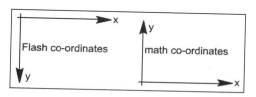

Feels like you're a puppet master controlling a mannequin doesn't it? But you won't be there when folks are looking at your content online, so you can't do it manually then. Instead you have another puppet master that you can leave instructions with about what you want to happen. Your proxy puppet master is Flash, and the instructions are ActionScript.

Dynamic animation with dot notation

You can now use your knowledge of levels, variables, and properties to execute a simple example of a new kind of animation and control. You'll create a dynamic animation that responds to user keyboard inputs.

1. Open a new movie, change the background color to black, and make sure that the stage is the default 550 pixels x 400 pixels.

2. Create a new movie clip symbol called spaceship, rename the movie clip symbol's default layer space and draw a spaceship that looks like it just emerged from a 1980s video game. Don't make the spacecraft too complicated because you're aiming for a retro feel here. Also, because Flash will be

moving your ship around the screen, it will be easier and smoother if the spaceship has a less complex shape. Make sure the center line of the spaceship is also the center of the movie clip (denoted by a little cross):

3. In the root timeline (remember, that's the timeline on the main stage), rename the existing layer ship and insert a new layer called actions.

4. In the new ship layer, drag an instance of your spaceship movie clip onto the stage. Position it at the bottom of the stage and scale it so that it looks like player 1's spacecraft from a Space Invaders arcade game. Using the Properties panel, give the spaceship movie clip an instance name ship_mc (you will see why you added the _mc to ship_mc in a moment):

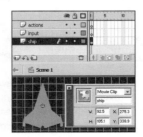

You want to be able to move this spacecraft left and right as it dodges the alien hordes in its epic battle to save the planet. To do this you need to know two things about this spaceship:

■ Its position

■ How fast it will move

To get this information, all you need to know is the spaceship movie clip's _x property, which is its position on the x-axis of the screen—how far from the right of the screen the spaceship is. The ship is at the extreme left when _x=0, and the extreme

right when _x=550. Once you have this value, you can assign it to a variable called shipPos, which you'll use to keep track of where the ship is.

5. In the root timeline's actions layer, at frame 1, open the Actions panel and type:

shipPos =

6. Click the Insert Target Path button (top of the Actions panel) and then make sure the Relative radio button from the Insert Target Path window is selected.

You'll now see that the paths are shown from _root, giving you an idea of where the ship instance is located from the main timeline of the movie.

7. Select ship_mc as the target path, and then click OK.

8. Flash has now added your path for you, and you now see

shipPos = this.ship_mc

Let's consider why you need this as your path to ship_mc. As we mentioned earlier, this is a keyword that is shorthand for the current scope in a code block. When you are outside a code block, you don't need it. Whether you keep it or not is up to you, but we will delete it.

> *Another way to think about this is the file structure analogy: you are already in the folder (timeline) containing your chosen clip, so you don't need a path.*

shipPos = ship_mc

9. Add a dot after _mc. As soon as you do this, you will see a drop-down menu appear. When you add _mc to the end of any instance name, Flash knows

you mean a movie clip, and this means Flash is able to provide you with more help than it usually does. Long-term users don't tend to use the _mc because it prevents them from using pure camel case, but because you are dipping your foot into longish scripts for the first time in this chapter, you will use it for now.

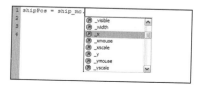

Find the _x and select it (you can use the keyboard up and down arrows to scroll, it tends to be faster). Your ActionScript should now read:

```
shipPos = ship_mc._x;
```

If you'd like to see the other properties available to manipulate movie clips and other objects, open the **Built-in Classes ➤ Movie ➤ MovieClip ➤** Properties book in the Actions Toolbox:

You'll use some of these in the next exercise.

The ActionScript you've added will equate the shipPos variable with the value of the ship movie clip's x (horizontal) position.

You need to assign two more variables: speed, to set how fast your spacecraft will move (in pixels per keypress) and shipDead, which will be either true or false depending on whether your ship is dead.

10. Still in the first frame of the actions layer, add the following ActionScript:

```
shipDead = false;
speed = 5;
```

This sets the value of shipDead to false, and the value of speed to 5, leaving this frame's finished ActionScript looking like this:

11. This is your *initialization* part of the code, so it is a good idea to label it as such. To do that, add a comment. A comment is any line that starts with two forward slashes (//). Add such a line at the start of the code so far.

```
// Initialize
shipPos = ship_mc._x;
shipDead = false;
speed = 5;
```

Notice that the comment code is grayed out, indicating that Flash will ignore this line.

Now you'll add the *input* and *movement* part. How should you do it? Because its something you want the ship to respond to *every frame,* you want to use the MovieClip.onEnterFrame event. This will run every time the play head enters a new frame interval.

The onEnterFrame *event is one of many event handlers that respond to an internal event. You can create basic interactivity with buttons that respond to user events, but for more advanced stuff, you need also to be able to run code depending on what Flash itself is doing, and internal event triggers is how this is implemented.*

The onEnterFrame *is the most used internal event in Flash because it is what you attach code to if you want the code to run every frame. Code that runs every frame can be used to create animation by moving a movie clip a little bit (by varying properties) every frame—the scripted version of what you did earlier in the Debugger.*

Although this event is called onEnterFrame, *it will occur even if you have a stationary play head. It will occur every frame even if you have a single 1-frame timeline and a playhead that doesn't move out of the current frame.*

12. It is customary to add your event scripts (and in fact, any code that uses the function block) as the first thing in a listing, so give yourself a little room above the current script by adding a few blank lines.

```
1
2
3
4 // Initialize
5 shipPos = ship_mc._x;
6 shipDead = false;
7 speed = 5;
8
```

13. Insert the following lines of code beginning at line 1. When you add the dot at line 1, you will see the drop-down menu appear again. This time, continue writing as far as ".on." You will see that Flash is constantly looking for the ending that best fits what you have started to write, and by the time it sees the ".on," it has picked the right bit for you. This feature is called *auto complete*. Guess why.

```
1 ship_mc.onEnterFrame = function(){
2
3 }
4 // Initialize
5 shipPos = ship_mc._x;
6 shipDead = false;
7 speed = 5;
8
```

This is your event handler block, and you will start inserting your code from the blank line at line 2. Note that you could have used the Insert Target Path window to add the ship_mc part of ship_mc.onEnterFrame if you wanted to.

Also worth noting is that you are now writing within an event block, and the scope has been defined at the start of the block as the movie clip ship. This means that if you want to access any of its properties, you should use this. If you want to access any variables on the main timeline, you should not use the this.

14. The first thing you should do is check that the left and right arrow keys are pressed. To do that, you can use the **Key** class. This is used to detect key presses on the keyboard. Add the following code at line 2.

```
if (Key.
```

Make sure you use a capital "K"—all classes in Flash start with an uppercase character, although it can be difficult to make out the difference between K and k. As soon as you hit the period, Flash reveals the auto complete choices again. Either scroll down to or add enough of the text for Flash to find isDown.

```
1 ship_mc.onEnterFrame = function(){
2     if (Key.isDown(
3                      Key.isDown( keyCode )
4 }
5 // Initialize
6 shipPos = ship_mc._x;
```

Wow! Even more help! Flash is asking you to enter a key code for the key you want to detect as isDown. You want the left arrow key. The keycode for this is Key.LEFT. Start typing it, and you will see auto complete come to your aid. When you have finished, make sure you have this line, and press the Enter key to start the next line.

```
1 ship_mc.onEnterFrame = func
2     if (Key.isDown(Key.LEFT
3     |
4
```

You are now starting a *decision* block. The code in the if will only be executed if the key you specified is down. You want to move the ship_mc to the left, and to do that, you have to subtract the variable *speed* from the currently scoped clip's _x value, which gives you the listing shown on the left of the following graphic. Press the Enter key and on the last line, close the decision block, and click the Check Syntax button and the Auto Format icon to correct and tidy up your code (shown on the right of the following graphic).

You can now test the movie. You should see that you can move the spaceship to the left.

15. Go back to the script, and repeat step 16 to add another `if` below the one you already have. This time, you look for a right arrow key and add speed.

```
ship_mc.onEnterFrame = function() {
    if (Key.isDown(Key.LEFT)) {
        this._x = this._x-speed;
    }
    if (Key.isDown(Key.RIGHT)) {
        this._x = this._x+speed;
    }
};
// Initialize
shipPos = ship_mc._x;
shipDead = false;
speed = 5;
```

16. Test your movie. You can use the *LEFT* and *RIGHT* arrow keys to move the spaceship left and right. How cool is *that*?

> *You can vary the speed value to get a faster ship movement. Set it to around 10 and increase the frame rate to 18 frames per second. (Double click the little box that gives the frame rate on the lower edge of the timeline to reach the Document Properties if you decide to do this.)*

This is a pretty basic movement, but you're using the main principles of dot notation to alter the properties of the spaceship movie clip and are

therefore able to move it at will—its movement is not fixed, as it would be in a simple motion tween. This kind of dynamic animation is often called **sprite movement**. Furthermore, you are mixing it with scope, using and omitting the `this` within the event handler to choose between the scope of the event handler (`with`) and the timeline the code is on (`without`). Although the former skill seems to be sexier at the moment, it's the latter that will make you an expert if you work on it.

You haven't finished yet. Next, you're going to simulate the effect of your spaceship being killed by the marauding hordes of alien invaders. You're not going to create the aliens themselves, but your knowledge will soon be sufficient for you to do that. When your ship is destroyed, you want to change the value of the shipdead variable you initialized in the movie's first frame: you want to change its value from false to true.

17. In the root timeline, select the keyframe in layer actions and open the Actions panel.

18. Add the following code to the lines:

```
if (Key.isDown(Key.SPACE)) {
    shipDead = true;
}
```

After correcting and formatting your script you will have the following:

```
on (keyPress "<Left>") {
    _root.ship._x = _root.ship._x-speed;
}
on (keyPress "<Right>") {
    _root.ship._x = _root.ship._x+speed;
}
on (keyPress "<Space>") {
    _root.shipdead = true;
}
```

You've set the movie up for the entire user input. Now you need to make the spaceship display change in response to the *SPACE* bar being pressed. You've just attached the code to the *SPACE* bar for the sake of this exercise. It's actually intended to simulate the outcome of alien fire hitting your spacecraft.

19. Open the spaceship movie clip and create a new layer called actions. Extend both to frame 11.

Select frame 11 of the actions layer and add a keyframe. Attach a stop() action on this keyframe.

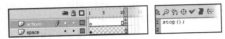

20. On the space layer, place a keyframe at frames 3, 5, 7, 9, and 11.

21. Delete the ship graphic on the keyframes at frames 3, 7, and 11. Your timeline should now look like the one shown in the following graphic. If you press play on the controller, you will see the spaceship flash in a typical bloop-bloop-blippity-bloop: *Game Over!!!* retro video game fashion.

22. You now need to add some code to animate to the death sequence when the *SPACE* is pressed. Go back to the main script on frame 1 of the root timeline. You should be getting good at this, so go right ahead and change the code as shown.

```
ship_mc.onEnterFrame = function() {
if (Key.isDown(Key.LEFT)) {
    this._x = this._x-speed;
}
if (Key.isDown(Key.RIGHT)) {
    this._x = this._x+speed;
}
if (Key.isDown(Key.SPACE)) {
    shipDead = true;
    this.play();
    delete (this.onEnterFrame);
}
};
// Initialize
ship_mc.stop();
shipPos = ship_mc._x;
shipDead = false;
speed = 10;
```

```
1  ship_mc.onEnterFrame = function() {
2      if (Key.isDown(Key.LEFT)) {
3          this._x = this._x-speed;
4      }
5      if (Key.isDown(Key.RIGHT)) {
6          this._x = this._x+speed;
7      }
8      if (Key.isDown(Key.SPACE)) {
9          shipDead = true;
10         this.play();
11         delete (this.onEnterFrame);
12     }
13 };
14 // Initialize
15 ship_mc.stop();
16 shipPos = ship_mc._x;
17 shipDead = false;
18 speed = 10;
19
```

So what do the new lines do? Line 15 stops the timeline of ship_mc, so it will sit at frame 1 until you press *SPACE* bar. When you press *SPACE* bar, the code block containing lines 9, 10, and 11 will run, of which 10 and 11 are new. Line 10 causes the timeline you stopped in line 15 to start playing. You also need to stop running the onEnterFrame script, and line 11 does just that by deleting the event handler. This means that the spaceship really is dead—the software "brain" that controls it via the onEnterFrame is effectively destroyed, and all that is left is the exploding ship hull...the flashing graphic that remains on the screen for a short time afterward.

Notice that you changed the speed to 10. This is because the ship didn't seem to be moving fast enough. It also shows an important point—you *could* have set lines 3 and 6 to:

```
this._x = this._x-5;
this._x = this._x+5;
```

To do that, however, you would have to find every 5 and change it to 10. That would have required a long script and been an error-prone and difficult task. It's far better to use variables for all your values rather than literal numbers because then you can change them in one place—the Initialization code section.

Some of you might be thinking "hang on though, what does the shipDead variable do? It is set to false when the ship is alive, but as soon as it dies, we set it to true, but shipDead is never used in the script to control my spaceship, and I can't see why it is even needed...what gives?"

Well, that is all true. shipDead *is not* needed by ship_mc itself. In computer graphics, one of the problems is that no graphic can actually "see" another graphic. You can't say "hey aliens, when you see the player is dead, you can all go back into formation and sit there gloating for a bit." The alien graphics are *blind* in that they only know what they are told through variables—they do not see the screen that you see, where it is obvious something has just happened. shipDead is such a variable. It is a signal or "flag" to other movie clips in the game that the player has just died. Other graphics "see" whether the player is still alive or dead through looking at *this variable* rather than the ship_mc graphic itself. In the next section, we will show you how to wire this flag to another movie clip that shows the standard "game over" message when the ship dies.

> *Although you are still beginners, in this example, we tried to show you some advanced techniques. The way you kill the spaceship by destroying its event handler is a powerful technique. The way the shipDead flag is used to signal a game condition to other graphics is also an advanced motion graphics technique. Finally, the way almost all the code for your animation is in one script is the preferred way of writing scripts in Flash MX 2004, and something that has been used by advanced coders since Flash MX. Readers of the last edition of this book will have noted a change of emphasis regarding the code, and this is for a specific reason—the standard of Flash coding has gone up considerably, and some previously advanced techniques can now be considered at beginner or intermediate level.*

Creating advanced animation communication schemes

Once you have seen how to create code for simple script based animations, you soon realize the next stage of interactivity is to get your various event handlers to talk to each other. There is an advanced scheme that allows you to do this via an event driven route, and this uses *listeners*. This is the scheme you will use when you have large amounts of code and need to start making it hyper-efficient. For now though, you will use shipDead as a flag that signifies that ship_mc is no more.

Creating a "game over" graphic

1. On the main timeline, insert a new layer named text between the ship and actions layers.

2. Insert a dynamic text field in the center of the stage on the new layer. If you have any retro-looking pixel fonts, use one of those later, but for now, you will use _sans. Set the text color to white, and make sure it is not selectable and doesn't have a border (via the Properties panel's Selectable icon and Show Border Around Text icon, neither of which should be selected.

3. Inside this text field, click the Align Center icon on the Properties panel then enter the text game over!! using italics.

4. The TextField class associated with out text field *does* not have an onEnterFrame event, so to attach one to your text you need to make it into a movie

clip (which does have this event). Select the text and press F8 to make it a movie clip. Call it Game Text.

5. Using the Properties panel, call the instance overText_mc. You also want to name the text field instance inside this movie clip, so double-click the movie clip, select the text field and name it overText_txt.

6. You can now start controlling this new clip. Add the following lines to the initialization part of the script on frame 1 of the root timeline:

```
// Initialize
ship_mc.stop();
overText_mc.overText_txt.text = "";
shipPos = ship_mc._x;
shipDead = false;
speed = 10;
```

This new line uses dot notation to find the embedded text field gameText_txt and make it show no text. The next step is to add an onEnterFrame to gameText_mc that keeps looking out for the shipDead flag and responds accordingly to it.

7. Insert the following code at the beginning of the script:

```
overText_mc.onEnterFrame = function() {
  if (shipDead) {
    this.overText_txt.text = "game over!!";
    delete (this.onEnterFrame);
  }
};
```

This code attaches an onEnterFrame script to overText_mc. This checks the value of shipDead every frame. If it is true, then the if block will run, causing the overText_txt text to change to game

over!! The if block then deletes the onEnterFrame (because there is no reason to continue checking).

8. Test the movie again. You'll see that when you press the SPACE bar, the spaceship will flash and the game over text will appear. (You can add the obligatory "blooop blooop…blooop blooop…ping!" noise later if you feel the need.)

(Note that if you try and publish the movie as it stands, the keys won't work until the user clicks the screen.)

What happens when you press SPACE bar is that the root timeline sets the shipdead variable to true. The gameText_mc movie clip is constantly looking at this variable's status via the onEnterFrame check that's attached to it. As soon as it sees that it's true, it changes the text embedded inside it.

Here is the full listing.

```
1  overText_mc.onEnterFrame = function() {
2      if (shipDead) {
3          this.overText_txt.text = "game over!!";
4          delete (this.onEnterFrame);
5      }
6  };
7  ship_mc.onEnterFrame = function() {
8      if (Key.isDown(Key.LEFT)) {
9          this._x = this._x-speed;
10     }
11     if (Key.isDown(Key.RIGHT)) {
12         this._x = this._x+speed;
13     }
14     if (Key.isDown(Key.SPACE)) {
15         shipDead = true;
16         this.play();
17         delete (this.onEnterFrame);
18     }
19 };
20 // Initialize
21 ship_mc.stop();
22 overText_mc.overText_txt.text = "";
23 shipPos = ship_mc._x;
24 shipDead = false;
25 speed = 10;
26
```

Let's summarize how it works. It may be a good idea to see if you can explain the code to yourself before looking at your description.

■ The Initialization section starts at line 21. It causes the ship_mc clip to stop at frame 1 (its "I am alive" graphic appearance) and sets the game over text overText_txt (which is embedded in overText_mc) to show no text. Finally, it sets variables shipDead and speed to false and 10 respectively.

- There are two onEnterFrame scripts that run every frame. The first one is for overText_mc. This constantly looks for changes in the flag shipDead, and sets the text overText_txt to "game over!!" when it changes to true. When this happens, the script also stops checking for changes.

- The second script moves your ship via changes to its _x property, depending on whether the left and right keyboard arrow keys are pressed. It also checks for the SPACE bar being pressed, which you are using to simulate the ship being destroyed. This causes the ship_mc timeline to start playing its death sequence. When this occurs, the script also sets shipDead to true to inform the rest of the code of its demise. It also stops itself from running anymore.

> Notice that the script was not written from line 1 down, but in the order that the script will actually run—initialization followed by the events. Also note that at the end of your animation, none of the code is left running.

In addition to controlling the spaceship's position on the x-axis, you could just as easily control any other property of the movie clip. For example, using the rotation property, you could get the ship to rotate clockwise and counter clockwise in response to the arrow keys. You could also create a slider and use its position to vary the alpha property of a movie clip instance.

We mentioned earlier the alien hordes you'll need to create in order to complete your game. Each alien would need to have variables such as invaderPos, invaderDead, and firePhotonTorpedo. Controlling the properties of all your invaders individually is much simpler than you may imagine, as the next brief example will illustrate.

> If you want to know more about advanced animation, games are a good way to do it. The skills used in creating Flash games are the same ones you use in creating advanced website interfaces. Due to the "show us how to create a space invaders game!" feedback we got from the early editions of Foundation Flash, we created a simple Space Invaders game in Foundation ActionScript. Then we got requests for instructions how to create a Flash version of a thousand games. In Flash Games Most Wanted, the author of this chapter takes the concepts shown here to their logical conclusion by writing a Flash version of the retro game Defender, complete with optimized game engine and dynamic backing soundtrack.
>
> Tip: You can download the source files of either of these books if you just want to have a look at the code—it's free, so take 'em while they're hot!
>
> Also included in the downloads for this chapter is a more advanced version of the same script, this time using optimized graphics and code. The file is called spacehip02.fla.

Armed as you are with your newfound knowledge of input text fields, dot notation, and 'sprite' animation, you're now ready to implement the changes for your Smiler movie.

Making Smiler age-sensitive

If you don't have your fully functional version of Smiler saved, you can download a ready-made Smiler in the downloadable files for this book on our website.

> On our website, you will also find the finished FLA you will be developing as smilerAge.fla, and a more advanced version (which shows how you can extend it a little as smilerAgeAdvanced.fla).

Guess Smiler's age

Let's remind ourselves what the requirements specification was:

- 1.1—Define a variable, *age*, with values between 1 and 99.
- 2.1—Input a numeric text entry from the user.
- 2.2—Assign this text entry to a variable called *guess*.
- 3.1—Create a new variable, *difference*, which is equal to *age—guess*.
- 3.2—If difference is negative, make it positive.
- 3.3—Go to a frame number that's equal to difference in the Smiler animated movie clip.
- 4.1—If difference is zero, then stop. Otherwise repeat from 2.1.

Let's walk through this step by step.

The first thing you need to do is get Flash to come up with an age for Smiler that it can compare to the user's guess. It would be a good idea to make this a random value, so that it's different for every run of the game. You can do this easily using Flash's Math.random() function.

Math.random() returns a number between 0 and 1. Because you require a number between 1 and 99, you'll multiply Math.random() by the maximum required number:

```
age=Math.random()*99;
```

This will return a number between 1 and 99 with decimal points. To force this to be a whole number, you use Math.floor(), which returns a rounded-down number:

```
age=Math.floor(Math.random()*99);
```

You want to generate the random number at the start of your game, during initialization, so that the age variable is populated, ready, and waiting for the user's guess.

1. In frame 1 of the actions layer in the existing Smiler movie, you already have this ActionScript:

```
1  leftButton.onRelease = function() {
2      if (smilerFrame>1) {
3          smilerFrame = smilerFrame-1;
4          face.prevFrame();
5      }
6  };
7  rightButton.onRelease = function() {
8      if (smilerFrame<15) {
9          smilerFrame = smilerFrame+1;
10         face.nextFrame();
11     }
12 };
13 face.gotoAndStop("neutral");
14 smilerFrame = 8;
15
```

You want to assign a new variable, age.

2. Delete the smilerFrame = 8; line, and replace it with the following code:

```
age = Math.floor (Math.random ()*99);
```

Testing the movie will not make Smiler do anything new at the moment, but you have completed 1.1, so let's carry on with the rest of your specification.

- 2.1—Input a numeric text entry from the user.
- 2.2—Assign this text entry to a variable called guess.

3. You need to change your FLA so that it can now accept text input. Delete the left button and its associated text "better." Move the enter button and its text label to the bottom right as shown, changing it so that it appears as shown:

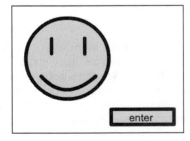

Change the instance name of the button to guessButton_btn. Make sure when you do this that you select the button and not the static text above it.

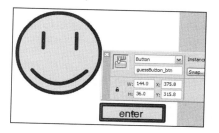

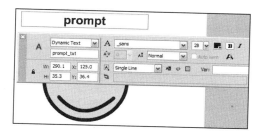

Add a new Input text field next to the enter button with properties as shown.

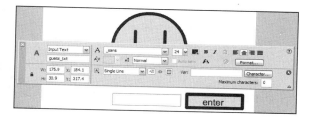

You also want to prevent the user from entering anything except numbers between 1 and 99, so set the maximum number of characters to 2 (Properties panel, far right) and click the Character button so the user can only enter the digits 0 to 9 as shown.

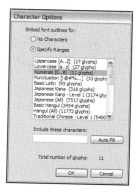

You could also do with some feedback from Smiler, so change the text above him to a dynamic text field. Give it an instance name of prompt_txt, and make sure it is not selectable. Enter the text prompt in it.

4. Delete the existing button scripts, add the following event handler for your new button guessButton_btn, and add a new line after your age definition at the bottom of the script.

```
guessButton_btn.onRelease = function() {
  userGuess = Number(guess_txt.text);
  trace(userGuess);
};
face.gotoAndStop("neutral");
age = Math.floor(Math.random()*99);
prompt_txt.text = "Guess my age!";
```

A pretty big change, there's only two lines left from the original! So what does it do?

■ The guessButton_btn onRelease handler converts the user's guess into a number and traces it back to you.

■ The last line causes the prompt text to appear with Guess my age! at the start of the game.

Not very clever so far.

In this step you will cover 3.1.

5. 3.1—Create a new variable, difference, which is equal to age—guess.

```
guessButton_btn.onRelease = function() {
  userGuess = Number(guess_txt.text);
  trace("your guess:"+userGuess);
  difference = age-userGuess;
  trace("you are out by:"+difference);
};
face.gotoAndStop("neutral");
age = Math.floor(Math.random()*99);
prompt_txt.text = "Guess my age!";
```

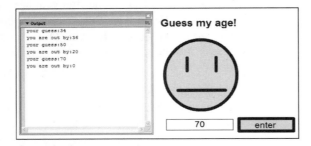

This time users can see the number they are inputting plus how far off they are, which is your variable difference.

Next up, 3.2 and 3.3.

- 3.2—If difference is negative, make it positive.

- 3.3—Go to a frame number that's equal to difference in the Smiler animated movie clip.

You want the Smiler movie clip to have 98 frames because that's the maximum amount you can be wrong by when you guess its age.

6. Inside the Smiler movie clip, add frames (using *F5*) to the left of the neutral keyframe to shift it up to frame 49. Then extend the layer to frame 98 as shown in the following graphic by adding frames to the right of neutral. Finally, extend the eyes and face layers up to frame 98:

Add the following new lines.

```
guessButton_btn.onRelease = function() {
  userGuess = Number(guess_txt.text);
  trace("your guess:"+userGuess);
  difference = age-userGuess;
  trace("you are out by:"+difference);
  if (difference<0) {
  difference = Math.abs(difference);
  }
  face.gotoAndStop(difference);
};
face.gotoAndStop("neutral");
age = Math.floor(Math.random()*99);
prompt_txt.text = "Guess my age!";
```

This time, you will see Smiler actually respond to your guesses by getting happier/sadder depending on how close you are to his age. Math.abs(difference) gives you the absolute value of difference, that is, the value as a raw number without a plus or minus. The number is always positive, so this line covers 3.2. The gotoAndStop() converts this positive number into a frame number (notice that you are using a variable containing a frame number here rather than a label). This gives you 3.3.

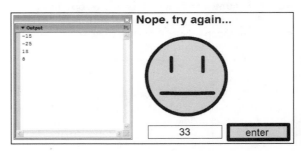

Almost there!

- 4.1—If difference is zero, then stop. Otherwise repeat from 2.1.

7. Add this code to do it.

```
guessButton_btn.onRelease = function() {
userGuess = Number(guess_txt.text);
trace("your guess:"+userGuess);
difference = age-userGuess;
trace("you are out by:"+difference);
if (difference<0) {
    difference = Math.abs(difference);
}
```

```
if (difference == 0) {
    prompt_txt.text = "You got it!!";
    face.gotoAndStop("happy");
    face.onEnterFrame = function() {
        this._rotation =
this._rotation+rotationSpeed;
    };
} else {
    face.gotoAndStop(difference);
    prompt_txt.text = "Nope. try again...";
  }
};
face.gotoAndStop("neutral");
age = Math.floor(Math.random()*99);
prompt_txt.text = "Guess my age!";
rotationSpeed = 10;
```

Well, actually, there's a bit more than you need.

The first thing you added is an `if` that looks at whether difference is zero. If it is, you prompt the user with an appropriately upbeat message. You also add an `onEnterframe` that makes the Smiler face do a little rotation trick to reward the user for getting the right answer. As part of this trick, you define a rotation speed at the end of the script.

> *The double equal sign (==) means "check that the left side is equal to the right side." It doesn't make the difference equal zero, as a single equal sign (=) does. You should always use the double equal sign within an `if` condition; using a single equal sign instead is one of the most common mistakes in ActionScript!*

The code that contains the instructions of what to do when the user doesn't get it right is now in an else block of the `if`—if the user doesn't get it right, you continue doing much the same as you did last time.

And that's it. You've followed your top-down requirements specification, solved your problem, and finished your game. Here's the listing after it has been polished up and made a little more user friendly.

```
guessButton_btn.onRelease = function() {
  userGuess = Number(guess_txt.text);
  difference = age-userGuess;
  if (difference<0) {
    difference = Math.abs(difference);
}
if (difference == 0) {
    prompt_txt.text = "You got it!!";
    face.gotoAndStop("happy");
    face.onEnterFrame = function() {
        this._rotation =
this._rotation+rotationSpeed;
    };
} else {
    face.gotoAndStop(difference);
    prompt_txt.text = "Nope. try again...";
  }
};
guess_txt.onSetFocus = function() {
    this.text = "";
};
//
//Initialize
face.gotoAndStop("neutral");
age = Math.floor(Math.random()*99);
prompt_txt.text = "Guess my age!";
rotationSpeed = 10;
```

You got rid of the trace() actions, added a little event handler that fires when the user clicks the text field ("gives it input focus"), and clears the last guess value.

You might want to give Smiler a bit more personality. For example, you could have a dynamic text box that displays a statement showing how Smiler feels about your last guess. If difference is greater than 30 it could say "Miles away!" If the difference is less than 30, it could say "Getting warmer!" And when the user guesses within 10 of the age it could say "Red hot!"

All this can be done by adding if and else actions that relate to the variable you've assigned to the text field. There are many other things that you can add to this program to make Smiler more intelligent, just using the commands and techniques you've now learned.

> We have added something like this in the FLA SmilerAdvanced. *Have a look at it if you want to see how to make Smiler's responses more appropriate.*

You've now reached the top of the intermediate learning slope. We haven't told you everything you need to know, but you now know all the basic principles and have had enough practice to allow you to quickly learn other structures that will increase your ability.

Case Study

In this section, you're going to finish the case study by completing the ActionScript. By the end of this chapter, you'll have a fully functional website that is ready to be uploaded to the Internet.

1. Open your case study movie.

2. Select the keyframe on frame 1 of the actions layer and open the Actions panel. The code begins like this:

```
1  webButton.onRelease = function() {
2      toOpen = "open web";
3
4      if (userHasClicked == true) {
5          content_mc.play ();
6      } else {
7          content_mc.gotoAndPlay(toOpen);
8          userHasClicked = true;
9      }
10 };
```

At the moment, you can click any button more than once, and the chosen rectangle will close and reopen. You need to change the code a little so that repeated button presses prevents any motion.

To initiate this, you need to change your if statements to do a few more crucial checks. You'll come to these in a moment. The first thing you need to do is store the previously opened page in a variable.

3. Add the following line of code in between the last two curly brackets of the first bunch of code:

```
1  webButton.onRelease = function() {
2      toOpen = "open web";
3
4      if (userHasClicked == true) {
5          content_mc.play ();
6      } else {
7          content_mc.gotoAndPlay(toOpen);
8          userHasClicked = true;
9      }
10     lastOpened = toOpen;
11 };
```

Line 10 of the code creates a new variable called lastOpened that is set to the value stored in toOpen. This will be used in a moment.

4. Insert the code on line 10 in the corresponding position in each button section.

Now whenever a button is pressed, you store the according frame label value. So when you click the webButton instance, lastOpened stores open web or specifically, the value of toOpen.

Many of you might be wondering here why both toOpen and lastOpened store the same value? It all relates to the new if condition that you are about to add. Let's look at it and then we'll explain further.

5. Add the following code as shown:

```
1  webButton.onRelease = function() {
2      toOpen = "open web";
3
4      if (userHasClicked == true && toOpen != lastOpened) {
5          content_mc.play ();
6      } else {
7          content_mc.gotoAndPlay(toOpen);
8          userHasClicked = true;
9      }
10     lastOpened = toOpen;
11 };
12
```

By adding an extra conditional, you are specifying that both conditions must be met for the code to run. If neither or only one of the conditions, say userHasClicked == true, is met, the else code statement is run.

The new condition added uses the not equals to operator. As you might have guessed, this is the exact opposite to the == operator, meaning that the condition is met only if the values toOpen and lastOpened are not the same. The reason you've added this condition is to prevent a page being selected two (or more) times in a row.

Before you can test this, you need to add a second condition.

6. Amend the following line of code as shown:

```
1  webButton.onRelease = function() {
2      toOpen = "open web";
3
4      if (userHasClicked == true  && toOpen != lastOpened) {
5          content_mc.play ();
6      } else if (userHasClicked == false) {
7          content_mc.gotoAndPlay(toOpen);
8          userHasClicked = true;
9      }
10
11     lastOpened = toOpen;
12 };
```

Why are you doing this? In case you didn't notice, there was a flaw in your previous code. Every time toOpen and lastOpened were the same, the else statement was run by default, meaning that button clicks sent the playhead to the toOpen frame label, kind of defeating the purpose!

This new condition prevents this from happening by running the code only if userHasClicked == false. In the event that userHasClicked is true and a button is clicked, nothing happens. Your conditionals are quite clearly defined for both scenarios.

Now all the buttons require the same code.

7. Highlight all the conditional statement code (as shown from line 4 to 9 here).

```
1  webButton.onRelease = function() {
2      toOpen = "open web";
3
4      if (userHasClicked == true  && toOpen != lastOpened) {
5          content_mc.play ();
6      } else if (userHasClicked == false) {
7          content_mc.gotoAndPlay(toOpen);
8          userHasClicked = true;
9      }
10
11     lastOpened = toOpen;
12 };
```

8. Copy the selection using *CTRL* + *C*.

9. Highlight the same code for each of the other button code sections and paste the copied code over it.

10. Test the movie with *CTRL* + *ENTER* (*COMMAND/APPLE* + *ENTER* on the Mac). Click a button more than once to see how the code has disabled the same page from closing and reopening.

That's it for the case study! Well done: you've built a complete portfolio website to display all your Flash and ActionScripting skills. You can now change the website content to display your own handy-work, and modify it by adding new pages or new content in the future. Once you are done, publish the website to the Internet for all to see.

Summary

In this chapter, you've explored the ActionScripting features that make Flash a powerhouse for sophisticated, powerful, web applications. Once you're comfortable with these principles, you can build the kind of websites you've dreamed of. We hope you've started to see that with ActionScript, the possibilities in Flash are infinite.

You saw that:

- The **top-down design** approach is a great way to plan complex programming and ActionScripting tasks
  - Define the general problem to be solved
  - Break the problem down iteratively into its smallest components
  - Reassemble these components in a logical list of **requirements**
  - Build solutions to each requirement. Test, integrate, and test again!
- Rudimentary user input can be captured using a simple **input text field**
- Input text can be assigned to a variable and redisplayed in a **dynamic text field**
- User input and variables can be manipulated with ActionScript. For instance, you used a big plus sign on a button to add together two numbers and display the result

- **Dot notation** gives you a secure and flexible way of targeting named movie clip instances inside your movies

- Dot notation gives you access to the **hierarchy** of movie clip timelines implicit in every Flash movie

- Movie clips have properties that you can target and modify using ActionScript, allowing you to alter a movie clip's appearance, behavior, and animation characteristics

- Movie clip properties and behavior can be modified based on user input and other movie events

- Variables can be **scoped** and targeted using movie clip timelines and dot notation

- Code also has scope, which can be either "here" or "in the timeline this code block is looking at"

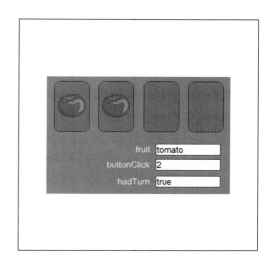

Chapter 16

INTERMEDIATE ACTIONSCRIPT PART 2

What we'll cover in this chapter:

- Fundamental concepts of **top-down** and **bottom-up** design
- Intro to advanced bottom-up design: **class-based object-orientated design**
- Bottom-down programming mindsets as a starting point for learning advanced object-oriented coding
- The creation of a simple Flash game using almost everything you have learned in the book:
  - The bottom up design mindset
  - Frame actions
  - Nested timelines
  - Event handlers
  - Decision making

The real power of Macromedia Flash MX 2004 over previous versions of Flash is in its code structures. Flash allows proper coding techniques to be applied to ActionScript, but you have to be fairly advanced to appreciate it. Although you are not yet ready to write code in the new class-based style, this chapter will show you the bottom-up coding process, and it is a fairly short step from there to the new class-based style.

In this chapter, you'll tackle scripting in Flash and move on to writing bigger code listings.

First though, consider the task of making a cup of your favorite instant coffee…*no*, I don't mean take a break; you've only started the chapter! I mean let's think about the process of making coffee.

Making coffee

First, let's think about how you'd analyze this in terms of the **top-down** approach that you considered in the previous chapter.

In top-down design, you take the problem and break it down into sub-problems. As you keep breaking it down, you make the individual functional items smaller and more compact until you can start to see the solution in the sub-problems because the sub-problems become more and more manageable and easier to understand. Take this problem definition:

To make a cup of coffee with milk and sugar

First iteration:

1. Boil some water
2. Have a cup ready with coffee and some sugar in it
3. When the water has boiled, pour the water into the cup
4. Stir mixture for 20 seconds and add milk

Second iteration:

1.1 Fill kettle full of water

1.2 Connect kettle to power, and switch on

2.1 Get one teaspoon of sugar from sugar bowl and transfer to cup

2.2 Get one teaspoon of coffee from jar and transfer to cup

3.1 Wait until kettle has boiled

3.2 Pour water from kettle into cup

3.3 etc.

You're breaking things down until the problem is so basic that its components can be coded. A system based on this kind of analysis would yield a set of steps that carry out each stage of the task. A computer system developed in this way will usually consist of a series of carefully targeted, tightly constrained code elements—*procedures*—that each performs a small piece of the overall task. This approach is fine until you want the system to do something different—say, make a cup of lemon tea, or an iced coffee. To reprogram the system to do this, you'd need to re-engineer multiple elements in the system to allow them to perform a different task. The top-down method of deconstructing the problem tends to "hard wire" the solution to the problem and make it less adaptable when your needs change.

A bottom-up cup of coffee

In bottom-up design, you try and look beyond the specific problem and analyze the nature of the building blocks that make up that problem. That means if you were looking at the process of making a cup of coffee in an object-oriented way, you'd ignore the brand of coffee, how hot the water needed to be, and how long you were supposed to stir the beverage. Instead, you'd think about the general processes involved, and try and conceptualize them.

The process of thinking from the bottom-up is a little like being in an episode of one of those TV shows where fantastically wealthy, stylish, and attractive thirty-somethings agonize over their inner torment, questioning the meaning and content of every aspect of their existence. Well, maybe not *that* bad, but you *do* have to philosophize—What is making coffee all about?

The generalized answers to this question would be: It is a process that entails liquid and powder, switching things on and seeing when they're done and moving things from one container to another.

You're deconstructing the problem-down into building blocks that are less specific to the components involved in the physical act of making a cup of coffee. You're not thinking about specific tasks any more, you are thinking about general principles like moving things from one container to another, liquid flowing, turning things on, and detecting when things have finished.

Once you can express the process in these generalized terms, you can start creating *generic* routines that embody these general principles. You might create, for example, a routine that describes the process called prepare the liquid. This routine would outline how to prepare a liquid, but it wouldn't be tied to preparing any particular *type* of liquid. Instead, this routine would perform the basic process using the values you supply to it when you start that process. For instance, you might tell it the kind of liquid to use and the temperature the liquid should be.

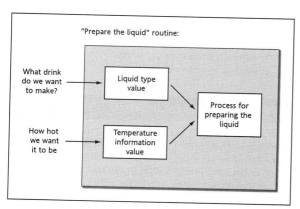

The generic routines are flexible, and because you've distilled them down to the very essence of their functionality, they can be applied to a number of different tasks—making tea, making an iced drink, making a milkshake, and so on. The "prepare the liquid" routine is the same, but the details of an individual implementation of this process—making *this* cup of coffee or *this* iced tea—can be specified in each particular instance.

The "prepare the liquid" routine is one part of the solution to the overall "making a beverage" problem, and it acts in choreographed collaboration with the other generalized routines to achieve the overall aim.

The generalized routines are templates for carrying out each aspect of the task. When you perform a beverage-making task, you initialize *instances* of each of these templates and provide the *specific* information required to perform this *specific* task properly:

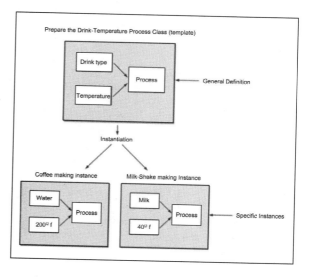

In one form of bottom-up code design, *object orientated design*, the template is called a **class**. The class describes the essentials of a process or an item, and specifies the characteristics of the process that make it different from any other kind of process. The definition of the "prepare the liquid" class might include: the capacity to specify a type of liquid; a variable that describes the amount of liquid, and a variable that controls the prepared liquid's temperature. The functionality for carrying out the task and for coordinating activity with other routines is encapsulated in this class, but it is *very* general. That's a good thing, because you can apply it as the starting point to many problems. This kind of class is called a *super class.*

To turn this into a more specific problem-solving process, you *extend* the super class by making it more specific. To modify one process to make coffee, you specify the liquid as water and a temperature range of 200 degrees F. You can modify the same super class to use milk at a lower range of temperatures. The extended classes still don't have everything you need to make black coffee instead of espresso, or a strawberry milkshake instead of a chocolate one**,** *but they are very close.* All they are missing is *values***.** These values or *properties,* when added to the classes, give you an individual cup of coffee the way you want it. The classes define methods of taking these values and working with them to provide real processes to form, in the case of our example, a *recipe* for which you specify *quantities* as well as the *methods* for making the raw materials into coffee.

> Notice that because our coffee and milkshake making structures share the same super class, they are both still structures for making a drink. The classes may be different, but they share the same super class.

This process is called bottom-up because you work from the general to the specific—you think about the specific aspects of your problem *last*. Unlike the top-down solution, in which you have to know *exactly* what you want at the start, in the bottom-up version, you start with a vague or abstract idea and build toward a more complete picture—in bottom-up you think from the bottom (general) up toward the more specific. The cool thing about this is that if your problem changes during the process, you don't really care—you can change the solution easily because it is just a set of *concepts,* which are easy to change.

> In real-world big programming jobs, the top-down approach requires that you define the full structure of the solution at the start. This is when you know the least about the practicalities of the problem, so you leave yourself open to having to start again because you missed something basic at the beginning.
>
> The bottom-up route allows you to step back and take an abstract view and add to it by extending, writing code from the start. As you extend, you understand the problem better. This time, problems you see on the way up are expected and act as signposts rather than hindrances—they tell you which way you need to extend the solution.
>
> This is why top-down design is rarely used in big projects, and when it is, it is only for the basic frameworks. Bottom-up is used when you are defining how to code up solutions because it is much more tolerant to changes in the understanding of the problem.
>
> The problem with top-down and bottom-up is that top-down seems to make more sense to our normal way of thinking—plan ahead and think of everything at the start. It works very well, but only for small projects. As you get bigger, the bottom-up approach is necessary to manage the uncertainty caused by increasing complexity. The concepts of abstraction and generalization don't sound as useful as the straight talking top-down process though, and that's where problems start—bottom-up programming techniques (such as object-oriented programming) get labeled as difficult.

In case this seems a little Zen to you and you're wondering where the Flash programming comes in, here's a simple example, and real code.

Working with raw ActionScript

We won't ask you to type this example out (although you can). Instead, you'll simply walk through it so those of you who are feeling a little brave can start looking at ActionScript 2.0 classes. After the initial confusion most beginners have with object-oriented programming, you will find the Flash MX 2004 implementation fairly easy to get into—as long as you can type without making mistakes. It is *very* unforgiving if you get either spelling or case wrong.

1. The first thing to know is that Flash MX Professional 2004 is geared more toward scripting than Flash MX 2004, and you will do well to use that version if you have it. Flash MX Professional 2004 has more document types than Flash MX 2004 including the ActionScript File (.as), as shown in the New Document window (File ➤ New).

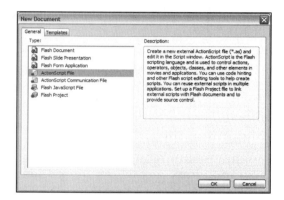

2. When you select an .as file in Flash MX Professional 2004, you will enter a new authoring environment that is specifically designed for editing and creating code-only files. Gone are the timeline and stage views, and you can also close the panel docking areas if you want—you won't be using them, and they are grayed out in any case.

Flash MX 2004 users can quit sulking because you can emulate the same big screen simply by increasing the size of the Actions panel's Script pane so that it occupies the same space. To create a .as file in Flash MX 2004, the process is to:

1. Open a new FLA

2. Select frame 1 of the root timeline

3. Create your script

4. Select **Export Script** from the Actions panel menu. To load a previous .as file, select **Import Script** from the same menu.

Creating the super class

The super class is a general definition of the problem. Recall that the basic problem is this:

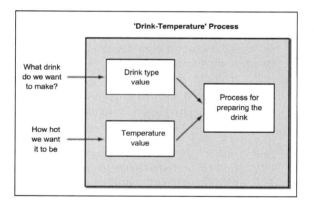

If you create a class for this, you would create a .as file something like this:

```
class DrinkTempProcess {
    // Define properties and type
    var liquid:String;
    var froth:Boolean;
    var temperature:Number;
    // Define constructor
    function DrinkTempProcess(arg_liquid:String, arg_froth:Boolean, arg_temperat
        // When a new Drink instance is created...
        liquid = arg_liquid;
        froth = arg_froth;
        temperature = arg_temperature;
    }
    // Create methods to solve the problem/define the process...
    function processIngredients():String {
        var doSomething;
        doSomething = "I have changed the temperature of "+liquid+" to "+tempera
        if (froth) {
            doSomething = doSomething+", then frothed it";
        }
        return doSomething;
    }
}
```

In this exercise, we are not trying to teach you object-oriented programming, only the basics of how it is structured, and what a class actually looks like in Flash. If you are already a programmer in another discipline, you can pick up the basic Flash file structures and conventions from this example. If you are new to programming, don't worry too much about the exact nature of the code, instead concentrate on what each .as file is setting up as part of the solution, and how the FLA is using these building blocks.

We will describe the main features of this code (rather than go through it step by step), which are the following:

- The class name starts with a capital letter and is defined on line 1—DrinkTempProcess.

- The file is called DrinkTempProcess—that is, it has the same name as the class it is defining. It *must* be called this to work.

- The class defines its own properties (lines 3-5) and methods (lines 14 on). The properties are "liquid," "froth," and "temperature." These are the parameters you have to define before you could process your drink. You would also have to answer the basic questions *what liquid are you using?*, *do you want it frothed?* and *what temperature do you want it?* The method defines the process you will use to make the *basic* drink.

- There is a *constructor* (lines 7-12). This is a function with the same name as the class (again, it *must* be the same otherwise it will not work). This is the part that constructs an instance of your class DrinkTempProcess.

How does this all tie in with the "Prepare the liquid" diagram? Let's run it and see.

Preparing the liquid

If you are feeling confident, you can create the .as file yourself, but note that almost every part of it has to be *exactly* as written, including spelling and case. If any part of it is wrong, the class will not work properly. We strongly recommend that you use our version of this file.

1. Create a new folder called drinkOOP either by using the DrinkTempProcess.as file in the downloads for this chapter, or by reading how to create .as files in the previous section, and then carefully typing out and saving DrinkTempProcess.as. Then place this file in the drinkOOP folder. This is your super class definition. Save this file before moving onto the next step if you are typing it.

If you choose to type it, you can get Flash to check for errors by clicking the Syntax Checker *button. In class-based programming, this may catch errors that the* Auto format *button misses, because not only does the* Syntax Checker *check the current .as file, it also checks the whole class based hierarchy, and classes in other .as files that form part of your definition.*

2. Create a new FLA called drinkTest01.fla, and save it in the same folder as the super class definition. Select frame 1 of the timeline and add the following script (you can also use our file from the downloads section of our website):

```
1  // test the Super Class...
2  testProcess1 = new DrinkTempProcess("water", false, 100);
3  testProcess2 = new DrinkTempProcess("milk", true, 4);
4  trace(testProcess1.processIngredients());
5
6
```

3. Test the FLA. Flash will pick up the class definitions, and will output the following:

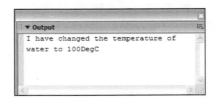

Flash is using your super class (well, at the moment it is just a class for reasons you will see in a moment) to create a solution to the basic problem—changing the temperature of a liquid. Here, you are getting Flash to do just that.

4. You can look at your class handling milk to form the basic process for a milkshake by altering line 4 as follows (change the 1 to a 2):

```
trace(testProcess2.processIngredients());
```

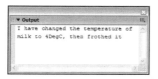

This time Flash cooled milk and frothed it.

You have the basic process of changing the temperature and using a straight or frothed liquid. If you think about it, that's the basic process you need to make all sorts of drinks: coffee, tea, cappuccino, or milk shake.

> *The important point to notice here is not the code you used, but the fact that although you do not yet have a complete solution on how to make drinks, you are already writing code to solve it! You have a vague idea about what the core process of making a drink is, but that hasn't stopped you from creating and testing this vague idea in hard code. In the top-down process, you would have to fully define your problem before you could start programming, hope that you had covered everything, and also hope that coding would not uncover problems you hadn't thought of in the specification. That's a lot of hope, and in most cases, you can safely assume that Murphy's Law will come into play.*

To make drinks rather than simply hot or cold liquids (frothed or otherwise), you need other ingredients. You need to *extend* your solution to include them. You do this by using the existing class DrinkTempProcess as a building block upon which you can add more specialized code to refine your solution.

Extending the solution

1. In the same way you created DrinkTempProcess.as, create another .as file, this time called MakeDrink.as

(or use our download file). Save it in your drinkOOP folder when you are done.

```
class MakeDrink extends DrinkTempProcess {
    //properties...
    var solid:String;
    //constructor...
    function MakeDrink(arg_liquid:String, arg_froth:Boolean, arg_solid:String, arg_temperature:Number) {
        //pass to superclass...
        super(arg_liquid, arg_froth, arg_temperature);
        //create here...
        solid = arg_solid;
    }
    //methods...
    function makeIt():String {
        return processIngredients(liquid, temperature)+" and mixed in "+solid;
    }
}
```

This looks similar to the last class, but is different in a number of ways.

- It refers back to the first class on line one with the word extends. This file uses the core from the basic class DrinkTempProcess and *extends* it toward the solution you want. By doing this, DrinkTempProcess becomes a super class because MakeDrink extends from it.

- You can see that MakeDrink extends DrinkTempProcess by adding a new property called solid. This is your solid ingredient. MakeDrink also creates a new method, makeIt. Notice that the code for this refers back to a method you saw in the super class, processIngredients—it is *changing* the basic method to heat/cool liquids by adding the solid ingredient into the mix—literally!

Let's give it a whirl.

2. Save both your .as files if either have an asterisk (*) on the tabs at the top.

3. Create a new FLA and attach the following script to frame 1 of its timeline (as you did in "Extending the Solution"). Save the FLA in your drinkOOP folder as testDrink02.fla.

```
// define our instances...
coffee = new MakeDrink("water", false, "ground coffee beans", 95);
milkShake = new MakeDrink("milk", true, "banana flavoring and sugar ", 3);
cappuccino = new MakeDrink("water", true, "ground coffee beans", 80);
//
// now test them...
//
trace("To make an instance 'coffee'...");
trace(coffee.makeIt());
//
trace("\nTo make an instance 'milkShake'...");
trace(milkShake.makeIt());
//
trace("\nTo make an instance 'cappuccino'...");
trace(cappuccino.makeIt());
```

If you now test this FLA you will see this.

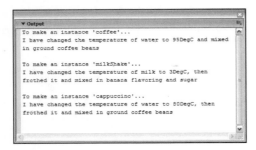

This looks *much* more like a finished set of drinks! What did you do? The class MakeDrink extends the basic "make hot or cold liquid" class DrinkTempProcess. MakeDrink uses the DrinkTempProcess to create liquids at the right temperature and adds to them with its own method makeIt, which adds the other ingredients to make a drink!

Reviewing the solution

Some of you might be wondering how this relates to reality. What *real* problem would this actually solve?

The code is not really modeling how you would make drinks, it is the way a *machine* would make them—you can conceptualize, but in the end, **code is for machines**.

When they first build new vending machines that dispense cups of coffee and soup and such, they start with the core components—the heater/cooler that pours the basic ingredients—hot water or cold juice, etc—down a spout. They test this with a microcontroller containing code implementing something very like DrinkTempProcess.

> *In real life,* DrinkTempProcess *would itself extend other classes below it, and these classes would interface to the machine's hardware, so you have layers of classes of the form hardware* ➤ classes *that can talk to the hardware* ➤ DrinkTempProcess.
>
> *When* DrinkTempProcess *says it is frothing something, its super classes would use this to make a whisk move around at some point in the heating process.*

The class above DrinkTempProcess (by "above" we mean closer to the solution) adds other things to your hot and cold liquids to make drinks. You've used a class that is a simplified version of it—MakeDrink—which refers to the same hardware-specific classes to pour coffee into the drink at the right moment and so on, so our simple text messages will be converted to *real* drinks.

What are the instances of MakeDrink? They are not the actual beverages—coffee, milkshake, or cappuccino. They are—see if you can guess what they actually are before reading the next bit—*instructions* to create the actual beverages, structured as software instances. The *properties* of the MakeDrink class are *ingredients,* and the one method of it, makeIt is the *recipe* that works on the ingredients to make your drink.

When you click the cappuccino button on a machine, the drink machine will be configured by the cappuccino instance of MakeDrink, and you will get a *real* cappuccino. Object-oriented programming is not vague at all—it's the way *most machines behave when you press one of their buttons*—from Windows XP/Mac OSX on your computer to the drink machine in the office.

What's the point of this? Why would you want to go through all this extra thinking and dip your toes into the world of object-oriented design? The answer is that object-oriented solutions are more robust and flexible, and they're easier to maintain and upgrade. Because you've designed the solution in terms of generalized and self-sufficient classes, you can reuse them in other tasks that have a similar element in them—maybe a "preparing a bath" task could reuse the prepare the liquid class DrinkTempProcess. Furthermore, as each class communicates with other entities using interfaces, you can completely change the instructions inside a class and not affect the overall solution—provided that you keep the same interfaces. Each class and the instances that are derived from it can be reworked in isolation. Here, in essence, are the benefits of the object-oriented approach:

- Reusability
- Encapsulation—functionality embedded in a self-contained object
- Maintainability
- Extensibility
- Flexibility

The object-oriented approach helps you build solutions that can change as the world that they're modeling changes, and the strength of OO design lies in its ability to generalize. Generalized solutions based on these design principles are not locked into the problem you initially set out to solve because elements can be used elsewhere and changed when different problems arise.

What's this got to do with Flash and you *as beginners*, given that you can't yet write classes on our own? As a beginner, it's a Very Good Thing that you at least looked at the class based coding stuff because:

- It's the way Flash works. You created your own classes instead of relying on one created for you! The only difference between the movie clip class and MakeDrink is that Macromedia wrote the movie clip class. If the movie clip doesn't do exactly what you want to do, you could make certain adjustments to it until it suited your needs better or you could extend movie clip to make a class that does Exactly What You Want. You would do this in very much the same way as you made object-oriented programming drinks—its not any harder. It is not that big of a leap in theory from this simple example to super classing movie clip to create your own Sprite class to write Flash video games with, or to write your own User Interface classes so you can make your websites out of already-built blocks.

- Macromedia already had the idea about already-built building blocks, and you probably already heard of them—they're called **components**. Knowing the basic framework of classes that underpin components will make you better at using them.

- You get the most out of Flash if you think in terms of classes. At the moment, you know there's a button class, and a movie clip class, and a sound class, and around 40 others! How will you ever get through them all? Simple—see them as the same thing. By adopting a class-based mindset, you quickly see that all classes are essentially the same. As soon as you understand one ActionScript class in terms of real class-based thinking, you don't just understand that one class—you understand ActionScript. When you do that, you certainly won't be a beginner, nor will you be an intermediate, you will be an advanced user of Flash, soon to be a new Master of Flash.

- Even if you don't use the rigorous, code-based object-oriented structures, it helps to at least think in a general bottom-up way in Flash, rather than the more structured and formal top-down design way.

In the rest of this chapter, you will break away from pure class-based scripting and move to a more general design thought process. Rather than code using classes, you will use standard ActionScript but think in a bottom-up mindset.

You are almost at the end of the *Foundation* part of your journey. You are an intermediate Flash user, and you have had a peek at the next mountain—it's a big one for sure. This is your starting point to that next mountain in the range. Think like a Master and you will become a Master, even if you don't yet have a Master's coat.

Flash and the built-in classes

Until now, your exposure to classes has been pretty limited right? Wrong. As you probably already know from the last discussion, Flash MX 2004 is fully OO-based (and unlike Flash MX, it also includes classes), so many of the elements you have already used in this book are classes. Typical classes in the Flash environment include video, sound, components, text, buttons, and of course, movie clips.

> *You can view a full list of Flash's predefined objects by using the Actions toolbox pane of the Actions panel and opening the Built-in classes book. Try not to be too intimidated by the list because the number of these that you will use at the moment will be minimal.*

It will help you a great deal in the long run if you begin to think that ActionScript is object-oriented and begin to think of elements such as video, sound, text, buttons, and so on, as classes, even if you do it without thinking too much about things like MakeDrink and super classing.

Let's explore the concept with a particular basic class that you're already really familiar with: **movie clips**.

A movie clip instance on the stage is essentially a specific named instance based on the movie clip class embodied in a symbol in the Library:

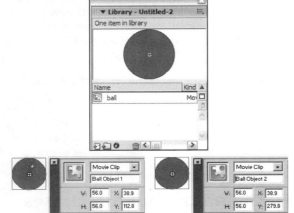

A movie clip object has standard, basic properties like size and number of frames, and once you've built the individual instance by adding a few actions and frames of content to it, it can start to do things.

A class has a standard general structure. At its simplest level, it calculates a certain small but well-defined chunk of a solution (or movie), and it has well-defined interfaces that allow it to communicate with the other classes that deal with the other parts of the problem (movie). Remember that to follow the object-oriented route you have to:

- Identify the basic elements of your problem in terms of what you can see happening (or what you *want* to happen in your movie).

- Identify what these basic building blacks *are* (conceptualize) and see whether you can generalize them into basic groups of building blocks so that each one builds on the previous one to extend your work toward the solution.

- Create movie clips in the Library that map to these basic groups and perform the functions associated with the group, thus making your movie clips your building blocks (rather than the classes in the last section). Instead of extending the movie clips, you can embed them into each other to create nested structures.

- Create an instance of (drag it out of the Library) these individual movie clip building blocks on the stage and if necessary, give them instance names so that you can target them with ActionScript.

The movie clips must be *self-contained*. They must be able to solve their part of the problem by themselves, and they must be able to do this independently of whatever else is also going on in the movie.

The process works best in situations where there are multiple instances of a few very similar processes to be performed. You can illustrate this with a graphical effect in a Flash movie. A lot of computer graphic effects use a few basic rules that are applied many times over to give the illusion of complexity. Here, you'll see how a very simple movie clip with a single process can be replicated many times on the screen to create a much more complex-looking effect.

A simple mouse trail

The great thing about bottom-up design is that it allows you to *play*—you don't even need to have a high-level problem or task to solve. You can just say, "This effect looks interesting, let's break it down into its parts and see what we can build from them." You can use this as a creative thought process, and not necessarily as a logical, analytical problem solving process. The reason for this is very simple: in Flash your most common classes are not long-winded and obscure data elements—they're visual movie clips with animation and sound, which can be much more fun.

A mouse trail is a little group of characters or text that follows the mouse pointer. An effective mouse trail usually contains some very complex math, using things like inertia and trigonometry to calculate the pointer position and the relative position of the trail. By stopping and thinking about it though, you'll realize that instead of using heavy math and shifting movie clips around behind the pointer, you could just use lots of static movie clips that *react* when the pointer moves over them. Basically, you're turning the problem on its head.

There are two stages to building a mouse trail: (1) building the basic movie clip object that you'll make multiple copies of later; (2) integrating the multiple copies into the movie.

Creating the basic movie clip

The first thing to realize is that all those fancy mouse trails have one thing in common: the character furthest away from the pointer is *least* affected by what the mouse is doing now, and the closest is *most* affected.

In essence, you've abstracted the problem down to a generalization of the type of animation that's required to create the desired effect. The animation on any particular character should get weaker based on: (1) increasing distance from the mouse; (2) how long ago the mouse was near it—longer ago means weaker animation effect.

> *If you were embarking on a code-orientated solution, this would be the vague idea that would create your super class. This is similar to the way the vague idea that all drinks have a liquid brought to a well-defined temperature is the core part of its super class.*

The only thing you've encountered so far that's affected by the mouse is a button symbol, so maybe if you had loads of buttons all over the screen, you could make Flash do all the hard work for you. That's all you need to know. It seems pretty vague, but that's OK, it allows you more room to experiment.

1. Create a new Flash movie and change the background color to black using the Properties panel. Also make sure that View ➤ Grid ➤ Show Grid and View ➤ Snapping >Snap to Grid menu options are both selected.

2. Create a new graphic symbol and call it sy.circle inside it, create a circle with a blue stroke and fill. Give the circle a diameter of about 90 pixels, and center it at 0,0. Make sure you have the middle dot in the Info panel's 3x3 grid.

3. Create a movie clip and call it mc.circle. Change the name of the movie clip's default layer to circle.

4. Leave frame 1 of this movie clip empty, but add a keyframe in frame 2. Drag a copy of sy.circle into this keyframe, and center it on the stage at 0,0.

5. Use the Properties panel to select Alpha from the Color drop-down menu and give the circle a value of **70%**:

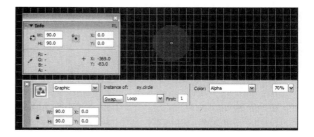

6. Add another keyframe at frame 20. In this frame, use the **Color** drop-down again, but this time, select Advanced and click the Settings button that appears to the right.

   The Alpha will already be set to 70% from before, but give the circle a red hue by moving the second **Red** slider (the one that's a *number* rather than a percentage) all the way up to **255**:

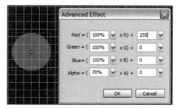

413

7. Using the Properties panel or Info panel, set the width and height of the circle to **1**. Then create a motion tween from frame 2 to frame 20.

8. If you drag this movie clip onto the stage and test your movie you'll see a circle that starts off big and blue and then gets smaller and red until it finally disappears.

You've now created your simple diminishing effect. Next, change the clip so that it'll run through once when the mouse pointer passes over it and stop until the pointer goes over it again. The more recently the mouse pointer was near it, the bigger the circle will be. This continues for 20 frames, by which time the circle is so small it disappears. Your movie clip building block must somehow get the mouse input that will control its appearance and behavior. You *could* get it to look at how close the mouse is to it, but there is a simpler option to try first.

9. Duplicate sy.circle by selecting it in the Library window and clicking the menu icon on the top right of the Library panel and selecting Duplicate from drop-down menu. Make the new symbol into a button via the Duplicate Symbol dialog box and call the button bu.circle.

10. The button should be transparent and the same size as the movie clip. In bu.circle, insert a keyframe in the Hit state, and delete the circle from the Up state. You now have a circular button that has no Up or Down state, but *does* have a Hit state, making it invisible but selectable:

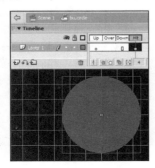

11. You want to add this button and some simple actions to mc.circle, so go into mc.circle and add two new layers, one named actions and one named button:

12. In the button layer, add the bu.circle symbol and center it. Then remove all the other frames from this layer so that the button only exists on frame 1. With the bu.circle button still selected, give it an instance name buCircle in the Properties panel.

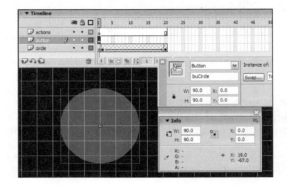

13. Type the following in frame 1 of the actions layer:

```
buCircle.onRollOver = function() {
    play();
}
stop();
```

You don't need to include a this reference on the second line (to give you this.play()) because your code is on the mc.circle timeline, and that's the timeline you want to stop.

14. Insert a keyframe in frame 20 of the actions layer and add gotoAndStop (1);.

That's it. You've created a movie clip that does the following:

- Waits at a blank first frame until it's rolled over
- When it's rolled over by the mouse, it plays
- When it has played once, it goes back to the blank first frame

15. Drag an instance of mc.circle onto the stage and test your movie. You'll see a blank screen until your mouse happens to move over the button. As soon as this happens, a circle appears and gets smaller as time goes by until it disappears completely. That was the basic object you started out trying to create: an effect that diminishes based on either time since it was started or distance the mouse is away from it.

Notice that you haven't even thought how you're going to use this building block. You just wanted to create something that waited until the mouse was near and then displayed a diminishing animation. You've set aside the initial problem completely and concentrated on creating this building block.

When you created your super class, you did not consider the class that would eventually extend it. In the same way, you did not consider what you would use your movie clip building block for—you simply generalized the current problem.

Although you are not writing complex class-based code here, you are thinking about the problem in a class-based way, which is a good place to start. Flash is one of the few environments where you can work in a loosely object-orientated way like this, and that makes it a good place to start playing with advanced, industry-strength programming techniques without actually writing in a strict, code-centric manner. Because of this, Flash is a great place for creative people to move over to a structured programming style. As you add more code to your simple building blocks and see what other folks are doing, you will likely move toward the pure, class-based code. Some of you will only go part of the way, but some of you will travel all the way up that mountain.

Building the movie

The next step is to see if your simple movie clip animation, repeated many times, could be used to produce the complex behavior you're looking for.

1. Drag instances of mc.circle onto the stage until you have built a single row of movie clips. Use the

grid to help you create a regular overlapping pattern:

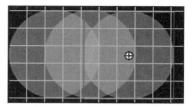

2. Keep dragging new clips from the Library until you have a complete row across the stage. To ensure the movie clips are aligned correctly, use the Align panel's **Align top edge** button.

3. When you have a full row, select them all, press F8 to convert the row into a new movie clip symbol, and call it mc.circle.row.

4. Continue adding rows above and below your starting row by dragging copies of mc.circle.row to the stage until you've filled the screen with a neat grid:

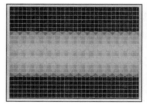

And now comes the moment of truth. Remember, you set the task of creating a trail that would start from wherever the mouse pointer was and gradually fade as the pointer moved away, or as time passed. Did you do it? There's only one way to find out—test that movie:

It seems to have worked perfectly. Cool. You can change the animation to be whatever you want—sparkling stars, jumping sheep—the possibilities are endless. The next step is to play and create!

Notice that in making this movie, all you've done is thought about an effect, decided what its most basic structure/building block was, and created a created movie clip that does it. Then you made a more complex-looking effect by making lots of copies of the simple effect. Although this movie isn't truly object-oriented, the thinking behind it *is*. The visual effect you created is based on one button in one movie clip. One of the fundamental advantages of objects is that they're self-contained, and therefore reusable. What's more, because they are generalized solutions, they can be rearranged to fit new problems. A bit like classes—same concept, different level.

We'll now show you how small, seemingly obscure ideas and the theories behind them can fleshed out in little experimental building blocks that grow slowly (a.k.a the bottom-up approach).

Putting it all together

You're going to look at a simple memory game sometimes called "Concentration." The first thing you'll do is define the basic rules:

- The player is presented with an even number of tiles with symbols on their faces. For each tile there is at least one other identical tile. All the tiles are positioned face down so their symbols aren't visible.

- The player has to match each symbol with a matching symbol by turning a pair of tiles over each turn. If the tiles match, the tiles are left face-up. If the tiles don't match, the tiles are returned back to their face-down state.

- The game is over when all tiles are face up.

This game can be implemented using either a top-down or an object-oriented approach. If you try it using the top-down approach, you're guaranteed to end up with a bunch of if-then-else statements as long as your

arm, and more variables than you would believe (we tried it just to make sure!).

Instead, let's look at it from a bottom-up approach.

Your first thoughts should be about what the fundamental objects of the game are. In this case, it's quite obvious—the only things being manipulated in this game are the *tiles*. If you can create a generalized tile object with an appropriate range of things it will do, you've cracked the whole game. What do you want the tile to be able to do?

At a guess, you'd want it to be able to do the following:

- Be face down when it's unselected.

- Turn face up when it's selected, and show the user and Flash its symbol.

- Ask Flash when the current turn has finished. If the selected tile does not match the other selected tile, it must turn back to its initial state. If the selected tiles match, each tile must remain face up.

Notice that there are a few things you *haven't* defined as necessary to know. Things like:

- How many tiles there are

- How many different tile symbols there will be

- How many tiles are face up

- How many tiles are face down

You don't need to know these things because the object you're creating will represent only *one* tile. All these bits of information don't apply to *one* tile, they apply to *many* tiles working alongside each other. So, using the bottom-up design method, you'll first create the tile, and when that's working fine, you'll move on to the next step up and build the game timing and control building blocks—you won't think right now how you will do that.

But wait a minute...

Part of this definition sounds strangely familiar. The mouse trail you just created stays still when it's not selected, and then does something when it *has* been selected. This is a subset of the same sort of behavior you want for our tile. The only difference is that the mouse trail circles were all identical, but the tiles you want to create will be different. Can you reuse part of the previous exercise? It might be a good starting point.

Creating the tile

1. Start a new Flash movie. Using the Properties panel, change the movie background to purple (enter a RGB value of **156**, **101**, **156** in the Color Mixer panel if you want to get the same color we used), and the dimensions to **800x800**. Change the frame rate to **18** fps.

   In the last exercise, you created a circle and a button that was the same size and shape as the circle to trigger the movie into action. You're going to do the same thing here.

2. Create a new graphic symbol and call it sy.tile.

3. Create a tile shape by drawing a blue rectangle with rounded corners and a black stroke, the same as you did for your playing cards earlier in the book. You could even reuse the playing cards, but remember to take the character off the front because you want them to be blank for now. Make your tile 80 pixels wide and 120 pixels high, and center it on the stage:

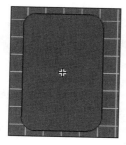

4. Use the **Option** menu from the Library panel to duplicate the symbol as a button, the same way you did in the last example. Call this symbol bu.transparent—the reason for this name will become clear in a moment.

5. Add a keyframe in the button's Hit state and clear its Up state to create a button that's invisible, but still hittable.

6. Now you need some pictures to go on the tiles. We've provided a set of graphics of fruit on our website that you can download and use (see tile game2004_graphics.fla, which contains the graphics in its library), otherwise feel free to come up with whatever you want. For this example, you'll use four different pictures: a tomato, an orange, a lemon, and a pear:

   Once imported, you will have four new graphic symbols in your Library: sy.fruit.tomato, sy.fruit.orange, sy.fruit.lemon, and sy.fruit.pear.

7. Create a new movie clip symbol and call it mc.tile.

   We know that you'll need to have a button and an animation in this clip, so you'll put them in now.

8. Rename the first layer tile, then create a new layer and name it button. Because you have a button, you will also need to define its event, so lets add the layer to do that as well. Make a third layer on top and call it actions.

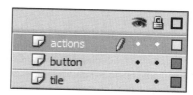

In the **tile** layer, you'll create an animation of the tile turning over, and to create this effect you'll use the same kind of illusion you implemented for the flipping face tween in Chapter 7.

9. In frame 1 of the **tile** layer, drag in a copy of sy.tile from the Library and center it. Add keyframes at frames 5 and 10.

10. The next thing is to create an animation of the tile flipping over. To do this, you'll make the tile get progressively shorter as it moves between frames 1 to 5, and then grow again until it's back up to its normal size in frame 10. This will give the illusion that the tile is flipping over. Click frame 5 and use the Properties panel (or the Info panel) to set the height (H) value of the graphic to 1:

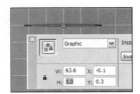

> If you find that the value doesn't want to go to 1.0 exactly (it may change to 0.9 or 1.1 after you enter it), try changing the value you enter. For example, if you get 0.9, enter 1.1 instead, and it should start playing ball. Of course, this doesn't really matter— 0.9 is still OK with us if it's OK with you!

11. Add two separate motion tweens between frames 1 and 5, and frames 5 and 10:

At the moment your flipping tile won't really seem very convincing as both sides look the same. After you've added a fruit picture to one side, the illusion will be complete.

12. Add a new layer between the two current layers and call it fruit. You want to make the fruit start to appear from frame 5 onward and grow until it's full size in frame 10.

13. Insert a keyframe in frame 10 of your fruit layer and drag a copy of one of your graphic symbols onto the stage—we're using the tomato symbol. Center your symbol and resize it until it fits nicely onto your tile:

14. Add a new keyframe at frame 5, copy the fruit from frame 10, and paste it in place into frame 5. Here's the trick: you want the tomato to be as thin as the tile at frame 5, so using the Properties panel, change the tomato's H value to 1, the same value as the tile. At frame 5, you should now have a squashed tile and a squashed tomato over the top of it.

15. Create a motion tween from frame 5 to 10. Your animation should now give a convincing impression of a tile flipping over:

The tile should start off blank and shrink to nothing, before growing back to full size again with the tomato image on it.

16. Once the tile has flipped over, the next thing you'll want it to do is flip it back over to its face down position. This motion would simply look like the animation you've created so far in frames 1 to 10, but in reverse. Create a new keyframe in frame 20 of your fruit and tile layers.

17. Select frames 1 through 10 on the **tile** layer and use the Edit ➤ Copy Frames menu option to copy them to the clipboard.

18. Click frame 20 of the layer and use the Edit ➤ Paste Frames menu option to paste the frames into the timeline:

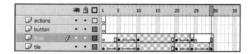

You don't need to reverse these frames—as you'll see, it looks fine if you play the movie clip.

19. If you were to do the same thing with the tomato animation though, it would be the wrong way round. Click frame 5 on the fruit layer and again use the Edit ➤ Copy Frames menu option to copy it to the clipboard.

20. Click frame 24 on the same layer and paste the frame there. Then set up a motion tween between frames 20 and 24:

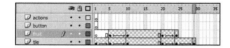

Now when you play back your movie clip, it should run through with no trouble.

You now have a tile that starts face-down, flips face-up, and then flips face-down again. The next things you need are the actions

Making the tile work

The tile should only flip when it's selected, so you need to incorporate a button into the movie clip to trigger this flipping.

The button will go into frame 1 of the button layer. This layer should have a single frame in it. Once the tile starts flipping, you don't want the user to be able to select it again because this could create problems later on in the game.

1. Drag the bu.transparent symbol from your Library onto the stage and center it on your existing tile. If you find it easier, you may want to hide and lock the other two layers by clicking the eye and lock icons on the timeline. Give it an instance name trans_btn.

The first thing you want the button to do when you click it is to start playing the movie clip, which you can achieve with some simple ActionScript.

2. Select frame 1 of the actions layer and add this script:

```
trans_btn.onRelease = function() {
  play();
};
stop();
```

This script will cause the tile to stay face-down until it is clicked. As soon as the tile is clicked, it will begin its animation. Frame 1 is also the face-down point in the animation, and the place you will have to get back to when the card flips back over for an incorrect match. Lets label it: with frame 1 of the actions layer still selected, enter a frame label of facedown via the Properties panel.

3. The other simple thing you want the tile to do is return to the first frame when it finishes running through the animation. You can do this by putting a keyframe with a **goto** action into frame 30 of layer actions. Enter the following code:

```
gotoAndPlay("facedown");
```

4. Go back to the main stage and drag a copy of your movie clip out from the Library. It doesn't matter where you place it because it's only there so you can test the movie.

5. Play your movie. The tile should stay blank until you click it, and then it will cycle through its animation and return to the face-down state. You should only be able to click it in the face-down state.

The next thing you need to do is to have the tile stop when it's face-up.

6. You'll need a little more than a **stop** action in this frame—you also want the tile to tell the user and

Flash what symbol it has on it. The user bit is easy—they can see the picture on top of the tile—but telling Flash is a little more complicated. The questions that you should be asking are:

- Who or what do you tell?
- How do you tell it, and what does it need to know?

One of the fundamental things about creating bottom-up programs is that you have to know which parts of the program fit inside one movie clip, and which parts fit into another clip or into external code. This is a difficult concept to grasp at first, but if you think *What's the game doing? What can a tile do, and should it be able to do that?* it quickly becomes obvious that the pieces of a game—the tiles—should not be the *controllers* of the action. The rules, or a referee who knows the rules, should control the game.

The referee for this game will be the main timeline, so that will be in control. The tiles are just performing their specific actions and nothing more. This is because you need to be able to add as many tiles to the final game as you like. This is the beauty of bottom-up design: the tiles are just building blocks that you can plug into the program any number of times without having to recode them. They are *self-contained*.

As you know, the main timeline is called _root. Although using the root would be fine for your movie, it would stop your code from being truly general. Remember what we said earlier about building blocks being reusable? Well, to keep this reusability as open as possible, you don't always want to tie things to the main timeline. The way you can get round this is to give control of the movie clip to the next level up instead. By doing this, you'll be able to move the code around within the levels of a movie and still have it work. The name for the next level up in Flash is the **parent**. By telling the movie clip to talk to the parent level, you're keeping it as a separate portable

object—wherever you place a tile in a movie hierarchy, this notation will ensure that it always talks to the next level up, irrespective of the name of that level's timeline.

That answers the first question—now you know you should be talking to the parent. What do you want to tell it? The parent needs to know what's on the tile, and in this case it's a *tomato*.

7. In the Actions panel for your bu.transparent symbol, add the following highlighted code, so the ActionScript for your button looks like this:

```
trans_btn.onRelease = function() {
    _parent.buttonClick += 1;
    _parent.fruit = "tomato";
  play();
};
stop();
```

The next thing to do is test if Flash can tell which fruit is on the tile.

8. Go back to the main movie timeline and draw a text field below the tile. Make the text field dynamic and non-selectable, and click the **Show border around text** button to make Flash draw a box around your text. Make sure the text color is different to your movie color's background and finally, assign it the variable fruit by typing fruit in the Var field.

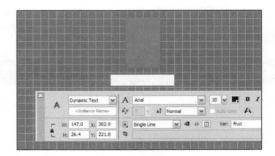

9. Test the movie.

This time, when you click the tile, you'll see the tile communicating with the _parent, telling it what the variable fruit is:

You now have one tile working pretty well, but the game won't be much fun with only one tile! Now test it with *multiple* tiles, and see what sort of problems arise.

Using multiple tiles

You now need to start thinking how you want each tile to work when there is more than one tile on the stage.

1. Add three more tiles to your main stage to make a row of four in all. You can tidy up the row by using the **Align** panel:

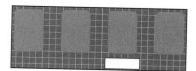

2. Test the movie. Notice the following:

■ Your text field won't change after you've selected the first tile because *all* the tiles are tomatoes.

■ It's possible to flip more than two tiles.

■ The first tile doesn't wait until the second tile has been flipped before it flips itself back round, so you'd have to be pretty quick to match a pair.

The first problem should sort itself out once you add different fruit symbols, so you don't need to worry about that.

For the second problem, you need to count the number of tiles that are now face-up. If it's two or more, you shouldn't allow any other tiles to flip. To do this, you'll need a variable to count the number of tiles that have been flipped.

To fix the third problem, you need to wait until a second tile is face up and the person playing the game has had time to look at both tiles before the tiles are flipped back over. You need to do a few other things before that becomes possible, so for now, simply add a stop(); to frame 10 of the actions timeline. This will make the tiles stay face up once they are turned.

3. Open the Actions panel for the bu.transparent symbol. You've already told the parent and the ActionScript that the fruit on this symbol is a tomato. Now add the following line of highlighted code and another closing curly bracket (}) under the **play** action, so that your ActionScript for the button symbol looks like this:

```
trans_btn.onRelease = function(){
  _parent.buttonClick += 1;
  _parent.fruit = "tomato";
    if (_parent.buttonClick<=2) {
        play();
    }
}
stop();
```

You now know how many times a button has been clicked. You have also told Flash to stop allowing more tiles to be turned when more than two tiles have already been flipped. What you haven't yet done is created a button click variable on the main timeline, so let's do that now.

4. Add a new layer called actions on the main timeline. In frame 1 of it add the following script:

```
buttonClick = 0;
```

421

The last line of code that you attached to trans_btn checks if you've already clicked any two other buttons and if so, says instructs the program not to respond to any more button clicks. The beauty of tying buttonClick to the parent and not to each tile is that all the tile objects will look at the same variable. They don't need to know *which* other buttons have been clicked, they will respond as soon as any two buttons are clicked.

5. Go back to the Test the movie to confirm this. You should see that:

■ Once you click a tile, it stays face-up.

■ You can turn tiles only if buttonClick is fewer than two. After that, they refuse to budge.

You can also check our version, tile game2004_part1.fla, which has a text field set up to show you the value of buttonClick and well as fruit. Note that after clicking the second tile, buttonClick will still increase in value, but no tiles will respond—the play() in the if is no longer been executed.

Getting the tiles to flip back correctly is a little more involved. You want to the following:

- Keep the first tile flipped until a second is face-up
- Decide whether the tiles match
- Flip both tiles back to face down or keep them face up based on whether they match

Hang on, the first part of that sounds a bit familiar: buttonClick already does that—it tells the main timeline how many buttons have been clicked so far. When that number is equal to two, you know that the player has picked a pair, and the current turn is over whether they match or not—you can't pick anymore tiles.

The next part of your task is to make the tile stay face-up until the referee says the current turn is over. You'll create a new variable called hadTurn to help you with that.

6. Back on the root timeline, name the existing layer the tiles are on tiles.

The first frame of the actions layer will set up the variables that apply to the whole game, and you'll insert a second keyframe that will actually control each turn.

7. Select frame 1 in the actions layer and add the following script, deleting what is there already (which will be buttonClick = 0).

```
resetTurn = function () {

};
```

resetGo is a function that you will run every time you want to start a new turn. What variables will you need? You would usually get out a pencil and paper and work it out, but we will tell you straight out for now.

You need one variable to tell Flash that the current go has finished, and one variable to say how many buttons have been clicks so far—both of which have already been discussed.

```
buttonclick = 0;
hadTurn = false;
```

One to show what is on the last turned tile:

```
fruit = "";
```

One to show what's on the first tile:

```
fruit1 = "";
```

One to show what's on the second tile:

```
fruit2 = "";
```

And a final one to show if they match:

```
match = false;
```

If you add all these variables in your function, you get the following:

```
resetTurn = function () {
    buttonclick = 0;
    hadTurn = false;
    match = false;
    fruit = "";
    fruit1 = "";
    fruit2 = "";
};
```

You still are not interested in the number of tiles and the number of different symbols there are on the tiles. They are not part of the problem even though they are part of the game. The important thing in this game is to find pairs, and it's this that determines our definition of the referee.

You'll start with a 4 x 4 playing board, which will include 8 pairs—you'll eventually have four pairs of our four different fruits. This will be constant for every game, so this value will go in frame 1 of the actions layer on the main timeline. This frame is blank at the moment, but remember that you decided this frame would contain the variables that would be initialized only once for each game.

Add the following line at the end of the script to complete the game initialization.

```
resetTurn = function () {
    buttonClick = 0;
    hadTurn = false;
    match = false;
    fruit = "";
    fruit1 = "";
    fruit2 = "";
};
pairs = 8;
```

That's your game initialization function done; now it's time to set up your turn logic and initialize for a single turn.

8. Add a new keyframe at frame 2 of layer **actions**. In it, add the following code, which resets for a new turn. Note that although you *defined* the function resetTurn in frame 1, you did not *run* it. Frame 1 initializes the game and runs once. Frame 2 initializes the *current turn* and runs a number of times depending on how many turns it takes to complete the game.

```
resetTurn();
stop();
```

Now you're ready to start a new turn...how do you implement it? The main timeline is the referee of the game, and the referee watches the game closely. To "watch closely," Flash would have to look every frame, and that implies an onEnterFrame script...but what to attach it to? Your script will not have to be attached to any particular movie clip, but it will be setting variables on the main timeline. How about attaching it to the main timeline itself, _root? _root is more like a movie clip timeline than you think—it is a movie clip. You may not be able to drag it from the library, but it uses the movie clip class, which means it has the same properties and methods...and that means it has the same events as a movie clip...understanding classes gives you some ideas that seem like little hacks and tricks to a non-class-savvy designer, but they are actually a consequence of knowing the class hierarchy well.

What is its instance name? Well, it's _root, but because you are actually on the main timeline, there is a better, more general name you can use—our old friend this.

You want to attach it to this timeline, the one your code is on.

> You can actually use nothing as well; just onEnterFrame = function() { *(because you are outside a code block when you use the* this, *and outside a code block,* this *is optional) but it tends to look a little odd having an event without an instance defined to attach it to—best to avoid that because it might confuse you later if you ever forget why you didn't add it!*

9. Add the following code to set up the event handler's block:

```
this.onEnterFrame = function() {
};
resetTurn();
stop();
```

You have defined your basic code for each turn, which will reset your variables for a new turn and stop. Some code will still be running though—the code you will put in the onEnterFrame.

10. Each turn can be split into three sections:

- The first tile flipping over
- The second tile flipping over
- Checking the result

  After the first tile click, you note what the first fruit is (i.e. you make fruit1 = fruit or make your first fruit equal to the fruit on the tile that has just been turned over). At the second click, you make fruit2 = fruit, but you also have to prevent any other tiles from been flipped over—each turn should only allow two tiles to be flipped. At the end of the second tile flip, you have to check whether the turn has been successful.

- It is successful if the two fruits flipped over are the same, or fruit1 == fruit2. If that is the case, you have to cause the tiles to stay face up.

- Otherwise, you have to make them return to the face-down state.

The variable that tells you whether the first tile of second tile has been turned over is buttonClick, so add the following:

```
this.onEnterFrame = function() {
    if (buttonClick == 1) {
        fruit1 = fruit;
    } else if (buttonClick == 2) {
        delete (this.onEnterFrame);
        fruit2 = fruit;
    }
};
resetTurn();
stop();
```

> Note that you delete the onEnterFrame at the end of tile flip 2. This is to stop the event from continuing to check when the turn is over. As you shall see, the end of turn logic involves playing the timeline rather than running an event. This is a good example of mixing event-driven code and frame-based code—the event handler runs when the timeline is stopped, and stops when the timeline runs. When the timeline stops, Flash is still running something via the event handler—it is waiting for a change in the variables, and these will be caused by the buttons in the tiles.
>
> You moved up a level with this code—Flash is not just running timelines on simple button clicks, it is looking at internal changes caused by button events. You are now making Flash think about what the user clicked rather than simply doing a fixed goto. This is what makes the game seem a little more intelligent than a simple website button menu. Flash is looking for combinations of button clicks, and reacting differently to different sequences. This implies that Flash is making intelligent decisions.

Step 9 covers you for the two tile flips, you now need to check the result. After you set fruit2 to fruit1, the user's turn is over and you check the result.

The first thing you have to do is check if the two fruit are the same.

```
if (fruit1 == fruit2) {
```

If they are, you have one less pair to find.

```
pairs = -pairs;
```

Because the current turn found a match.

```
match = true;
```

Add the following code:

```
this.onEnterFrame = function() {
    if (buttonClick == 1) {
        fruit1 = fruit;
    } else if (buttonClick == 2) {
        delete (this.onEnterFrame);
        fruit2 = fruit;
        if (fruit1 == fruit2) {
            pairs = -pairs;
            match = true;
        }
    }
};
resetTurn();
stop();
```

So by the match = true line, you know whether a match was made in the current turn. If a match was made, you need to see if that means the game has finished (that is, the last pair has been found) or if the user still needs to turn more tiles.

There are several ways you can do this part, some of which are very hard (and involve adding an ActionScript pause) and some of which are very easy (and involve simply jumping to two sections of the timeline—one for "Try Again" and one for "Game over, you've won.")

Add the following lines to the listing so far.

```
this.onEnterFrame = function() {
    if (buttonClick == 1) {
        fruit1 = fruit;
    } else if (buttonClick == 2) {
        delete (this.onEnterFrame);
        fruit2 = fruit;
```

```
        if (fruit1 == fruit2) {
            pairs = -pairs;
            match = true;
            if (pairs == 0) {
                gotoAndPlay("won game");
            }
        }
        play();
    }
};
resetTurn();
stop();
```

This last bit of code causes a branch in the timeline depending on what your onEnterFrame (the referee) sees. If it sees that the game has been won, it will go to a frame labeled "won game." If it doesn't, you simply restart the timeline from this frame, frame 2. You still need to add these two frames, which you will do almost immediately, after this word from our sponsor.

> It is interesting to note that after the timeline is restarted, it is now acting dumb. You added the intelligent "gateway" that is the referee code that decides which of two outcomes the game is at and restarts the main timeline at two different points depending on what it sees. When that occurs, the referee is switched off (via the delete(onEnterFrame), you are back to the free-running linear timelines you looked at in the beginning of the book.
>
> You have actually mixed the two styles of creating Flash—the intelligent code, and the standard dumbly running timeline. You will see more of this throughout this game.

Completing the main timeline

You now need to complete the main timeline. If the main timeline simply continues playing from frame 2, you want it to eventually come back to frame 2 to start the next turn. You want it to run for long enough for all the tiles to be flipped, and then you want to go back to frame 2 and start another turn.

1. Select frame 2 of layer actions and give it a frame label of start turn. At frame 10 of layer actions, add a keyframe. On it, add the following code:

   ```
   hadTurn = true;
   ```

   Place this further down the timeline to allow both tiles to be flipped. This frame tells the tiles that the turn is over. It is up to the tiles to find out if they need to turn back around (no match found) or stay face-up (match found). You will look at this issue when you return to completing the tiles.

2. At frame 20, add a keyframe and give it a frame label of //end turn. The two forward slashes instruct Flash add a comment rather than a label, the difference being that a comment is for *our* benefit and doesn't go into the final SWF (and so saves you a few bytes).

   At frame 20, attach the following line of code:

   ```
   gotoAndPlay("start turn");
   ```

3. Extend the actions layer to frame 50, add a keyframe at frame 50, and label it won game. Your actions layer should look like this.

When the timeline runs, it initializes the variables at frame 2 (using a function defined at frame 1), and then stops and runs an "referee script" that controls the players turn, allowing the player to flip two tiles. If there is no match, the referee simply restarts the timeline. If this occurs, the timeline will turn hadTurn to true at frame 10, and jump back to frame 2 at frame 20. This will restart the referee—you start a new turn.

If the referee decides the game is won, you jump to frame 30 and start playing from there, bypassing the "next turn" loop. At the moment, nothing happens when you get there, so let's fix that.

4. Add a layer named finished and insert a keyframe in frame 50. Extend layer tiles to frame 49. On frame 50 of layer finished, add a suitable "You have won" message—don't worry if it's a bit basic right now, you can embellish it later!

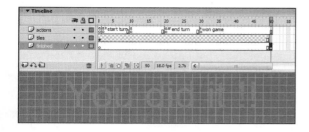

5. Select frame 50 of layer actions and add a stop();
action. Test your movie.

You'll be able to flip over a tile, and then Flash will
wait for you to flip over another tile before continuing. When you've flipped over two tiles, Flash will
start back at the beginning of the turn.

You can see what is happening by running our
second text movie, tile game2004_part2.fla.
buttonClick never increases beyond 2, and hadTurn
changes from false to true for a short period after
each pair has turned. When the turn is over, the
fruit field and buttonClick are both reset to 0, and
the referee is waiting for you to try again with
another turn. The problem is that none of the tiles
have flipped back over because they haven't been
wired to do so.

Adding the final touches

The only thing left to do is tell your tiles to stay face-up
when they are a pair, and you'll also put in a little animation to make them look different when they're
matched.

Back in the **movie clip**, the crucial frame is frame 11.
This frame is the brains behind the whole game

because it decides what the tile is going to do after it
has flipped face up. At the moment, it just looks for the
root to tell it whether there are already two tiles
turned over via buttonClick. It needs to start looking at
hadTurn as well as match. If hadTurn is true, the tiles
know that the current turn is finished. They know what
they are required to do by looking at match. If the latter is true, they are a matching pair, and they should
stay face up. Otherwise, they should flip back to the
face down position.

Sounds like a new problem, right? Well, not really—you
want something like what the main timeline is already
doing—a bit of code rather like the referee that causes
a branch. This time you want to branch between two
outcomes—a timeline that keeps the tiles face up, and
one that flips them back over. It's the same problem as
the one you just worked on in the main timeline!

> *The entire problem on both timelines is one of
> branching between two possible outcomes. If you
> used a more rigorous programming route, you
> would have written this branching code only once,
> either as a class, or as some other encapsulated
> package. You won't in this exercise, but the impor-
> tant thing you should note is that the basic func-
> tion of the tile is the same one as the umpire code
> below it!*

1. The main timeline works by having an
onEnterFrame at the start of each turn. The only
difference is that you are not controlling a complete turn, but a smaller part of it—a single tile flip
that makes up part of a single turn. So the question
is "where does the onEnterFrame have to go on the
tile timeline?" right? Wrong!! If the problem is the
same, you should really be asking where the branch
point is this time because that is where the intelligent referee code needs to go. The tile will always
do the same thing as it flips over, but once it has
fully flipped face-up, it can branch two ways—stay
face up, or flip back. The branch point is when the
tile is fully face-up. More specifically, it's frame 10
on the tile timeline. Select frame 10 on the actions
layer. This currently has a stop() on it.

427

Change it to now read as follows.

```
this.onEnterFrame = function() {
    if (_parent.match) {
        delete (this.onEnterFrame);
        gotoAndPlay("done");
    } else if (_parent.hadTurn) {
        delete (this.onEnterFrame);
        play();
    }
};
stop();
```

It's essentially a cut down version of the referee but with different variables. If you have a matching pair, you go to a "done" frame, and this will run a bit of timeline that keeps the tiles face up. If you have had the current turn and there is no match, the tiles need to turn back over. All you have to do now is add those timeline animations.

2. Because frame 10 is the branching code, you should point it out as special. You can't call it a referee so how about *controller*? Cool. Describes it perfectly—the code on frame 10 controls the tile timeline's branching intelligence. Select frame 10 and add a frame label of // controller, which is a comment to remind you of your code structure six months from now when you have completely forgotten about it all.

3. Add a keyframe at frame 20 and label it // down. This is the frame where the tile is back to face down, and is displayed if there was no match. The controller has simply restarted the timeline to show the "flip back" animation from frame 11 to 20. You are done for this turn when you get here and you want to go back to the start, so attach the following to frame 20:

```
gotoAndPlay("facedown");
```

4. Add a keyframe at frame 40. Because you actually jump to this frame, Flash needs a label, so enter done as the label. You *could* simply add a "face up" graphic here, but instead you will have a five-frame victory animation. Add a keyframe at frame 50 and attach a stop() to it. This is the state of play at the end of this step.

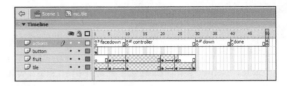

You need to add an animation for a match being found.

5. On the tile layer, insert a keyframe at frames 40 and 50. Select frame 10 in the fruit layer and right-click it to display the context menu. Select Copy Frames. Select frame 40 in the same layer, right click it as before and select Paste Frames. Finally, extend this layer to frame 50.

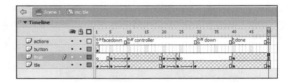

6. On the tile layer, use the Color drop-down in the Properties panel to set the Brightness of the tile in frame 50 to 100% and then put a motion tween between frames 40 and 50 to make it glow when a pair is found.

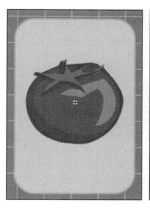

You can test this glow effect now by playing the movie and turning over two tiles. You can also see our work in progress version _tile game2004_part3.fla.

It's time to add the rest of our fruit and get the game working fully.

7. You need a new tile graphic for each of the four fruits—the one that you've been using so far has got a tomato on it, so rename mc.tile to mc.tile.tomato.

8. Duplicate this object three times in the Library, and name the copies mc.tile.lemon, mc.tile.orange, and mc.tile.pear.

    We'll change the lemon movie clip now, and then you can go back and do the same to the orange and the pear clips. There are two things that you need to do to make the transformation complete: change all the pictures of tomatoes into lemons, and change the ActionScript that tells the timeline which fruit it is.

9. Start by locking all the layers except for fruit. You know that all the keyframes on this layer currently contain a tomato, and you need to change them even when they're squashed so much that you can't see them.

10. Click the first keyframe in frame 5, select the fruit (you will be hardly able to see it, but clicking in the center of the tile should select it) and use the Swap button on the Properties panel to change the tomato for sy.fruit.lemon.

11. Run through the rest of the keyframes in the animation and perform the same operation on each so that all the tomatoes are swapped for lemons.

    Once you've done this to all five keyframes, your tomato will look like a lemon, but it will still *think* it's a tomato. So, you need to retrain it—luckily this isn't as hard as it sounds.

12. On the actions layer, select frame 1, and in the Actions panel change line 3 from:

    ```
    _parent.fruit = "tomato";
    ```

    to:

    ```
    _parent.fruit = "lemon";
    ```

    That's it. Now you just need to go back through the two fruit conversion stages for your pear and orange movie clips, and you're ready to make the game board. If you're feeling lazy, have a look at tile game2004_part4.fla

13. Go back to the tiles layer of your main timeline and delete everything that's currently on the stage in the tiles layer (lock the other layers to do this) Randomly place four of each movie clip into the stage in a 4 x 4 grid. Use the Align panel to tidy up the tiles and get them into neat rows:

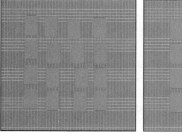
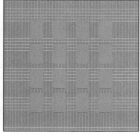

That's it. You're now ready to show off your first complete Flash game. Congratulations. Our final game is included on our website as tile game2004.fla.

Possible improvements and modifications to your game

You're probably staring in disbelief at the title for this section. It's taken you long enough to get the game working, and there's *no way* you're going to change it now. At the back of your mind though, there's a niggling little voice saying, "It would be nice if there were a few more fruits so I only needed *one* pair of each, and maybe a few more tiles, and while I'm at it, the victory screen could really do with improving. This section has been dictated by that voice.

- You can add as many tiles as you want, creating a 16x16 or even a 32x32 grid if your eyes are up to seeing tiles that small. All you have to do is change the initial value of **pairs** (in frame 1 of the main timeline's actions layer) to how many pairs there are to find. This is actually a nice consequence of the way the game was built—the referee doesn't care how many tiles there are because it only looks at a *single turn,* and the tiles don't care how many other tiles there are—it just looks to the umpire via the variables it changes.

- You could make a timer or a turn counter to score each game.

- You could make a scoring system where the player scores 5 points for each correct tile, but loses 2 for each wrong tile.

- For those feeling really confident, you could figure out how to make the game deal a random set of tiles every time a new game is started. To do this, you would have to

  - Start with a blank stage.

  - Use ActionScript (via `this.attachMovie()` from the stage) to place tiles onto the stage in pairs and following the grid layout at runtime. You would probably need to use an array for Flash to know where it had already placed tiles as it does this.

If you want to get Flash to place the tiles randomly, you will probably need to use a `for` *loop that runs eight times, and each time this should place two tiles of the same fruit.*

This game is more advanced than the simple mouse trail it's derived from. You can use it as the basis of other, even more advanced games. You could, for example, take the basic `mc.tile` and because it allows you to model a generalized playing card object, make some rather cool card games.

But what has this to do with website design? Websites and games are two branches of a tree called *interactivity.* There is an offshoot from the website branch that's very close to the game branch, and that offshoot is called *advanced website design.* Both use lots of clever bits of ActionScript to create their animations, interfaces, and effects. By learning simple games, you're priming yourself for the design and coding of *complex* sites.

There's another very basic reason for including games on a website. Web marketing studies have shown that games cause a visitor to return to a site even if the games have little to do with the site's subject matter.

In particular the following:

- The way you mixed event handlers and timeline animation is no longer beginner stuff. You are no longer a beginner—you are well into *intermediate.*

- The way you solved two seemingly different problems (i.e. you found that a game turn is fundamentally the same as a tile flip) is an advanced concept. It's the type of thinking that will make classes and object-oriented programming seem like child's play once you have worked out the syntax.

The next chapter will start to look at website design and point you on your way. You've reached base camp one on the ActionScript Mount Everest, and armed with what you've learned so far and that little niggling voice that keeps on asking questions and tells you to try new things, the only way is up. Never lose sight of the main goal and keep having fun—it'll be worth it.

Summary

In this chapter, you've dipped your toes into the vast ocean that is object-oriented design and programming. You looked at the basic principles of the OO programming approach and seen how you can map this onto the movie clip objects you use in Flash.

You saw that:

- Object-oriented design and programming delivers solutions that are:
  - Reusable
  - Extensible
  - Flexible
- The key to OO design and programming is the ability to conceptualize the surface detail of a problem until you can define its absolutely essential components.

- A class defines the characteristics of one of those components—what it is, what it can do, what its characteristics are, and how it communicates with other components. The class is a template.

- An object is an individual instance built using the class template.

- In Flash, you can think of a named movie clip instance on the stage as an object. This object is derived from the original Library movie clip symbol. All instances of the symbol on the stage will share the same essential properties, but you can customize them so that their behavior and properties individualize them.

- Simple movie clip objects can be combined to produce complex effects.

In the next chapter, you're going to look at the considerations you need to take into account when you're **designing** your Flash site.

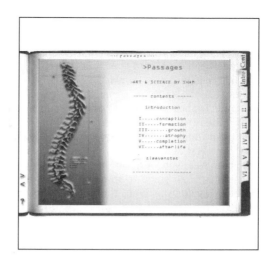

Chapter 17

HIGH-LEVEL SITE DESIGN

What we'll cover in this chapter:

- The principles of good design
- Website file structure and management
- Dynamic website design
- Recommended websites

At this point in the book, you can afford to congratulate yourself on your new status as a Flash programmer/designer. It's been a hard road, but it's worth it. Before you rush off into the crowded world of web design, there are a couple more things to think about. So far, this book has been about the technical implementation of your ideas inside Macromedia Flash, but this chapter will run through some tips on what to do when you have that first spark of inspiration and how to make sure your ideas will work on the Web. This chapter will give you a rough guide to some of the dos and don'ts of designing for the Web, both by reminding you of some of the considerations we've discussed earlier in the book and by drawing new ones to your attention. At the end of the chapter, Kris recommends some sites that will fire your imagination and get those designs flowing. First, Sham is going to discuss some of the principles he follows when creating his designs.

The principles of good design

When I was in my early twenties, I worked in a design team that created VDU display screens for nuclear power plants. The plant's operators would use the screens as their primary point of reference to see what was going on all over the plant. In an emergency, the reactor engineers had to be able to access the information they needed as quickly as possible, so the VDU display screens had to present that information in a form they could understand immediately. It was important that the screens never showed too much information—just the relevant information that the engineer requested.

The rules I followed to resolve this project are just as important to the work I do today because now, as then, my projects have the same basic requirements: **usability** and clarity. Of course, websites have to be engaging, interesting, and entertaining as well, but that has more to do with the content than the design. Before users can be engaged, interested, and entertained by the content, they have to be able to *find* the content. There are sites out there that intentionally break the rules and are entertaining because of it, but the people who design those sites can get away with this because they are always aware of the rules they're breaking.

These principles, important as they are for the usability of your site, will not bring you success on their own: *originality* is another defining feature of good web design. Sites that don't catch the eye and draw in the mind with good ideas and solid graphic design will get fewer visitors.

Flash is a cost-effective and bandwidth-effective design tool with loads of features that enable you to engage your visitors with compelling visuals and sound. One of the reasons that Flash is so prevalent on the Web is its high number of creative options, all of which are viewable with the small and simple Flash Player. However, viewers will leave your site if they've already seen it all before or are fed up with the two-minute download time. There's a fine line between multimedia and junkmedia, and designers must always be aware of which side they're on. In your design career, you're must balance creativity with practicality—in this chapter, we talk about both.

File structure and file size

Whenever you create anything for the Web, you have to be aware—even if it's only in the back of your mind—of what the Web is and what it will do to your presentation as your files are downloaded or streamed. We talked about these issues in the Optimization and Publishing chapters, but we'll reiterate some of the main points again here:

- Be aware of download times and optimize as much as possible to lower them.
- Differentiate between what's central to the message you're trying to get across and what's just eye (or ear) candy. If download times are an issue, you should know which parts of your movie should be the first to end up on the cutting room floor.

- Consider a multiple **loadMovie** download strategy to avoid a large initial download (see Chapter 13, Publishing, for more details).

- Take special care with bitmaps and sound. Optimize them all individually and don't rely on the global export settings to do the job for you.

- When using video, consider making a number of Flash files in various sizes for different user bandwidths. Load these in with **loadMovie**.

- Choose your symbols carefully and use a "one symbol often" approach instead of using lots of symbols once.

- Remember that ActionScript-based "sprite" animation is particularly bandwidth friendly. It requires far fewer frames than the corresponding tween-based animations.

The chapters on Optimizing and Publishing explained how to structure your movies correctly, but we'll reiterate the main points because your increased understanding of ActionScript will help you understand the basis of more advanced solutions.

Preloaders

We introduced you to **preloaders** earlier. I work with three levels of preloader so I'll give you a brief reminder of their varying degrees of complexity.

Basic: timeline-based loader

We introduced this basic preloader in the Optimization chapter. I recommend this option if you don't want to get your hands dirty with ActionScript or if you have a relatively simple and small SWF.

Intermediate: ActionScript-based loader

You can build a very efficient ActionScript preloader by looking at the **_framesloaded** and **_totalframes** properties of your movie. You can view these two properties of the main timeline just like any other variable by using the Properties tab in the Debugger window:

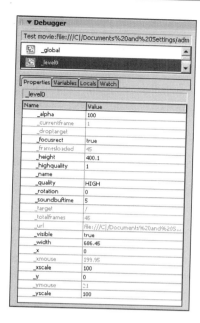

You want to create a simple animation that keeps the user interested while the main site loads. You use ActionScript to stop playing the animation and display the main site once the movie properties _totalframes and _framesloaded are equal to each other. When these two values are equal, the whole of your SWF has been loaded.

Intermediate/advanced: bandwidth manager object

The most sophisticated preloader I have is a "loading manager" object that I coded. It constantly looks at what's being loaded, and if nothing is, it looks for any other SWF levels to load via loadMovie and then loads them in the background. All the loaded SWFs have a blank frame 1 with a stop command in it so they just sit there, hidden (because the first frame is empty) until the lowest level sets them off with a play command You can tell that nothing is being loaded if _totalframes and _framesloaded are equal for the last level of SWF that you loaded.

If you decide to embark on this kind of approach, remember **never to unload an already loaded SWF level**. Instead, send it back to its first (blank) frame where it will remain invisible to watching eyes. A problem arises if the user requests a SWF other than the one that the manager is currently loading, but explaining that is beyond the scope of this chapter.

Intros

What you show during your preload is another major concern. A good intro (the animation that hides your preload) will draw the viewer into the main website, whereas a poor one is like a cheesy rock band's guitar solo—it goes on for *far* too long.

As a general rule, always have something interesting going on while the main site is loading. As we've said, the average Internet surfer will not stay long if you display a "please wait, loading" screen. Your intro must:

- Show the user what will be missed if they exit the site
- Give an indication of the quality of the actual main website
- Give viewers the option to skip past the intro if they want to

Different types of website require different intros. If you are creating a website advertising yourself as a website designer, you'd want to show off your technical ability and give the potential client a showcase of your advanced understanding of complex animation and graphic design ability. If you are designing an information service for a bank, however, you would not spend time showing fancy animations. Viewers of a site like that want to see the information they came to look at, and they want it *fast and clear*. They should be attracted to the site by a cool and slick Flash design, but once they decide to open an account, the route to the "Sign me up" page must just be a click away and free of over-indulgent Flash animation and tricks. Making your design appropriate to your client and audience is a vital consideration.

Tailoring your designs

There are several constraints and features that you need to be aware of when building a website. Here is a number of checklist items that you should be aware of when you are ready to build your main site.

Timeframe

We all want to build the coolest Flash sites possible, but if you are doing this for a living, you need to think about how soon the site needs to be completed. A good, delivered-on-time site will always yield a satisfied customer, whereas a brilliant, cutting-edge site delivered three weeks late *won't*. Remember, it's very difficult to change a site once it's up because people tend to get accustomed to the navigation and style. So be careful—unless, of course, the change is the *client's* idea and they're paying by the hour!

Style

The style you choose for the site is defined in part by the content and the impression that the client wants to get across to the viewer. When defining a style, be careful to choose one that's suited to the message rather than one that's easy to create in Flash. A lot of the time, the client already has a brief or advertising campaign that the site will be part of, so you should be flexible enough to incorporate your client's ideas and jump between styles.

Content

Unless you're creating a site based on a very specific brief in which the client provided all the site graphics and type, you'll have to find a way to hold the audience's attention long enough to get the site's message across. The coolest visual Flash interface will be ignored if it's not properly integrated with something *interesting*.

Navigation

The content of your site will greatly influence the navigation you create for it. In some (especially commercial) sites, there's often a route that you'd prefer the visitor to take—the one that'll most likely result in a sale or a click-through to your sponsor. Your navigation must make this route clear. Other sites are based around a central hub with numerous links going out to subtopics. In these sites, it's important that users can quickly access *any* area of the site, and as a general rule, they should be able to do it *within two clicks*.

Because there's no substitute for practical experience, I've included a walk-through of some site designs to illustrate the different methods of visualizing and creating a website.

Case study 1: online showcase

A few years ago (which equates to several decades in Flash years), I found a weathered poetry book dating back to Victorian England. Reading it, I was particularly taken by how different the thinking was from that of the 21st Century: whereas we live in an age where everything is out in the open (especially on the Web), they had a much more closed and hidden society.

I decided to put an updated and fully interactive version of the book onto the Web using all the new technology available to me. I wanted to create a website with the same look and feel of the book to give viewers a sense of the cultural and behavioral beliefs in that bygone world. But I wanted to present it via Flash animations.

Before I went into the Flash implementation, I had to have a very clear idea of what I wanted to create because I could see this being a very large project. I'd have to do two things:

- Create a set of storyboards and sketches that gave me a graphical direction and template
- Create the text, making sure that it matched the graphical style

Storyboarding

I had to define the look of the final website before I could begin. For the site to work, I knew it would have to be true to the original concept. I decided that the original book would play a part in the final look.

However, I had a problem: to navigate through a book, you turn pages. Going to a particular page is easy when you're holding the book because you can feel the paper's *thickness*, so you know if you want to go a point a third of the way into the book, you just open the book at a third of its thickness. You can't do that with a 2D representation on a monitor. Here's the rough sketch that solved the problem:

By looking at the way address books use tabs to help you quickly find a particular section of names—the Newmans and the Newton-Johns under "N" for example—I was able to create a 2D representation of a book that was still easy to navigate. Each tab would represent a chapter of the book.

To get the effect of old book pages, I used a cheap flatbed scanner to scan an image of a small notebook I'd carried with me in my coat pocket for close on a year. Then I got some newspaper that had faded to yellow in the sun and scanned that in too. I cobbled it all together in Photoshop so that it looked like this:

I now had an idea of what my open book would look like. The animated poems would appear in the page area as SWF files. Next, I needed to create my navigation tabs.

I also needed something to allow users to move between the individual pages of each chapter. I needed **last page** and **next page** buttons. I also needed a **help** button somewhere, so I sketched that in as well:

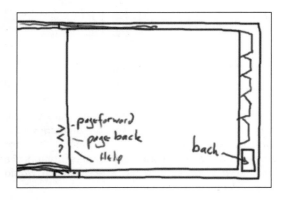

These sketches were created using a Wacom pen tablet. It's a quick way to make initial sketches, and it helps workflow because you can import the image directly into Flash (or whatever program you're using), rather than having to scan it and then fiddle with image resolution, color depth, and so on.

With my basic site structure worked out, I needed to make sure I could create a convincing set of tabs for navigation before I started devoting time to Flash programming. I went back into Photoshop to mock it all up:

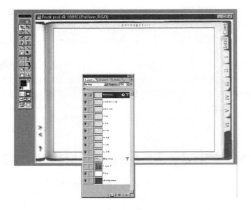

I put each tab in a separate layer to simulate the effect of a page being turned. I also used Adobe ImageReady, a web page preparation tool, and some JavaScript to create a simple HTML version of the book to see if the navigation was workable—and thankfully it was:

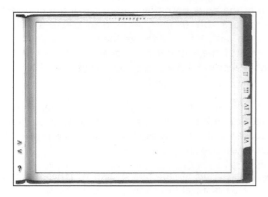

As you can see, removing tabs gives the impression that we have moved further into the book. Luckily, the fact that our virtual book still has the same number of pages left no matter how far into the book you are doesn't seem to kill the illusion.

By mocking up my ideas in Photoshop first, I proved to myself that the concept of a virtual book was a viable one before spending my time trying to get it working in Flash. As an added advantage, I now also had some bitmap images I could trace into Flash.

Content

The book would be called *Passages*, and it would be about the one journey we all make—the journey through life. Victorian society was full of double standards, and had a very rich upper class and a chronically poor underclass (maybe things haven't changed *that* much…). Using this as a starting point, I wanted the book to liken an individual's lifetime to a child who is secretly in a rich man's mansion, seeing what's there and taking whatever he can.

Here are two initial storyboards done in Photoshop:

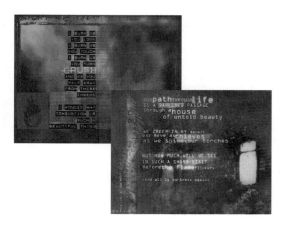

The first page is an introduction to the book, and the second is called *crush*. Both of these compositions are multi-layer Photoshop files. By moving the individual layers around in real time, I gave myself a good idea of how the text should appear and how the individual elements should move. These shots show the last frame in each animation. There are approximately 40 animations for the whole *Passages* sequence, which follows our young thief through an entire lifetime using the metaphor of his trip through the mansion.

By now I had lots of images, sketches, and text, and I was ready to mold it into a site. Time to start looking at Flash.

Integration

The book had to look *real*. It had to have pages that turned. Contemporary native Photoshop files can be imported into Flash, but with such large file sizes, you are better off splitting the layers and exporting them as separate GIFs or JPEGs, as I did in this project. The separated Photoshop images were first converted to vectors and rebuilt as fully animated movie clips. Here's the final Flash symbol of the front of the *Passages* book, which is a fairly faithful reproduction of the original book's cover:

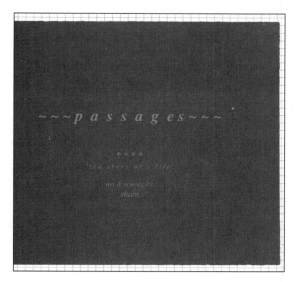

The pages were also made to turn with a simple tween animation, which you can see in this "under construction" shot:

439

Here's the finished, open book in Flash. The whole book and associated animations comes in at a little over 20K:

Next I built a simple intro to play as the book animations and graphics loaded. (The individual poems would come in as onLoad movie levels, using the loading manager I mentioned earlier.)

I wanted to introduce specific symbols to represent the themes of *Passages*: the Victorian ideas of *life* and *mortality*. For *life*, I chose a butterfly, and for *mortality* I scanned in an image of a human spine from *Gray's Anatomy*. There were two advantages to this second choice: it was written in the Victorian period, and its engravings are royalty free—providing you don't copy the whole book. Neat.

> *New designers need to pay careful attention to issues of copyright and royalties to avoid getting themselves into unwanted, and perhaps costly, trouble.*

The butterfly appears in the introduction, and flits through the book as you turn certain pages. The image of the spine is shown as a recurring theme throughout the book as well.

figure 1a
Existence

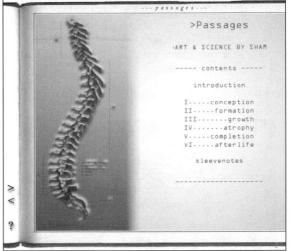

Summary

This case study demonstrated how Flash can be used in a creative way to make websites that are unlike anything else on the Internet. At its lowest level, *Passages* is nothing more than an online showcase of related Flash movies. However, by creating an overall *style* and *ambience*, the site will hopefully become much more than its individual components. I hoped users would forget that they're viewing a Flash website and become drawn into its strange and beautiful world—in the very way I was when I first found that old book.

The best thing about something like *Passages* is that it has no heavy ActionScripting; it's all about basic artistic skills and ideas. Those of you who are coming into Flash from a Photoshop or graphic design background could create something like this now because you already have the basic Flash skills required to pull it off.

Mocking up the site and prototyping it in Photoshop and ImageReady was one of the most important parts of this site's creation. Flash doesn't have the tools to take in bitmaps and other scanned data in the same way Photoshop does, and for this reason a lot of professional designers use Photoshop for the initial design and storyboarding. Even when used in the simple ways shown here, Photoshop and Flash form the basis of a very powerful set of visualization tools for the designer—whatever he or she is designing.

Case study 2: my Flash home site interface

Designing your own home site is when you get to *play*. Some designers use it to show off and compete with other designers, but I think that's just asking for trouble—whenever another designer uses a new technique, you'll have to go one better. That kind of technological "arms race" is not my idea of fun—I prefer to be creative.

The first example was all about design—how to get those vague ideas in your head onto a digital canvas by creating a plan and then animating the elements in Flash.

The next example looks at the sites that start as a folder full of half-finished ideas and uncompleted FLA files that you don't know what to do with—and then something in your head links them all together and an idea hits you out of nowhere.

Random idea #1

As I was driving down a busy highway, I noticed some large billboards by the side of the road. It put the idea in my head that sometimes size really "makes" a picture—wouldn't it be nice to have a browser that was as big as a billboard?

I decided I would try to do just that. But if you had a really *big* site, how would you see it all? The browser is way too small. Then I remembered book called *Fahrenheit 451* by Ray Bradbury. In it, cars moved so fast that the only way people could read the ads they drove past would be if the billboards were miles long and the images and text on them were stretched out to that length. At that speed, the stretched images would look normal. I decided to try and do the same with my site design: stretch it out horizontally into a really long billboard site.

I created a new movie, modified it to have 2880 pixels by 600 pixels, and then set the publish width to 300% by 95%, just to see what would happen. It looks nice as a design concept because the user would have to scroll from left to right to get to the actual website at the end, where they'd get an eye full of oversized logo (I've used one of mine as an example). Because this is a novel format (or will be until you all try it yourselves), the average web user will remember the first site that used it. As we said at the outset of this chapter, originality is an important component of your sites.

Random idea #2

Another thought was buzzing around my head at around the same time as I was thinking about the long billboard: my VCR was broken so whenever I played anything on it, I got a horrible picture that was totally unviewable. It was the kind of snowy, fuzzed, picture you get when you play a video that's a copy of a copy of a copy. In a funny way, though, I liked the mangled image on the screen. I imagined, somewhat dramatically, technology breaking out of our control and refusing to be mastered.

With this on my mind, I happened to walk past a shop that had a lot of TVs on at the same time in a 4 x 4 grid. No two screens showed exactly the same picture: one was brighter than the others, one was more red, and one had a lower saturation, and so on.

I imagined the same effect in my browser window—separate "TV screens" each doing its own thing, and I decided to create this effect.

I used an array of little movies that sit on top of an underlying SWF, similar to the grid in the following graphic. If you read the chapter on masking, you'll no doubt have a good understanding of how this is done:

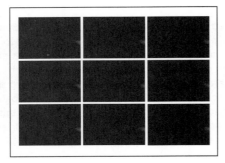

All I needed now was my broken VCR effect in each segment:

I built a set of little objects that randomly applied distorted noise effects to the underlying SWF. Remarkably, the whole thing worked! It looked a little bit like the video walls you still see in some bars or clubs that show one picture on a grid of TVs—each TV showing a separate square portion of the image.

I now needed something to tie my two media related ideas—the billboard and the TV grid—together.

Integration

I don't know what made me put the television grid on the end of my billboard, but I did, and it worked. I was just playing around, putting this grid idea over other SWFs and looking at how it mangled everything up. I was just having fun. Even when the underlying SWF was motionless, there was still plenty of movement going on.

I needed a menu bar to really tie it all together, and I was still in love with the test patterns I mentioned earlier, so I created a row of rectangles that approximated the color bars. It's shown in grayscale here, but it is in fact the color progression you see on a color TV—white, yellow, cyan, green, magenta, red and blue:

This menu bar is made up of little button objects that the user can press to navigate the site. The buttons wobble—when you press one, it expands and contracts and moves as though it were made of Jello. These wobblers are wrapped within a parent object called "menu." When one wobbler expands, the others contract (and vice versa) to preserve the overall length of the menu bar:

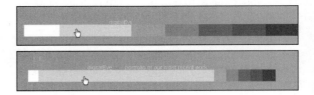

The menu bar buttons wobble with a delay so it looks a bit like a big plastic band, producing a bouncing effect that's fascinating and disorienting at the same time.

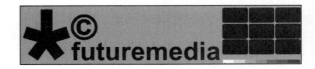

So here's my idea for my new Flash home site. You have to scroll in from left to right, going over the oversized billboard logo. Once you get to the far right end of the site and the mouse passes over the TV screens, they spring to life and play their test patterns and video noise until you click something. If you click a link to another website, you don't see it in a new window...it appears in the TV screens! Every now and again one of the screens gets a little brighter or loses synch or something, and the longer you leave the mouse still, the more pronounced the effect becomes.

The screens also display images even when the user hasn't clicked anything: little MTV-type animations, Japanese Manga cartoons, or the grainy video footage taken from the cameras in missile nosecones during the first Persian Gulf war. I want to add things in those screens that are possibly *better* than the things the visitor came to see—I want my visitors to say "Never mind looking at the websites...missile command just showed up in the top left corner! Quick...figure out the keys before it disappears!"

Summary

I hope that walking through these examples made you enthusiastic about creating your own innovative sites. Most of what you need to learn to achieve something like these sites is covered in the ActionScript chapters.

Don't overlook Flash as a tool for just trying out ideas. Maybe you'll start a collection of effects that you like but that have been done to death. You can take the best aspects of each and create something unique to use on your own site.

Most designers have a little box of collected effects, but unfortunately, some never change what they keep in it. The best designers are always on the lookout for new coding ideas. When they can offer a client the chance to be the first site to use a particular effect, they can ensure themselves a better chance of getting the job.

Dynamic Websites

Even before Flash MX 2004, building dynamic websites in Flash was fast becoming one of its key uses. In essence, Flash MX 2004 and Flash MX Professional 2004 have significantly built up the dynamic armory and has cemented Flash as a prime tool for producing dynamic websites and applications.

Even though only some Flash users will grab hold of the dynamic beastie, it is well worth being aware of some of the considerations involved.

Case study 3: a dynamic visual guestbook

One night I had an idea to build a guestbook that would build an archive of the visitors' names. But unlike standard guestbooks, this archive would provide a *visual* representation of the visitors' names.

A dynamic site in Flash works by pulling in information (such as variables) from a data store, called a database, and displaying or processing the information in Flash. Usually, when fetching or sending information to or from the database, a server-side scripting language is used:

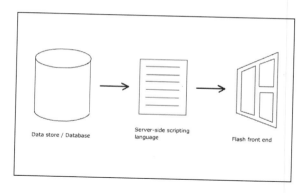

Data store / Database   Server-side scripting language   Flash front end

You might have already heard of a few server-side scripting languages such as PHP, ASP.NET, Java or Macromedia's ColdFusion software. Server-side scripting languages are beyond the scope of this book, but there are many different ways to develop your knowledge in this area. However, I'd advise that you get comfortable with ActionScript before attempting to integrate these languages with Flash.

For the guestbook, I decided to use a complex line-to-line structure to represent the names visually, a little like the way constellations are depicted in astronomy books. Each letter of the name would have a point, and two lines would connect one letter with the next. The first letter would start off the lines, the last letter would be the ending, and each letter is randomly placed:

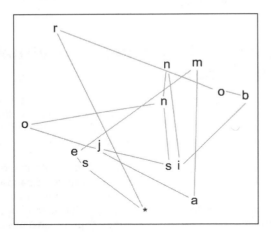

Rather than stick to a dull black and white canvas, I decided to incorporate a little color and different stroke widths. I came up with a set of simple rules to create some diversity:

- The color of each line is determined by the position in the alphabet of each letter of the user's name.
- The number of lines drawn is proportionate to the number of letters in the user's name.
- The stroke size and positioning of each letter is random, so no two names have the same visual representation.

All these factors are set using ActionScript in Flash, stored as variables, and are then sent to the database for storage.

Given the stated rules, "Stephen" looks like this:

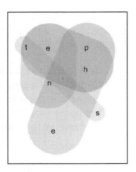

Once the user has seen his or her name in shapes, it is randomly placed with all the other "nameshapes" of previous visitors. The more people who sign the guestbook, the bigger the collective image will be, until all the layers are so thick that the stage is a mass of color and the guestbook needs to be cleared.

However, if I chose to clear the guestbook every month, an archive of all the previous months could be placed on display, forming a totally different image for each month. When a visitor views the guestbook, all the names and the visual information for each one are pulled in from the database, and the composition is drawn in Flash.

If all this dynamic stuff sounds a little complicated, don't be put off. It's not an essential learning component for a designer...phew! However, as you advance with ActionScript, you might also find yourself interested in learning other technologies. There is plenty of documentation available on the Web and in numerous books.

If you really don't want to learn all this back-end stuff, fortunately there are programmers dedicated to making all this stuff happen. In this case, the communication between you and the back-end programmer is crucial. You must be sure that you both agree on naming conventions for variables and such, and you both need to understand how the two elements will tie together. (It goes without saying that you both will meet your deadlines of course.)

Either way, dynamic sites are the next big thing, and Flash MX 2004, in particular Flash MX Professional 2004, has a lot of added functionality specifically designed for building dynamic web applications, so it pays to be familiar with some of the concepts involved.

Suggested sites

Now that you have a better understanding of how websites are created, the best place to start looking at Flash sites is the Web itself. As promised at the start of the chapter, here are some suggestions:

- **www.presstube.com** This site is packed with loads of amazing linear and interactive animations. You might notice that most of the Flash files are published with the quality set to low, giving them an altogether different kind of texture.

- **www.yugop.com** Yugop's creator, Yugo Nakamura, is always one step ahead of the pack, and his current pickings are better than ever. The creations on this site are truly amazing, and set the standard for other Flashers.

- **www.threecolor.com** This site has a number of sweet animations that will make you think differently about ways to work with the basic shape and motion tween tools in Flash.

- **www.levitated.net** A massive archive of beautiful Flash experiments showcasing the power of ActionScript combined with logic. This site has all kinds of advanced elements from basic interactivity to behavioral OOP. Many of the Flash files shown on this site are also available to download (be warned—this is advanced scripting).

- **www.modifyme.com** Modifyme has some amazing sounds and interaction which, when combined, make it a kind of futuristic sound mixer. You'll doubtless spend hours here trying different combinations of settings to see what you can make those pesky nodes do. Sometimes curiosity can keep the user from leaving your web page.

- **www.vectorama.org** This multiuser design pad allows a number of players to create a digital composition—working on the same canvas! Whereas the premise is to encourage collaboration with the other designers, this usually turns sour and the **kill** command comes in handy for destroying other people's hard work. For those of you who want to go out and imitate this site, be aware that it is built in both Flash and Director and has a pretty hefty back-end too.

- **www.friendsofed.com/fmc** Not a friends of ED plug at all, but a demonstration of how ActionScript can be used creatively to design some beautiful compositions. Although the experiments featured in the book were written way back in Flash 5, they still look absolutely marvelous.

- **www.derbauer.de** This site is just amazing. These people really know how to put their images to use. The programmers and designers have created a well-designed site. Even though the file sizes are large, the site is easy to navigate and is extremely interactive.

- **www.banja.com** Great animations and a great game. Islands, treasures, pirates—the whole bit. Excellent interactivity and well thought out design that loads fast for such a large game.

Summary

The summary for this chapter is short and sweet:

- Learn
- Work
- Explore
- Plan
- Play

Great Flash design comes from continually honing your design and Flash skills, from innovation, and from trying things out as you go. Remember that time spent monkeying around with little movie clips and effects can pay dividends later.

In our final chapter, we're going to look at some other Flash areas that are ripe for exploration as you build your Flash future.

Chapter 18

FUTURESCAPE

Where next?

Flash has come a long way from being just a superb animation package. Macromedia Flash MX 2004 is capable of producing fully functional web applications that are rich in graphics, sound, video, and interactivity. As a complete web application in its own right, Flash is rapidly becoming the web developer's tool of choice for creating the whole range of e-commerce, entertainment, and community sites. Flash can talk to web servers in a highly sophisticated way, meaning that dynamic content is within everyone's reach using ActionScript, and Flash has become integrated with other web-standard technologies such as XML.

You've now learned the basic skills required for Flash competence. In the space of a few hundred pages, you've gone from a ground-level beginner making a mushroom grow to an intermediate programmer coding an interactive game.

Mastering these new skills completely will keep you occupied for many months to come as you explore the full range of your powers. But before too long you're going to want to do more. You'll be hungry for new knowledge and new skills, and you will want to wring every possible design opportunity from Flash and from the Internet as a whole.

Using and improving your Flash skills

There are numerous Flash tutorial sites out on the Web, and most have beginners' sections. Most new Flash effects and interfaces seem to end up being deconstructed and presented as a how-to tutorial within a very short time, so if there's a particular design effect you want to know more about, check out the Web first. Be sure to try the Macromedia newsgroups as well; these tend to be a good way of picking up the knowledge of some of the older hands. Our advice, though, is to check out the FAQs of these groups before asking questions of your own as most beginner questions will have been covered.

Here are some good starting points for Flash resources on the Web:

- http://www.macromedia.com/support/flash
- http://www.friendsofed.com/forums
- http://www.flashkit.com
- http://www.flashmove.com
- http://www.flashmagazine.com
- http://www.ultrashock.com

Flash web design presents the user with a large number of different fields to look at. You only have to look at a few sites created by the Flash masters to realize that the variation in Flash sites is larger than that exhibited by any other web technology currently on view. From cartoon sites to futuristic-looking 3D, Flash has a large amount of the best of the Web covered. To give you an idea of some of the areas you may want to find out more about, we're going to briefly introduce them to you now.

Flash games and toys

Getting noticed as a designer is hard work, and you need to find a way to get your skills recognized. One way to attract attention is by designing quality games because games and toys can be a good way to hold a viewer's attention. You could add them to an existing site that's in need of new blood, or make them into a site in their own right where people can witness your

Flash experimentation. If this is the area you're interested in, perhaps existing sites that need perking up with some Flash interaction would be willing to incorporate your work—if you give them enough of a nudge.

Check out http://ferryhalim.com/orisinal/ as a top example of the kind of interactive games you can create in Flash.

Flashed cartoons

As a pure animation tool, Flash should not be underestimated. Managing the timeline with the skills you've learned in this book can produce highly professional looking animations. You can generate drawings within Flash itself, scan in photos or drawings you've generated by hand to give a less computerized appearance to your work, or import work from other applications that give you more flexibility when creating your images (as you saw in the walk-through in the previous chapter).

The animation features of Flash are used in preliminary work for TV production, for mocking up commercials, and they are also now being used to produce content for the Sony PlayStation 2. Take a look at the Flash webisodes at http://www.s4studios.com, one of which is a Flash animated trailer for Sony's Twisted Metal: Black game.

Using Flash with other software

In addition to using Flash in isolation, many designers use Flash in conjunction with other software, such as Macromedia's Multiuser Server included with Director. Using this application, designers can set up interactive sites—for example, enabling real-time multiuser online gaming and interaction—without having to learn new server-side scripting languages. Combinations such as this allow you to extend the use of Flash even beyond whole web applications and into standalone programs.

Although Flash has its own drawing tools, there's a lot to be said for using programs such as FreeHand, Photoshop, and others to enhance the available options of Flash presentations. Many designers take this initial approach when designing their web projects. However, always make sure to optimize anything you bring into Flash because some of these image manipulation applications are not quite as web savvy as Flash can be.

Using sound effectively in Flash is another exciting area to investigate. Although creating sound can become very expensive, there are many entry-level options available by using a good sound card as the main device, and shareware or freeware tracker and sequencer software.

3D in Flash

As some of the examples in this book— as well as many of our recommended sites—have shown, adding a 3D element to your work can achieve impressive results, and give your sites an extra edge over conventional Flash work. The applications available are well worth getting involved with; if a client wants a 3D version of their logo on their site, you want to make sure you're in the running for the job.

As the demands placed on websites increase and become more varied, 3D rendering skills are highly desirable. Adding this ability to your impressive Flash résumé will do you no harm at all. Flash is well suited to the use of 3D images and whether you're trying to make your name as a designer, or merely using Flash for fun, you'll find that using 3D objects will add to your success. Check out **Swift3D** as a Flash-friendly 3D tool that can output SWF files which you can then load in your movies:

- http://www.swift3D.com

Advanced ActionScript-based Flash interface designs

ActionScript is now a major force in web programming, and now that you know the basics—more than just the basics in fact—thanks to this book, you will no doubt be bursting to know what other possibilities are offered by this web wonder. ActionScripting is a skill in itself and knowledge of it will be a tremendous benefit to your designing. You saw in the later chapters of the book what effects can be achieved, but you've only seen the tip of the ActionScript iceberg. When you really flesh out your ability, the Flash designs you create will be sure to please and astound you. The sister

book to this one, *Foundation ActionScript*, shows you how to create the home site of one of the authors of this book, a complete ActionScript heavy website. See http://www.futuremedia.org.uk and/or the download page for the Foundation ActionScript MX 2004 book, where you can have a sneak peek of the files as soon as the book is published.

Dynamic content

With a good knowledge of ActionScript, you can go on to combine server-side architectures with Flash front-ends to create dynamic websites. You can pass data between the browser and web server using ActionScript in conjunction with a whole range of server-side scripting languages such as PHP and ASP/ASP.NET. You can also use a middleware package such as Macromedia ColdFusion. This is Macromedia's server back-end of choice for combining with Flash and we're expecting even closer integration of these products in the future.

XML

Flash MX 2004 includes support for the eXtensible Markup Language (**XML**), which is already a web standard for disseminating data in a form that can be interpreted anywhere, on any device, and rendered according to the abilities of that device and the needs of the user.

Because XML tags can be used to tell a browser something *about* the included information rather than just *how to display it*, XML is taking off in a number of areas, including e-commerce, intelligent search engines, and wireless devices. Flash's ability to deal in XML data in ActionScript, coupled with the rich multimedia features that Flash is famous for, mean that Flash can be a powerful player in a world where XML and data-driven web applications are becoming evermore popular.

Flash is branching out into a whole new set of contexts: for all kinds of wireless and non-PC web devices, such as PDAs and cellular phones.

Starting a career in Flash

Flash has now become the standard for dynamic animation and sound on the Web. It follows, therefore,

449

that it's also a discipline that can be used to form part of a career in web design. The question many people tend to ask is *how do you get your foot in the door?*

If you are so taken with Flash that you're considering attempting to earn a living as a Flash designer, you'll have to stop a moment and consider the following issues:

HTML

Most employers and agencies expect you to know something about HTML. This is something that's becoming less of a constraint as time passes and the majority of operations adopt site/HTML creation packages like Macromedia Dreamweaver. However, a lot of Flash web design positions still require you to know HTML. Even if this is not the case, we'd be very surprised to find Flash positions that did *not* require an understanding of Dreamweaver. Some understanding of JavaScript is usually an advantage too, as ActionScript is based on JavaScript—good news for you as it means there's less to learn to achieve competency.

Graphic design

Web design is an offshoot of a much wider discipline called graphic design. As a web designer, you won't be expected to get your pencils and paints out, but a knowledge of computer based graphic design and layout packages is usually a distinct advantage—Adobe Photoshop is usually stipulated as a competency. It's also worth your while considering a point that the earlier chapters alluded to: with the ever-increasing competition for web surfers, your potential clients are going to take it for granted that you can produce a functional site. They're going to want something that's visually appealing *as well*—so your artistic skills need to be up to the job.

Getting in

Having an impressive home site is one of the best ways to get noticed on the Web. There are a number of well-known Flash designers who started out by building a killer home site. Having a cutting edge site does not necessarily mean that you have to be an ActionScript or 3D guru: there are plenty of other site styles that will appeal to users—humor, animation, innovation and a distinctive style spring immediately to mind.

There are of course other, more stealthy ways into Flash design and these seem to be the routes that most of us tend to end up following.

One of the things we'd recommend is that you look at what is in your area's local businesses and organizations that are physically nearby and have a website in need of some renovation—but make sure you have a good portfolio of personal Flash and some HTML work before you approach them. A good starting point when looking for your very first site job (after your own of course) is charities. They tend to be run and organized by volunteers, and many won't turn away a volunteer Flash expert who asks to re-engineer the existing HTML site to full Flashed status, with the promise of a much more entertaining site and therefore more visitors. This is the way many designers start out, doing odd website jobs in their spare time and keeping up the day job, slowly increasing their portfolio and gaining a good reputation.

Although your first few Flash sites may be more in the solid-but-dependable ballpark, it won't be long before you have a few sites that you're actually proud of. That's the time to start looking at full time **freelancing**. This is much easier to do now that the Web has really taken off, and there are a number of websites in America and Europe that will e-mail you with weekly lists of contract positions, but be aware that the market for this type of work is *very* competitive, and many jobs ask for Flash as part of a range of skills that are increasingly including server side technologies.

A good tip is to add Flash, HTML, Dreamweaver, Photoshop, and JavaScript to your résumé's list of keywords. If you choose this route, our advice would be to find a few websites that allow online portfolios, and add links to your three best sites. You'll find that a lot of traditional employment agencies now scour such entries, and you sometimes find e-mails from agencies you have never worked with imploring you to get in touch about a contract!

Applying directly to web design houses is another option. However, unless you've already created a stir on the Web with your home site or other work, be prepared for a disappointing starting salary. There's a lot of money to be made from the Internet, but junior web designers seem to be seeing a minimal part of it. A lot of people may choose this option despite lack of initial pay because it can create a very good portfolio of work very quickly. Working with the right company, the work can be very satisfying and you can move up to more senior positions, or into freelance work, after a couple of years. There's much less uncertainty when starting out on this route than there is with freelancing, where you may not be employed all year round (at least, until you have a good freelance portfolio).

Flash farewell—for now

The end of this book is very much the beginning of your Flash career—whatever you choose to do with your new skills. You now have a platform of knowledge that'll allow you to branch out into a variety of areas—all with their own pitfalls and possibilities. Flash is now a major force on the Web, and it is destined to increase its power and influence. There's an opportunity now to ride the crest of Flash's wave and make your mark in the world of web design. Don't rest on your laurels: practice the skills you have and search out new ones and new ways to apply them.

See you on the beach.

INDEX